PROBLEMS
OF AMERICAN
SOCIETY

VALUES IN CONFLICT

fourth edition

JOHN F. CUBER Ohio State University

WILLIAM F. KENKEL Iowa State University

ROBERT A. HARPER Washington, D.C.

*Holt, Rinehart
and Winston, Inc.*

NEW YORK CHICAGO SAN FRANCISCO

TORONTO LONDON

To the memory of

R I C H A R D   C .   F U L L E R

whose vision has broadened the purview

of the realistic observer

Copyright 1948, 1951, © 1956, 1964 by Holt, Rinehart and Winston, Inc.

All rights reserved

Library of Congress Catalogue Card Number: 64-12925
September, 1964

21630-0414

Printed in the United States of America

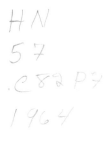

PREFACE

This fourth edition of *Problems of American Society* is not a revision in the ordinary sense. A major part of the text is new. At least three complete chapters dealing with problem areas not previously discussed have been added. The point of view, however, remains the same, namely, that the key focus for understanding social problems in a somewhat free and democratic society consists of an examination of "who wants what and why."

Nearly thirty-years ago Richard Fuller conceived and partially formulated what he regarded as a realistic, democratic and at the same time quite sociological frame of reference for studying social problems. He acknowledged indebtedness to prior work by Lawrence Frank and Willard Waller. Fuller decried the tendency to make of the almost universally taught social problems course an omnibus of facts, pronouncements on social problems and their remedies, a hodgepodge without explicit statements indicating how social problems are defined or the role of the sociologist in the many-sided task of analyzing and treating them. In its most terse form Fuller's position was that the sociologist is first and foremost an analyst of the collective situation as it *is*, that the various groups and individuals in the society through *their* evaluation of *their* society set up the dimensions of each social problem. Thus, a social problem is the condition about which there is a conscious discontent. It is obvious to almost anyone that in a pluralistic society like the American, judgments vary radically as to what conditions *are*, whether or not they warrant a negative appraisal, and what, if anything, ought to be done if the appraisal is negative. Since the term *value*, vague as it acknowledgedly is, generally connotes the goals, purposes, and/or criteria involved in judgment and consequent action, and since values are as a rule not uniform for the entire society, Fuller's approach has come to be called the "clash of values" frame of reference.

The value conflict position holds the social analyst to a hard realism. Unlike sentimentalists and some humanitarians who seldom get further than a kind of muck raking, the value-conscious analyst soon sees that problem conditions are stubborn precisely because they are rooted in the fabric of society—in those relatively uncompromisable ought-structures, cultural norms, values, call them what we will. This forces the student to come to grips with the irrationalities of conduct and judgment that, buttressed by ethnocentric circular thinking, turn out so often to be the real stumbling blocks toward getting something constructive done. Realistically he must come to appreciate the typically mammoth task that human ingenuity must face if practicable solutions to social problems are to be invented and "sold."

This frame of reference is a good vehicle for focusing attention upon the interest group conflicts that are so often at the heart of problem definition and problem solution. It points up the fact that expert and lay opinion as to what social problems are may be very diverse. It is rather pointless to rail against the "stupidity" and "ignorance" of the laymen. Since laymen sit in the legislatures, preside over the schools and churches, and do the bulk of the voting, it becomes rather manifest that what we proudly call "professional opinion" must in some way reach the verbal arenas in which the values clash—the pulpit, the class room, the editorial page, the coffee breaks, not to mention legislative halls, committee meetings, and the court chambers. Whatever expertness the sociologist and other specialists in analyzing social problems may have must be diffused into the channels of lay communication; it must find champions who can rationalize, to use an emotive word, professional opinion in terms of preexisting value positions. If social problems research is to have any practical utility, it must find its way more often and more favorably into the channels of communication than is now the case. One of the effective ways in which to gain skill in accomplishing this is to function within a labeled framework that explicitly reminds us that we are dealing always with human values, embarrassing and frustrating as this may at times be.

At times this point of view seems trivial. Publics are fickle as well as superficial. Some of them can show more interest in the Supreme Court's reaffirmation of the separation of Church and State than they can ever quite muster to face the problem of potential annihilation by nuclear devices. Moreover, the logic, the cause-and-effect presuppositions are often ludicrous, if not insulting to mature intelligence. But in a democratic society, one in which the fiction is maintained that all intelligences are equal at the polls, it may be well not to underestimate outrageous logic and inane semantics.

The value conflict analysis of social problems documents and underscores one of the growing anomalies of the democratic mass society. In the mass society practically everyone functions in groups with which he more or less identifies, but the perspectives of which are exceedingly limited. It is difficult, if not impossible, for most to see much beyond the immediate limits of their own participations.

Since the first edition of the present book was published in 1948, subsequent editions have somewhat embellished the original treatment. This edition we believe to be much more sophisticated than its predecessors in that it takes more into account some of the larger contexts within which the clashes of values take place. Liberal use is made of such concepts as the mass society, the affluent society, and similar realities of the cold war world. The level of difficulty has been materially raised in line with current efforts to make the educational adventure more demanding and (hopefully) more fruitful for the student. In the fifteen years since the first edition, new value positions have appeared in American society, older ones have been modified, and research has opened up more avenues of fact and interpretation.

This revision has been the responsibility of Professor Cuber and Professor Kenkel. Although a great deal of collaboration has taken place between us, each is primarily responsible for specific chapters, Cuber for chapters 5, 8–10, 16–18, and 20–22 and Kenkel for chapters 1–4, 6, 7, 11–15, and 19.

To write a book about the values of various groups in a modern society is almost a pretentious undertaking. We are sociologist enough, however, to believe that we have achieved sufficient objectivity so that divergent values have each been faithfully presented. This does not mean that we maintain the polite fiction which passes among some that we ourselves are value-neutralized, that our own views on a number of matters have been completely expurgated. We know they are not, they cannot, and they should not be. We have, however, tried assiduously so to present description and analysis that the student may come to appreciate the prima facie reasonableness of a wide variety of value positions and also to acquire the habit of subjecting assertions and positions to rigorous empirical and logical scrutiny. The American dialogue about social problems is in many respects pathetically naïve, in other respects brutally cynical. We have tried to point out bluntly many of these naïvetes and cynicisms where evidence and reasonable inference from evidence has permitted. Like many other educators, we operate with a faith, a set of beliefs that taken together seem to mean that we believe man to be at least somewhat rational and somewhat educable, that within limits a fair and open-minded mental stance can be taught. We offer this fourth edition of *Problems of American Society* as one effort toward such an objective.

J. F. C.
W. F. K.
R. A. H.

Columbus, Ohio
Ames, Iowa
Washington, D.C.
February 1964

CONTENTS

PREFACE   iii

LIST OF TABLES   ix

LIST OF FIGURES   x

part one ORIENTATION TO THE STUDY
OF SOCIAL PROBLEMS   1

1   A Dynamic Society   3

2   The Nature of Social Problems   26

3   The Treatment of Social Problems   40

part two FOCUSES OF SOCIAL PROBLEMS
IN AMERICAN SOCIETY   61

Introduction   63

4   Economic Problems in an Age of Abundance   65

5   Adapting to Major Economic Change   86

6   The City   102

7   Population Problems: World and National   118

8   Marriage   134

9   Education   154

vii

10 Religion 176

11 Leisure and Recreation 193

12 Race 213

13 Physical Health 234

14 Mental Health 252

15 Old Age 277

16 Crime and the Criminal 301

17 Juvenile Delinquency 325

18 Some Conventional Deviations 347

19 Pressure Groups 360

20 Broader Implications: The World Background 381

part three   OVERVIEW 391

21 Rationalism and Value Analysis 393

22 American Ideology and the Hope for Rational Action 404

AUTHOR INDEX 411

SUBJECT INDEX 415

LIST OF TABLES

1   Changing Occupational Composition of the United States   10

2   Projected School Enrollments, 1960–1980   11

3   National Income in the United States, 1929–1961   68

4   Changes in Dollar versus "Real" Income   69

5   Income Distribution in the United States in 1961   71

6   Unemployment in the United States, 1947–1962   76

7   Fuel Production: 13 Years of Change   88

8   Farm Employment—Annual Averages   89

9   United States Farm Price Index   89

10 Farm Mortgage Debt   90

11 Percent of Population Living in Cities, 1900–1960   103

12 Number and Size of Cities, 1900–1960   103

13 Population and Population Growth by Continents, 1930–1959   122

14 Population Growth in the United States, 1790–1960   129

15 Federal Government Funds for Education, 1959–1960   172

16 Extent of Chronic Illness in the United States   236

17 Family Income and Family Health Expenses   242

18 Family Income and Number of Doctor Visits per Year   243

19 Patients in Mental Hospitals, 1935–1960   258

20 Ratio of Mental Patients to Personnel in Public Mental Hospitals 272

ix

21	*Life Expectancy at Birth and Selected Ages, 1900–1960*	*278*
22	*Total Population and Population 65 and Over, 1900–1963*	*279*
23	*Income of Older Persons and Families, 1961*	*287*
24	*Proportion of Older Workers, 1900–1960*	*288*

LIST OF FIGURES

1	*U.S. Population Growth since 1800*	*7*
2	*Increasing Farm Output per Man-Hour of Work*	*9*
3	*How the Total Income is Distributed*	*66*
4	*World Population Growth, 1650–1960*	*120*
5	*Sources of Public School Finance, 1960*	*171*
6	*Population and Income*	*382*

PART I

ORIENTATION TO THE STUDY OF SOCIAL PROBLEMS

A DYNAMIC SOCIETY   1

Recently it was reported in the press that the "bride price" in an African tribe had spiraled upward. The size of the customary gift to the bride's father had become so great that many young men could not afford to marry. Here indeed are the ingredients for an emerging social problem. Yet no one should try to solve this problem until he knows considerably more about this society where inflation was threatening romance. We should learn something about the history of this society's experiences with the custom to discover what function in the society bride price serves, how and by whom the price scale is set, what seemingly has caused it to rise, and how the giving of a substantial gift to the bride's father fits in with other customs, beliefs, and values of the society. Not until these and many other questions are answered could we even begin to address ourselves to the matter of what to do about the problem.

There is a lesson to be learned from considering this specific problem in a society remote from our own. It illustrates the infeasibility of trying to study a social problem out of the context in which it occurs and of which, in actuality, it is a part. It helps us appreciate the need for sound understanding of the social history of the society and, ideally, the need for some insight concerning the direction in which the society is moving. Given a proper perspective, our understanding of the problem should be more complete and any corrective action more reasonable and effective.

Because the problems with which we will be dealing in this book occur in our own society and in our own time, it does not follow that we can dispense with the task of struggling to see them in societal perspective. On the contrary, the contemporary student may be so accustomed to today's problems and "things as they are" that he does not recognize that some of the familiar issues are relatively recent occurrences or that others have long been with us. With all of the concern for juvenile delinquency, for example, and the need to help our youth to use their spare time wisely, it is difficult to remember that not so long ago "the problem" was that children worked too long and too hard. Again, with the general recognition that inflation is one of the economic realities of our life, memories of depressions become less vivid. The sight of our vast cities with their sprawling suburbs makes it very difficult indeed to appreciate the fact that less than a hundred years ago ours was a distinctly rural nation. And so on.

AMERICAN SOCIETY IN PERSPECTIVE

Even our few examples above make it clear that American society has changed and is changing—and rather dramatically at that. The fundamental lesson of human history is that *all* societies are dynamic. There is no such thing as a static, never changing society. It is true that in some eras and in some places change may appear to be slight, while at other times and in different societies change may be rapid and all-encompassing. Even after one has studied a considerable amount of social history and mastered the general proposition that human society is ever changing, he may still easily underestimate the true *extent* of the change through which he has lived or the many different aspects of his society that have been significantly modified. To get the full impact of the amount and nature of change in our own society, relative to other times and places, it would seem desirable to take a panoramic view of all human societies over time and then to move in closer, so to speak, and examine in more detail some of the important changes in our relatively recent past.

A Panoramic View of Human Society

It has been estimated that the species of man we call *homo sapiens* has been on this earth 100,000 years. Here on our own continent, which was relatively late to welcome human inhabitants, it is now thought that man was dwelling 30,000 to 40,000 years ago. Surely we would all admit that "times have changed" over this relatively long span of years. But how can we visualize this difference and appreciate it fully?

There is one view that depicts civilization as a gradually sloping line, representing an ever upward and onward progress in civilization from man's beginning, through his long history, and leading on into the future. Another view sees social change in a cyclical fashion. Great civilizations rise, reach an apex, and then decline. The experience of the Roman Empire is probably the most frequently cited example of this viewpoint. Yet even if we go back before the founding of the Republic, the whole Roman period is something less than a thousand years. In a sense, studying but a thousand years is taking a short run view of the history of mankind, and it is no wonder that the rises and falls in civilization stand out so clearly.

A third view of the history of human society is a little more difficult to visualize. Perhaps an analogy would be useful. In the biological world we have gradual changes in the species as they adapt to their environment and, side by side, sudden mutations caused by a "freak of the genes." Under certain conditions these mutations or abrupt changes can become fixed or inherited. And so, by analogy, social change can be visualized. Intermingled with the gradual changes in man's societies over the long course of 100,000 years, there have been abrupt and radical changes, or mutations, which then became fixed.

Looking at the entire span of time, it has been posited that there have been only three great mutations in civilization. The first occurred tens of thousands of years ago and was marked by man's learning to use tools and fire, and developing a true language. Imagine the vast range of activities now opened to man. With his fire, he could protect himself better from the elements and could create better tools. His chances for survival increased. With his language, man could transmit all that he learned to the next generation. For thousands of years, man gradually became better and better equipped to cope with his environment. Building on the past, he developed ever-better ways to shelter himself from the elements, to gather his food, and to protect himself from his enemies. Still, these fundamental necessities occupied most of his time.

A second mutation then occurred, this one a mere 6000 to 7000 years ago, when man learned how to *raise* food. Consider the tremendous impact of this. Food became more abundant and the chances for survival increased dramatically. Homes could become fixed, for no longer was it necessary to roam great distances in search of food. With more available food, and food that could be stored, hunters, fishermen, and food gatherers were released for other activities. In this period men began to smelt and work metals, invented the wheel, developed writing and built small cities. Within a thousand years after this mutation the rudiments of civilization as we ordinarily think of it were laid down, and for a long time thereafter only gradual changes took place.

The third great mutation occurred only recently, in the mid-1700s. It was marked by the great *industrial revolution* and in particular by man's learning how to derive power from heat. In the years immediately preceding, there was, of course, some industry. Hand powered looms existed and various arts and crafts were practiced. But these industrial activities were for the most part conducted in the home or in small shops. Substituting steam power for human power called for radical changes in industry and had ramifications for the entire social order. Steam proved to be quite efficient and relatively cheap, but it has the quality of not being capable of transmission over great distances. The only feasible system, therefore, was to collect all the workers in a great place and feed to each of their looms and other machines the magic power of steam. Thus was industry removed from the home, city living encouraged, and new roles developed for family members.

In the two hundred years since the onslaught of the third great mutation we have, of course, improved upon our power, and inventions have followed inventions with remarkable speed. It is interesting to note, in this connection, that atomic energy has not yet been used directly, but is a new method of creating heat from whence is derived power. Automation is in actuality an improvement and expansion of previously existing industrial techniques, rather than something entirely new. It would seem that we are still living within the tidal wave of the third great mutation and, indeed, there is no indication that we have passed the peak in this third surge.

It is fascinating, but a little awesome, to be living at the time of one of the three great upheavals in human affairs. As contrasted with the longer periods between the peaks, these are times of swift and dramatic change. Change is of such magnitude, occurs with such relative suddenness, and affects so many areas of life, that it is only with difficulty that those not living in such a period could imagine it and those within the period can accept it. In times of rapid change, habit and tradition are no longer completely acceptable guides to action, accustomed patterns of behavior are replaced by nuances, and the familiar is superseded by the unfamiliar. The many and far-reaching effects of rapid social change are well kept in mind as we turn now to look at the relatively recent past of American society.

THE RECENT PAST OF OUR DYNAMIC SOCIETY

It is not our intention in this section to attempt an encyclopedic account of the myriad changes that have occurred in our society. Rather, we want to investigate a sample of the many different aspects of American society that have shown pronounced change in the last 100 to 150 years. Our stress will be on the magnitude of the changes. Since many of these matters will be handled in greater detail in subsequent chapters, at this point we will not dwell on the implications of the changes.

People and More People

Looking back over the last century or century and a half of our society, one is struck at once by the tremendous increase in the number of people.

FIGURE 1   U.S. POPULATION GROWTH SINCE 1800

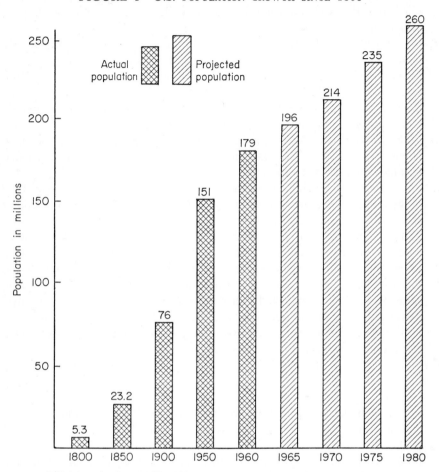

NOTE: Official projection, 1965–1980.

SOURCE: U.S. Bureau of the Census.

A little over a hundred years ago, in 1860, there were but 31 million people in this country; now we number almost 190 million. There are more people today in two of our states, New York and California, than there were in the entire country at about the time of the Civil War.

It is difficult to appreciate all that is implied when a society adds 160 million people, an increase of 600 percent, in about 100 years. In the early decades of this period, our rate of growth was over 25 percent. At each census period, in other words, there were over a fourth more people than there had been ten years previously. Gradually the rate of growth declined somewhat, reaching a low in the 1930s. The census year of 1960, however, found that the population had increased about 18 percent during the preceding ten-year interval.

A simple listing of some of the more gross effects of a continuously increasing population is enough to stagger one. As the present rate of growth is reflected at different age levels, we will find that each year about 3 million more children will be starting school, 3 million more persons than the year before will be searching for jobs, getting married, needing homes, and purchasing the many, many goods and services our society has to offer. When this type of growth continues for a time, it calls for expansion in almost every area of life that can be imagined, and soon expansion itself becomes familiar and expected.

There is every indication that our population will continue to grow in the immediate future. As we indicate in Figure 1, the official projections show us passing the 200 million mark in the late 1960s and having over 250 million people ten years after that! How long can this kind of growth continue before it produces difficulties and, later, real hardships? Should we attempt to slow down our rate of growth and, if so, how should we try to do it? How can our economy, geared as it is to continual expansion in so many spheres, be adjusted to a modest rate of population growth only? These are some of the questions that the present generation will have to answer. They cannot be ignored. But even tentative attempts to answer them will reveal a diversity of value positions within our society.

Rural-Urban Population Shift

Within the last 150 years we have evolved from a nation made up almost entirely of rural inhabitants to one in which over 70 percent of the people live in cities. Even within the last sixty years or so we can notice profound changes. At the turn of the century there were about 30 million Americans living in cities; now there are over 125 million urbanites in America. The enormity of the change that has taken place becomes even more evident when we consider the *size* of the cities in which millions of Americans live. Over 50 million people are living in cities with populations of 100,000 or more. If we consider metropolitan areas, which consist of a central city and the surrounding places that are sufficiently integrated with the city, we find that about 113 million Americans are in metropolitan areas with a central city of 50,000 inhabitants. In cities of a million or more are 17.5 million people. By way of contrast, in the entire country there are about 20 million people, or about 12 percent of the population, living on farms. There can no longer be any doubt but that we are a distinctly urban society.

Changing Occupational Patterns

Becoming an urbanized society affects people's occupations as well as the kind of place in which they live. As we might expect from the urbanization rates, there has been a pronounced decline in the number of farmers and farm laborers over the last fifty years. Today a scant 7 percent of the labor force makes its living by farming, as opposed to 31 percent in 1910. Despite the great increase in the number of people that need to be fed, we have had a noticeable decrease in the proportion of workers required to meet this need. The answer, of course, lies in the fact of greater farm efficiency and greater production per farm worker.[1] Using index numbers that

FIGURE 2   INCREASING FARM OUTPUT PER MAN-HOUR OF WORK

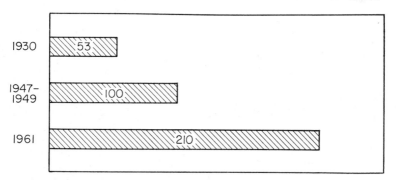

NOTE: Farm products available for human use divided by index of man-hours worked.

SOURCE: U.S. Bureau of the Census, *Statistical Abstract of the United States: 1962* (Washington, D.C., 1962), p. 644.

are based on available farm products and number of hours worked on farms, we note that even within the last thirty years farm output per man-hour worked has increased almost fourfold. Obviously there is some minimum number of farmers necessary to provide the food and fiber for our population of almost 190 million, but from all indications this minimum has not yet been reached.

Another dramatic shift that has occurred is the increase in the proportion of professionals, proprietors, and sales and clerical personnel, and the decline in proportion of laborers of all types. With the present stress on automation and mechanization generally, the increase in skilled and semi-skilled workers is not pronounced. As time goes on, we can expect that the

[1] See Chapter 5.

trend toward more "white collar" occupations will continue and that the "blue collar" jobs will demand increasingly better trained personnel.

Table 1 Changing Occupational Composition of the United States

Occupation	Percent in 1910	Percent in 1960
Farmers	16.5	4.4
Farm laborers	14.5	2.9
Professionals	4.4	12.2
Proprietors and officials	6.5	11.5
Clerks, sales, and kindred workers	10.2	22.8
Skilled and semiskilled workers	26.4	31.6
Laborers	14.7	4.4

SOURCE: U.S. Bureau of the Census, *Statistical Abstract of the United States: 1960,* Washington, D.C., 1960, p. 217.

Occupational shifts, finally, have not only affected the male bread-winners, but have also been evident in the increasing employment of married women. At the turn of the century, less than 6 percent of all married women were employed outside the home; today almost a third of all married women are so employed. Almost half of the married women without children are now working outside the home. Women's work has thus changed its nature every bit as much as has men's work.

A More Highly Educated Nation

In the last fifty years significant changes have occurred in the educational attainments of Americans. In 1910 about 3 percent of the people who were then twenty-five to twenty-nine years of age had completed college; 10 percent had completed high school. Almost a fourth of them had completed less than five years of grade school. Of those who were twenty-five to twenty-nine years old in 1960, and presumably finished with their schooling, about 13 percent had completed college and 41 percent had completed high school. The relatively unschooled, those with less than five years of grade school, has shrunk to less than 3 percent.

Fifty years is, in actuality, a short time in which to accomplish the change in educational achievement that we have witnessed. When change is so swift and so dramatic, it is not hard to understand that there are many problems associated with it. Keeping pace with the increasing demand for more schools and more teachers is an understandably difficult task, and one that our society has not really accomplished.[2]

Table 2   Projected School Enrollments, 1960–1980
(in millions)

	1960	1975	1980
Elementary school	32½	37–42	41–48
High school	10¼	15–16	15–17
College	3½	6–8	6½–9

SOURCE: U.S. Bureau of the Census, *Current Population Reports,* Series P-25, No. 232 (June 22, 1961), p. 2.

Projected school enrollments for the immediate future of ten to fifteen years indicate continued increases. We cannot see in the immediate future any time when we will be able simply to "catch up" with the backlog of demand for more and better teachers and educational facilities. By 1980 grade school enrollment is expected to increase about one third, high school enrollment by at least a half, and enrollment in college will probably be more than double what it was in 1960. The expected increase in grade school attendance is, of course, a function both of the high birth rate and compulsory school attendance laws. At the high school and college levels, however, the projections take into account not only that there will be more people of the appropriate ages but that a higher proportion of them will want and need more education. The question remains whether we will be able to adjust our thinking and shift our resources so that we will be able to meet the demand with a minimum of confusion.

An Older Population

It is paradoxical that at the same time that our society has had to meet the needs of more and more children and youths, it has also been confronted with an increased number of older people.[3] As is often true when change occurs swiftly, it is difficult to appreciate the magnitude of the growth in the number of aged in our society. Today it would take the cities of Chicago, Los Angeles, Philadelphia, Detroit, Washington, D.C., Cleveland, Baltimore, Boston, St. Louis, and San Francisco to house all of the old people in the United States; the aged of 1900 could have been housed in *one* of our present-day cities, Chicago.

While the sheer number of old people is important, it is likewise neces-

[2] Chapter 9 deals with the social problems of the American educational system.
[3] For a fuller discussion of the social problems of old age see Chapter 15.

sary to realize that the older segment of our population has been growing significantly faster than the population in general. The 17½ million older people of today represent over 9 percent of the total population—more than double the proportion of older people at the turn of the century. By 1980 about 10 percent of our population will be sixty-five years of age and older and this will increase to between 13 and 15 percent by the year 2000.

Our society has barely begun to address itself to the imposing catalogue of problems related to its aged. We need the productive efforts of our capable older citizens, yet, increasingly, we are fostering the policy of compulsive retirement at age sixty-five. Housing, health, and recreation are three additional areas which will have to receive a decidedly different emphasis if we are to meet the needs of this rapidly increasing segment of the population. At present, it seems unlikely that the immediate future will see much relief in these problem areas, and it is probable that some of the problems of the aged will become intensified before, as a society, we can make the necessary adjustments in our thinking and our policies.

Inventions and Innovations

While it is impossible to do justice to the topic, we cannot ignore the new material objects and ideas that have been produced by our society in the recent past. Faster and more efficient methods of travel and communication are but two examples. Together they have enabled persons in any one part of the country to be closely in touch with those in every other section. They have spread the common culture, or at least knowledge of it, more evenly throughout the society than has heretofore been true. Families in the northeast consume food that cannot be grown in their climate, farmers in the midwest have at least some idea how factory workers in the urban east live and earn a living, and all over the country people can watch the same television programs, see the same motion pictures, and read the same syndicated columns in their so-called local newspapers. Events and happenings in one section of the country are quickly disseminated throughout the land. A labor strike in Detroit, a forest fire on the west coast, racial troubles in the South, the marriage or death of a celebrity, rapidly become in some respects a shared experience of Americans. Thus, the "homogenizing" and other social effects of the innovations in travel and communication are staggering and, in truth, our knowledge of them is meager.

Almost any adult American could draw up an imposing list of "wonderful inventions" and "new things" that have been produced within his lifetime. Probably he is unaware, however, how profoundly such innovations have changed his life and the life of those around him. In terms of the billions of people who have lived throughout the long course of human history, it is a unique experience to have so many and such major changes occur within a generation.

We must not ignore the various social inventions that we have witnessed and are witnessing. As a matter of fact, it may well be that in the long run our period will be better remembered for its inventions of ideas rather than "things." Already we can see that there is much truth in this proposition. Take, for example, the contributions of one of our first industrialists, Henry Ford. No one will deny the importance of his technical contributions, particularly his refinements of the principle of assembly line production and interchangeability of parts. At the same time, Ford's "radical idea" that the worker should be paid a wage that would allow him to buy an automobile did much to make his technical inventions practical. The idea of mass consumption is certainly a major social invention and one that is not yet found in many, many parts of the world.

Among other social inventions we would number the extension of the ballot to women, mass public education, and our attempts at racial equality, meager as they sometimes appear. These are but a few of the multitude of "new ideas" we have witnessed in recent years and it would require considerable space even to list the many areas of life in which their impact has been felt.

THE MASS SOCIETY [4]

People with sufficient maturity and education to read this book already know a good deal about contemporary human relations and society. College students know, or ought to, that the modern world is one of massive organization and that the coercive power of large organization over the individual is definitive. Even if we had to rely upon television and movie interpretations, we must by now realize, despite the oversimplifications, that we are living in a kind of world in which a remarkable sameness pervades the people and the situations in which they participate. To be sure, there are still some regional variations and sometimes some telltale reminders that one's classmates have come from different national groups or have distinctive religious convictions. But chiefly these are impedimenta to be lived down or to be kept under wraps in the modern world—not adhered to in the prideful way in which these differences were worn in the past.

Everyone knows, or says he does, that things were not always this way, that the kind of human relationships which we now have evolved in a complicated historical process which is at least vaguely understood. But vague understanding is not enough for a sociologist—a trip to the zoo does

[4] John F. Cuber, *Sociology: A Synopsis of Principles* (5th ed.; Des Moines. Copyright © 1963 by Meredith Publishing Company), pp. 62–76.

not make one a zoologist. We need to look more closely, to analyze more precisely and with greater objectivity than is ordinarily achieved, in order to understand what the present human mélange really is.

It has been observed that the last thing that a creature in the ocean would identify would be water. Carrying this notion to our own sphere, it is equally true that some of the last characteristics that contemporary Americans—or for that matter, contemporary Russians—would recognize in their own society would at the same time constitute that society's most salient characteristics as seen by someone from the outside.

Probably the most fundamental features that have transformed the historical Western society, which is now called a "mass society" by many professionals, are growing homogeneity and conformity. One of the reasons why the layman is likely to underestimate the extent to which his potential individualism is atrophied is due to the many and subtle ways in which society influences his desires and rewards his conformity, thus tending to obliterate his individualism. For example, one says he earnestly desires to own a recording by a new television star, but he is likely not to recognize that he desires this particular recording because, usually through no effort or choice of his own, he was exposed to it by society and not to something else as a result of his own curiosity or exploration. He desires to conform to the latest fad; he is not, as he sees it, coerced or unduly influenced. He maintains the illusion that this is his own choice. Curiously enough, Americans are typically very sensitive about being what they call brainwashed, yet are all living in a society in which more and more of us are being brainwashed every day in innumerable ways of which we are largely unaware.

What are the sources of this "great sameness" which has settled increasingly upon the American society and also upon much of the Western world?

Mass Communication

The external influences which play upon people are becoming increasingly standardized. For example, in the United States four national television networks and four national radio networks supply virtually all of the important television programs and commercials, including the so-called public information and public affairs services. Anyone even remotely familiar with the radio and television industry is aware that there are few, if any, significant differences among the services of these four so-called competitors. The major reason for this sameness is, of course, that these networks are all trying to reach the maximal audience, and thus they scrupulously avoid offending any religious, occupational, regional, or social group, since this would reduce the number of viewers and reduce the value of the program to the sponsor, to whom, of course, it represents a costly investment.

The effect is to play down differences of all kinds as far as possible and to accent the common denominators of opinion, taste, and values.

Newspapers represent a similar influence in the direction of accenting uniformity and playing down differences. Between 1925 and 1955, for example, the number of English language newspapers in the United States decreased by 248, while the circulation of newspapers increased from 34 to 56 million. In 1900, 42 percent of the cities of the United States had daily newspapers with noncompetitive ownership; by 1954, 94 percent had noncompetitive ownership. In other words, at the present time only 6 percent of American cities have local daily newspapers with competing ownership.[5]

There are many reasons, chiefly economic, that explain the concentration of our sources of information, entertainment, and education. We are not here concerned with these reasons—simply with the facts which together support the inescapable conclusion that uniformity in taste and information is exceedingly hard to escape, unless one turns to sources other than radio, television, and the newspapers for his intellectual stimulation. Not many do.

A number of students of contemporary society have been exceedingly critical of some of the personal manipulation that this kind of concentration of influence makes possible. One best selling popular book [6] has richly documented the effectiveness of the standardization of taste and intelligence that presumably results from such concentration of influence. Probably no one book, however, could succeed in giving a sufficiently complete picture of the great extent to which one or another kind of thought control shapes the minds, the aspirations, the tastes, and the world view of the great mass of the American people.

Mass Production and Distribution

As every schoolboy knows, we live in a "mass-production economy." With the modern production and distribution systems which we have, we make vast numbers of identical units, and so it is possible to sell them at prices low enough that the items are available to great numbers of people of even modest financial circumstances. At the same time it is possible to pay wages to the great mass of partially skilled laborers that enable them to buy commodities that in previous times would have been reserved for the rich.

But the cycle of increasing production, it was found, needed further stimulation and so there was invented, and firmly established in American society, a practice known as installment buying. Very few durable items of

[5] Wilbur Schramm, *Responsibility in Mass Communication* (New York: Harper & Row, Publishers, 1957), p. 4.

[6] Vance Packard, *The Hidden Persuaders* (New York: Pocket Books, 1958).

consumer goods now need to be purchased outright by persons with steady incomes. In fact, it has become customary to advertise only the down payment and the monthly installment when trying to attract customers. This has had the effect, as intended, of greatly increasing, at least in the short run, the amount of goods that the public is able to absorb. Whether or not in the long run installment buying greatly increases the volume of goods that a society can absorb, is a question about which economists are not in complete agreement. There is, however, no disagreement that installment buying of identical mass-produced goods is an entrenched part of the American way.

It is easier to describe the practice of installment purchasing of goods and services than it is to appraise its subjective influences upon the people who live such budgeteered lives. It is not our purpose here to attempt such an evaluation. We are simply making the point that not only does almost everyone own the same collection of gadgets, but everyone has the same anxieties about down payments and monthly payments and is aware that everyone else is in the same boat with him. Thus, not only the external materials are mass produced, so are the anxieties and the concerns and the skills of making one's way in the world.

Stronger Government

In the modern mass society the citizens have come to rely more and more on the government to provide services that formerly were supplied either by persons for themselves or by some kind of private contract with a supplier. The "welfare state," which to some traditionalists has become a form of polite profanity, is not the whole issue. Many of the numerous and increasing rules, regulations, and controls no one seriously expects even a "conservative" government to abolish. Traffic tickets to jaywalkers, licenses for dogs which never leave the owner's premises, compulsory liability insurance for auto drivers, are merely token illustrations of the increasing number and the increasingly restrictive nature of collective controls over the conduct of people. And the end is by no means in sight.

Part of the continued pressure to pass more and more laws requiring more and more people to do more and more things more and more alike goes on apace. One of the obvious reasons is that it is more convenient that way. If everyone is required to act in a certain way, then it becomes easier to "get along"; one always knows what the other person will do, because he has to do it. The real awkwardness, the real nuisance is that occasional person who insists on being different; the way to take care of him is to make a rule that will require him to do as others bid.

There are undoubtedly many other factors that would help to explain why the homogeneous-conformist accents, which are the essence of the mass society, have come to be what they are. Simply focusing on mass communication, mass production and distribution, and increasing government regulation, nevertheless, goes a long way to reveal the underpinnings of the contemporary order.

CONSEQUENCES

The mass society, whether one likes it or not, has had a number of consequences. The daily lives of people, their hopes and fears, their way of coming at life, are strongly influenced by the configuration of circumstances which we have just described. A few of the consequences of these mass influences deserve brief preliminary consideration.

A Sense of Affluence

Ever since J. K. Galbraith, then (1958) a well-known Harvard economist, wrote *The Affluent Society*,[7] this apt phrase has been a part of the daily discourse of informed people. The gist of the point is that following a decade or more of depression and slow recovery in which unemployment, financial reverses, modest incomes, and considerable austerity occurred, America, and to some extent much of the rest of the Western world, has experienced what appears in contrast to be bountiful times. Very probably World War II was the greatest single factor in bringing about the remarkable reversal. Nevertheless, the reversal occurred and in comparison to the thirties and forties, life in the fifties and sixties has seemed affluent indeed. This does not mean, to be sure, that everyone is rich and certainly not that financial problems for many people are not still the cardinal problems of living. The essence of the affluent society lies in the abundance of goods and services that the great mass of Americans and other people in Western civilization are enjoying, and the rather remarkable freedom from serious ups and downs in business cycles that the last two decades have brought.

Some critics have complained that Americans have thereby become a more materialistic people, that we revel not in our good deeds or our pure hearts, but rather in our inventories of installment-ridden goods. Whether or not there has been an appreciable increase in materialism as a result of current affluence, is something which is exceedingly complicated and difficult to pass quick judgment upon in an objective evaluation. It is, of course, quite possible that these critics are right. Nevertheless, the modern citizen lives his life accustomed to a prima facie luxury which the older person finds strange by comparison to the conditions of life that he can recall from his own past, just twenty or thirty years ago.

[7] John K. Galbraith, *The Affluent Society* (Boston: Houghton Mifflin Company, 1958).

Fragmentation

The mass society appears to require a fragmentized life for the participant in it. Work is increasingly specialized so that when one explains "what he does," he finds very few people who can really understand him. Often the best answer to the question is at the same time the vaguest one, "I work for Coca-Cola." Life at work and the rest of life are typically very, very different from each other, and there is little feedback from one to the other. There is a very general view to the effect that except for the professions, and not always then, work is no longer supposed to yield much satisfaction; the rest of life is to provide a kind of therapy, or at least diversion, to make the work world bearable.

High Mobility

Within the mass society there is a great deal of personal movement. Part of this is coerced. Practically every male youth is required to spend some time in the armed forces and it is not at all unusual to be "shipped" around the world. Many corporations have a policy of moving important as well as secondary personnel from one part of the country to another for a variety of efficiency reasons. But a great deal of mobility is also voluntary, either for financial betterment or because the climate may be better or just because it may be fun to move. Many people move from one part of the country to another with little fear of feeling strange in the new place, because people and circumstances have become so standardized that it takes but a short time, if any, to feel at home again. Every census shows a smaller and smaller percentage of population living in the states of birth.

The Organization Man

A few years ago William Whyte, Jr. wrote an extremely influential and provocative book called *The Organization Man*.[8] This phrase has become a byword. Whyte's inimitable portrait of the man who "takes the vows of corporation life" and the wife who must come to accept the fact that "her husband belongs first to the corporation" is to many millions of people nothing more than a blunt description of what they had already come to realize. For the Organization Man the central facts of life are belongingness and togetherness, and his success may well depend quite as much on his facility in adopting this way of life as upon any other skills he may have developed or talent he may possess. Putting the matter as we have may lead

[8] William Whyte, Jr., *The Organization Man* (New York: Simon and Schuster, Inc., 1956).

to the inference that there is a general resentment against the Organization-Man psychology. Except for occasional instances, this seems not to be the case. The overwhelming mass of people seemingly accept this mode of life as altogether natural and acceptable under the circumstances, and many of them are quite grateful for the protecting arm of the corporation with its abundant fringe benefits such as health insurance, life insurance, recreational programs, pensions, educational programs, and a whole host of protections against individual adversity. The consequence, again, seems a reinforcement of what we have pointed out several times before: a blurring of individual difference and an accenting of common problems, common orientations, and common satisfactions.

Individual identity is increasingly submerged in the larger mass of organization. Not only is this true at work but also in religious organizations and community associations. Thus, at work and at play the typical American is submerged in categories of organization and, insofar as he thinks much about it, seems rather grateful for the large amount of security that this kind of life has brought him.

"Other Direction"

David Riesman's *The Lonely Crowd,*[9] is another contemporary classic. One of the main threads in this original and highly respected interpretation of American life is the condition which he calls other-direction. Putting it tersely, other-direction means that a person looks to his immediate associates for his standards of correct and incorrect behavior. In contrast, the inner-directed and/or tradition-directed person looks to longer standing "principles" and "authorities" for answers to questions of morality, propriety, etiquette, and other proscriptions for the good life. Riesman's research convinced him that other-direction has become the prevailing morality, if it can be so called, in American society and thus has added a further and telling evidence of encrustation of conformity. The other-directed person, the prevailing person-type according to Riesman, is not a conformist simply in the things he owns, or in the recreation he follows, or in his artistic tastes. He is a conformist to the immediate group in a far deeper sense— his concepts of right and wrong, the important and the unimportant, the permissible and the disapproved. Since the other-directed person is not geared in his moral precepts to any kind of eternal verities, he typically possesses an elastic conscience. But the elasticity is not of his own contrivance; rather it is that of the group with which he "runs around." The immediate group of his peers is the final arbiter of what is right or wrong, approved or disapproved. As the group changes, he changes. The greatest

[9] David Riesman, Reuel Denny, and Nathan Glazer, *The Lonely Crowd* (New Haven: Yale University Press, 1950).

breach of morality is to break with the group; the act in question is secondary.

Riesman is careful to emphasize that not everyone is other-directed and that some people are a mixture of other- and inner-direction. But he seems to insist that other-direction is the prevailing psychology of man in the modern mass society and that more and more we are producing other-directed men.

Amorality

Another aspect of the mass society which has attracted the attention of many observers is a seemingly growing casualness about traditional moral precepts where the collective enterprise is concerned. A dramatic incident which comes to mind is the election of an ex-convict to the mayorship of Boston in recent years. The man's crime was no impulsive crime of passion but a rather deliberate and continued violation of tax law. The concept "white collar crime" has come into wide usage to describe the activities of persons engaged in seemingly legitimate businesses and professions, but who in the course of their work systematically and more or less openly violate not only the modern laws but the time-honored religious and moral precepts concerning proper conduct. The line between "smart business" and gross immorality has come to be so badly blurred that for millions there is no line at all.

In the *Power Elite,* C. Wright Mills [10] coins the phrase "the higher immorality" to characterize the rather cynical disregard for moral precepts that he says typically characterizes elite persons in the high military, governmental, and business echelons. Perhaps more telltale, however, is the far more general characteristic in American society of "the public relations front"—the deliberate use of falsehood and misrepresentation, even by institutions supposedly dedicated to high purposes, when making bids for public acceptance or covering up a scandal.

These are probably simply extensions of a more diffuse amorality, such as falsification, on oath, of the rate of speed at which a friend's auto was traveling when it struck a pedestrian. The essential point seems to be that in the large, impersonal society, many people, who are scrupulously moral toward persons they know and care about, are notably callous and unmoral where the victims of their behavior are removed by time and space and less intimate relationships. For whatever reasons, the historical precepts fostered by the church and incorporated in our basic law seem not very convincing to large numbers of people when the consequences of their acts are not immediately visible to them.

[10] C. Wright Mills, *The Power Elite* (New York: Oxford University Press, 1956).

Racketeering

Closely tied with the foregoing several points and in some degree simply a special case of some of them, is a widespread occupation known as racketeering. Racketeering practices are so normal in American society that for the most part they are no longer reported in the press, except now and then when a homicide or particularly sensational scandal comes to light. In the more genteel modern practice of racketeering, the crude methods reminiscent of the 1920s are in ill-repute. There are better ways in today's racketeering that do not stir up much opposition and get the job done as effectively.

> Business and industrial rackets in American cities have principally developed in the distribution of services and commodities. The racketeer has found that the soft spot in the American competitive system is the point of distribution of services and goods in the urban community, for it is in this area that competition is keenest and demand is greatest. Milk must get out. Bread must be distributed. Newspapers must go on the streets. Fish and poultry must be disposed of quickly. In other words, the racketeer found the vulnerable place in the American system of free enterprise and took advantage of it in the absence of effective laws and law enforcement.
>
> Very few fields of distribution of services and goods in the large American cities have been able to stay out of the clutches of racketeers. Taking the outstanding rackets in New York City as an example, Thompson found that there were rackets in the clothing business, in the running of taxicabs, in the distribution of fish, in the poultry business, in the building and construction business, in the milk dealers' business, in the distribution of artichokes, and in the operation of movie houses.[11]

> The racketeer, therefore, became a new type of middleman dictator who was able to control and enforce the conditions of doing business. He set up a monopoly. He also became a stabilizer of business through his enforced regulations and prices. He became the illegal policeman of the distribution of services and goods. He is the invisible government of urban distribution who cannot be touched by legal government.[12]

The important aspects of the situation, which are insufficiently noted, seem to be these: (1) There is very little attention paid to the large amount of racketeering that has infiltrated into at least fifty fields of business, as the

---

[11] Craig Thompson and Allen Raymond, *Gang Rule in New York: The Story of a Lawless Era* (New York: The Dial Press, Inc., 1940), p. 220.

[12] Walter C. Reckless, *The Crime Problem* (3d ed.; New York: Appleton-Century-Crofts, 1961), pp. 191–192.

Kefauver Committee [13] investigations pointed out. (2) Present methods of enforcement are notoriously ineffective in curbing racketeering practices. (3) Most important of all, there is little sense of public outrage when the vast extent of racketeering activities is made public, as, for example, by the Kefauver Committee investigations in 1951.

It should not be inferred from the foregoing that a blanket indictment of American society is intended. Quite the contrary. No indictment whatsoever is implied—we intend simply a candid camera description of a number of aspects of American society which are well known among professional social scientists but which are not widely recognized by many people who consider themselves well informed. There prevails today a kind of schoolboy conception of life which prefers to pretend that old platitudinous descriptions are true and offers reassurances, largely detached from reality, that the real world is something other than what it is. One certainly has the moral right to such views, but abdication of intelligence is not conducive either to informed citizenship or objective scholarship.

MASS SOCIETY AS A WORLD-WIDE CONCEPT

Up to this point we have discussed the mass society as if it were distinctly American. It is, of course, not so. Most of the European nations, increasingly even including Russia, show many of the same characteristics. If it were not for the barriers of language and a few remnants of pluralistic origins, people from the United States would find, and some of them already have found, that the conditions of their lives and their attitudes and tastes are quite congruent with those of persons of similar class position in other nations of Europe, South America, and even here and there in Asia. This is what some observers have meant by the emergence of "one world."

But there are really still two worlds: (1) the modern-urbanized-mass society, as exemplified by the United States and increasingly approached by Russia, and (2) the so-called underdeveloped areas. The latter are essentially rural and derive their sustenance from the soil, chiefly by what seem to us to be archaic, almost superstitious modes of cultivation, and fabrication of raw materials for human use. Despite nominal nation-states, the great mass of people in the underdeveloped areas have been relatively untouched by the more cosmic political considerations which are of so great importance to the nations in the mass society. Numerous observers have pointed out that most of the rank and file in the East and in Africa, for example, are often oblivious to the changes in political fortunes of the nations

[13] *Third Interim Report of the Special Committee to Investigate Organized Crime in Interstate Commerce,* United States Senate, Report No. 307 (Washington, D.C.: Government Printing Office, 1951).

of which they are presumably citizens. They typically have no part in formulating political decisions, are illiterate or nearly so, and by and large could not care less whether their nominal leaders are allied with the East or the West or hold a capitalistic or Communist political philosophy. The urgencies of existence are so stark and the life risks are so apolitical that only a very few ever find their way intellectually beyond the immediate exigencies of existence.

It hardly needs mentioning that the so-called underdeveloped areas are rapidly being developed. Both the United States and Russia, the two principal world powers, are spreading technical "know-how," first in agriculture and simple medicine, and later with industrial techniques, as a means of aligning the various underdeveloped areas with its respective side. Each sees this as a necessary condition to winning what is called the Cold War.

One should not lose sight of the fact, however, that underdeveloped areas have been served by various agencies in this country and others for a long time. Much of the activity of early missionaries was, in practice, as much educational and economic as it was theological. Thousands of hospitals and agricultural demonstration stations dot the world as evidence that for various reasons, chiefly humanitarian, efforts have been made to change the modes of life of simpler people to accord with Western ideas. Success in these respects has been very limited for reasons that will be made much clearer in the remaining chapters of this section. Nevertheless, whether motivated by political expediency or humanitarian zeal, the long arm of the mass society is increasingly encircling the globe, and it is no pipe dream to envision the passing of the "simpler" societies in the "underdeveloped" areas.

In the current popular simplicities of our time, it is fashionable to think of the "two worlds" as the Anglo-American and the Russian. Actually these two have far more in common—and this may be what sharpens some political issues—than they have by way of difference, as far as the prevailing life modes are concerned. The real contrasts in the present world are between the mass societies and the underdeveloped ones, and, as we have seen, the mass society is rapidly expanding.

CONCLUSION

In describing the mass society as we have, a certain degree of unreality may have been suggested and so needs to be corrected.

1. The mass society is *not yet a completed thing;* it is in process of emergence, and the traditions with which it has broken are by no means completely extirpated.

2. Furthermore, the mass society *affects people in different circumstances differently.* To take an extreme illustration: to an Amish farmer

in Lancaster County, Pennsylvania, or Holmes County, Ohio, life is still essentially rural, human relations are comparatively simple, and the mid-twentieth century has not yet quite dawned. Yet a close look at these and other dramatic remnants of the pluralistic past indicates that even they are having great difficulty maintaining their traditions, despite vigorous efforts to do so. More to the point, however, are the run-of-the-mill farmers and small-town dwellers for whom there is considerable illusion that the old order is still with them. But the illusion is increasingly hard to maintain as the inroads of uniformity, centralized government, and technological organization press more and more heavily upon provincial custom, strong religious conviction, and independence of thought and action.

3. In short, what we have been saying in the above paragraphs, as earlier, is that *the mass society is a generalized interpretive and descriptive idea,* like the phrase "the American way of life" or "the industrial revolution," and that it is not a completely literal description of reality for every last person with complete consistency. It is, nonetheless, increasingly true as a relentless impersonal force whittling away at the older pillars of pluralism.

4. Nor is there any intention to deny the *strong sentimental appeal,* again particularly for older people, *of the older ways and the supporting ideas and ideals which better fit our national origins than our current realities.* One of the interesting social realities of this period of history is the continuing inconsistency between what people *say* about interpersonal relationships and society and what they, in fact, *do.* Thus, people who say, "Honesty is the best policy," are nevertheless forced to use the "public relations front." Persons who believe in individualism, if they wish to find employment, must submerge their separate identities and become organization men. And persons with genuine Christian conviction feel that they are faced with no real alternative but to hold to policies of personal living that are at best badly compromised versions of the principles they feel to be right.

5. All of this, then, by way of saying that *the mass society is a growing and engulfing system of human relationships for which few, aside from the present generation of youth, have much compatible precedent.*

6. The foregoing certainly should not be taken to mean that there is necessarily anything eternal or inherently good about the mass society. *Very probably the mass society, like all of its historical precedents, will one day become something else. But for our time and for the immediately foreseeable future, it appears to be here to stay.* All realistic considerations for individuals and groups must be worked out within the confines imposed by the mass society. There is, of course, especially among some older people, much sentimental nostalgia for the pluralistic society or some parts of it, and occasionally some individuals by one device or another can escape at

least some of the impact of the mass society. But fewer and fewer want to and fewer and fewer are able to. The mass society is the inescapable backdrop against which life in the twentieth century must be lived by people in the Western world.

SUGGESTED READINGS

BRONOWSKI, J., "Planning for the Year 2000," in Elgin F. Hunt and Jules Karlin, *Society Today and Tomorrow*. New York, The Macmillan Company, 1961, pp. 470–475.

DUNLOP, JOHN T., ed., *Automation and Technological Change*. Englewood Cliffs, N.J., Prentice-Hall, Inc., 1962.

NORDSKOG, JOHN ERIC, *Social Change*. New York, McGraw-Hill Book Company, Inc., 1960.

ROSENBERG, BERNARD, and DAVID M. WHITE, *Mass Culture*. New York, The Macmillan Company, 1957.

SALISBURY, HARRISON E., *The Shook Up Generation*. New York, Harper & Row, Publishers, 1958.

THE NATURE OF SOCIAL PROBLEMS

2

Probably anyone who reads these pages could give an *example* of *a* social problem, but few would want to provide a defensible *definition* of social problems. One could, of course, begin with the dictionary definition of "social" and of "problem" and then simply put the two together. From a similar excursion into Webster one could also discover that a tumbleweed is "an economically useless or unsightly plant that rolls over or to and fro," or, in other words, that a tumbleweed is a weed that tumbles. While such a definition may be accurate, it does not seem to contribute much to our understanding of the nature of tumbleweeds. In a similar manner, to understand the nature of social problems, to understand why some conditions are and others are not social problems, we need more than a simple definition of the phenomenon.

Our approach to understanding the nature of social problems will first take the form of a critical investigation of various conceptions of "social problems." In this way we will learn more about the nature of these "perplexing situations of society," and we will learn, too, the extent to which the various conceptions constitute a suitable and realistic sociological approach to the study of social problems.

SOCIAL PROBLEMS AS
UNDESIRABLE CONDITIONS

It would seem simple enough to regard social problems as undesirable social conditions. But when we ask *Undesirable to whom?* and *Undesirable by whose values?*, we face difficult and complicated considerations.

To probe one of these questions—undesirable to whom—let us consider the position of the Women's Christian Temperance Union. This group holds that the consumption of alcohol, in any amount, is highly undesirable, harmful, and, in fact, immoral. Does this make the use of alcoholic beverages a social problem? Apparently not to the majority of Americans who occasionally or regularly drink alcoholic beverages nor even to many others who are nondrinkers. *It is a problem, then, to persons who evaluate human behavior in the way in which the Women's Christian Temperance Union does.* Until or unless a sizable or influential group becomes convinced that some social condition is "really" undesirable, then that condition cannot be considered a social problem. While, to continue with our example, we might approach unanimous agreement that *alcoholism* or *excessive* use of alcohol is undesirable, apparently a large majority of people seem unconvinced that *any use of alcohol* is a seriously harmful condition in American society. It therefore, for the present at least, cannot be accurately referred to as an *"American* social problem."

Let us examine the other aspect of our question—namely, what values are to be used to determine the "desirability" or "undesirability" of a social condition. Is the Negro's inferior status in American society, for example, "undesirable" and a social problem? Many Negroes, social scientists, and a growing number of civic groups consider it one of the most serious social problems in American society today. According to many other persons and groups, the inferior status accorded the Negro is desirable, is "his proper place." Or, again, is it desirable or undesirable that cities can and do add fluoride to the community drinking water? It is desirable to those who hold that their children's teeth are thereby benefited, but it is undesirable to those who believe they are being slowly poisoned to death.

The foregoing illustration of the fluoridation of water leads us to a consideration of the role of experts in defining social problems. Surely, one would contend, there are bodies of experts in the fields of dentistry and medicine who could determine once and for all whether the addition of fluorides to drinking water is harmful or beneficial, desirable or undesirable. To a large extent, American people have followed the advice of the experts with regard to this issue. Some people, however, do not acknowledge that experts have the ability to give sound advice on fluoridation and dispute the facts presented by the experts. The citizens of Columbus, Ohio, in a 1954 popular referendum rejected a fluoridation proposal by a decided negative vote!

In many other "problem" aspects of everyday life, we seem willing to follow the dictates of the expert. If, for example, the construction engineer states that serious "problems" prevent the location of a dam at a particular point in a stream, we accept his evaluation of the "problem situation." While we may call in another engineer to corroborate the findings of the first, we stay within the expert system, so to speak, and do not call for a popular vote on the question of the exact location of the dam. If the physician diagnoses the patient's "problem" as diabetes, the patient accepts this "expert opinion" without insisting on a public opinion poll in regard to the matter.

Such "expert opinions," however, are used as criteria in "problem" situations only where the public has accepted the "experts" as such or where value agreement is so complete that no other course of action is open. In the trouble areas of our society generally labeled social problems, we have no such popularly approved experts. For problems relating to race relations, unemployment, international conflict, old age and health security, crime and juvenile delinquency, who are to be regarded as "experts" with public recognition comparable to the acceptance that is accorded physicians, engineers, physicists, chemists, and others in their special fields? "Expert opinion" as the basis for decision regarding the presence or absence of a problem situation rests ultimately upon public acceptance of the "expert."

From all that we can determine, the vast majority of Americans accept dentists and physicians as the experts with regard to the fluoridation of water, even though a small minority refuse to grant them expert status. With broader social conditions, the situation is quite otherwise. There is probably a small minority of Americans who genuinely feel that social scientists are the appropriate experts in their fields and are therefore capable of defining what is desirable or undesirable about society. Most Americans, it seems, are unwilling to grant expert status to social scientists insofar as their ability to diagnose the state of society and to recommend appropriate action is concerned.

We have seen that the same condition can be desirable or undesirable, depending upon who is doing the evaluation and the value position from which the evaluation is made. We have seen, too, that *at the present time* society fails fully and consistently to accept experts on societal phenomena. It is for both of these reasons that "undesirability" is not a suitable criterion for determining what is a social problem. It is well-nigh impossible to apply the criterion of undesirability in a rigorous, consistent, and objective way to social conditions and reach a meaningful conclusion as to what are the society's social problems.

HUMANITARIAN CONSIDERATIONS AND SOCIAL PROBLEMS

Related to the criterion of undesirability, by which to judge which situations are problems, are those considerations that we can think of as humanitarian. In some ways humanitarian considerations make for a more explicit definition of a social problem and they seem to have a certain logical, or perhaps merely charitable, appeal. The question becomes whether humanitarianism constitutes, in various ways, an adequate basis for determining what is and what is not a social problem. We need further to investigate how humanitarianism can be applied in remedying situations judged, on the basis of its own criteria, to be social problems.

The essence of humanitarianism is that pain, suffering, and extreme unhappiness are intrinsically bad. Societal conditions that produce these effects on one's fellow human beings constitute problems for the society in that they need either to be eradicated or their unsavory effects mitigated. Humanitarian ideas are, of course, not new. They recur repeatedly in the teachings of Christ, and they were and are found in times and places unaffected by Christianity. One does not have to search hard in our own society to find many who have some humanitarianism, and some who have much of it. There are those who devote their lives to caring for the mentally retarded, helping the leper, or ministering to the poor; groups have been formed to protect the widow and orphan, to befriend the ex-criminal, to abolish child labor, and so on.

It should by no means detract from humanitarianism as an ethical principle to say, as we feel we must, that it does not constitute *for our relatively affluent society* an adequate basis for determining what are our problems. There are several serious difficulties with the concept as an objective, scientific orientation to social problems, and we encounter no less serious difficulties when we try to apply it to the treatment of social problems.

In our affluent society, with its high average personal income and the tremendous average consumption of goods and services, some types of suffering and discontent are produced by *relative* rather than *absolute* deprivations. With our many public and private sources of relief, for example, no one in the United States need die of starvation or suffer because of lack of food. Nor, of course, is this the problem, save for an occasional recluse or a person sufficiently isolated so that no one knows he is in need.

Each month the federal government makes available tens of thousands of pounds of meat, butter, eggs, lard, and other "surplus food" to the needy. For the most part, those who receive it are in need of the food not in the sense that they would die without it, but because they cannot afford to consume food in accordance with the high standards of nutrition, variety, quality, and quantity that prevail today. The relief measures allow them to approach these standards, even if they cannot reach them. Undoubtedly millions of the people in the world who are chronically threatened with starvation would feel that we were making a mockery of the term "suffering" if we were to apply it to those who are in need of food in the sense that "need" is used in an affluent society.

Similar illustrations could be provided in the areas of clothing and housing. From humanitarian as well as other considerations, a strong case can be made that our affluent society should eliminate *absolute* poverty, *absolute* hunger, and *absolute* need for clothing and shelter. But how do we apply humanitarian ideals to the suffering produced by *relative* needs in these areas, or to "needs" beyond those essential for maintaining life? Does love of humanity demand that the suffering caused by the lack of spacious housing, up-to-date clothes, or a good automobile be removed? Is it morally right, according to humanitarian ideals, that thousands of Americans cannot afford a good automobile and that each year thousands of others are forced to return their new television sets because they cannot meet the monthly payments?

Other than the extreme types, therefore, pain, suffering, and unhappiness become fuzzy and hard-to-measure criteria by which to judge the conditions of a relatively wealthy society. We are not contending that the frustration experienced by being deprived of something one's society has deliberately taught one to "need" is unreal, or that it does not hurt to dress onself or one's children in poor, but warm enough, clothing. The point is that pure humanitarian considerations would have to be unduly stretched to include the moral necessity for eliminating all of the new varieties of suffering ushered in by the growth of affluence.

More than likely, once we went beyond the extreme and traditional forms of suffering, we would experience considerable disagreement in society concerning who is suffering, and how much, and whether or not it is right that they should continue to do so. There is a real danger, in other words, that humanitarian considerations would cease to be pure but would get all mixed up with lots of other values. It would seem likely that sooner or later conditions would be labeled social problems merely because some people did not like them, and not because it could be demonstrated that a certain amount of suffering was being produced by them.

Another difficulty with the humanitarian criterion can be illustrated by reversing the logic and asking if *lack of suffering* indicates that no problem exists. For several reasons this is difficult to accept. First of all, we know that there is a certain plasticity to human nature and that, therefore, human beings are capable of adjusting even to inhuman situations. The "lifer" who is pardoned after thirty years in prison, but chooses to remain there, obviously adjusted to his confinement and probably for many years did not suffer from it in any real sense. Again, throughout much of human history peoples have developed a passive acceptance of disease, pestilence, premature death, and so on, because they have been visited so regularly by these misfortunes as to consider them ordinary. In other words, merely because people can or do learn to live under certain social conditions without undo suffering, it does not mean that *judged by other criteria* these conditions are not problems, even for the society in question.

Finally, if the removal of pain and suffering were our major objective in the treatment of social problems, the implications could be frightening.

There are many ways in which "the masses" can be kept reasonably happy, most of the time. They can be kept in ignorance and remain oblivious to the potentialities they have as human beings. For that matter, the masses could be soothed into a "contented cow" type of existence through the administration of drugs by the ruling elite. We are reminded of Aldous Huxley who, writing before the days of mass use of "tranquilizing pills," had the masses in his *Brave New World* kept free of tensions and anxieties through the liberal use of "soma." [1]

In sum, humanitarian considerations *by themselves* seem to present critical, logical difficulties when used to define social problems or to treat them. The potentialities of man go far beyond the absence of pain and suffering and it would be setting the goals for our affluent society too low if we failed to recognize this.

DISAPPROVED DEVIANCY AND SOCIAL PROBLEMS

In every society there are norms governing the behavior of people in multitudinous situations and, just as surely, there are in every society individuals whose behavior or characteristics depart markedly from the norms. Such individuals are called *deviants*. The imbecile is a deviant, and so is the genius. Likewise the chronically ill are deviants and so are those few who possess a degree of well-being and vigor probably unattainable by the masses. It is already apparent that deviation of some types, and in a given direction, is "good," while deviation in the opposite direction, or of a different type, meets with social disapproval.

Almost by definition, the existence of even a moderate amount of disapproved deviancy in a society will cause friction. Because of this, it is easy to equate the problems of a society with the types and amounts of disapproved deviancy. One could classify the disapproved deviants as the physically sick, the criminal, the financially needy, the mentally ill, and one could go on to study the severity of the various disapproved deviancies. While it is probably true that valuable insights into human behavior could result from this type of analysis, it seems that the approach has some serious weaknesses *insofar as it concerns the sociology of social problems*.

Deviancy, of course, is a relative matter. The behavior or characteristics of a deviant differ from what is normal and approved in degree rather than kind. The behavior of a man who occasionally throughout his lifetime committed petty thievery deviates in the disapproved direction from the societal norms, and so also does the behavior of the professional criminal. The severely mentally retarded are obviously deviants, but they are devi-

[1] Aldous Huxley, *Brave New World* (New York: Harper & Row, Publishers, 1946).

ants, too, whose intelligence is only somewhat below the normal range. The fact that so much of disapproved deviancy is a "more-or-less" rather than an "either-or" matter is not unsolvable, but it does complicate the use of the concept of disapproved deviancy. For example, how many delinquent acts can one commit without being considered a deviant, and how many more need be committed before one is singled out for special treatment as a criminal? Where does one draw the line between the criminal and the law-abiding citizen, the sick and well, the needy and the self-sufficient? We are left with the confusing situation that with some types of behavior some deviancy in the disapproved direction is tolerated and it may even be "normal" to be "a little deviant"!

A more serious difficulty with the concept of deviancy arises when we ask, "deviant from what norms?" While we have referred to *the norms* of "a society," it is clear that in many cases there are competing and conflicting norms within the society that nevertheless refer to the same behavior. A child in the city slums who has a highly negative attitude toward teachers, school, and anything connected therewith obviously deviates from the norms of middle-class society. It is quite likely that in the group in which the child lives, the group, in other words, that is most important to him, he has a normal attitude toward education. When he "plays hooky" or fails to prepare his homework, his behavior may deviate not at all from that commonly found and *approved of* in his group. Is he normal or a deviant?

Undoubtedly, there is such a thing as absolute deviancy, in the sense that the behavior or characteristics of the individual precludes meaningful interaction with his fellows in any society or in any type of social situation.[2] The extremely mentally retarded and many of the severely mentally ill would be cases in point. Much more deviancy is culturally defined with the result that even within the same society, as we have seen, a person may be a deviant in one group but normal in another. Confusions such as this make it difficult to apply the concept of disapproved deviancy to the study of social problems.

Perhaps the most serious difficulty with the personal deviation approach is that *for the sociology of social problems* it tends to focus too much attention on the behavior of *individuals* and too little on the conditions of the *society*. The social problem of crime becomes the problem of a certain number of criminals, the problem of mental illness becomes the problem of so and so many mentally ill persons. In a sense this approach begs the question of why certain conditions are social problems and deals, instead, with a collection of deviant individuals.

The problems of a society do not, of course, exist in an ephemeral sense. They are reflected in and acted out through the behavior of individual

[2] For a good discussion of absolute and cultural deviancy see John P. Gillin, *The Ways of Men* (New York: Appleton-Century-Crofts, 1948), pp. 589ff.

members of the society. If a society has problems in the areas of race relations, alcoholism, and marriage, for example, we would expect to find the problems reflected in how some of its people act or fail to act. The behavior of individuals and the problems of a society clearly are related, but they are not the same phenomenon.

Failure to distinguish between the problems of a society and the behavior of its members, or too great emphasis on the deviant individuals, has implications for the treatment of a condition. One may be led, for example, in the direction of finding a way to change existing criminals, rather than attempting to discover what it is about the society that regularly produces a predictable number of criminals and seems to interfere with their rehabilitation. Treating deviant individuals may be necessary for the welfare of society, but one is not thereby treating the social condition that produced the deviancy in the first place.

SOCIAL PROBLEMS AND SOCIAL DISORGANIZATION

There is another view of social problems that draws its definition from the concept of social disorganization. Social problems, in this sense, are seen either as symptomatic of imminent disorganization or as direct manifestations of an existing state of disorganization. It would follow that the treatment of social problems basically would consist of ridding society of its alleged disorganization and becoming "organized" once again. Since it is difficult to think of social disorganization without reference to its logical counterpart, we will turn first to the concept of *social organization*.

Long ago it was observed that man is a "social animal." Wherever man may be, and whatever may be the other circumstances of his existence, he has a need to associate with and to interact with others of his species. Interaction that is to be more or less frequent and association that is to be more or less enduring demand that there be some rules of behavior. Orderly social interaction requires also a certain consensus about the meaning of the societal rules and an agreement to abide by them, just as an orderly game could not be carried on unless the players knew the rules, agreed upon them, and agreed to abide by them. This is the essence of social organization. It makes social living possible and provides some degree of regularity and predictability of the behavior of people within a group.

The history of industrial societies has been marked by an increasing degree of specialization in the activities of their members. Specialization, in turn, implies interdependence. The network of social rules necessary to coordinate the activities of the many interdependent people necessarily becomes more intricate. Any American home gives a vivid illustration of the degree of specialization in our division of labor. To make the specialized services of the many men in the shops, factories, and on the construction site available to any one man in the form of a completed house requires organization of no simple sort. In countless other spheres of life the orderly coordination of the behavior of the specialized, interdependent members of a mass society is clearly demanded. It is obvious that we have some degree of social organization in our mass society.

The expression social disorganization suggests the disruption of previously existing organization. When traditional behavior patterns no longer prevail and confusion is apparent among the participants in a social situation because of this nonfunctioning of customary patterns, a state of social disorganization is said to exist. If, for example, the instructor of a college class walked into the classroom dressed in boxing tights and began engaging in setting-up exercises, the resulting situation might or might not be one of social disorganization. If he happened to be an instructor of physical education, he would probably be following the behavior patterns considered appropriate to his role; his students would be attitudinally prepared for such behavior and would themselves act in orderly fashion. If, on the other hand, the class were prepared for instruction in, say, political science, the behavior of the instructor would be considered inappropriate for the social situation. Established traditions of conduct relating to a class in political science would have broken down, confusion would undoubtedly result, and a state of social disorganization would be in effect.

Situations more complicated than, but comparable to, our simple classroom illustration are said to exist in many of our basic social institutions in the United States today. It is true that our society is in the process of change, some of which is radical, and that a concomitant of this change is, at times, confusion. Since proposed criteria for judging disorganization consist of such conditions as "breakdown of social controls over the behavior of the individual," modifications in social roles, experimentation with new roles, and confusion in the individual's behavior, why show any reluctance about using the term? Stated briefly, the answer to this question is that the term "social disorganization" connotes something temporary and something undesirable. When a society is "disorganized," it is in a "bad" condition, and, because organization is essential to a society, it will have to get "reorganized" in a hurry in order to survive.

The usefulness of social disorganization as a concept for delineating social problems and determining corrective action for social problems so identified is seriously limited by the fact that specific value judgments underlie the application of the social disorganization concept. The term implies disapproval and abnormality, temporary undesirability, a trend which (if unchecked) will lead to institutional dissolution. In economic, government, family, and other institutions, we have made profound changes as a society. Quite evidently we are in the process of making many more. To hold, however, that contemporary changes are symptoms of social disorganization is to imply that the formerly established patterns in these areas were "good" and that the conditions toward which current changes are moving are known to be "bad." It can be expected that a certain amount of confusion, discomfort, inconvenience, longing for the old patterns, and name-calling of the new ways will accompany any marked social change. Yet certainly it is not to be contended that all marked social change is social disorganization.

Our concluding thoughts on this matter, then, are that the concept of social disorganization is of dubious utility in identifying, understanding, and treating social problems because it (1) contains implications of moralization rather than objectivity, (2) fails to distinguish between "disorganizing" and other types of social change, and (3) may lead to suggestions for treatment which are essentially recommendations that we return to the "old ways."

VALUE CONFLICTS AS THE SOURCE OF SOCIAL PROBLEMS

The various criteria for defining a social problem that we have so far discussed seem ultimately to come to the matter of human *values*. From the value position of some groups, certain societal conditions are clearly "undesirable." Using other criteria, social change of a pronounced sort is labeled disorganization because it threatens the values of an earlier time. Humanitarianism is clearly a value position, even though those who claim to embrace this ideology would disagree among themselves when it came to applying humanitarian considerations to a specific social situation.

The sociologist studying social problems could, of course, simply endorse a given value or set of values and use it as a frame of reference by which to judge all social conditions. Those conditions that seemed in accord with the value position would be labeled good, while the "social problems" would be those conditions that threatened or competed with the values. Such a sociologist would have an exceedingly difficult time deciding whether he should use as a frame of reference *his values,* what he thinks are *sociologists' values,* or what he believes are the *values of most Americans.* Once having chosen the value position, it would be manifestly necessary and fair to point out to the readers which value position was adopted and to attempt to explain why it, rather than any one of others, was chosen.

There is another way of handling the matter of values as they relate to the judgment of social conditions. Instead of *advocating* a value position, the sociologist can *treat values as data.* From this point of view, the sociologist steps back a pace, as it were, and looks both at the objective conditions of society and how these conditions are evaluated by the various groups and individuals within the society. In his role as a social scientist, he is not himself the judge of the worth of a specific condition. Rather, he determines in the most objective and able manner he can how society's members judge the condition. He attempts, also, to understand the value positions that lead to such judgments.

When the sociologist assumes the stance of an amoral analyst of society, he is struck at once by the fact that some of the most perplexing and difficult to solve societal questions are those that are engulfed in a conflict of values among society's members. Sometimes he sees the existence of strong value disagreement with regard to the desirability of the condition itself, sometimes he notes more or less agreement that a condition is undesirable but strong value clashes or even competing systems of logic when it comes to the "solution" of the problem that is defined as undesirable. Observations such as these led to the formulation, by the late Professor Richard Fuller, of the "clash of values" approach to the study of social problems.[3] That is, the essence of a condition considered to be a social problem is that there is in society serious disagreement regarding the evaluation of a given condition or regarding what should be done about a condition.

The clash of values frame of reference seems to have stood up well to the test of time. It was applied provocatively and with insight to the problems of the late depression era, when the early formulation was made, and it seems, if anything, even more appropriate to the problems in a time of relative plenty. While in actuality this entire book is an illustration of the clash of values framework, perhaps a few examples will clarify how it can be used in delineating and dealing with the problems of our time.

TWO MAIN PHASES OF VALUE CONFLICT. As we have indicated, *value conflict tends to center around two main phases of a social problem.* First, the clash of values often relates to the issue of *whether or not a problem really exists.* A given condition is a "problem" only when it has come to be regarded as a problem. There are numerous examples from history of times when floods, famines, pestilence, and other "undesirable" conditions were defined as inevitable aspects of the human environment. According to earlier values held in our society, such conditions as slavery, poverty of the masses, child labor, and dangerous and unhealthful working conditions were not social problems; they were considered inevitable and acceptable patterns of human living.

Today many authorities on human behavior are concerned with what they see as the threat to personal integrity and identity in a mass society. Living in an age of relative plenty, the danger is that life loses much of its meaning, or at least that it is difficult to find meaning in life. Self-realization and self-respect accordingly are threatened. While it is probably true that a

[3] The discussion of the clash of values framework that constitutes the remainder of this chapter is based on Fullers formulation. See Richard C. Fuller, "The Problem of Teaching Social Problems," *American Journal of Sociology,* 44 (1939), pp. 415–435.

growing proportion of Americans admit to a "mental health" problem in the sense of the serious mental illness that affects the few, it appears doubtful whether many recognize the more subtle emotional difficulties with which the masses are faced. Since these latter threats are largely unrecognized, one could scarcely say that they are "problems" in the minds of rank and file Americans in the same sense that crime or the automobile accident rate is a problem to them. The actual danger of harmful effects to the average person may be greater, and more serious, from the threats to his self-realization than from many conditions more generally recognized as problems. But the problem of maintaining identity in a mass society, as is the case with most problems before they are widely recognized as such, must go through this stage of value conflict as to its existence as a major problem before there can be broad consideration of what ought to be done about the condition.

Second, once considerable agreement has been reached that a certain condition is undesirable, the value clash shifts to *what society can and should do*. Several possible courses of action usually emerge in this stage of the conflict of values. One course invariably recommended is to do nothing at all. This argument is often phrased in some such way as these: (1) granting the undesirability of the conditions, proposed actions would make for "worse conditions than those existing," or (2) the problem is "too large and complex" to handle, or (3) the existing undesirability is "just human nature" and the proposed treatment is contrary to human nature. While the sincerity of the "do-nothing" advocates is sometimes indisputable, there is evidence that some interests taking this stand are not loath to misrepresent difficulties involved in proposed "solutions." Owners of real estate in slum areas, for example, have been known to exaggerate the difficulties of constructing better housing because some of them, at least, have considered it to their financial interest to keep the slums. In other words, if the argument could be shifted from discussion of the seriousness of the problem to the magnification of the difficulties of solving the problem, the same end would be attained—namely, inaction. Thus the opponent of change would remain, in the eyes of some people at least, a person who is not insensitive to the plight of the slum dweller.

But even among those who sincerely wish the problem attacked and solved, there is likely to be disagreement as to a course of action for reaching the desired end. Values are often involved here, too. Many persons, for example, feel that a large portion of our population receives inadequate medical attention. Numerous surveys give indisputable factual substantiation for this feeling, and few deny the "undesirability" of conditions thus exposed. It is at the point of what to do about inadequate medical treatment that conflict arises. The means to the desired end of improved medical care differ widely and reveal sharp conflicts of values. Some advocate the government's taking over medical facilities; others recommend compulsory health insurance with practice still in the hands of private physicians; still others propose voluntary insurance; and some defend a continuation of present conditions as better than the socialism, which, according to them, would inevitably follow upon "tampering with private medical practice." Better medical care for more of our people, yes, we agree; but on the methods, bearers of conflicting cherished values, we fight. On this social problem, as with almost any other you choose to consider, disagreements as to methods are numerous; much discussion and much compromise must generally precede action in relation to the condition.

The utility of the clash of values framework for the sociological study of social problems can be summarized through the following considerations.

1. It is consistent with the amoral position of the sociologist-analyst. The admonition not to engage in the propagandizing of particular value positions is a well-established one in the sociological tradition. It is held, by no means exclusively, for example, by positivists. We feel that for our time, at least, the sociologist is better suited to the role of *interpreter of values* than to the role of *value advocate*.

2. This frame of reference seems to be a good vehicle for the realistic study of value positions in regard to interest groups, classes, and other group advocates of points of view. Fuller puts it as follows.[4]

> So the core of the social problem is a multi-sided conflict of interests with humanitarian interests joining forces with organizational interests to combat other humanitarian and organizational interests. The job of the sociologist is to isolate and define those conflicting value-judgments which are the *modus operandi* of the problem. He must chart the oppositions and co-operations between the warring pressure groups. He must lay bare the issues of policy which in their conflict deter the public in its solution of the problem. His findings should revitalize our theories of social control. After his spadework is done, he should be in a position to say to the social planners, "Attitudes and values being what they are today, you may (or may not, as the case may be) expect success with the program you have in mind"; or, "Before your plan will work you will have to change the attitudes and policies of this or that interest group."

3. This frame of reference makes explicit the needed emphasis that problem areas may emerge in a society as a result of changes in the value structure per se, and not simply as a residuum from biological or economic changes as has too long been inferred from the Ogburn cultural lag hypothesis and the social disorganization theory. The point is not that these earlier frames of reference denied the possibility of a more or less independent variable of values, but rather that their emphasis tended to direct attention away from such an important possibility.

[4] *Ibid.,* p. 423. Reprinted by permission of the University of Chicago Press, publishers. Copyright 1939 by The University of Chicago.

4. Such a mode of treatment as that advocated by Fuller assists us in keeping data and theory in better perspective *for a sociological treatment* of social problems. Sociologists are not the only ones who study social problems. Nor are they the only ones who have a vital interest in the outcome. What seems to be needed, and what sociologists seem best able to perform in an ultimately practical way, is to exploit the role of understanding social problems *from the point of view of their relation to group-related values,* both instrumental and more ultimate. So long as we use this point of view, we seem less likely to get "bogged down" with reams of tables and charts on mere technological aspects of social problems. We do not mean to depreciate the technological aspect of social problems *on the professional level of research.* We do advocate keeping the *introductory* treatment of social problems on the level of such conceptions as "What are various groups really fighting for?" and "Why are they fighting for them?" and "What are the results of these value clashes?"

It would be less than accurate, finally, to fail to point out that there are difficulties in applying the clash of values framework to the study of social problems. The objective determination of the values of a group or an entire society, even with regard to a fairly specific issue, is not an easy task. Because of this, the decline of older values or the emergence of newer ones may, temporarily, go unnoticed. Some of the real values of a group may, at times, escape the researcher. These and related difficulties, however, essentially are technical problems of improving our measurement techniques and clarifying our concepts, meanwhile recognizing that something less than the desired degree of precision prevails. Such difficulties do not seem to be inherent weaknesses in the clash of values framework and, for this reason, make it no less defensible as a sociological approach to the study of social problems.

SUGGESTED READINGS

BROWN, LAWRENCE GUY, "The Normal and the Abnormal," in John F. Cuber and Peggy Harroff, *Readings in Sociology.* New York, Appleton-Century-Crofts, Inc., 1962, pp. 159–166.

FULLER, RICHARD C., "The Problem of Teaching Social Problems," *American Journal of Sociology.* 44 (1939), pp. 415–435.

FURFEY, PAUL H., "The Social Philosophy of Social Pathologists," *Social Problems.* 2 (October 1954), pp. 71–74.

GILLIN, JOHN, "Cultural Deviancy and Absolute Deviancy," in John F. Cuber and Peggy Harroff, *Readings in Sociology.* New York, Appleton-Century-Crofts, Inc., 1962, pp. 167–169.

KOLB, WILLIAM L., "The Impingement of Moral Values on Sociology," *Social Problems.* 2 (October 1954), pp. 66–70.

THE TREATMENT OF
SOCIAL PROBLEMS

3

Social problems exist, as we have seen, because there is in society no unanimous feeling with regard to the desirability of things as they are. To understand these value issues and to consider corrective action for them means that we must have as complete and objective data about them as is possible. Since it is a clash of values that makes the problem in the first place, one could anticipate a certain amount of difficulty in obtaining factual information. It is not unlikely that strong values can blur one's objectivity with regard to the sheer facts about a social problem, and it can well be imagined that individuals and groups with opposing value positions will *interpret* differently even those facts on which they agree.

Even when factual information about a social problem exists and is agreed upon, and even when the various interpretations of the data are understood and somehow rationalized, it is frequently not possible to move directly to effective treatment. One of the reasons for this lies in the clash of values that often occurs when it comes to determining what, if anything, should be done about a condition. Some are content with treating the most annoying symptoms of a problem, rather than the problem itself, others feel that with regard to certain problems nothing really can or should be done, still others are quick to propose drastic and expensive frontal attacks on a problem, and so on.

In this chapter, therefore, we will investigate the various difficulties associated with the treatment of social problems. We will turn first to those that have to do with the facts about a problem and how these facts are obtained and presented. Following that, we suggest that facts *do not* speak for themselves, and we attempt to show why this is the case. We conclude the chapter with a more general discussion of competing viewpoints and values regarding the treatment of social problems.

GATHERING AND PRESENTING FACTS

Almost everyone has heard the cliché, "Figures don't lie, but liars can figure." Sometimes we do fail to appreciate how thoroughly misleading a set of "facts" may be and how the same facts can be manipulated so that contradictory conclusions are reached. While it is manifestly impossible to investigate all of the ways in which objective data can be distorted, it is well to be aware of some of the more common techniques.[1] Whether these are the "tricks of the trade" of the propagandist out to "prove his point" at any cost, or whether they are honest errors, the result is frequently the same —a clearly distorted impression is received from a set of so-called facts.

Lies—Honest and Otherwise

Many people have heard of the technique called "the big lie" and somehow associate it with Communists, Fascists, and other groups not usually discussed at good American dinner tables. It is true, of course, that various special interest groups have deliberately invented a mistruth that was eventually accepted as a truth because it was repeated often enough and loud enough. But a "big lie" can be equally as preposterous and equally as wrong, even when it is the result of an honest error.

When Chicken Little, of nursery story fame, announced that the sky was falling, we can assume that it was nothing more than an honest misinterpretation of what had actually hit her on the head. None of the other animals to whom Chicken Little related the fateful event, however, bothered to question the original fact. Each was content to tell others the awful news and to join in the trek to the king who presumably could "do something" about it. All around us we see examples of "honest big lies" which have been repeated by so many for so long that their factual basis goes unchallenged.

Judging by articles in the popular press and magazines, and readers' responses to them, it is "common knowledge" that the sexual morality of American youth has reached an all-time low. Like the friends of Chicken Little, few bother to question the facts, but repeat the shocking facts to all who will listen and then go on to posit the reasons for them and how the situation can be remedied. In the first place, our knowledge about generational differences in sexual behavior outside of marriage is not sufficiently

[1] For a good discussion of the ways in which "facts" can be mishandled see Darrell Huff, *How to Lie with Statistics* (New York: W. W. Norton and Company, Inc., 1954).

precise to allow anything but gross comparison. More than likely there is a built-in bias in the matter since our knowledge about the behavior of the present generation is more complete and more accurate than it has ever before been. With our more thorough studies and our greater willingness and ability to disseminate the information, there is undoubtedly a greater *awareness* of the sexual behavior of the unmarried youth of today than there was in his parents' and grandparents' time. More important still, however, *our best available knowledge indicates that the assertion of a recent and significant increase in nonmarital sex relations is simply not true.* While our facts on the matter could certainly be improved, those that we do have show a remarkable stability in the sexual behavior of intergenerational males and that the change in the proportion of women having nonmarital sex experience occurred not recently but at about the time of World War I.[2]

There are many other instances of "common knowledge" that is indeed common but may be absolutely false or nearly so. We may well ponder how many Americans have ever troubled to question allegations regarding such things as the increase in juvenile delinquency, the decline in the physical fitness of youth, the lowered academic standards of schools, or, for that matter, the extent of Communist activity in the United States. We have deliberately chosen hard to measure phenomena, and we are certainly not contending that these facts can be "proved" to be false. The fact remains that there does seem to be a body of "common knowledge" about these things that is infrequently challenged, but that in the interest of honest accuracy, should require "hard" factual evidence before being accepted.

Sampling

Many times, the knowledge we have about a particular aspect of a social problem is gained from one or more studies which, in turn, investigated only a portion, or a sample, of the society. Some people are immediately suspicious of all samples and wonder how a study that is made of only a small proportion of the population can possibly tell us anything about the entire society. But it is both legitimate and necessary to use samples in much of our work. At the same time it is true that even gross errors can result from improper sampling methods.

Imagine that a man is presented with a barrel of various colored marbles and told to come up with a reasonably close estimate of the proportion that are red, blue, white, and so on. Most people would immediately realize that it is unnecessary to count the thousands of marbles. Discovering the proportion of each color in a sample taken from the barrel would more

[2] See William F. Kenkel, *The Family in Perspective* (New York: Appleton-Century-Crofts, 1960), pp. 269–278.

than likely yield results that would be reasonably close to those that would be obtained by counting each and every marble. But if the blue marbles were slipperier and tended to fall from the sampler's hand, or if the red ones were heavier and tended to settle to the bottom, or if the white ones were extremely few in number, even a fairly large sample could result in erroneous conclusions about the color make-up of the marble population.

Sometimes a sample is too small to give a reliable picture of the total group of which it is a part. Frequently it is *the way in which the sample is taken* that biases the results. If a sample of women were interviewed in their homes between the hours of nine and four, we would not expect that their attitudes toward working women would be typical of *all* women. We might not know in which direction the exclusion of working women biased the matter, but we would have good reason to suspect that the results of the survey would be strongly influenced by the time at which the sample was taken. The science of sampling is a technical one, and it is not possible to discuss the various types of errors attendant on improper methods. One can, however, become alert to this phase of "fact gathering" and can learn to spot at least the more obvious biases and imprecisions in sampling.

Tricks with Trends

One common method of giving meaning to numbers and rates is to make a time comparison, to determine, in other words, whether there is now more or less of the phenomenon than in the past or whether the rate is increasing or decreasing. This is certainly a legitimate operation and at times it is a crucial one. Much depends on the time period that is selected as the base or starting point to which other years or periods are compared.

Recently we heard a lecture on the state of the American family that illustrated well the problem of the base year. Among other things, the speaker stressed the point that the divorce rate was "going down." Such a conclusion is technically correct if one uses, as did the speaker, the immediate postwar period as his base year. But the years 1945–1946 were quite unusual ones as far as divorce is concerned. These were the years in which the hasty, furlough marriages of World War II demonstrated their brittleness. To use this admittedly atypical high-divorce period as a point for comparison is to invite misinterpretation. Over the last 100 years or so we have gone from a time when there were about three divorces for every hundred marriages to a time when there are about twenty-five divorces per hundred marriages. The *long-run* trend has been for an ever-increasing divorce rate, precisely the opposite conclusion from that which the lecturer in question managed to get across to many of the audience to whom we later talked.

Reckless Extrapolations

A difficulty related to the foregoing arises from the assumption that a given trend will continue indefinitely, or even for a specified length of time. Sometimes it is reasonable to assume that a trend will continue and to use this assumption in planning and preparing for the future. At other times, however, there may be no good reason to assume that a trend will continue and there may even be every good reason to predict that it will *not* continue. A case in point is the age at which dating begins in our society. If we were recklessly to extrapolate from the present trend toward younger ages at first date, we would be forced to conclude that very soon our little ones would be arranging a quick orange juice date after nursery school!

Another example of reckless extrapolation is contained in the following prediction based on the prevailing rate of decline in the number of farmers: [3]

> It was easy to see that the U.S. was losing farmers at the rate of 35,539 a year. Blackenschultz simply divided the number of farmers counted by the census taker in 1950 by the number who were leaving farming each year and arrived at the figure 151.44. He added 151 years to 1950 and came up with the year 2101 as the last one for the farmer. Carrying the number to two decimal places was very shrewd; 44/100ths of a year was 160.6 days. This figure made it possible for him to predict that the last farmer would disappear at twenty-four minutes past two in the afternoon of June 9 in the year 2101. The twenty-four minutes past two gave his prophecy a terrible feeling of exactness that made people believe it even though others came out immediately with contradictory dates.

It is unlikely that many will take seriously the above forecast, for somehow it does not seem logical that within fifty years there will be no farms and no farmers. Other extrapolations, however, deal with trends that *theoretically* could continue indefinitely or with matters about which the general public lacks adequate information. Some years ago, for example, the psychologist Terman discovered that about 86 percent of the women in his study who were born before 1890 were virgins at time of marriage, but that only about half of the women born after 1900 were virgins at marriage. He then pointed out that if the drop continued at the same rate, virginity at marriage would be close to the "vanishing point" for women born after 1940.[4] Later studies, however, have shown that the trend did not continue at a constant rate. Women who were born at the turn of the

[3] R. J. McGinnis, *The Good Old Days* (New York: Harper & Row, Publishers, 1960), pp. 251–252. Used by permission.

[4] Lewis M. Terman *et al.*, *Psychological Factors in Marital Happiness* (New York: McGraw-Hill Book Company, Inc., 1938), p. 323.

century reached adolescence and early adulthood at the heyday of the feminist movement, at the time of World War I, and the subsequent "roaring twenties." Apparently this was the time of a big change in sexual behavior among unmarried women and since that period the pattern has been more or less stable.[5] As we begin to understand the phenomenon, we realize that there were no sound reasons to expect the trend to continue and that simple extrapolation was quite misleading.

Confusing Correlations

In statistics there are ways of determining the degree of association between two sets of quantitative data. When variables are found to be statistically associated, so that where one is the other is likely also to be, we speak of the variables as being "correlated." The essential point, more frequently missed than might be imagined, is simply that *correlation is not the same as causation*. While it may make the matter confusing, we must also add that *correlation may indicate causation*.

If a study were made of the relationship between throwing a certain switch and the burning of an electric light connected to it, a perfect correlation would be discovered to exist between the two events. In this case, of course, we would impute a causal relationship in addition to the associational one and say, in effect, that the turning of the switch caused the light to burn. Since events causally related in the sense of the switch and the bulb are also always statistically correlated, it is easy to reverse one's logic and assume that events correlated to one another are therefore causally connected. A few illustrations will indicate that such is not necessarily true.

There happens to be a good correlation between the sale of Bibles and the consumption of alcoholic beverages. Anyone can repeat the study and he will find that when the sale of Bibles goes up so also does the sale of liquor and, conversely, when there are fewer Bibles sold the sale of alcoholic beverages also is lower. Now which causes which? Does heavy consumption of alcohol make men turn in remorse to the Bible, or does Bible reading turn men to strong drink? The answer, of course, is that there is no direct causal relationship between these two rates despite the fact that they are correlated. The sale of Bibles, liquor, and a host of other things vary according to economic conditions. Put differently, people buy more things of many kinds when they have money than when they do not!

Recently a student facetiously reported in class that he discovered the cause of high birth rates. In studying the phenomenon he had used countries with a high birth rate, India and Egypt, and "selected" European countries with a low birth rate. He found that the countries with lots of babies also had many storks, while the places with fewer infants had fewer or no

[5] Kenkel, *op. cit.*, pp. 277–278.

storks! We trust that the admittedly biased selection of only certain European countries was not the only error in this "study."

From the example above we can see that events or rates can actually be correlated but yet have no causal relationship or any other genuine linkage to one another. In the case of the sale of liquor–sale of Bibles the relationship existed because both rates were affected by a common factor. It is possible, too, that when phenomena are found to be correlated, the conventional interpretation of which causes the other should be reversed. Some years ago, for example, it used to be said that smoking cigarettes caused "nervousness." Assuming that reliable studies could show a relationship between the two, is it not equally as plausible that nervousness causes smoking? Even if we suspect a causative link between two correlated variables, therefore, we cannot discover from the correlation alone in which direction the causation goes. Finally, we must remind ourselves that a correlation *could* indicate causation. Indeed, discovering whether there is a statistical association between two events is often the *first* step in determining the cause of one of them. But it is not the only step.

Perplexing Percentages

In Chapter 4 we learn that there are over 14 million families in the United States with a yearly income of less than $4000. Surely most will realize that 14 million is a lot of families, but just as surely our understanding of this problem would be severely hampered unless we also realized what *proportion* of American families have to manage on an income of this size. It makes a big difference whether we are talking about half of all families, or 10 percent, or, the actual percentage, 30 percent. Similarly, the fact that there are currently about 400,000 divorces each year takes on additional meaning when we relate it to the number that could have occurred, that is, the number of marriages in existence that year, or to the number of marriages that were performed. Expressing data in terms of percentages or rates is often quite useful and sometimes it is about the only way that the facts can be seen in their proper *perspective*. At the same time, however, many errors of interpretation can result from improper uses of percentages.

It was once pointed out that shortly after Johns Hopkins University opened its doors to women, one third of the coeds had married a member of the faculty. True enough. At the time in question there were three women students in the University and one of them did marry a staff member. Computing percentages on a small number of cases can be quite misleading even if technically accurate. A general principle for understanding percentages is to understand as completely as possible the size and other features of the base on which the percentage is computed. Consider the following case.

Mr. Jones has a neighbor who can never remember to buy cigarettes. Each day, Jones buys a package for twenty-four cents and sells them to his neighbor for a quarter. A penny a day sounds like a modest profit and expressing it as about a 4 percent daily return also sounds reasonable. If Jones kept this practice up for just one year, his original twenty-four-cent investment would net him a profit of 1521 percent! But yet this "fantastic profit" does not seem so large when we remember that Jones made exactly $3.65 for his year's service!

According to our most accurate information, about two thirds of all babies born to American mothers under fifteen years of age are illegitimate. In an entirely proper manner this percentage could be compared with the ones for earlier years, or, perhaps, for the parallel ratio in some other country. But without a good deal more information, this particular rate tells us practically nothing about the general problem of illegitimacy. We would need to know, first of all, that these young mothers bore a total of 4000 illegitimate children. This represents about 2 percent of all illegitimate children born that year and, furthermore, it constitutes about 0.1 percent of all babies born. It need not detract from humanitarian considerations toward the 4000 young unwed mothers and their 4000 illegitimate children to recognize that the behavior of girls of this age has very little effect on the total illegitimacy pattern of our society and an almost indiscernible effect on the annual birth rate. Usually, of course, nobody claims that it does have these effects. Sometimes, in this and other areas, a person with his private "axe to grind" will seize upon a percentage that sounds impressive, even though it is quite misleading. Somehow, it sounds "worse" or more "shocking" to state that *66⅔ percent* of babies born to very young mothers are illegitimate than to state that *2 percent* of illegitimate births occur among the very young mothers.

Averages

Following a class during which examination papers were returned, a student remarked to her friend that most of the class did better than average. This was neither wishful thinking, nor a stereotyped example of "feminine logic." Such a statement could well be true because of the imprecise way in which the term *average* is used.

An average is the measure of the "central tendency" in a series of quantitative data. As such, it provides a sort of summary for the array of scores, heights, incomes, or whatever else is being studied. Thus, we can compare the average test scores of men with the average for women, the average family income at two different periods of time, and so on. Actually, however, there is not one, but *three* averages. One of these is more technically called the *mean,* and is computed by summing the scores obtained by all of the cases and dividing the sum by the number of cases. Average is also used to refer to the *median,* or middle case. If the scores of thirty-three people were arranged in order from highest to lowest, the seventeenth case would have the median score. Half of the group scored higher and half lower than the median. Finally, another measure of the central tendency of an array of scores is the *mode,* or the most frequently occurring case. When a distribution of scores approaches a "normal" or bell-shaped curve, the mean, median, and mode give much the same picture of the central tendency of the array. But distributions are not always normal. Sometimes there is a tendency for the scores to cluster near the high or the low end of the curve, rather than at the middle.

Returning to our example of the class grades, the arithmetic mean was sixty-five, brought about in part by a few students who scored extremely low. The median grade, however, was seventy-five. While exactly half of the class scored above the average in the sense of the median, more than half, of course, did better than the average in the sense of the mean. Deliberately choosing the kind of average that best "proves" one's point is not at all uncommon. In the above example, a student may want to use the mean the better to illustrate that his own low grade was the result of a too difficult test. His instructor, however, will realize from the median score that the test was eminently fair.

Another difficulty with averages is illustrated by the remark of an architecture student in a sociology class to the effect he would not design houses for the average family because the majority of people would not fit in that size house. While this is similar to the previous situation, the problem here is mainly that the mean family size is not the most appropriate measure *for the purpose at hand.* The average family household in 1962 consisted of about 3.4 members. Ignoring the fact that no household has four tenths of a member, if this average were taken literally there would be a gross overbuilding of two-bedroom homes. The average family size, is of course based on *all families,* including young couples without children and older couples whose children have left home. The designers of homes undoubtedly would do better dealing with such figures as the percentage distribution of families of different sizes, the decline in the proportion of married couples who never have a child, and the relative increase of three- and four-child families. These facts, of course, account for the popularity of three- and four-bedroom homes.

An average, therefore, can serve as a useful summary for a series of data. At times, however, an average may conceal more than it reveals or one type of average may give a distorted view of the facts. Averages may be used by the unscrupulous propagandist precisely because they make possible concealment and distortion!

We began this section by pointing out that we could not hope to exhaust the ways in which objective facts can be distorted so that they seem to show something which is not true. What we have tried to do is to illustrate some of the biased methods of manipulating data and, in so doing, to produce a certain amount of scientific skepticism with regard to factual data. At the same time we have emphasized that the understanding of a social problem necessarily begins with a sound body of factual knowledge. But facts, while necessary, are not worth much in *themselves*. The reason for this is that facts are only the raw materials of knowledge or understanding, as the bricks, lumber, and nails are the raw materials of a house. Facts, then, are basic but insufficient. What more is needed to complete one's understanding?

What Do Facts Mean?

Facts must be interpreted in order to have meaning. Facts may be interpreted in more than one way. Let us take, for example, the fact that in more or less prosperous times there are about 4 million American wage earners who are unemployed. That means that nearly 32 million man-hours of work are wasted each day and nearly 8 billion man-hours of unused skill and effort are lost during a so-called prosperous year. Now what does this set of facts mean? Obviously, it means different things to different people. To the unemployed workman, or to his wife or children, it means hunger, insecurity, and countless daily frustrations; to the employer trying to get a job done as cheaply as possible, it probably means getting work done for somewhat lower wages than would prevail if everyone were employed; to the social worker it means more clients; to the merchant it means more customers who are unable to pay their bills; to the courts it means people to be evicted for nonpayment of rent; and so on and on. Somewhat more profoundly, does an unemployed group of 4 million workers even during "good times" mean that we have a "good" or a "bad" economic system? Do these 4 million people "count"—or are they merely the price that some people have to pay in individual misery in order to keep an economic system going? Or does it mean simply that the Holy Bible is good prophecy because we note there that "Ye have the poor with you always"? Or does it mean that the threat of falling into the ranks of the unemployed is the spur that makes men work; we need the unemployed as a living example to the man who is tempted to be lazy that this too would be his fate. We could go on endlessly with the problem of interpretation, but our purpose has probably already been achieved—namely, to demonstrate that a simple statistical fact may mean many different things to different people or to the same person who considers it in several different contexts. What makes up these "different contexts" for interpreting facts? And what basically different contexts are there? These, and other similar questions we shall try to answer throughout this book.

Which Interpretations of Facts Are the Correct Ones?

Here, again, there is no easy answer, in fact there may be no answer possible. Correct *to whom?* Rich or poor? Old or young? The religious or the irreligious? Obviously, again, the legitimacy of using a term like "correct" is in serious doubt, unless one is so bigoted or so ignorant that he does not recognze the existence and the legitimacy of varying frames of reference for determining correctness. Only the naïve and the misinformed expect that there is only *one* correct interpretation possible; the wise man knows that there are several—maybe an infinite number—of correct ones. To be sure, all of us are not equally naïve in our assumptions of correctness, nor are we equally intolerant of the existence of interpretations opposing our own, but the interpretive horizons of all of us are to some degree at least limited by our knowledge of other facts and nonfactual understandings and intentions.

Isolated Facts Mean Almost Nothing

Any fact derives its significance from its relationship to other facts in the knowledge of the person. The fact of a normal reservoir of 4 million unemployed men in the United States, *when added to other facts,* begins to take on meaning. Moreover some of the related matters that supply the perspectives to which we have referred, are not facts at all but are, instead, pertinent ethical principles such as justice. Thus, many of the disagreements among us in regard to the significance of some fact which we all know arise from differences among us in regard to the number and kind of *other data* with which we are acquainted.

THE IMPORTANCE OF A "POINT OF VIEW" OR A "FRAME OF REFERENCE"

As we have seen in the foregoing paragraphs, much depends upon the point of view from which factual matters are observed. We also must recognize that the given fact itself is only a valid fact from some one point of view. Suppose two men observe an arc from two sides of a room, thus.

Joe — — — — →) ← — — — — Jack

What, now, is the "fact"? Is the arc convex or concave? It is neither, or both. From Joe's point of view it is concave; from Jack's it is convex. They could, with honesty, argue from now till doomsday as to which was "correct" regarding the "fact" of the nature of the arc.

The interpretation of social facts—especially those pertaining to social problems—is often like our illustration. We disagree as to the facts themselves as well as to their meanings, because we reason often from different points of view. Catholics often differ from non-Catholics regarding the divorce "facts"; Republicans disagree with Democrats, and both with Socialists, regarding the facts of wage rates and especially the interpretations thereof.

A Sociological Point of View

In this book we shall try to maintain what might be called a "sociological" point of view. The chief characteristic of the sociological point of view is the deliberate attempt to see both—or all—points of view from which the various persons and groups "see" social problems. Going back to our previous illustration of Joe and Jack and the arc, the point of view that we shall attempt to maintain is that of a somewhat detached observer who can understand why Joe argues that the arc is concave and why Jack argues that it is convex. But having the *perspective* that we do, we have a greater understanding, because we have the advantage of *all* of the various—or at least *several* of the various—points of view.

This objective, detached, sociological point of view is not easy to achieve. Anyone can get the point regarding the arc in the above illustration, but it is an oversimplification of the kind of objectivity on social problems which is readily attainable. Everyone can see that both Joe and Jack had good reason for his "view" because Joe and Jack are abstractions with which we do not identify ourselves. But if the illustrations were, instead, the points of view of Catholics and most non-Catholics on birth control, then it might be much less easy to recognize that there are two "good" sides because each one of us is already more or less committed to one view or another, and the other one seems not very tenable, "logical," "realistic." So it is with almost every social fact that we shall attempt to interpret or to evaluate.

VALUES AND VIEWPOINTS ON THE TREATMENT OF SOCIAL PROBLEMS

We have already discussed two obstacles to effective treatment of social problems: (1) the "facts" about a problem, on which obviously depend what is done about it, are frequently unavailable, misleading, or downright distorted, and (2) these facts cannot stand alone and are subject to more than one interpretation. A third major difficulty lies in the fact that there exist competing philosophies with regard to the treatment of the problems of a society. We are not referring to specific remedies for a given condition but, rather, to conflicting systems of ideas about the course of action society should take with regard to its admitted ills. The following are some of the major value positions concerning the general approach to the treatment of social problems.

Laissez Faire versus Purposive Control

The laissez-faire philosophy originated in Europe as a protest against excessive government regulation of society, especially of business, during the eighteenth century. It means, literally, let [people] do, or make, [what they choose], hence noninterference. The implication is that social problems are "inherent in the scheme of things" and cannot, therefore, be successfully treated by collective, especially by governmental, action. The historic quotation, "That government governs best which governs least," has become a laissez-faire slogan with which almost everyone is familiar. The laissez-faire concept is also found in the Holy Bible where the somewhat cynical statement, "Ye have the poor with you always," is embedded in a body of otherwise largely idealistic writing. The modern person who opposes almost every attempt to attack poverty, immorality, or squalor finds little difficulty in pointing out that we not only have the poor always with us but so also the weak, the blind and the lame, the criminal and the prostitute, the racketeer and the exploiter, and that in spite of all collective efforts to stamp out vice and misery, they seem to recur in one form or another with heart-rending vitality.

CONSISTENCY IN ADVOCACY OF LAISSEZ FAIRE. It should be emphasized, however, that some of our loudest advocates of laissez faire in modern times have been anything but consistent in their advocacy of this policy. Certain business groups in recent years have protested loudly against subsidies for the agricultural industry, pointing out that subsidies create "artificial prices" and "encourage inefficient production," while at the same time they advocate protective tariffs, which almost in identical ways create artificially high prices and encourage inefficient industry. Similarly, many industrialists oppose governmental measures that fix prices or in other ways tend to restrict the "free operation of the competitive system," and yet these same industries have shown a tendency for the last seventy-five years to form trusts, mergers, chains, and other devices designed precisely to eliminate competitors and prevent the operation of a free competitive system. Likewise, labor groups at times cry out in protest against any government support of the monopolistic tendencies of big business, while building for themselves the best monopoly they can and doing their utmost to prevent government from interfering with that monopoly by some of the same tactics as those used by big business to protect its monopoly. The situation is such that it is easy to conclude somewhat cynically that everyone is an advocate of laissez faire, so long as it is to his advantage to be free, but comes quickly whining for governmental or other protection whenever the existence of a laissez-faire policy is in the leastwise hurtful. Although there is lip service paid to the laissez-faire philosophy by many groups in American society at any one time, a more careful examination of the same groups' past and present actions almost always reveals that either now or recently they have pressed for governmental or other collective action when it is to their advantage.

Thus the laissez-faire philosophy, though easy to phrase in academic language, is in practice a "glittering generality," if not a deliberately misleading "red herring." Many propagandists, sensing the Americans' long-standing adherence to the concept of freedom, have used the laissez-faire generality as a propaganda device to win friends to some cause, either unknowingly or unscrupulously using it in such a way as to mislead. Laissez faire no longer exists in fact, if it ever did. As laws and other kinds of collective control come into being and pass out, there is no returning to or departing from laissez faire. Laissez faire is gone—the only remaining question is not *whether* there shall be influence by organized groups, but *what kind* of influence and *which groups* shall have it.

Amelioration versus Curative Treatment

Many social problems are of such a nature that they can be handled either by a direct attack upon the basic source of the trouble or by leaving the source untouched and providing palliative assistance to the victims of the condition. Let us take a simple illustration from the field of public health to sharpen the distinction. Suppose there is a lake in the vicinity of a city. The water in the lake serves as a breeding ground for mosquitoes that carry malaria. The malaria menace can be attacked in two basic ways: the city can build hospitals to help malaria victims recover from the malady and inoculations may be offered or required of the population to reduce the vulnerability to malaria. Or, the malaria problem can be attacked at source and cured more or less permanently. The stagnant lake can be drained or the water can be treated with some chemical that would destroy the mosquito larvae.

Now suppose we take an illustration of a social problem of another scope—for example, the baffling problem of caring for the children of divorced parents. The ameliorative method would suggest the use of skilled child guidance and placement experts to assist the court in the best possible placement of the children. Moreover, the children of divorced indigent parents might need to be supported by the state in whole or in part. The curative approach, on the other hand, would get at the root cause—namely, the divorce. Every husband-wife estrangement that can be prevented means one less case of children who will need ameliorative treatment.

In using divorce as the illustration in the above paragraph we have deliberately chosen one of the knottiest problems for illustration. This was done in order to show that curative treatment of social problems can be a very difficult if not an almost impossible task. But it would be an error to end our discussion at this point because not all social problems are as complex as the divorce problem. As we shall see in subsequent chapters, we now have conclusive evidence to show that many problems can be efficiently and successfully attacked by direct curative means.

Amelioration is usually justified as a "less costly" approach. But it is not always such. If the full facts were known, we might easily come to realize that it is much cheaper, especially in the long run, to cure a social problem outright rather than merely to give the victims some "first aid," so to speak, which will tide them over until the next attack to which they will be more vulnerable because of the first one.

In the analysis of specific social problems throughout the rest of this book, the student will do well to direct his thinking to the crucial question of curative over against ameliorative treatment. Caution should be observed, however, not to regard amelioration and curative treatment as mutually exclusive categories. A society may and possibly should attack its problems by *both* procedures. Usually it will be necessary to use ameliorative measures until curative measures have been perfected. Sometimes the final curative program is not discovered until after various ameliorative measures have been tried. Some ameliorative work will probably always be necessary no matter how perfect a social system may be, for there are always unusual circumstances or unusual persons who need assistance under almost any conceivable curative program.

Coercion versus Persuasion

It has been said that the American's first reaction to an undesirable condition is to assert that "we ought to pass a law against it." This is an altogether common initial attitude. If someone is doing something that is inimical to the general good, then he ought to be prevented from continuing the practice. Thus, we prohibit people from driving at excessive speeds, printing counterfeit money, and selling their children.

It is obvious, of course, that the legislative-coercive approach has serious limitations. Sometimes, even though there is rather general agreement that some persons are doing things that are contrary to the public good, it is difficult, if not impossible, to enforce the law that prohibits the unlawful act. The Prohibition experiment of 1919–1933 constitutes an excellent illustration. So also did the price control and rationing experiment of World War II.

Another difficulty with legislative coercion is that the remedy may be worse than the disease. The cost of enforcing the law may be burdensome, if not impossible, to bear. The infringement upon personal freedom might be so great that the people would rebel. The change in basic patterns of living might be so radical that, despite the harmfulness of the social condition, many people would rather contend with it than with the substitute. Many people throughout the country felt this way about price control and rationing after war. Finally, there are many social problems concerning which we lack sufficient knowledge to treat by coercive methods because, frankly, we do not now know whom to coerce into doing what. The great problem of war is a case in point.

At the same time it is well to recognize that there have been instances in which legislative-coercive action did seem to result in changed behavior. The Fair Employment Practice laws of some of our states, which forbid racial and other discrimination in the hiring, firing, and promoting of workers, are a case in point. While it is certain that some discrimination still takes place, it seems equally as certain that the few states with such laws have a method of keeping employment discrimination to a minimum. Forcing people to behave democratically, in other words, does seem in this instance to have produced the sought-for effect. In a similar manner, the Supreme Court interpretations with regard to racially segregated schools seem to have made it quite difficult, but not impossible, to discriminate against the Negro educationally and have greatly speeded up the integration of schools. At times, therefore, even laws in emotionally charged areas, and *apparently* running counter to the wishes of many people, can produce a change in behavior.

Educative or persuasive approaches to social problems are sometimes offered as a substitute for coercive ones. Thus many persons argue that while Prohibition failed, a long, slow process of education concerning the effects of alcohol would dissuade people from using it—at least to excess. Similarly, during the war it was frequently argued that price control and rationing were not necessary, that if the government simply appealed to the people's patriotism and was honest in presenting the facts and the need, a "self-discipline" would be observed by the people and the problem would be solved. Most unbiased observers would probably disagree with both of the foregoing. A knowledge of the effects of alcohol is now widely diffused in American society and seems not to deter many persons from alcoholic consumption—even to excess. Likewise, the existence of the "black market" both during and after the war demonstrated that, despite persuasion, many persons would not discipline their wants, even to win a war in which their sons were fighting.

It would seem, then, that there are definite limitations both to coercive treatment and persuasive treatment of social problems. Certainly both approaches have their place. No one would seriously argue that capital and labor could at present work out their difficulties without any legislation whatsoever, so that both sides would be free to do whatever they wanted and required to do nothing. On the other hand, particularly where enforcement of coercive measures is impossible, too costly, or too inconvenient, education may remain the only solution. Finally, coercive and persuasive methods may be used simultaneously on the same problem, each buttressing the other. The toll of automobile deaths can be reduced in part by forcing people to drive more slowly, but also by educating them to drive better.

Evolutionary versus Revolutionary Procedures

Frequently the people of a society have a choice with respect to the relative speed and relative completeness with which to attack a given problem. Almost invariably in such cases, some voices will counsel that "we should proceed slowly, not rush into a radical, untried program," while others will advise that if we do not proceed with haste, "we shall be caught fiddling while Rome burns." Obviously, you can rationalize either position, and even though you try to be objective and unprejudiced in your judgment, you may find it extremely difficult to determine, all things considered, which is the better approach.

Generally speaking, one of the chief impediments to revolutionary change by democratic procedure is the apathy of the great mass of the people, their unwillingness or inability to function outside of traditional grooves. Under conditions of dictatorship, of course, the consent of subordinates need not be secured in support of a revolutionary change, but the inertia of subordinates may create so many resistances and other nuisance inconveniences that the person in position to make the decision often decides against radical change in favor of the path of less resistance.

While in general the above can be demonstrated to be true, there are exceptions, and conspicuous ones at that. The Bolshevik revolution in Russia at the end of World War I, the coup d'état of the Fascist regime in Italy and Germany are well-known examples of a radical remaking of a social system by revolution. In the crisis of 1933 the Roosevelt New Deal regime, through democratic means, enacted sweeping legislative changes by the so-called 100-day Congress which altered the structure of American social and economic life at numerous crucial points.

It is always difficult, however, to interpret these seemingly revolutionary changes. It is quite possible, as some contend, that they only represent a sort of "catching up" by a people on reforms which have long been in demand but were held back by the overly conservative government in power. Thus what seems to be a revolution is really only the accumulated impact of accumulated evolutionary plans for change. Others interpret revolutions essentially as plots contrived by a small group of clever men who, regardless of their motives, succeed in foisting a radical program upon a powerless people. In interpreting a revolutionary change, it is very difficult to maintain one's objectivity. Prejudices based upon vested interests and other factors reach extreme intensity in part because of the magnitude of the change.

Frequently, of course, the only difference between evolution and revolution is the interpretation of the change. As one reads the history of American law, he is entertained by the manner in which people in the past viewed what we now regard as very minor, evolutionary changes. Many, for example, thought that a revolution had occurred when Andrew Jackson became president; many others thought so when Abraham Lincoln signed the Emancipation Proclamation. Perhaps they were right, but as we look today at the history of the United States in the past 100 years, we see certain long-run trends, which some historians call "the emergence of the common man," and the administrations of Andrew Jackson, Abraham Lincoln, Woodrow Wilson, and Franklin D. Roosevelt seem simply to be a series of not too radical steps in the 100-year-old evolution.

Piecemeal Attack versus Total Attack

Another ideological variation in attacks on social problems pertains to the inclusiveness of the proposed program. Many observers feel that one of the major weaknesses (and wastes) of the "typical American" approach to social problems is the tendency to tackle only one aspect or only one problem at a time, when there really are several aspects of one problem or several problems which can most advantageously be handled together. For example, in one midwestern state there are currently six separate divisions of the state government that are concerned with the problems of conservation of the state's natural resources—the divisions of game and fish, water, parks, forests, soil, and minerals. These various agencies were created at different times and with different purposes. Better, it is argued, that the whole problem of conservation of natural resources be attacked at once, thus avoiding the waste, duplication, and other interagency inefficiency which is now said to exist. The conservation of forests, soil, and water, certainly, are intimately interrelated, and a sound program that achieves one purpose automatically achieves the others at the same time.

The clearance of slums over against the separate treatment of juvenile delinquency, health conservation, family disorganization, and immorality is another illustration of the distinction between piecemeal and total attack. We now have abundant and conclusive evidence to show that there is an intimate and causative relation between these several problem areas of modern urban life. The root problem is housing; the root solution is the elimination of slum dwellings. And yet for many years we have had numerous agencies, programs, and movements each designed to treat one separate problem at a time as if that one were largely distinct from the others. We in America are notably deficient in the ability and willingness to see social problems in their real relationships with one another. Our professional leadership (social workers, sociologists, and others) has long known and advocated the more total approach, but its appeals have fallen largely upon deaf ears so far as legislators and the general public are concerned. Both continue to think largely in terms of the nonexistent separateness of these social problem areas. The cost of such ignorance—especially in the long run—would be tremendous and staggering if fully known. In the long run —and not necessarily very long—the cost of a concerted, organized attack on groups of related social problems such as those mentioned above and others might be less than the cost of separate, piecemeal attacks. Or, to put it otherwise, per dollar spent the nation would, it is argued with considerable logic, get much more for its money by a total approach than by a piecemeal one.

The Results of Value Diversity

On the preceding pages we have, if anything, oversimplified the extent and nature of value diversity with respect to the treatment of social problems. A fuller appreciation of the true dimensions of the situation can be gained when it is realized that the same person or group may hold contradictory viewpoints, either at different periods of time or, at the same time, toward different types of problems. For example, the person who accepts the idea of "over-all attack" on the problem of conservation of natural resources may not be able to see the point at all with respect to our example of slum housing. Another may be all in favor of coercive action for a given problem but refuse to accept it as a reasonable alternative for another. While all of this may seem to add up to a rather dismal picture of the treatment of social problems, it is not meant to be discouraging. Realistically, however, an important ingredient in the problems of our society is precisely this intellectual diversity with regard to their treatment. It is the ideological climate in which American social problems live, breathe, and have their being.

SUGGESTED READINGS

GARDNER, MARTIN, *Fads and Fallacies in the Name of Science*. New York, Dover Publications, 1957.

HAGER, DON J., "Housing Discrimination, Social Conflict and the Law," *Social Problems*. 8 (Summer 1960), pp. 80–87.

HUFF, DARRELL, *How to Lie with Statistics*. New York, W. W. Norton & Company, Inc., 1954.

MCKEE, JAMES B., "Community Power and Strategies in Race Relations: Some Critical Observations," *Social Problems*. 6 (Winter 1958–1959), pp. 195–202.

SCHNORE, LEO F., "Social Problems in the Underdeveloped Areas: An Ecological View," *Social Problems*. 8 (Winter 1960–1961), pp. 182–201.

PART II

FOCUSES OF SOCIAL PROBLEMS IN AMERICAN SOCIETY

INTRODUCTION

One does not need to be a professional analyst of social problems to discover the problem focuses in a society—certainly not in his own. He learns about them from the barber shop sage as well as the "public service" features of radio and television; they are ubiquitously reported in the news columns as well as the editorial pages. The selection of a particular group of problems for presentation within one book, however, is not so easy. Consciousness of social problems varies by region, by educational level, and certainly in response to the sophistication level of the evaluator. In parts of the South, for example, the problem of race, whether from the point of view of the self-conscious Negro or the equally self-conscious white, can hardly be missed. Even where there is agreement upon a list of social problems there is often sharp disagreement with respect to the order of importance. One could find a fair representation in American society of the view that the number one social problem is mental health; to another group it is the nuclear bomb, while to a third the "school prayer" issue seems of preeminent importance.

The problem of selecting social problems for treatment here is somewhat simplified, however, because we are writing for a uniform age and educational level, treating them from the point of view of the total society rather than any particular region, and addressing ourselves to a sophistication level that makes it possible largely to ignore minor ramifications of value conflict and also obviates the necessity for spelling out certain elementary considerations.

The logic of order of presentation is essentially arbitrary. Our order of treatment is guided by the following considerations. The first two problem nexuses grow out of our supposition that economic considerations not only loom large in the consciousness of many people but are also intrinsically at the heart of a good deal of the troubles of human living together. The "long arm of the job" has a way of circumscribing the purview as well as the freedom of overt action. Other hard facts of life grow out of the panorama of urban living and the biological facts of population. Another set of backdrops are the traditional institutions—the family system, educational institution, organized religion, and formalized leisure. These traditional modes of structuring human action both present problems in themselves and affect other problems. From these we move to considerations of a more immediately personal type, social aspects of problems which impinge, or are likely to, upon everyone—physical health, mental health, and old age. Less universal but no less personal are the social problems subsumed under the familiar rubrics of crime, juvenile delinquency, and such disputed practices as alcoholism and gambling. Finally, we return to larger considerations with concluding chapters on the pressure group structuring of value issues and the reciprocal world-wide impact of what we tend to think of as strictly American problems.

ECONOMIC PROBLEMS IN AN AGE OF ABUNDANCE

4

A foreigner coming to our land notices the tall office buildings, the rolling college campuses, the new shops and suburbs, and the seemingly endless miles of paved highways. Never before, probably, has he seen so vast an array of material things, so that it is not to be wondered at if he concludes that the cornucopia has been turned over and poured out on America. We, too, sense our great abundance. Our expenditures on space craft alone seem to make it impossible to deny that we must be an affluent society.

AN AFFLUENT SOCIETY: FACT OR MYTH?

It is by no means easy to arrive at meaningful statements about the economic well-being of a country. To begin with, the common confusion between wealth and income must be avoided. Both ought to figure in one's assessment of how a nation stands, but they are quite different concepts. Wealth is a *stock* of things—such as houses, factories, railways, automobiles, furniture, paintings, school buildings, and so on and on—from which benefits are drawn. Income is a *flow* of goods and services that can be measured only over a period of time. Neither is money, though both are measured in money terms. Both have to do with a family or a country being rich or poor, but wealth is a difficult concept to measure. We shall rely here mainly on income, the figures for which are more available.

Another pitfall in any discussion of "richness" is that it is a relative notion. That is, to label a society as rich we require some points of comparison, which might be its condition at some earlier period in its history or the condition of other societies. Caution must be the byword here, for

FIGURE 3   How the total income is distributed

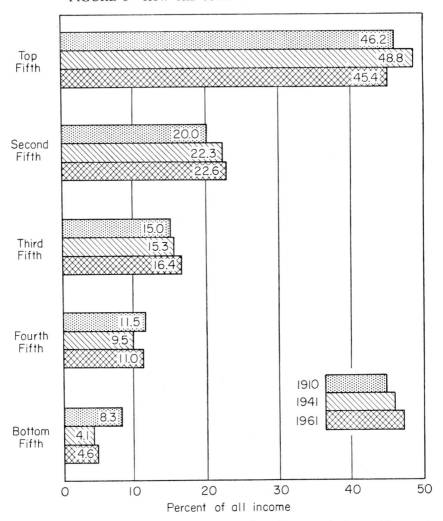

NOTE: While generally the distribution has remained the same, the lowest 20 percent of income recipients now receive a smaller share of the national income than they did in 1910.

SOURCES: Data for 1910 from Gabriel Kolko, *Wealth and Power in America* (Frederick A. Praeger, 1962), p. 14. Other data from the U.S. Bureau of the Census.

the greater the time spread or cultural differences between the two entities being compared, the less meaningful is the comparison. Finally, we need to be careful about the unit we are describing as rich or "wealthy." A given quantity of material things may be quite differently divided among the members of a society, so that the distribution of the total becomes a crucial factor in deciding how well off the whole body is.

Our first task, then, is to get a reliable picture of how our income is allocated among our families. We need next to know what getting a certain share of the total income means in terms of level of living in the mid-1960s, and how many Americans can be labeled wealthy, poor, and so on. Following that, we will be able to investigate the economic problems of the different segments of society.

The Trend in Income Distribution

A convenient way of determining whether changes have been occurring in the distribution of the national income is to compare the shares received by various income groups at different periods of time. We can thus discover, for example, whether the 20 percent of the families with the lowest incomes now receive a larger or smaller share of the national income than they did ten, twenty, or fifty years ago.

From Figure 3 it is apparent that a pronounced unequal distribution of income has been characteristic of our society for the last fifty years. The top *20 percent* of income recipients get a larger share of the national income than does the lowest *60 percent*. The lowest income fifth has experienced a definite loss in its share of income as compared with 1910, and the next lowest income fifth receives a slightly smaller share now than it did fifty years ago. The second and third highest income fifths have improved their relative position. The top income fifth has lost a little of its 1910 share of the income. Most of the people in the highest income fifth, however, either have maintained their relative share or have increased it, for more detailed analysis shows that the loss for the entire top 20 percent was borne by the top 1 to 5 percent of income recipients.

It would be a safe general conclusion to say that the poorest segments of our society are at least as poor as they were fifty years ago, and the rich as rich as they were, if in both instances we added the qualifying words: *relative to the rest of society.* As most people realize, the total income of our society has increased, so that we need also be concerned with the absolute dollar incomes received by American families. First, however, we need an accurate analysis of *how much* the national income has increased.

Total National Income

A convenient way to describe the relative prosperity of our society is in terms of its total earnings at different periods of time. The *national income,* computed yearly, is the total of the earnings by employees (wages and salaries), proprietors (profits), corporate profits, owners of real property (rents), and lenders of funds (interest).

Table 3   National Income in
the United States, 1929–1961
(in millions of dollars)

Year	Income
1929	87,814
1931	59,708
1933	40,159
1935	57,057
1937	73,618
1939	72,753
1941	104,710
1943	170,310
1945	181,248
1947	198,177
1949	217,690
1951	279,313
1953	305,573
1955	330,206
1957	366,503
1959	400,500
1961	427,800

SOURCE: Department of Commerce, *Survey of Current Business,* July 1959 and December 1962.

From a glance at Table 3 it can be seen that the national income has risen phenomenally over the last several decades. The total earnings of our society are almost five times as much as they were in 1929 and are over twice as great as in 1947. Of course, now there are more people among whom the national income must be divided, and our currency has been inflated. While the pronounced rise in the national earnings is no meager achievement, it is nevertheless necessary to determine how this rise has affected the purchasing power of families.

Real versus Money Income

Almost all thinking about wages and income is confused by the failure clearly to distinguish the number of dollars received and the amount of goods and services that the income will buy. The number of dollars a person receives as cash income is important only for what goods and services the cash can purchase for its owner. If a man earns $100 per week and pays

$25 rental for his apartment, for example, he would be no better off should his wages be increased to $125 and his rental to $50. In both instances he would have $75 left for other purposes. The same holds true, of course, for expenditures for goods, clothing, taxes, or any other item. Wages are important only as they relate to prices of goods purchased with them. Doubling wage rates is of no value to the worker if the prices of the goods and the services he buys are also doubled. Thus, wage rates may be going up, but the persons who receive the increases may be getting poorer because prices have risen more rapidly than have the wage rates. The reverse trend may also, of course, be true: wages may be going down but prices may be dropping even faster. It becomes very difficult, therefore, to discover the significance of constantly changing wages and prices upon the level of living of the worker and his family. And yet unless and until one relates these two interdependent items, he cannot accurately determine the status of the income recipient or the actual trends in the level of living which are taking place.

Table 4   Changes in Dollar versus "Real" Income

Year	Average family income	
	Current dollars	1962 dollars
1929	$2340	$4250
1948	4130	5450
1950	4350	5430
1952	4170	5250
1954	4360	5990
1956	6010	6580
1958	6280	6560
1960	6810	6930
1962	7140	7140

SOURCE: Department of Commerce, *Survey of Current Business,* April 1963.

The data in Table 4 illustrate the point. From 1929 to 1962 money income per family increased 205 percent. But let us adjust the figures to take into account the price changes since 1929. This can be done by converting dollar figures for all years into dollars of 1962 purchasing power. It is now evident that "real" income increased but 68 percent. While not as spectacular as the 205 percent increase in dollar income, it is by no means a small matter when the average family's purchasing power increases 68 percent in about three decades.

The Distribution of Family Income

The average family income represents what conditions would be like if the total of the income of all families were divided equally among these families. It is true that the total to be divided has increased greatly, but we must be careful not to assume that the rising prosperity has affected all wage earners equally, or even proportionally. Our next task is to determine the number of families at various income levels. To make this more meaningful, we need also to know what a certain income means in terms of the absolute well-being of a family in the 1960s.

It has been calculated that a family consisting of a husband, wife, and three children requires a yearly income of $5000, after deduction of federal income taxes.[1] Such a family would be able to "get by," and probably would not be eligible for welfare assistance. If we define as "poor" any family whose total income, before taxes, is less than $4000 a year, we would have a conservative definition of poverty. That is, in view of today's costs of food, clothing, and shelter, there can be little doubt that a family with an annual income of less than $4000 is poor, but use of this figure would tend to underestimate the extent of poverty in our society.

At the opposite extreme, family incomes in excess of $15,000 a year would provide more than just a comfortable level of living. Such families could be labeled affluent, although only a small proportion of them would be truly wealthy. Between the extreme types of the poor and the affluent, we can designate families as deprived if their yearly income is more than $4000 but less than $6000, and as comfortable if their incomes range between $6000 and $15,000. While these designations of income levels are somewhat crude, they should provide us with reasonably accurate working definitions of the meaning of a certain yearly income in terms of what it can provide a family.[2]

While as a nation we may be experiencing an age of abundance, it is nevertheless true that millions of Americans are living in poverty. The extent of poverty is startling. As shown in Table 5, over one fifth of the nation's families have an annual income of less than $3000 a year, and about 30 percent receive less than $4000. Taken together, this means that over 14 million American families are living in poverty. There are an estimated 36 million people in these families.

[1] For a discussion of minimum family budgets, according to size, age make-up, and other characteristics of families, see James N. Morgan *et al., Income and Welfare in the United States* (New York: McGraw-Hill Book Company, Inc., 1962), p. 188ff.

[2] For other attempts to define poverty and related concepts see Morgan, *op. cit.,* Chap. 16. See also *Poverty and Deprivation in the U.S.* (Washington, D.C.: Conference on Economic Progress, 1962).

Table 5   Income Distribution in the United States in 1961

Total yearly income of families (all family members), or unattached individuals	Percent of families	Percent of unattached individuals
Under $1000	5.0	32.4
$1000–1999	7.7	22.0
$2000–2999	8.7	12.6
$3000–3999	9.4	9.7
$4000–4999	10.5	7.9
$5000–5999	11.7	6.0
$6000–9999	30.9	7.0
$10,000–14,999	11.3	1.5
Over $15,000	4.7	0.9

SOURCE: U.S. Bureau of the Census, *Current Population Reports,* Series P-60, No. 39 (February 28, 1963).

Above the level of poverty but with insufficient income for a comfortable level of living, are about 10 million families. Almost one fourth of the nation's families fall into the "deprived" category, with incomes between $4000 and $6000. When the poor and the deprived are combined, we account for about 53 percent of the families in our society. Living comfortably or in luxury are 47 percent of the families, certainly a significant portion of the nation.

The foregoing are the facts, as best we know them, regarding the distribution of family income in the United States. While from time immemorial societies have had "economic problems," the situation in present-day America is admittedly unique. By any reasonable definition, a sizable portion of our society is living in comfort or opulence. Both absolutely and relatively, the purchasing power of just under half of our families is high, and they can enjoy the many material conveniences and comforts our society has to offer. At the same time, there is another sizable group of Americans living in poverty. Nor are they merely poor relative to the rest of Americans. The fact is that the millions of families with an income of $2000 or $3000 a year do not have enough money to meet the minimum needs of all of the family members. In a sense, then, American society in the mid-1960s has two distinct kinds of economic problems. The one is more traditional, and concerns the causes, effects, and solutions to the problem of poverty. But affecting as many people in our society is the newer problem of discovering how best to use abundance. While we will treat separately these two groups and their problems, we will strive not to lose sight of the fact that it is a *single society* with which we are dealing.

In closing this section, we should not wish to leave the implication that the problems flowing from the unequal distribution of income have been entirely ignored in our country. On the contrary, a number of steps taken by our governments—to say nothing of private philanthropy—have the primary or secondary result of redistributing income. Sometimes the effect is to redistribute upward, though this is often unintentional. Usually the deliberate purpose is to redistribute downward—that is, to take some from the more well-to-do and give it (in various forms) to the less favorably placed. A few examples of such action are these: a progressive income tax, which takes larger proportions of higher incomes; the "free" provision to all of such services as public schools; social security payments; old-age benefits; grants-in-aid to the poorer states.

The over-all effect of many such devices on the distribution of income is positive, but not very large. Most experts feel that *some* further steps could well be taken in the direction of greater equality, and that good economic (and even better social and political) reasons exist for so doing. At the same time, there is less feeling than a couple of decades ago that a *great deal* can be accomplished in this direction without encountering severe problems. Rather, the consensus now seems to be that the poorer segments of our economy would be more helped by plentiful job opportunities and a higher total income than by much more redividing of what we now have.

Finally, it might be noted that the distribution of *wealth* has received much less attention. It is possible that wealth is more unequally held than income. Few steps have been taken directly to correct this state of affairs, nor is there reason to think that we will soon have policy proposals along that line.

THE POOR IN AN AFFLUENT SOCIETY

As we have seen, about 30 percent of all families are living on incomes of less than $4000 a year. But sheer numbers and dollars are difficult to grasp, and may disguise what it really means to be poor in American society in the mid-1960s. Our first intention, therefore, is to deal with the physical, more or less tangible, effects of poverty and, following that, with the psychological toll exacted for being poor in a time of plenty.

Many Americans find it difficult to imagine how their fellow citizens can possibly support a family on a wage of $40, $50, or $60 a week. They wonder how such a sum can provide adequate housing, decent clothing, and sufficient and proper food for a family with several children. The fact is that it cannot. The poor in our society necessarily do without those things that other Americans consider necessities.

It is not only that the poor are forced to accept unsanitary and overcrowded housing, worn and shoddy clothing, and inadequate diets from a nutritional standpoint. In American society one's life chances are in large measure determined by his financial status. The goods and services necessary to maintain life must be bought and paid for out of the accumulated wealth or current earnings of the person or his family. Broadly speaking, quality varies with cost. The principle is the same whether the person is buying potatoes, securing music lessons for his child, or purchasing medical care. The better potatoes cost more, so do the music lessons taught by more competent teachers, and so do the services of medical specialists.

Life itself can frequently be preserved only at considerable expense. We have long known, for example, that a larger percentage of the babies born to parents in the higher income groups survive the first year of life than among persons of lower income. Not only is infant mortality affected by income, so also is the incidence of various illnesses. Accident statistics also show that life is safer for persons of higher income.

So far we have been talking about those families that, in actuality, do not have a minimum adequate income. Even many families a little better off financially cannot afford such "common luxuries" as central heating and good lighting in their homes, a short vacation away from home, and mechanical appliances of various sorts. These deprived families, as well as the very poor, are exposed to the mass media advertising which tells them that they should buy these items, and that every home "needs" many more than we have named. But they cannot afford to buy them. Some, of course, contract to buy them anyway, and thereby go into debt.

Because most Americans are not poor, and because most of the poor are not as destitute as the poor in other societies, it is likely that we have become callous to the emotional meaning of poverty. When one must watch his children go to bed hungry or go to school with ill-fitting, worn clothing, it is little comfort to be told that they are better fed and clothed than many children in the world. When one's early teenage son or daughter drops out of school to look for a job, it is really no answer to be told that already he has had more education than millions of adults in other countries. It is no answer, because our poor are not living in these "other countries." It is this society, and not some underdeveloped country on the other side of the globe, that our poor know best and whose standards of living they use as a point of comparison with their own.

Poverty, therefore, has a special significance in a wealthy society. To be poor in a time of plenty means that one must daily witness a sizable portion of his society visibly display its luxuries. This robs the poor of any possible solace that elsewhere they might find in being representative members of their society. Here they are failures. Since financial success is highly valued in our society, and since so many have been able to "make the grade," it is little wonder if the losers in the race for affluence lose also their sense of self-worth and self-respect. While Americans are quick to remind one another that "it is no disgrace to be poor," it is understandable if it is disheartening, discouraging, and even degrading.

REDUCTION OF POVERTY AND VALUE CONFLICTS

Presumably, most Americans would like to see poverty reduced, and presumably we have the talent and knowledge in our society that could be applied to this persistent problem. What, then, is being done to reduce poverty? How effective is our present treatment? What else could our society be doing?

It should be recognized at the outset that there is no "guaranteed cure" for poverty in our own, or for that matter in any other society. Particularly when we are dealing with a large, highly industrialized, and highly complex society, we must admit that various corrective programs, frequently operating simultaneously, are required to deal effectively with poverty. What is more, such corrective programs are not simple remedies which affect only the poor. It is precisely because they are complicated and because they have implications for everyone that measures for the reduction of poverty are met with strong reactions.

On the following pages we shall set forth some of the frequently made proposals for reducing poverty. It is our intention to describe the nature of each proposal and to draw attention to some of the implications of each. In this way we should be able better to understand why, instead of merely accepting the expert advice, we have so intense a clash of values.

Higher Wages

Many people react negatively to the proposal of simply increasing wages. In times of prosperity it is feared by some that a wage increase will produce inflation, and in times of depression it is held that society cannot afford an increase in wages. And yet if in the long run wages did not go up faster than prices, or if prices did not go down faster than wages, we would have no real increase in the general welfare.[3] In order to have a higher level of living, it is necessary for there to be an actual increase in the ability to purchase goods and services.

The economic principle that wages need to rise faster than prices to permit a real increase in purchasing power is hard enough to accept in the abstract. But there is even more reluctance when the principle is applied

[3] For a general discussion of the relationship between wages and prosperity see *Wages and the Public Interest* (Washington, D.C.: Conference on Economic Progress, 1958).

to the problem of reducing poverty. Some of the reluctance is due to an honest misunderstanding of the results of the proposal, but it must also be admitted that in other instances the implications are understood well enough but they are not considered "good" or "right."

One clash of values centers on the issue of a minimum wage. While many Americans may subscribe to the idea that any worker, as a citizen of a wealthy society, has the right to a "decent" minimum living wage, there is still an uneasiness when it comes to full acceptance of the principle. At today's price levels, for example, full acceptance would mean that the minimum wage should be well over two dollars an hour and that a method be found so that it would apply to all workers, and not just those currently affected by federal minimum wage regulations. What is more, to be an effective partial remedy for poverty, the minimum wage, whatever its initial amount, would have to rise faster than prices.

If the minimum wage was such that any full-time regular worker could support his family above the level of poverty, it is possible that the lower income groups would receive a larger share of the national income than they do now. There is much to recommend this result from an economic standpoint, for putting more money into the hands of more people would result in a greater consumption of goods and a continued need for workers. But because of certain difficulties beyond the scope of this book, most economists no longer think that a large step-up in the minimum wage would alone provide an adequate solution.

Reduction of Unemployment

Among the experts, a more widely accepted remedy for poverty is to maintain as close to full employment as is possible. For the most part, Americans seem unwilling to admit, in times of national prosperity, that we have an unemployment problem. But like other problems, it does not "go away" when we look the other way.

Our tendency to ignore unemployment has meant that too few understand the magnitude of this problem and its persistence. As shown in Table 6, since the close of World War II there has been a general rise in unemployment. Consistently, year after year, millions of potential workers have been idle. It is also apparent that not only sheer numbers but also the rate of unemployment has been increasing. Furthermore, from Table 6 it is evident that the average number of weeks of unemployment has been increasing over the last fifteen years.

More detailed analysis shows that almost 30 percent of the unemployed, or about a million and a quarter people, are without work for three and a half months or longer. In a typical recent year, at least a half million people were without work for over six months. It must be recog-

Table 6   Unemployment in the United States, 1947–1962

Year	Number of unemployed in civilian labor force	Percent unemployed	Average number of weeks unemployed
1947	2,356,000	3.9	9.8
1948	2,325,000	3.8	8.6
1949	3,682,000	5.9	10.0
1950	3,351,000	5.3	12.1
1951	2,009,000	3.3	9.7
1952	1,932,000	3.1	8.3
1953	1,870,000	2.9	8.1
1954	3,578,000	5.6	11.7
1955	2,904,000	4.4	13.2
1956	2,822,000	4.2	11.3
1957	2,936,000	4.3	10.4
1958	4,681,000	6.8	13.8
1959	3,813,000	5.5	14.5
1960	4,206,000	6.1	14.2
1961	4,806,000	6.7	15.5
1962	4,382,000	6.2	16.5

SOURCE: U.S. Bureau of the Census, *Statistical Abstract of the United States: 1960,* p. 206, and *1962,* p. 217, Washington, D.C.

nized that during times of relatively high unemployment the official figures and rates consistently understate the true extent of joblessness. That is, the relative difficulty in securing jobs has kept hundreds of thousands from continuing to seek work, and since they are not actually looking for work, these potential workers are not defined as being "in the labor force." But even the official rates on unemployment, and the duration of unemployment among the jobless, are sufficiently high to indicate that we cannot deal effectively with poverty without attacking the problem of unemployment.

In a large industrial society continually marked by technological change, it is no easy matter to assure that there are jobs for all those who want to work. At the same time, there are value implications regarding the steps that could be taken to move us further in the direction of full employment. One way to create more jobs, for example, may be to heighten the demand for consumer goods, and thus increase the need for workers to produce the goods. Increasing the size of unemployment benefits and extending the period of time over which they could be claimed would not only help to relieve poverty temporarily but should result in some increased demand for goods and services. But here again many are quick to hearken back to the dictum of an earlier time, "he who will not work, does not eat," forgetting that in today's world it is not personal preference that keeps at least 4 million people jobless. Another measure for the relief of unemployment is a sound retraining program for workers in "depressed areas" and for those who find themselves without a job due to automation, but our current programs are designed for tens of thousands of workers when at least a half a million are in need of additional training so that they can qualify for modern jobs. Admittedly, the potential results of a full-scale drive are not yet known, for our efforts to date have been small and hesitant.

The remedy for raising the national income and keeping it high that is most broadly agreed to by economists involves the use of a tool called fiscal policy. Briefly, this is the deliberate use of the power of government (federal, state or local, but especially the first) to tax and spend so as to alter the level of national income. Spending at once becomes income, while taxing directly affects the ability of people and business firms to spend. The impact of the government can be, indeed *is,* tremendous—as witness the large role played by federal spending on defense in our present (qualified) prosperity. Were that suddenly to cease altogether, we would be plunged into a severe depression with many millions more jobless.

Another device in the hands of government is monetary policy—the control over money and credit, and hence, indirectly, over what people and businesses have to spend. Just how powerful a tool this is has given rise to dispute among the experts. Monetary policy tends to be more favored by those with a conservative bent. At any rate, almost all economists agree that a combined arsenal of several different fiscal *and* monetary measures can be very effective in maintaining a high and stable national income. Not all unemployment and poverty can be liquidated in this way (at least not within the framework of a free enterprise economy), but much of it can.

In fact, much of it has. Our government does employ fiscal and monetary policies. Why are not these pressed further and carried out more consistently so that we eliminate the substantial poverty that persists amid plenty? There are several reasons. Partly, those in positions of power are confused by the disagreements among economists over the *details* of policy. Partly, there is a widespread concern that government not become too active or powerful. There is also some general apathy about the problem, which affects Congress where it takes the form of saying that "government can't solve all problems."

Presumably, no one really wants our relatively high rate of joblessness and the poverty that follows in its wake. Unless we are willing to take bold steps toward a real reduction in unemployment, however, we cannot expect to escape from the perplexing paradox that in "the wealthiest nation on earth," 36 million people are living in poverty.

Effective Treatment of Special Problems

While keeping unemployment to a minimum and reducing poverty are urgent goals, they are not the only areas of concern. From time to time there will arise special economic problems, or there will be segments of the population that are uniquely affected by current trends so that they find themselves in adverse straits. In a rapidly changing society marked by continued technological improvements we should expect these special problems.

Today, for example, migrant farm laborers are trapped in a system in which they work for an extremely low wage, and as they follow the crops, they are forced to live in shanties of the worst sort. Their children are scarcely in one place long enough to attend school, and even when they are, local laws may prohibit them from attending. Consequently, at a young age they join their parents in the fields. Yet because of his poor education and his lack of marketable work skills, the migrant farm laborer finds it infeasible to seek another type of work. And so his misery continues, and what is more, the poverty of one generation is transmitted to the next.

Another special problem area is the plight of our older people. Since we deal with the problems of the aged in Chapter 15, we will merely take note that a large fraction of them are in economic trouble. For the most part they would not be much affected by the measures suggested for the relief of general poverty. Some special effort is required to relieve the poverty of those in their later years.

Still another group requiring special attention are the slum-reared youth. Unemployment and consequent poverty run high in such groups, with 30 to 50 percent of those under twenty-four years of age who are not in school being without work. Fuller employment nationally would undoubtedly help them, but probably there would continue to be local pockets where young people drop out of school too soon, only to find themselves unemployable.

It is not our intention to investigate the various ways in which these special problem cases can be handled. Rather, it is to indicate that the problem of poverty in our society cannot be dealt with fully unless we are able to find remedies for these and other unique situations, and for still others that undoubtedly will arise. A society truly bent on reducing poverty would be extremely sensitive to the presence of special problems, it would be quick to determine what corrective action was necessary, and it would be quick to apply it. That such special problem cases as those of the migrant farm laborer, the older person, and the slum-reared youth persist suggests that our society does not fully accept them as problems worthy of much societal effort.

THE COMFORTABLE AND
THE AFFLUENT

Throughout the long course of human history, most of the people in the world have been poor. They have been poor in the sense that food and shelter were scarce and, while they worked hard, they were barely able to provide themselves with the fundamentals for survival. Here in our own society, as we have just seen, an estimated 36 million people are still living in poverty. And yet in the same towns and cities are about 68 million people living in comfort or affluence. From an historical perspective, it is a unique experience to find such a large proportion of a society's population living well above the subsistence level.

Apparently, no one is wholly sure from whence the abundance which makes possible the comfortable and affluent classes came, and there is equal uncertainty as to how to assure ourselves that it will continue. There is the notion that it is tied up with our industrial and economic systems in the sense that we have found the way to produce more and more consumer products and to create a sufficient demand for them so that the factories are kept busy producing still more goods. This explanation for our national prosperity seems to have given rise to a way of thinking and feeling about material goods that we will label *the consumption morality*.

The chief characteristic of the consumption morality is the attitude that it is good to consume goods, to use them up, and then to replace them or buy newer things. The value position holds that it is good to consume because it brings happiness and pleasure, and that it is also good "for the economy" to keep the demand for products relatively high.

Of course, many of the poor accept the consumption morality, and the more they do so the more they are doomed to disappointment and frustration. Our concern at this point, however, is with the effects and implications of the consumption morality on the comfortable and the affluent, that is, on those who can do more than just "believe in" the consumption morality—who can afford to make it a working value in their lives. There is some concern, as we shall see, over some of the by-products of the consumption morality and what this approach does to people as human beings rather than as consumer units.

Decline of "Traditional Virtues"

It is paradoxical that one of the reasons our abundance exists at all is because our ancestors did not believe in it. Theirs was a sterner approach to life and to the meaning of material possessions. As the adage had it, one was supposed to "use it up, wear it out, and do without." Thrift was considered a prime virtue. Most of all, there existed a strong measure of the deferred gratification pattern, that is, the feeling that it is right and proper to postpone pleasures in the present in order to get more of them at some future time. This made it possible to accumulate capital.

Clearly the consumption morality is at odds with the traditional virtues of thrift, deferred gratification, and saving. Today, the moral superiority of the ant over the grasshopper is questioned, if not denied. For some people saving for future pleasures has been replaced by an "enjoy it now" philosophy, and this, in turn, has been stretched to include seizing present enjoyments whether or not one has the ability to pay for them, the familiar "buy now, pay later" slogan of the advertisers. Some people seem unable to satisfy their desires for more and newer "things." This is the consumption morality at its best—or at its worst. (To be sure, a number continue to save a portion of their incomes.)

The decline in the "traditional virtues" has had some curious effects. The emphasis on enjoying increasingly more consumer goods here and now, and its value counterpart of the decline in deferred gratification and saving, has led to an inability, at least for those designated as "comfortable," to make purchases requiring a fairly large sum of cash money. It seems to have led, too, to an unwillingness to make *certain kinds* of purchases. Both of these effects are felt in the financing of higher education. The seeming inability of many to save for the purchase of this particular service has led to a more sympathetic attitude toward "federal aid" to education. To be sure, many voice their objections to such "government interference." Such people are in a value trap of their own construction—they do not want to save for their children's higher education or for security in their own old age, yet they are not quite comfortable with the alternative of the government providing these things for them.

A Belief in Waste

As we have noted, the consumption morality assigns a place of extreme importance to consumer goods. Yet the true attitude toward goods can better be described as a strange mixture of positive and negative values. While they are highly desired, one cannot afford to become too attached to his purchases, for the new, the brighter, and the different should automatically be rated higher still.

The consumption morality includes, then, a belief in waste. If the purpose of the economy is to produce an increasingly greater amount of consumer goods, then it is necessary that these goods be purchased, used for a time, and then thrown away, so that new purchases are continually necessary. If it is good in itself and good for the economy that more and more people have new things, then it is better still if these new things are soon obsolete or worn out and have to be replaced.

On an ethical and philosophical level, one could certainly question whether it is good for people to have, and to be encouraged to have, such wasteful attitudes towards the things that they and their fellow men have worked to produce. There is also the practical matter that sooner or later people will begin to see a basic incompatibility in their attitudes toward material goods—they cannot be so desirable that they *must* be purchased and, a little later, so undesirable that they must be replaced. It is common today to talk of the declining *pride in workmanship,* in that goods are produced without care, thoughtfulness, and a desire to make the best possible object. But there is an analogous attitude of *pride of ownership* which would include carefully choosing objects, and then caring for them, respecting them, and in a sense cherishing them. Is it possible, then, that the consumption morality is self-defeating, in that the decline in the pride in ownership it unwittingly fosters can only go so far before people cease to "believe in" consumption? What then will keep our factories humming?

Abundance and the "Good Life"

Whether or not there is yet a noticeable discontent with consumption itself, there is some evidence that high consumption has not led to the "happiness" it so blatantly promises. The real concern is whether the consumption morality is capable, under any circumstances, of providing a sense of purpose and meaning to life. We are dealing now with such time-honored questions as "Why are we here?," and "What is the purpose of life?" But certainly the comfortable and the affluent in present-day America, who need not be concerned with *if they can live,* can afford to ask themselves *what kind of life they wish to live.*

The problem, put bluntly, is that our technological and economic success may be a failure in the sense of what it has done to human beings. Among those who consume most of the fruits of our technology, there is ample evidence of tension, boredom, uneasiness, aloneness, and a feeling that somehow life has lost its meaning. The poor can still delude themselves into believing that if only they had a better car, more gadgets, and a nicer home then life would be serene and happy. The comfortable and the affluent know better. They have engaged themselves quite seriously in the acquisition of things, and are coming to realize that things are not enough.

So runs the charge of the modern "social critic." To claim that our societal emphasis on consumption of material goods can only lead to boredom and aimlessness is a serious indictment. Strangely, it does not seem to be considered so. Witness how few people dare to question the consumption morality, or are willing thoughtfully to ponder that for all our rotisserie sets in backyards and butterfly chairs in family rooms, the good life may be escaping us. Fewer still seem willing to consider whether our current emphasis can go on and on, or what will happen to us if it does. Perhaps Riesman is correct in his analysis that "a serious discussion of the future is just what is missing in the United States." [4] And perhaps he is correct again when he claims that what we are afraid lies in the future is even worse than total destruction, for it is *"total meaninglessness."* [5]

REDUCING THE PROBLEMS OF ABUNDANCE AND VALUE CONFLICTS

What, then, is the "way out" for our affluent society? Some, of course, contend that what we all need is a "touch of poverty" or "a good depression." Yet it would certainly seem to be possible to preserve the best of our abundance, even while reducing its undesirable features.

One important proposal for dealing with the problems of abundance that has attracted many serious thinkers would involve a redirection of our national energies. It would mean, in short, devoting more of our productive efforts to providing public services and less to providing consumer goods.[6] Proponents of this solution envision a shift in the balance between the public and private sectors of the economy, rather than a drastic reduction in the production of goods. Even so, the proposal has evoked a value clash of major proportions.

Proponents of Extended Public Services

Those who support the proposal for extending public services hold that such action is in keeping with our democratic principles, that a need exists, and that it would benefit the entire society if such a proposal were adopted.

In the preamble of the Constitution of the United States, part of our national purpose is stated as to "promote the general welfare." Historically, the government at all levels has provided services that the people need and want and that they cannot provide at all, or as well, through their individual efforts. The provision of public services is thus both legal and traditional. The critical question is *how many* services should be provided, in terms both of the need for them and of the effects on our economy of providing them.

---

[4] David Riesman, "Abundance for What?" *Bulletin of the Atomic Scientists,* 14 (April 1958), p. 139.

[5] *Ibid.*

[6] The economist Galbraith has defended this proposal most ably. See John K. Galbraith, *The Affluent Society* (Boston: Houghton Mifflin Company, 1958), particularly Chap. 18.

It is not difficult to document the contention that the affluence of our society is lopsided, that we are rich in consumer products but poor in public services. Privately, for example, many Americans can afford to buy a good automobile, but we have failed to provide adequate roads and parking facilities. These same automobiles help to create a serious problem in air contamination about which, realistically, the individual can do little. Privately, many Americans can afford a vacation trip to our national parks, only to find that they must travel to them on clogged highways, and that when they get there the facilities are overcrowded and the streams are polluted.

There are other public services that from a certain value position are more important than roads and highways, parks and fresh streams and which, from the same position, our country needs. As long as a sizable proportion of our population cannot afford medical attention, it can be said we need to provide such service to them. As long as an estimated one half of the intellectually capable cannot afford to remain in school, a need exists in this area. As long as there are millions of workers unemployed, we need to provide them either with jobs or adequate unemployment compensation. And as long as we have real poverty in the midst of our abundance, we need to remove it and to prevent its recurrence.

Most of all, it is contended, we need to provide a deeper sense of purpose and meaning to the lives of our people. Some of the proposals mentioned above are said to be capable of filling the current uneasy emptiness. Instead of orienting our lives to the production and consumption of ever more things, we could strive to become an ethically superior nation in which all children had an equal access to quality education and all people an equal opportunity for good medical care. Combatting air pollution in our cities and creating more beautiful cities would not only be good from a health and aesthetic standpoint, but also would provide a sense of importance and meaning to working and living. Developing programs for the care and enhancement of our natural resources would cultivate greater meaning to life than our present attitude of waste and disrespect for produced things. It would be more satisfying, both personally and societally, to work on the elimination of poverty rather than on the creation of a product that differs from last year's model only by the addition of a functionless protuberance or on one which nobody really wanted until he was psychologically coerced into "needing" it.

Proponents of increased public services for the general welfare contend that such a proposal is economically sound. More than this, they hold that it is our best hope for assuring that our age of abundance will continue. Providing the "good life" in nonmaterial ways is held not to be competitive with providing material necessities, comforts, or even luxuries.

Critics of Increased Public Services

The mildest criticism of the foregoing approach to our economic problems is meted out by those who believe it is a little risky to depart too much from the status quo. While admitting that we have problems, such people emphasize the positive features of our abundant society and adopt a "don't rock the boat" attitude. For the short run such critics very likely have a point. Certainly, as we have indicated often, there is much that is good with things as they are, and maintaining the status quo would not be all bad. We even have ways, now in use, to deal with some of our economic problems, such as preventing an economic slump, reversing a recession that occurs this year or next, or otherwise handling our short-run problems. More serious consideration, however, should be given to the longer run. After all, if a major redirection of our economic system is needed, it takes time to study, to prepare, and gradually to put the plan into action.

It is scarcely necessary to point out that the proposal for more attention to public services draws more violent reactions than we have so far indicated. For some, the proposal is too "radical" and too "socialistic", even to warrant consideration. Indeed, it would be dismissed as a preposterous daydream were it not defined as constituting a serious threat to "the American way of life."

While the local, state, and federal governments over the years have provided more and more services for the people, it is true that the proposal under discussion calls for an accelerated rate of production of public services. In a sense the proposal could be labeled radical, for it constitutes a departure from the accustomed, even though it is by no means a "new idea." As we have used it, the term "radical" is not in itself an evaluation, but merely a description of the degree to which the proposal is new or different.

The provision of more public services necessarily would mean that taxes of various sorts would be increased and that more purchasing decisions would be made by representatives of the people, rather than by the people as individuals. Some individual purchasing power, in other words, would be surrendered to the local community and to the state and federal governments. With regard to the portion of his income he uses for taxes, the individual is no longer free to purchase the particular consumer product that he prefers. Of course, if he does not surrender some of his purchasing power as an individual, there is no *practical* way in which a community could prefer to enlarge a school, to build a dam, or to increase relief payments to the needy aged.[7] The city, state, and the federal govern-

[7] *Ibid.,* p. 267.

ments each can perform services that the individual scarcely can provide for himself, but to do so these governments need money. If a city combats the problem of air pollution and thereby furnishes its citizens with fresh air to breathe, it is difficult to see how this constitutes a dangerous drift to socialism or is a threat to "the American way of life." And so with other specific public expenditures. As long as the people need and want them, and as long as they can better be provided by the society than by individuals, there would seem to be nothing intrinsically wrong with this system of furnishing services.

Undoubtedly the most serious criticism of the proposal for a shift in emphasis toward more public services is that it will not alleviate our societal ills. Some consider it economically unsound, and talk of the infeasibility of "spending ourselves out of poverty." Others doubt whether the shift in productive efforts is really capable of providing a richer, fuller, more purposeful life for individuals. And so the clash of values continues.

It is difficult to believe that we are too ignorant to alleviate poverty, to assure our continued societal abundance, and to help our citizens find a more meaningful and significant life. It is more plausible to conclude that most Americans at least unconsciously recognize that the essence of our social problems, economic and otherwise, is the threat to cherished values. This same threat keeps us at odds with one another concerning solutions, for it becomes a question of whose cherished values shall be trampled upon, and whose respected, as we seek and apply corrective action.

SUGGESTED READINGS

DUNLOP, JOHN T., *Automation & Technological Change*. Englewood Cliffs, N.J., Prentice-Hall, Inc., 1962.

GALBRAITH, JOHN K., *The Affluent Society*. Boston, Houghton Mifflin Company, 1958.

HARRINGTON, MICHAEL, *The Other America*. New York, The Macmillan Company, 1962.

HUGHES, CHARLES C., et al., *People of Cove and Woodlot*. New York, Basic Books, Inc., 1960.

KOLKO, GABRIEL, *Wealth and Power in America*. New York, Frederick A. Praeger, 1962.

MILNER, ESTHER, *The Failure of Success: The American Crisis in Values*. New York, Exposition Press, 1959.

MORGAN, JAMES N., et al., *Income and Welfare in the United States*. New York, McGraw-Hill Book Company, Inc., 1962.

NOSOW, SIGMUND, and WILLIAM H. FORM, *Man, Work, and Society*. New York, Basic Books, Inc., 1962.

ADAPTING TO MAJOR ECONOMIC CHANGE

5

According to one school of interpretation, practically all social change is simply adaptation to economic change, chiefly as a result of technological innovation. This concept, often termed the economic interpretation of history, is usually credited to the social theory of Karl Marx, but it is by no means so limited. The idea of technology as the prime mover in human affairs is very widely held, both by social scientists and by laymen. Long standing theories of culture change, like Ogburn's well known theory of culture lag,[1] are at heart conceptions of social change as derivative from technological modification. Our concern in this chapter, however, is not with such large-scale concepts as the economic interpretation of history or the primacy of technology, although value judgments stemming implicitly from them constitute an important idea source from which many more specific judgments and ideas flow. The concern here will be with particular kinds of economic change, their effects upon collective living, and the kinds of value judgments involved in their interpretations and proposed treatment.

Many contemporary critics have made the point, correctly, we think, that there has been a pronounced tendency, both in academic circles and elsewhere, to deal with the economic aspects of social problems with a "depression orientation." This is understandable historically, however inappropriate it may be at present. Thirty years ago, for a period lasting almost a decade, the people of the United States experienced one of the most generally disruptive economic reverses that this country has ever known. The "dismal thirties" were regarded then, as now, as one of the most profound and lasting influences not only upon the economic aspects of American life

[1] William F. Ogburn, *Social Change* (New York: B. W. Heubsch, 1922).

but upon American character itself. But historical importance should not be permitted to overshadow contemporary reality to which the affluent society, as we have pointed out in earlier chapters, provides the backdrop. Present-day college students are a generation or more removed from the thirties and even many of their parents remember that decade only through a misty adolescence. Present-day socioeconomic problems appear to require analysis within the perspectives of the affluent, not the austere, mystique.

The affluence of the present mass society, however, is by no means universally shared. (See Figure 3.) Substantial segments of the society, certain occupational groups, and regions particularly dependent on certain economic complexes have suffered serious disruptions. Contemporary economic distress can be even worse, particularly psychologically, than were the deprivations of the thirties, because at that time unemployment, diminished trade, and other root causes of individual deprivation were general. Everyone knew that there was a depression and what its awesome effects were, if not directly, at least through the experiences of associates. Continued attention to the problem in the newspapers, and tell-tale landmarks like soup kitchens and bread lines in the cities, foreclosures and abandoned farmsteads in the country, could not be ignored.

KINDS OF ECONOMIC DISTRESS

More specifically, economic distress in our time results from at least the following factors:

1. *Chronic unemployment due to the obsolescence* of many unskilled and semiskilled jobs as manpower continues to be replaced by machinery. *Automation,* it is called by some, and technological progress by others— but not by those for whom it has ended a mode of livelihood. Occupational obsolescence is a continuing process and few occupations are immune from its threat. Office personnel have been displaced by business machines, computers, and other technological instruments, in addition to the better-known kinds of obsolescence of manpower in the heavy industries.

Coexistent with this chronic unemployment and underemployment for the semiskilled are abundant job opportunities for the more highly skilled. On the surface it would seem that all that would be needed would be to educate or reeducate the unemployed, the unskilled, and semiskilled to fill the more technical jobs which are open. At least two limitations present themselves—cost and native capacity. It often takes several years of advanced and costly education to accomplish the needed personal retooling. How is the individual and his family to be supported during the interim, and where is he to get the funds for the added education? Even if, by some miracle, funds were made available for such a purpose, substantial numbers of the unskilled could not, despite effort, acquire the necessary intellectual and kinesthetic skills required. This is a continuing and growing enigma, and except for dramatic success stories here and there, the problem promises to grow rather than diminish.

2. The phrase, *a sick industry,* is, of course, a literary license. What is called a sick industry is one that, again chiefly because of changes in technology, is unable to compete as effectively as previously, and consequently is unable to pay conventional wage rates or to employ a labor force comparable to its own immediate past. One well-known sick industry in America is coal mining. Many of the uses to which coal has previously been put are now met by other sources of power and heat, chiefly petroleum products and to some degree hydroelectric power. (See Table 7.) In order to sell coal the industry must set prices that are competitive with oil, gas, and electric power, but such prices makes it difficult, if not impossible, to pay wage rates that are in line with other industries. Looking to the future, the prospects for improvement are exceedingly dim; the situation seems more likely to worsen.

Table 7   Fuel Production: 13 Years of Change

Year	Anthracite coal (in thousands of short tons)	Bituminous coal (in thousands of short tons)	Natural gas (in millions of therms)	Crude petroleum (in thousands of 42-gal. bbls.)
1949	42,702	437,868	55,770	1,841,940
1951	42,670	533,645	76,660	2,244,529
1956	28,578	500,505	108,381	2,617,432
1957	25,476	489,996	114,810	2,616,780
1959	19,548	406,870	129,496	2,572,000
1961	17,808	399,996	140,922	2,986,800

SOURCE: U.S. Department of Interior, U.S. Department of Commerce, and American Gas Association, 1963.

Another sick industry is agriculture. (See Tables 8, 9, and 10.) The causes here are a little different but the consequences much the same. Improved technology is again at the root. Fewer and fewer people using bigger and bigger machines are able to meet the needs for food and fiber. One agricultural economist recently pointed out, by way of comparing hand labor and machine labor, that a man shoveling ear corn with a scoop shovel (a traditional way of loading and unloading vehicles) earns $1\frac{1}{2}$¢ an hour when compared to the cost of movement of ear corn with mechanical equipment. Even the use of tractors of moderate size has now become of doubtful economic efficiency when compared, on many kinds of farms, with gigantic tractors that can do three or four times as much work and still require only one man to operate them. For twenty-five years there has been a continuing exodus of manpower from agriculture into other employment, and the end is nowhere in sight. There remain today millions of underemployed and inefficiently employed persons in American agriculture whose standard of living, despite various government subsidies, is appreciably below that of urban workers of comparable ability.

Table 8   Farm Employment— Annual Averages

Year	Average number	Index (1910–1914 = 100)
	1000 persons	Percent
1940	10,979	81
1945	10,000	74
1950	9926	73
1955	8364	62
1960	7118	52
1961	6990	52

SOURCE: Agricultural Marketing Service, U.S. Department of Agriculture, 1963.

Table 9   United States Farm Price Index (1910–1914 = 100)

Year	Paid * by farmers	Received ** by farmers
1945	189	206
1948	259	285
1950	255	256
1952	286	288
1955	281	236
1960	299	238
1961	301	240
1962	305	244

* Commodities, interest and taxes, and wage rates.
** All crops and livestock.
SOURCE: U.S. Department of Agriculture, 1963.

Superficially it would appear that the problems of a sick industry are simply solved, namely, by accelerating movement to other employment, and thus restoring a "balance." Difficulties, however, are numerous. This kind of mobility is "sticky." Employment in agriculture, for example, is different from almost all other kinds of employment offered in the urban setting.

Table 10   Farm Mortgage Debt
(in thousands of dollars)

Year	Total farm mortgage debt
1945	$ 4,940,915
1950	5,579,278
1955	8,288,837
1957	9,907,623
1958	10,507,032
1959	11,254,264
1960	12,288,759
1961	13,089,276
1962	14,195,348

SOURCE: Economic Research Service, U.S. Department of Agriculture, 1963.

Many farmers, particularly middle-aged and older ones, do not have the skills for urban employment. The entire mode of life, not just the job skills, is foreign, and many resist bitterly so sharp a wrench in their way of life. Furthermore, no one in the city is looking for a well-trained farm hand. The farmer needs vocational rehabilitation, but how is he supposed to get it? Moreover, there is for many a deeply sentimental attachment to the land, to local loyalties, and to the rural way of life. These roots go back for generations, and many are hopefully hanging on to a set of traditions that they understand and value. There is often the hope, despite the doubt of the experts, that the government may yet come up with a farm "policy" that may make it possible to survive.

The effects of a sick industry, it must be understood, spread far beyond the threat to the standard of living of the worker in the industry. They spread quickly and summarily to the whole community. If the coal miner or farmer has a diminished or irregular income, he has less money to spend at the store, his credit contracts. What may be more important than either of these is that he does not have the necessary financial surplus to ease even his own children out of the collective plight. He and his neighbors have progressively diminished ability to pay taxes, which means that the schools his children attend get worse compared to the schools of the children with whom they must later compete for urban employment. The whole institutional base of the community in the sick industry feels the impact. Schools, churches, and civic organizations must get along with poorer and poorer personnel, more and more restricted programs, and poorer physical surroundings in which to function. This is the matrix of the so-called distressed areas, where virtually everyone in the community, even though he is not engaged in the primary distressed industry, suffers the fate of those directly involved in the industrial sickness.

One important qualification is that not every sick industrial establishment, farm, and community is affected equally. By reason of some exceptional ability, or some advantage, or simple luck, some mining communities fare better than others. Certainly everyone has noticed that some agricultural communities have excellent schools, thriving business establishments, modern and inviting homes, and acres of shiny automobiles. Seemingly, there is little distress in these local areas. There may not be. Usually the community less affected by societal transitions such as these is one whose leadership recognized the emerging order early and made adaptations to it. Thus, the more mechanized agricultural communities have jumped the gun, so to speak, and are further ahead. Whether and how long they can stay ahead is another question. It must be realized, however, that with an overproduction problem such as we have in farming and coal mining, any gains by occasional individuals, communities, or industrial concerns simply worsen the situation for the rest, since all must compete for whatever market remains for their commodities.

3. There is yet a third category of depressed economic base in which the industry rather than being sick, is simply changing so rapidly that there is serious dislocation in particular communities. Cottrell's inimitable portrait of "Death by Dieselization" [2] is a graphic account of one kind of such recurring individual and community crisis. He describes the consequences of a transition from steam-driven to diesel locomotives. Since its fuel carries a diesel unit many more miles than can the conventional coal tender, many communities that formerly existed as refueling and repair centers for transcontinental railroads have been bypassed by the diesels. The unemployed workers could not turn to other employment. Most of them preferred to remain railroad employees and tried to move to other places. The results were devastating. Many houses were for sale, prices fell precipitously and there were still no buyers; homes were simply abandoned. Business after business enterprise collapsed because there were no customers. Churches closed. There was insufficient tax money to support the schools; the newspapers ceased publication because there was not enough advertising to sustain them. All this because of a single technological change from coal-driven to petroleum-driven locomotives.

This is not the only kind of "ghost town" that dots America. Many communities approximate ghost towns. Wherever an entire community relies upon one single mode of economic activity, the ghost town specter is an

[2] Fred W. Cottrell, "Death by Dieselization," *American Sociological Review*, 16:3 (June 1951), pp. 358–365.

ever-potential reality. Sometimes regional competition, which attracts enter-prises from one part of the country to another, creates this situation. The promise of tax advantages, lower labor costs, and other inducements to industry is fine for the area of ingress but devastating for the area of egress. The textile industry in many of the smaller New England cities is an illustration. Not only has it been hit by competition from synthetic fibers and foreign mills, but also by southern communities that, eager to industrialize, have enticed plants to move. The potential threat of additional movements casts a pallor of pessimism and uncertainty upon many communities, which is certainly not conducive to optimal living. Even the highly technical areas of production are sometimes caught in chronic uncertainty. In a press conference in early 1963 President Kennedy pointed out that one of the reasons the government found it difficult to abandon an obsolete weapons system costing billions of dollars a year was the fact that whole communities were dependent for their economic sustenance on its production. He explained that great pressure had been brought to bear by local communities upon their senators and representatives and also upon him to continue the obsolete weapon in order that they not be thrust into economic chaos! This is no isolated problem. With so large a percentage of our population engaged in the production of implements of war and with these changing so rapidly because of technological advance, it is exceedingly difficult for individuals or communities to plan with confidence so far as their economic base is concerned.

These are some of the facts of life on the underside of the affluent society. These conditions are real, stubborn of solution, and certainly no one needs to be told, frighteningly serious. What are we doing about them? What can we do? And why?

VALUE CONFLICTS

Probably the major divisions of judgment in American society concerning problems of this sort are traditional: laissez faire versus government interference, melioration by governmental policy versus collectivization (the Socialist proposal). Despite noisy and periodically aggressive minorities, collectivization has not attracted any large number of followers. The Socialist party has upon a number of occasions run a presidential candidate, but has never polled an appreciable popular vote and only occasionally has elected congressmen. For all practical purposes, as of this writing, the value judgments of collectivized solution may be ignored. This leaves the real issue one of laissez faire versus melioration, one way or another, by government. We shall examine these value clashes somewhat more fully.

Laissez Faire

The laissez-faire position has a strong sentimental appeal to many, quite possibly to a majority of Americans. The traditional virtues of self-reliance, freedom from government regulation, minimal taxation, are part of our cherished ideological heritage. Numerous politicians, spokesmen for business groups and agriculture, indeed nearly everyone, when called upon to make a public statement, wax eloquent about these precepts. But despite verbal adherence to the philosophy of Adam Smith, not many seem willing to *act* on it any more. Everyone it seems is against "subsidies"—for others, and everyone wants freedom—for himself. Spokesmen for industry complain about the monopoly power vested in large labor unions, yet monopolistic tendencies arose in industry a half century, at least, before the large-scale use of this technique by organized labor.

Actual adaptations of lassez faire to economic change, as distinct from verbal labels, have been and will probably continue to be essentially meliorative, that is, will consist of government action, regulation, and income redistribution intended to soften some effects of economic dislocations. Both state and federal (but especially federal) government show every likelihood of continuing these efforts regardless of the party in power. Few persons have any real comprehension of the full scope of the federal enterprise. Furthermore there is a great deal of opposition to almost everything that is attempted. Propaganda techniques utilized by both proponents and opponents of specific measures and general programs make the full truth about them difficult to establish. Several issues with respect to meliorative efforts by government concern us here.

1. The problems themselves are technical and so therefore must be the solutions. A great deal of technical expertness is required to understand the question adequately and to treat it effectively, *but* legislation is largely in the hands of people who are not expert on the problem at hand, nor can they be expected to be, in the light of the multiplicity of problems about which they must legislate. In the practical situation, then, the expert recommends, but has no authority to do anything but try to persuade the lay legislator.

2. The legislators, as well as the representatives of the executive branch, are elected by popular vote. Their political fortunes depend upon pleasing (or at least not displeasing) constituents, very, very few of whom are in any sense expert. But the voters often know what they want; if they don't get it, there may be a new legislator next time. This is no less true if they "want" something that is uneconomical or unwise. Some legislators have admitted the seriousness of the fact that "political considerations" rather than economic wisdom have had to guide their voting.

3. There is almost invariably a conflict of interest involved. However tragic the effects on the coal-mining town of a shrinking market for coal, it is certainly no cause for regret to an oil-producing community in another part of the country. Provincialism still dominates the perspective of many people. Legislative action is necessarily a majority decision and it is sometimes very difficult to get a majority interested.

4. So-called expert judgment is often affected by different value positions in such a way that more than one "expert" opinion emerges. This is nicely illustrated in the conflicting expertness of agricultural leaders. The American Farm Bureau Federation, for example, has for some years taken the position that the agricultural revolution should simply be permitted to work itself out in terms of supply and demand, government subsidies be substantially withdrawn, and the individual farmer be left to sink or swim on the basis of his own ability to reconvert to an economic and competitive mode of production. The Farm Bureau, of course, does not stand for the majority of farmers—no organization does. The Farmers Union, another minority, takes an antithetical stand that is logical too. What is seldom made explicit is that these two organizations speak with different economic philosophies, and what is more important, for farmers with exceedingly different capacities for survival in the rigors of the current situation. For the successfully mechanized cornbelt farmer with adequate credit and other necessary conditions for a capitalistic enterprise, the Farm Bureau's position does make sense. But to another kind of realist who wants to see the transition come more slowly, with less sudden and painful personal dislocations, a continuation of subsidy may not be as altogether ridiculous as it is sometimes made out to be. Again, what are the underlying values? If one wants sheer economic efficiency, one course of action may be sound. If humanitarian considerations enter, then another course may be sound. Compromise is, of course, possible, and this seems to be the way in which the federal agricultural program has evolved. The Farm Bureau is dissatisfied because there is more subsidy in American agriculture than it desires, and so also are the opponents who want more subsidy than at present is granted.

5. Conditions change, making unrealistic many current value positions. Yet a great many people continue to operate with values that are no longer appropriate. Some, for example, who have read the discussion of agriculture in this chapter may have stereotyped, possibly historically accurate conceptions of what agriculture is like, but these conceptions belong to an era already passed. Others have never seen, much less tried to function in, a depressed agricultural economy, a sick coal-mining town, or a city made ghostlike by the obsolescence or the emigration of its major industry. Others may have had such practical experience but lack sufficient technical economic understanding of the nature of the problem or the practically of proposed solutions to enable them to take and justify a truly intelligent position.

Yet everyone has opinions, has judgments, is for or against this or that. In fact, in the American value system one is *supposed* to have judgments, whether or not he is knowledgeable about the technical aspects involved. This is the climate of political philosophy and stern economic reality within which these social problems press for understanding and solution.

VALUES AND MELIORATIVE EFFORTS

Unclarity in the Cultural Heritage

Meliorative decisions involve, of necessity, a conflict of values, not only between participants in the decision-making process, but often within the personality of the individual himself. As Robert Lynd pointed out so ably almost thirty years ago, American society typically holds to opposite values at the same time, without quite facing up to the fact that the various positions when juxtaposed are in fact in conflict.

> 2. Individualism, "the survival of the fittest," is the law of nature and the secret of America's greatness; and restrictions on individual freedom are un-American and kill initiative.
>
> *But:* No man should live for himself alone; for people ought to be loyal and stand together and work for common purposes. . . .
>
> 7. Religion and "the finer things of life" are our ultimate values and the things all of us are really working for.
>
> *But:* A man owes it to himself and to his family to make as much money as he can.
>
> 8. Life would not be tolerable if we did not believe in progress and know that things are getting better. We should, therefore, welcome new things.
>
> *But:* The old, tried fundamentals are best; and it is a mistake for busybodies to try to change things too fast or to upset the fundamentals. . . .
>
> 14. Science is a fine thing in its place and our future depends upon it.
>
> *But:* Science has no right to interfere with such things as business and our other fundamental institutions. The thing to do is to *use* science, but not let it upset things.[3]

Thus, typically, when an agriculture bill is before Congress, members of the legislature, lobbyists, experts in the Department of Agriculture, and others make statements supporting or attacking it. The positions taken seem clear and unequivocal paragraph by paragraph, but are often utterly confusing when seen in toto. Those who want efficiency in agriculture desire the most food and fiber produced per acre that is possible at the lowest possible cost, thus ensuring the great mass of consumers the lowest possible price for

[3] Robert S. Lynd, *Knowledge for What?* (Princeton, N.J.: Princeton University Press, 1939), pp. 59–62. Copyright by the publisher.

agricultural produce. This is clearly the efficiency value. To accomplish this quickly could, of course, be facilitated by the removal of all subsidies. Inefficient farmers, that is, farmers unable to produce at a profit on a competitive market would go bankrupt and be forced to make a living wherever else they could. Marginal (that is, inefficient) land would be retired from production in a year or two, because it would not be profitable for anyone to till it. Efficient producers, with knowhow, adequate financial backing, and credit would make a profit at the lower prices, and the consumer would thus gain too.

But the farmers and their families thus displaced raise another problem. How are the displaced farmers' children to be supported? More than that, how is the farmer and his children to be occupationally rehabilitated for some other employment? Obviously, these questions are not strictly economic. They raise considerations of public policy that are humanitarian rather than strictly related to efficiency. There are political implications too. Displaced farmers and their wives, their friends, and adult children also vote. Thus, for either (or both) humanitarian and practical political reasons, legislators who hold efficiency ideals find themselves voting for the continuance of subsidy. Thus, they often speak of "gradualism" in solving the problems of converting agriculture from a traditional to a technological basis.

The Case of Subsidies

To those who attempt to evaluate the farm subsidy program realistically, the situation is indeed vexing. Even from a strict efficiency point of view contradictions emerge. The federal government through the Agricultural Extension Service, is teaching farmers efficient ways to apply technology so as to increase production per acre, per man, and per dollar, thus increasing the volume of goods for the market. Another arm of government is paying farmers through one or another of the "soil conservation" programs to allow land to remain idle. In various ways the several programs appear to be at cross-purposes. But are they?

From the point of view of meliorating the effects of sudden social change, the subsidies may be effective. Because scientific methods make it possible to produce more food and fiber per acre than we can consume, this overproduction can presumably be eased by paying some people to withhold land from cropping. In turn, this allows them some time to seek other employment, acquire other skills, or simply wait for retirement age to take them off the agricultural job market. If the farm family system is an important national resource, some small subsidy added one way or another to the farm family's income may make it possible to maintain for some additional years a mode of life that many people believe is intrinsically important and worth continuing.

Considerable disillusion with meliorative effort, of course, results from the ability of some persons to turn an idealistic program to narrow personal advantage. It is impossible apparently to anticipate the ingenious ways that unscrupulous people will invent to pervert a government program intended for some special group's assistance, as the Billy Sol Estes scandal in the early sixties showed. (This is by no means limited to agriculture subsidy. Scandals of similar magnitude have occurred in other government programs that involve politically manipulatable large sums of money. In the minds of many people this is prima faci evidence that the programs are ill advised.)

A similar dilemma is posed when attempts are made to render assistance to unemployed people in distressed areas or obsolescent occupations. Some individuals, for any of a wide variety of plausible personal reasons, will not exert themselves effectively to find other employment, preferring any kind of government relief, however modest, to solving their own problems. No one knows what percentage of displaced persons act like this; laissez-faire advocates exaggerate their numbers and others minimize them. Undeniably there are some, and this group offends self-reliant individuals. Because the unemployed man usually has a wife and children who need the basic necessities of life, even though their husbands and fathers may be somewhat deficient in ability or character, the familiar dilemma arises. In order to protect children from the effects of economic displacement, we may tend indirectly to encourage a perpetual dependency of some breadwinners who may be willing to settle indefinitely for a parasitic role. Conversely, to "get tough" with the breadwinner is to impose penalties on wives and children that are not only unfair but have baneful effects on the community at large.

Costs of Meliorative Programs

The best meliorative programs generally cost a great deal—first of all, to administer effectively. The history of many government agencies that have been involved in unfortunate waste of public money shows this was in demonstrable degree due to the poor quality of their personnel. Because of widespread aversion to a large public payroll, the short-sighted tendency has been to employ substandard personnel at substandard rates, resulting in an inefficient and more easily corruptible program. The "penny saved is a penny earned" adage may have a juxtaposed antithesis. A penny spent may be several pennies earned, particularly when the spending is an investment in competent administration. Paradoxically, therefore, our cultural image of the public employee as a parasitic individual, inefficient and overpaid can be made a true one by a penny-wise policy of public administration.

This does not mean that there have not been bonafide instances of "gold bricking" in governmental employment, but only that penury in carrying out programs encourages rather than discourages the very substandard public service that is so frequently decried.

Traditionalism

Other value conflicts and confusions grow out of the human propensities to attempt to solve tomorrow's problems by yesterday's wisdom. In fact, however, such time honored virtues as thrift, for example, may be inimical either to personal success or the public interest under certain conditions. To the extent that it is necessary to maintain a high level of public consumption in order to avoid depression, the individual who does not save, who in fact is willing to practice deficit financing by buying services and goods now that he pays for later, can easily serve the economy better than can the austere individual who insists on saving money for that rainy day. Similarly, the individual who is able to suppress his individuality and blend his talents quietly and gracefully into the regimentation of the "organization man" may do both himself and his organization more good, as it is now defined, than the individual who insists on being himself, an eager beaver, disturbing the calm "togetherness" of the workforce.

These individual actions have their counterparts in the collective enterprise. In many instances it has been demonstrated that by a willingness to expend public moneys even at the expense of temporary deficits, the resultant stimulation of the economy as a whole can many times over repay the initial cost. But deficit financing is a concept rejected by many people because they equate it with financial irresponsibility in terms of a family budget. For example, the per capita indebtedness of the federal government is computed by dividing the total indebtedness by the number of people. It obviously falls unequally on all people, depending on the amount of income or property which they have. To be meaningful, however, this per capita debt figure should be accompanied by a second statistic, the per capita wealth of the nation against which the indebtedness is a claim. When this is done, it is clear that the national debt, however computed, is backed up by national assets many times greater. To revert to the analogy, a doubtful one to be sure, a family with assets several times its liabilities would consider itself well off.

IS OBJECTIVITY POSSIBLE?

For all of the foregoing reasons and additional ones as well, it is exceedingly difficult to achieve the seemingly modest goal of "clear thinking" on the question of whether or not, and if so, how much government involvement in adaptation to economic change there ought to be. It is possible to isolate from the caldron of claim and counterclaim at least four reasons for the continuing unclarity.

1. On the part of many, laymen and legislators alike, there continues to be a remarkable innocence about the real conditions which are faced. Our society is a highly diversified one, and people in different regions, occupations, income and educational levels, may be quite ignorant of the circumstances of others. In addition there is often a seeming callousness toward the plight of people somewhat removed. Ordinarily not much concern for the submarginal farmers in southern Illinois can be expected from people in Brooklyn, nor is it too surprising if the problems of a dying coal-mining town in West Virginia seem remote and unimportant to people in Iowa. And even if "conditions are bad" there, it is somehow "up to the people involved" to use their own self-reliance to find a way out.

2. Vested interests in American society are highly differentiated and possibly increasingly so. The stockholders of a corporation manufacturing missiles are interested in dividends, and dividends are augmented by ever larger government contracts. This is about all there is to it, except perhaps that Congress ought to see to it that the contracts do not get cancelled. In a vague way, of course, the stockholders, like everyone else, want a good national defense, but with predictable certainty they can be counted on to believe that the particular missile manufactured by the company in which they hold stock is the one most to be relied upon! Illustrations could be multiplied.

3. "Eternal verities" loom large in the thinking of many, particularly when the problem under discussion is not close to home. Simple answers to every problem can be found in George Washington's farewell address, the writings of Adam Smith, or the pronouncements of some cleric. If these should fail, there is always some aphorism, some hallowed cliché which covers the subject. This is not to deny that there may be wisdom from the past, but there may also be a good deal of nonsense in this same source in terms of a *current* problem. It requires the wisdom of a Solomon many times to know whether the time-honored advice will bring solution to today's problem if heeded or whether it will worsen it. But most men are not philosophers to this degree. It is reassuring to find some cliché, some hidebound concept, or some revered name that suggests or points a course of action on the basis of which "things should fall into line."

In addition to those who misuse the past by using it inappropriately, there are those who know better, but exploit the reverence for tradition in order to facilitate their own vested interests. This has the effect of compounding the problem for the hard realist who wants to face today's problems in terms of today's realities, utilizing today's knowhow, and interested in achieving today's goals.

4. The goal of competent analysis, as we have indicated previously in this chapter, can be vexing. Despite the tendency of many to oversimplify

problems, simple candor points in the reverse direction—problems are increasingly complex, technical, and difficult of solution. The so-called average man to whom such deference is paid in political oratory for his "common sense" is typically ill equipped to participate competently in the vast majority of political-economic decisions. They are simply beyond him, even though they are problems in which he is vitally involved. In pointing this out there is no intention to disparage the rank and file. The point is that they do not have access to the relevant facts, are misled and bamboozled by various propagandists whose intention it is to confuse them, and they lack the kind of technical understanding of complex matters that can come about only as a result of careful objective and formal study. This baffling complexity, unfortunately, is not limited to the "average citizen." It is a problem also to the legislator who is typically asked to vote in a single session on several dozen highly technical questions concerning which no one man could be adequately informed.

Consequently there has been a tendency to rely, probably not enough, on so-called experts. This sounds rational and intelligent—let the expert on agricultural economy advise on economic policy, the space scientist on satellite policy, similar experts elsewhere. But this presents problems too. In the first place, it is one thing to be an expert in fact, and often quite another thing to be accepted as one. There is a strong tendency to accept the advice of experts when it adheres fairly closely to one's own views or to tradition, but to distrust him otherwise.

This is further complicated by the well known, and overpublicized, fact that the experts do not always agree. This may be so because of differing (but unstated) value premises from which even experts may proceed, or because they have selected for emphasis differing sets of facts out of a large universe of facts that may bear on an issue.

Nevertheless, in this increasingly technical world in which so many problems entail esoteric knowledge, there is more and more need to rely on specialists. A democratic society does so only reluctantly, for the greater the role of the expert the more removed from control over decisions is the voter and his representative. Thus the theory of popular control, which justifies democracy, is threatened—giving rise to a source of deep conflict in our system. It is a conflict that invades the individual, as well as dividing people into opposing groups.

CONCLUSION

Solutions to problems such as those we have discussed in this chapter could be realistically anticipated *if* there were some way in which, in the interchange between value positions, each could be required to be (1) honest about his reasons for advocating what he advocates, and (2) thoroughly informed on the matters at hand. Issues could then be clarified much more quickly, and policy objectively formulated.

Lacking this, for the foreseeable future the tradition of legislation by gross approximation seems the most realistic anticipation. Meanwhile it is to be expected that social change, particularly when sparked by technological change, will continue apace, and that dramatic dislocations of occupations and industries will occur from time to time. It is well to remember that all gains are made at a price and that one of the prices paid by a society for its rapid change and sometimes miraculous accomplishments is a continued dislocation of its parts. In this process, the real expendables have been, and probably will continue to be, the individuals and families who get caught in the backwash of changing technology. Obsolescence can set in very quickly; it is no longer a mechanical concept.

SUGGESTED READINGS

ALLEN, FRANCIS R., *et al., Technology and Social Change*. New York, Appleton-Century-Crofts, Inc., 1962.

BUSH, VANNEVAR, "Automation's Awkward Age," *Saturday Review,* August 11, 1962, pp. 10–11, 47.

COTTRELL, FRED W., "Death by Dieselization," *American Sociological Review,* 16:3 (June 1951), pp. 358–365.

DRUCKER, PETER, *The New Society*. New York, Harper & Row, 1950.

GALBRAITH, JOHN K., *The Affluent Society*. Boston: Houghton Mifflin, 1958.

RIESMAN, DAVID, "Styles of Response to Social Change," *Journal of Social Issues,* 17:1 (1961), pp. 78–92.

ROGERS, EVERETT M., *Social Change in Rural Society*. New York, Appleton-Century-Crofts, 1960.

THE CITY

6

The city is a paradox. Cities are the seat of man's greatest cultural achievements, and of his severest problems. It is in the city that we find magnificent cathedrals and high rates of crimes, the beauty of art treasures and the ugliness of slums. Great medical centers are found in the city, but so also are found organized prostitution and traffic in illegal drugs. People come to the city for excitement, but the city dweller is said to be bored and unhappy.

While cities have been eulogized and at least one has been wept over, it is not our intention to produce a balance sheet of the good and bad that is found in the city. It is our aim, rather, to focus on some of the social problems that are distinctly urban, as opposed to the wider variety of problems that are found in cities. As a background for the focus on urban problems, we begin with a few comments on the growth of urban living in the United States.

URBAN GROWTH IN THE UNITED STATES

Urban Population Growth

So urbanized are we today that it is difficult to realize that less than 100 years ago ours was a distinctly rural society. In 1860 only about 6 million people in the country were living in places classified as "urban." Urban dwellers, furthermore, constituted less than one fourth of the total population. By the turn of the century about 40 percent of Americans were living in cities, then about 50 percent in 1920, and 57 percent in 1940. The 1960 census found that urban people make up about 70 percent of the population.

Table 11   Percent of Population Living in Cities, 1900–1960

	1900	1920	1940	1960
Percent in cities 500,000 and over	10.7	15.5	17.0	16.0
Percent in cities 100,000–500,000	8.1	10.5	11.8	12.5
Percent in cities under 100,000	21.0	25.3	27.7	41.4
Percent in cities, all sizes	39.7	51.2	56.5	69.9

SOURCE: U.S. Bureau of the Census, *Statistical Abstract of the United States: 1962,* Washington, D.C., 1962, p. 21.

Decade by decade, rural America has been diminishing in size. Almost forty-five years ago we passed the point where a simple plurality of the population lived in cities. Today, the America where about seven out of every ten people live is urban America.

Number of Cities

Furthermore, the United States has become more urbanized in the sense that there are a greater number of cities and a greater number of large cities. There are now about three times as many places classified as cities as there were at the turn of the century. In 1900 there were but 6 cities in the United States with populations of 500,000 or more, in 1960 there were 21. At the turn of the century there were 38 cities with 100,000 or more in-

Table 12   Number and Size of Cities, 1900–1960

Size classification	Number of cities						
	1900	1910	1920	1930	1940	1950	1960
1,000,000 or more	3	3	3	5	5	5	5
500,000–1,000,000	3	5	9	8	9	13	16
100,000–500,000	32	42	56	80	78	88	111
50,000–100,000	40	59	76	98	107	126	201
25,000–50,000	82	119	143	185	213	252	432
Under 25,000	1577	2034	2435	2789	3052	4257	5276
All urban places	1737	2262	2722	3165	3464	4741	6041

SOURCE: U.S. Bureau of the Census, *Statistical Abstract of the United States: 1962,* Washington, D.C., 1962, p. 21.

habitants, while now there are 132. Today there are 333 cities of 50,000 or over whereas in 1900 there were but 78 cities of such size.

Metropolitan Area Growth

Of course, it is clear that the term "city" used in the preceding paragraphs has referred to the political city, with its geographical area and boundaries legally defined. As everyone knows, in many ways the city extends beyond its legal boundaries. The functional network of people, institutions, services, and places of employment can encompass a large area which can be conceived as concentric rings about a central city.[1] The basic interdependence of the entire urban area is reflected in such expressions as "Greater Chicago" and "The Los Angeles Area."

A further manner in which the United States has become increasingly an urban society is in the growth of large urban areas. The Bureau of Census uses the unit *Standard Statistical Metropolitan Area,* abbreviated as SSMA, for describing the largest and economically most important urban areas in our country. An SSMA is a county or group of contiguous counties that contains at least one city of 50,000 inhabitants. Counties adjoining the one that contains the central city are included in the SSMA if they are economically and socially integrated with the central city and if they are essentially metropolitan in character.

The number of people living in Standard Metropolitan Areas has risen from 84 million in 1950 to 113 million in 1960. More than six out of every ten Americans now live in a place that is metropolitan in character and that is integrated with an important city. About 80 percent of the population increase between 1940 and 1960 occurred in the SSMAs. There can be little doubt that metropolitan America will continue to grow.

The increasing urbanization of our society is reflected in the number of urban dwellers, the number of *large* cities, and the growth of sprawling metropolitan areas. These are, of course, related phenomena. The total increase in the urban population, the rate at which it has occurred, and the fact that recently much of the growth has been beyond the legal boundaries of cities particularly affect urban social problems.

VALUE CLASHES IN THE AMERICAN CITY

The range of value clashes in any American city could extend from its art museum to its zoning policy, with more specific issues in between than could be included in an entire volume. The fundamental problems of

---

[1] For an excellent treatment of the growth and structure of the urban region see Alvin Boskoff, *The Sociology of Urban Regions* (New York: Appleton-Century-Crofts, Inc., 1962), chap. 7.

the city could easily be missed by undue concentration on specific issues, almost regardless of their intrinsic importance. Our attempt to impose an order on the seemingly endless problems of the city considers them as problems of human needs, of service needs, of management needs, and of governmental needs. The four are in reality inseparable, but it is hoped that the classification scheme will allow for concentrating on *types* of major urban problems, rather than getting bogged down in the details of specific issues.

URBAN LIVING AND INDIVIDUAL NEEDS

In many ways the city is far superior to any other social organization when it comes to meeting the needs of human beings. The element of choice provided in a city in so many areas of life is a case in point. There is a wide range of employment alternatives in the city, with the result that one should have more possibilities of finding a job in keeping with his preferences and personality. Many different types of housing are available at a fairly wide range of prices. Cities are noted for their recreational and leisure opportunities. Swimming pools, parks, art museums, bars, libraries, night clubs, theaters, dance halls—the list is almost endless. Surely there must be something for every taste and purse.

Even the population size of the city provides a wider range of choices than found in rural areas or small towns. One's chances of finding agreeable friends and associates, or for that matter a compatible spouse, would seem to be enhanced due to the sheer number of people available.

While one of the lures of the city is the freedom of choice that it allows the individual, paradoxically, urban living is only possible if certain curtailments of individual freedom are made. One of the basic difficulties is that the freedoms gained are not the same as the freedoms lost. Cities are made up of people culturally not more than a generation or so removed from the rural area. Perhaps they find it easier to accept the newly available freedoms of the city than to relinquish the different sorts of freedom that prevailed in their own or our society's past.

One of the precious values in our pioneer and later rural background was that of "individualism" in the sense that a man's home was his castle, and if he wanted to keep a pig in the parlor, it was no one's concern but his and the pig's. That such an outlook on life was acceptable, in fact necessary, in an earlier day is obvious enough. It is equally obvious that such ideas work havoc when large numbers of people with conflicting ideas have to live close together. When and how loudly one plays his radio, how he disposes of his garbage, where his dog chooses to roam, and where and at what his children play may have a vital influence on his neighbor's health, safety, and convenience, and most assuredly on his temperament. Obviously, a man's freedom of activity and his property rights are conditioned by the effects that they have on neighbors, but numerous problems arise from the practical application of this principle to specific acts and specific neighbors. How much quiet, for example, is it normal and reasonable to expect of children—of one's neighbors' children, that is—the courts have never been able to decide satisfactorily, any more than they have been able to determine what constitutes "unreasonable" barking of a dog or "undue loudness" of a radio.

In spite of the difficulties, however, marked strides have been made in circumventing the cultural tradition that a man's home is his castle and that he can keep a pig in his parlor. The community now reserves the right to quarantine a man in his home for illness and to prevent his being buried by his relatives until a burial certificate has been obtained. Cities have the right to stipulate how a man's home should be wired for electricity, what kind of plumbing it should have, and how much footage must exist between his home and his neighbor's. Some cities have passed "curfews" which require that children under a specified age cannot be on the streets later than a certain hour at night.

The demands of communal living mean that freedoms of an earlier stage need to be curtailed, even if in the process new freedoms are achieved. It seems not overly facetious to generalize that for most urban dwellers the problem of city living resolves itself into how to live *in* the city without being *of* the city. Thus they seek to work out their living arrangements with as much defiance of the logical urban living pattern as their financial condition and ingenuity will allow. Thus, generally speaking, a house is preferred to an apartment of the same size because "the house gives us more freedom and the children like the yard." This urban phenomenon reaches its logical extreme in the case of the suburban dweller who lives as near to the open country as the time and cost of commuting will allow. Thus, in effect, he holds to the advantages of the city occupationally, but escapes from it for most of his, and especially of his family's, actual living. In the more developed suburban areas there are suburban schools, suburban churches, and suburban trading centers, thus providing a whole constellation of institutions that in many ways more nearly resemble a rural community than they do an urban satellite. For many urban dwellers, then, not merely for the suburbanite alone, urban living resolves itself into escaping from the city for living but remaining close enough to the city to secure its occupational and other advantages.

At the other extreme, the cooperative-housing dweller accepts the requirement of close living and works out a pattern of life that maximizes the advantages of such living. Between the suburbanite who solves the problem by escaping it, and the cooperative-housing dweller who solves the problem by capitalizing on it, are the majority of urban dwellers who work out a life pattern consisting of a combination of escapist measures and practical expedients. They capture what measure of solace they can by cultivating a garden ten feet square, with two rose bushes and an elm tree, worrying each day whether Junior or Bowser will create a neighborhood crisis by intruding into "that cranky Mr. Jones's" dahlia garden.

Part of the difficulty today is the unnecessary assault on individualism by city authorities who are either insensitive to individual needs or who see their task more as that of running an efficient machine than of leading a human grouping. But part of the difficulty can be traced to the inability or unwillingness of the urban dweller to recognize the requirements of large-scale group living.

SERVICE PROBLEMS OF THE CITY

The most apparent urban problems are those that involve inadequate services for the people who live, work, or spend their leisure in the city. Human beings deserve an environment that is clean and reasonably quiet, but most of our cities are noisy and many, in entirety or part, are dirty. As we will see in Chapter 13, the air that urban dwellers are forced to breathe is often polluted by industrial and other gaseous wastes and threatens the very health of the city person. City slums are almost universally found. Movement into and within the city is laborious, time consuming, and annoying. At peak times particularly, recreational and cultural facilities are overtaxed.

The list of inadequate services of most American cities could be continued. Each particular service failure in some ways presents a unique problem, but frequently its remedy demands a more total view. The symptoms of urban service failure that are treated below, traffic congestion and slums, are notoriously commonplace and extremely complex. Both illustrate, too, how value conflicts impede remedying conditions that probably almost all urban dwellers, workers, and visitors define as undesirable.

Traffic Problems

Each day tons and tons of goods are brought into our cities—food, household supplies, and raw materials, parts and equipment for the workers. Finished products are sent around the city and out of it. Millions of people travel into a city each morning and out again each evening. Making the movement of people and goods possible is an obvious housekeeping function of the city. Just as obvious are the complaints about traffic and transportation that are registered in almost all American cities.

Presumably everyone who travels into, around, or out of the city would like to do so as quickly, as economically, and as pleasantly as possible. To most Americans this suggests using a private automobile. Urban planners most frequently favor public transportation. In practice there has been a compromise, with the bulk of the city's money and effort going toward making it possible to use private automobiles. At the root of the traffic problem in our cities, then, is the fundamental clash of values over the merits of public versus private transportation.

That most people see the virtues in the automobile is apparent to anyone who has ever watched the stream of slow-moving cars on their way out of the city at night, or for that matter to anyone who has ever searched for a parking place within the city. At the same time, others feel that the automobile is literally strangling the American city and is producing major dilemmas.

As more and more automobiles pass their homes, the noise, dirt, and congestion make the city dwellers' homes less desirable to them, and those who are able to do so move "out a ways." Every move to the suburb adds one more car to the traffic problem. Freeways and expressways are added at great cost, but the relief they provide is temporary. The faster a route from the suburbs they provide, the more suburbanites will switch away from public transportation.

As we follow the traffic from the expressways, we see the self-defeating nature of the scheme that allows more cars to be whisked from the urban fringe. Once in the central city, of course, they overtax the streets and parking facilities. And the system continues to be self-defeating. The more land that is allocated to wider streets, expressways within the city, and parking lots, the less available for offices, stores, and factories. If automobiles could be driven around the city at ease and could be parked wherever desired, there would be no need for anyone to come to the city, for there would be nothing but streets and parking lots.

Many people who admit to the general inadequacy of the present urban transportation system discouragingly conclude that not much can be done because of the love of Americans for their automobiles. It may be that people are not as irreconcilably wed to private transportation as has been assumed. At any rate, public transportation is not today an attractive alternative. Buses and commuter trains are slow and uncomfortable. Subways are faster, but grossly overcrowded at rush hours. The cost of public transportation continues to rise so that relative to the ease, convenience, and sometimes even the speed of the automobile it is no bargain. Somehow the suggestion that general city funds should be used to provide modern, rapid transportation at low cost to the user can always be made to sound by its opponents as prohibitively expensive and undemocratic. Meanwhile, private transportation is subsidized by the building of streets, expressways, bridges, and tunnels, by the provision of numerous personnel to direct and control traffic, and by the loss of potential tax revenue by allowing street parking.

The public and private transportation systems of our major cities can be patched up and kept functioning for some time to come. This will continue to be expensive and inefficient, but it will be familiar. Its annoyances will be the familiar ones of slowness, congestion, noise, and dirt. Presumably this is presently preferred to the annoyance of having to make fairly radical changes in thought, habit, and custom, that would be required by a forthright endorsement of public transportation.

Slums

Although by no means an American invention or monopoly, the slum is a much publicized problem of most of our cities. Physically, slum areas constitute some kind of low in urban living. Slum housing may be of the multifloored, walk-up, tenement variety, the once private home long since converted into many unbelievably small "housekeeping rooms," or still some other type, but in any case, it accurately fits the census category, "delapidated." Overcrowding abounds, with whole families or even several families sharing a couple of rooms. And it is paradoxical to find in our most up-to-date cities that there are dwellings that lack running water, toilets, and sometimes even electricity.

But the physical conditions of slums are not their only problem characteristics. It can be readily demonstrated that phenomena such as drug addiction, alcoholism, and certain types of mental disorders are more prevalent in slums than in other areas of the city. The slum has been called the "cradle of gangsters" and the "school of crime." A high infant mortality rate, a high incidence of tuberculosis, and a high venereal disease rate are but a few other distinguishing features of slums. It is difficult indeed to substantiate a precise cause and effect relationship between physical conditions and disease, and it is even more difficult to so relate slum conditions and deviant behavior. There is, of course, a certain amount of "drift" of deviates or near-deviates, the chronic unemployed, and the like, into the slums. It is nevertheless true that from many objective standpoints there is much that is undesirable about slums. And society is fairly well in agreement that the slum conditions of our cities are distasteful. There is little value conflict, then, regarding the definition of slum conditions as a problem. But there is likely to be a rather sharp clash of values and interests when someone proposes to "do something" about the slums that no one wanted in the first place!

On the one hand, there is the individualistic, almost fatalistic attitude toward slum conditions and slum dwellers epitomized by the cliché, "You can get the people out of the slums, but you *can't* get the slum out of the people." Thus, although they dislike the sight of slums and talk of them as a "blight" on our cities, there are some who hold that such conditions are more or less inevitable due to the "sifting and sorting" of people according to their "ambition," "ability," "character," or whatever else the proponent happens to think contributes to what he loosely terms "degeneracy." Such individuals, who are frequently more loquacious than scientific, would strenuously object to spending "good taxpayers' money" on the rehabilitation of slums. Slums are a problem of slum dwellers; they need simply to remove themselves from their environment, and those with the proper "determination" do just that! It scarcely needs to be pointed out that many slum dwellers cannot afford to pay higher rent or, if their skin happens to be a little darker than most, they cannot find another place to live even if they can afford it.

There is, at the same time, the competing idea that slum conditions are a community responsibility and that any amelioration of the problem must take place through the concerted effort of all city dwellers. Without necessarily attaching blame or cause to the conditions, adherents to this philosophy feel that the city as a whole would profit from better and more healthful conditions for all of its citizens. But even within this group there may well be strong disagreements concerning the means and methods of removing slum conditions. Should the city elicit support of the federal government for redevelopment, or is this "too socialistic"? Should the slum housing be removed and municipally owned housing erected on the same sites, or should slum dwellers be relocated in outlying areas? And what about the owners of property classified as "slum"? What are their responsibilities and rights? At whose price should they be reimbursed even if they are willing to sell their property? And so on. These are some of the areas of conflict and disagreement that can harass city officials and citizens bent on "cleaning up" their slums. It is sometimes surprising that actually so much has been done in recent years to alleviate the slum conditions of our cities.

MANAGEMENT PROBLEMS OF THE CITY

The city, like any other large-scale organization, requires management. Funds have to be derived to run the city, decisions have to be made on the allocation of the resources, a system of determining and meeting the service needs of the city has to be in force, and planning for tomorrow, next year, and the longer run has to be performed. Inadequacies or difficulties of the modern city in these areas can be thought of as management problems. They are not as visible as such housekeeping problems as dirty streets or inadequate transportation, but these and other service failures indicate a breakdown in one or more of the management functions.

The management problems considered below are those concerned with financing the city and planning for its orderly existence and inevitable change. Our interest is partly with how well these functions are now performed but more with an evaluation of the present legal and political systems for performing them.

Financing the City

Under the American system of separate federal, state, and local governments, the city has found it exceedingly difficult to maintain a sound financial base. Traditionally the city has derived its revenues from taxes on real estate. The old theory was that people who owned their own homes and businesses should pay taxes to support the city services such as police and fire protection, maintenance of parks and playgrounds, and education. Persons who lived in rented properties would presumably pay taxes indirectly, since the landlord could shift his tax to the renter. This system worked reasonably well prior to the advent of the automobile and the resulting suburban trend. Now with easy transportation by automobile and bus, larger and larger proportions of the workers in the central city live outside the city. Since they do not live in the central city, a land tax on the property they own or rent does not accrue to the coffers of the central city. And yet the central city has the expense of providing police and fire protection and other services that benefit the worker from the central city. The effect of suburbanization is to increase the burden of taxation for the decreasing percentage of the population of the greater city that still lives in the city limits and pays taxes to the city.

Many American cities already have serious financial difficulties. To operate at all they are forced to reduce their services and increase their property taxes. The urban dweller, paying higher taxes for fewer services, becomes increasingly convinced that it is a poor bargain. And so the trek to the suburbs continues.

Three general schemes are used to broaden the base of revenue to the city and relieve the burden to the real estate owner, namely, (1) the city income tax, (2) the city sales or transaction tax, and (3) annexation of the suburbs and outlying areas.

CITY INCOME TAXES. Although varying from one another in important details, city income taxes are usually on the incomes of all persons who live in or work in the central city, to the extent that the income is earned in activities performed in the central city. The legal basis for such laws is not entirely clear, since the income-tax principle, as we have seen, breaks with some important traditions of taxation. In some states it is unconstitutional to tax the incomes of workers who do not live in the city, and in other states it is unconstitutional for cities to levy income taxes at all. The trend, however, seems clearly in the direction of city income taxes.

CITY SALES OR TRANSACTION TAXES. The logic behind the city sales or transaction tax is essentially the same as that behind the city income tax; in other words, the purpose is to spread the burden of taxation so as to reduce the load on the real estate owner and to increase the burden on the nonresident who benefits from the city's services but does not otherwise pay for these benefits. In general, business interests favor the income tax rather than the sales or transaction tax because they fear that the transaction tax, unless all cities adopt it, will tend to discourage nonresidents from trading in the cities with the taxes. Most tax experts would tend to favor the income tax over the sales tax because it is more clearly based upon the ability-to-pay principle, which is now generally regarded as the soundest fundamental principle in taxation.

ANNEXATION. The city's financial plight, though alleviated, is not solved by the income tax or the sales tax or any other single expedient. These devices do not solve the problem because they do not get at the root of the trouble, namely, the territorial basis for tax collection. As long as people move very freely over large areas as they do now, and large numbers can therefore live and work in different political jurisdictions, it is relatively easy to escape taxation deliberately or otherwise.

Many cities have attempted to solve their problems by the direct method of annexing their suburbs, making them legally a part of the city. But this does not always work out to the advantage of either the central city or the suburb.[2] Since people move to the suburb to escape the city, it is understandable if they are less than eager to become again, through annexation, a part of the city. Suburbs can resist annexation by incorporating themselves as municipalities, and by other means. In this way a suburb that functionally is but a residential part of the city may remain legally a separate entity.

When a suburb is annexed, the city is then required to provide services for this new section of the city. Sometimes the cost of providing these services outweighs the tax returns and other anticipated advantages to the central city. For the most part, annexation has been haphazard, adding a geographic bit here and there, more in accordance with the political, legal, and financial aspects of the situation than the functional realities. Annexation, of course, sometimes has provided temporary relief for cities, but increasingly it seems to be recognized as just that—a stopgap measure but not a real solution to the city's problems.

Urban Planning and Zoning

It has long been obvious to civic leaders as well as to laymen that property owners in the city, even more than in the country, must have their rights somewhat limited by consideration of the rights of those living near by. Although the principle has not been easily or quickly accepted, it is now rather clearly established in law that only certain uses of land and

[2] The Editors of *Fortune, The Exploding Metropolis* (New York: Doubleday & Company, Inc., 1958), p. 105.

buildings are appropriate in each part of the city, and that only certain kinds of new construction can be allowed. Thus there are not only residential, industrial, and commercial areas marked off ("zones"), but there are also different classifications within each of these areas. Thus in some residential areas apartment buildings cannot be constructed, and in others only houses of a certain cost, size, and architectural type, can be built.

One of the persistent problems of zoning, however, is that of adjustment to the dynamic character of the city. Suppose that a certain area is set aside as a commercial area. Later the city grows, and the commercial area is inadequate to the needs of the population. The commercial interests wish to expand into areas designated as residential. How can this be done without working a hardship on people who have built homes in these areas on the supposition that they would remain residential? How can the adjustment be made equitably and with a minimum of community conflict?

City planning is a more fundamental concept than mere zoning.[3] City planning comprises a wide variety of aspects including zoning, location and maintenance of parks and playgrounds, financing and organizing welfare services, organizing and modifying traffic plans, establishing parking areas, and so on and on. Most cities of any size have planning commissions under one name or another with more or less power to implement their suggestions in practice. These have often been attacked on the ground that they are undemocratic, that is, that the planning is done in terms of upper- and upper-middle-class needs and values to the total or partial neglect of the working classes, Negroes, and other groups, or that they have served property owners and business groups rather than the community as a whole. Such charges are not difficult to understand in view of the power structure of the community, based as it is so largely upon wealth and those occupations associated with business and commerce. Regardless of these criticisms, many cities have made marked strides in improving their over-all physical plan and activities, and have achieved a working philosophy that balances collective community needs and traditional property rights with reasonable justice and a minimum of community conflict.

One of the biggest obstacles to effective urban planning today is that it must be done on the basis of the political entity that is the city, rather than the functional whole that would embrace the suburbs and perhaps much more. A city's forthright plans for orderly growth in residential areas, for example, may be offset by new housing developments outside the city, whose inhabitants, however, will work in the city and use many of its facilities. Plans for a rapid transportation system may go awry or may never leave the drawing board due to the city's inability to anticipate and to control what goes on immediately outside its present legal boundaries. The

[3] See Boskoff, *op. cit.*, chaps. 15–18.

inability to secure financing from the broader base of metropolitan residents, rather than from only those who live within the confines of the city, further hampers creative planning. Some of the problems of urban planning, thus, are related to the previously discussed problem of city financing and to those of city government, to which we now turn.

CITY GOVERNMENT PROBLEMS

The city of today is faced with two major problems with respect to its government. Problems of the first sort stem from the alleged breakdown of the familiar partisan system of city government. The need is seen for an improved, more businesslike way of running our cities, backed by a more responsible citizenry. The second value issue is more extreme, for it deals with the creation of a new governmental unit encompassing the city and its environs.

Efficient Government and Responsible Citizenship

The American political system, as everyone knows, is bipartisan, on the theory that the people can best decide vital issues by choosing one or the other of the parties on the basis of what they offer with respect to vital issues. Although this does not result in an entirely responsible government, even on the national level, it works reasonably well there. With respect to the city, however, the theory breaks down completely. A city government does not concern itself, except in very rare and exceptional instances, with policy matters. The government is simply a big business enterprise consisting of important service departments like those for police and fire protection, parks and playgrounds, education, health protection, and the like. There is, obviously, no Republican way or Democratic way of sweeping the streets, controlling disease, regulating traffic, or fighting fires. All that a city needs is an efficient, businesslike handling of these services with a minimum of waste, political patronage, and inefficiency. Accordingly there has arisen a great deal of dissatisfaction with the bipartisan method of selecting officials in city government, and several devices have been invented, presumably to increase the efficiency of the city business enterprise. Among these, the city-manager system, in one form or another, is the most radical departure from our traditions, but it is widespread enough to warrant special treatment.

The logic of the city-manager plan is as follows. Since the city government is almost exclusively a set of services, it should be run like any business under an executive head who is chosen for his business ability rather than for his party affiliation or skill in vote getting. Thus, the city manager is hired rather than elected in much the same way as is a superintendent of schools. He is then, presumably, retained or discharged on the basis of the efficiency and honesty with which he handles the city's business.

The high hopes of the early advocates of the city-manager system have not been completely realized, although there is little doubt that city managers have provided a tremendous improvement in the administration of city governments. In those cases where city managers have not been altogether successful, aside from purely personal considerations, they have failed for the same reason that the traditional city governments have failed —because of some combination of public ignorance and apathy and organized corruption. As we have pointed out previously, corruption in city government is traditional in America. Fortunes have been made by methods more closely resembling those of the racketeer than those of legitimate business, through such devices as overcharging the city and setting up fictitious purchases by the city. The mere replacement of a partisan mayor and council by a city manager cannot automatically guarantee efficiency and honor in the administration of the street-paving department, unless the citizens know and care how their money is being spent. For decades corrupt business practices involving police departments with gambling interests, prostitution, and paving contractors especially, have gone on in many American cities with considerable openness, and with little challenge either from the public press or from any other potentially powerful group. The central problem of city government seems to be one of arousing citizens to a more realistic understanding of the nature of city government and of its relation to their own individual life problems and, then, of exposing the business dealings of their city government and its officials to constant public scrutiny. This is a far cry from present practice, but it appears essential if democratic government in the American city is to be retained.

Need for Metropolitan Government

The central city, its suburbs and exurbs, and, many times, even smaller satellite cities can constitute an economic and social whole. When such is the case, why not make it a political entity as well? In short, the idea of *metropolitan area government* has been advanced as the only real solution to many urban problems.[4]

A metropolitan government would involve some level of merger of the various governmental units in existence in a metropolitan area. Supporters of the idea contend that it would permit more orderly and rational plan-

[4] For some of the benefits and problems of metropolitan area government see Luther H. Gulick, *The Metropolitan Problem and American Ideas* (New York: Alfred A. Knopf, 1962), chap. 4. See also Scott Greer, *The Emerging City* (New York: The Free Press of Glencoe, 1962), pp. 178–192.

ning and, with the duplication of many efforts removed, would result in better, more efficiently supplied services in the entire metropolitan area. New services, such as a rapid transportation system, art galleries, or a metropolitan area college or junior college, could be provided if the population that would finance them would be the same as that which would use them. Various problems resulting from haphazard proliferation of autonomous units would be avoided. Today, for example, an industrial tract may be developed contiguous to a quiet residential area, if it happens that the tract is also outside the city or county line. Or a small suburb may allow inadequate storm sewers, which then causes flooding problems in another suburb or the central city. The advantages of a metropolitan area government are many and are widely extolled by the supporters of the system.

On the other hand, there is well-recognized opposition to the idea of a metropolitan governmental unit. Some of it stems from a fear that "bigness" will result in an inefficient government remote from the people. There is also the matter of existing pride and loyalty to a place, be it the city or one of the suburbs. People, it is held, just cannot give up such loyalties easily or transfer them to some vague "metropolitan area." Resistance is expected from the major and minor public officials whose jobs depend on the existence of the many small municipalities in towns.

Metropolitan government plans have been proposed for some cities as early as 1933.[5] As of now, there is only *one* comprehensive metropolitan government in existence in the United States, and that is the Dade County, Florida, District System which makes a single unit of Miami and its suburbs. Quite apparently, then, other efforts over the years to provide legal recognition and governing power of the metropolitan area—to create, in a sense, a supercity—have failed. Nor is there any indication of a change in temperament. As social phenomena, metropolitan areas now exist. Political and legal admission of the reality of metropolitan areas await the resolution of many and serious value conflicts.

[5] Greer, *op. cit.*, p. 181.

SUGGESTED READINGS

BOSKOFF, ALVIN, *The Sociology of Urban Regions*. New York, Appleton-Century-Crofts, 1962.

CHURCHILL, HENRY S., *The City is the People*. New York, W. W. Norton & Co., 1962.

GOTTMANN, JEAN, *Megalopolis*. New York, The Twentieth Century Fund, 1961.

GREER, SCOTT A., *The Emerging City*. New York, The Free Press of Glencoe, 1962.

HAWORTH, LAURENCE, *The Good City*. Bloomington, Ind., Indiana University Press, 1963.

JOHNSON, THOMAS, *Renewing America's Cities*. Washington, D.C., The Institute for Social Science Research, 1962.

ROSSI, PETER H., and ROBERT A. DENTLER, *The Politics of Urban Renewal*. New York, The Free Press of Glencoe, 1961.

SCHORR, ALVIN L., *Slums and Social Insecurity*. Washington, D.C., Government Printing Office, 1963.

SIRJAMAKI, JOHN, *The Sociology of Cities*. New York, Random House, 1963.

SOFEN, EDWARD, *The Miami Metropolitan Experiment*. Bloomington, Ind., Indiana University Press, 1963.

STRAUSS, ANSELM L., *Images of the American City*. New York, The Free Press of Glencoe, 1961.

POPULATION PROBLEMS: WORLD AND NATIONAL

7

In the classical example, it is supposed that goats released on an island will multiply until their numbers reach the level allowed by the supply of grass. If at that moment wolves are released on the island, they, too, will multiply as long as there are ample goats. As the wolf population increases, the supply of goats will diminish, and soon after the last goat is eaten the wolves will die.

It makes for an interesting game to alter the various conditions and then to speculate on what the effects will be on the "population problem" of the wolves. If the wolves were technologically sophisticated, for example, they could devise ways for the goats to reproduce more rapidly. The same world of the wolves could thus be made to yield a living for an ever-higher population. Even so, if their numbers increased indefinitely, eventually there would be "standing room only" on the island, and soon the wolves would die of suffocation! The wolves, of course, could practice birth control and keep their numbers at a level where there would always be enough goats for dinner and enough also to be producing meals for future generations of wolves.

For some time people have been fascinated with playing a sort of "population game" that involves the human species. This island in the solar system we call the earth has boundaries, and there must be a limit to the food supply it can be made to yield. If, therefore, the population of the world increases at the rate of x, then by the year y the population of the world will be z. If the player has a flair for the dramatic, the total population, z, is astronomical and the year y is close at hand.

Games aside, the prospects of an overcrowded planet are not pleasant

118

to contemplate. But how likely is it that this will happen? Are there other, more immediate problems associated with the world's population growth? And what about our own society? Is America in the throes of a "population explosion"?

The population question is a serious matter, but it is also an extremely complicated one. Some, it seems, refuse to take it seriously, while others take it seriously enough, but proceed recklessly from inadequate knowledge to unwarranted conclusions. Our concern in this chapter is with the number and growth of the population in the world and in the United States, to the extent that both can be considered problems of our society. A great deal of knowledge and "facts" are required before one can begin to understand the issues involved in the current population problem. In the section that follows, the population growth of the world and the factors responsible for it are reviewed. While it constitutes a minimum background, it should provide for better understanding of the population issues in our world and our nation.

World Population Growth

In the year 6000 B.C., it has been estimated, there were probably only a few million people on the entire earth.[1] The total world's population at that time would have fit comfortably in one good-sized modern city. At the time of Christ, the world's population probably was about 250 million. The tremendous increase over the preceding figure reflects the development of true agriculture, but even so it took 6000 years to produce the tenfold increase. It took over 1600 years from the time of Christ for the world's population to double, making it about 500 million by the year 1650. Two hundred years later, however, in 1850, it had doubled once again and the population of the world was close to an even billion. Today we number almost 3 billion people.

While population figures, particularly for the earlier years, certainly lack precision, there is no mistaking the fact that the world's population has increased dramatically, that the *rate* of population growth recently has been many times greater than in the past. The lowest rate of population growth expected in the immediate future is 1 percent per year. Anyone with a rudimentary knowledge of arithmetic can demonstrate what *could happen* if that rate continued indefinitely. By the year 2000, the world would have about 5.7 billion inhabitants, and a hundred years later some 31 billion. Another hundred years would bring the total to 170 billion! There is no need to continue the impressive projections, for at best all they can provide

[1] John D. Durand, "World Population: Trend and Prospects," in Philip M. Hauser, *Population and World Politics* (New York: The Free Press of Glencoe, 1958), chap. 2.

FIGURE 4   WORLD POPULATION GROWTH, 1650–1960

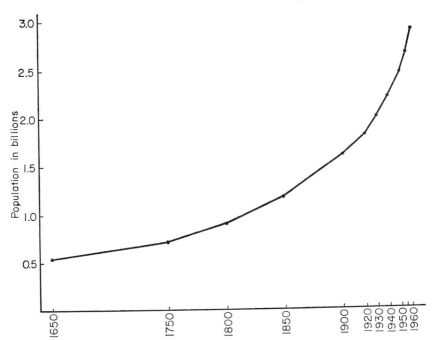

is a mathematically precise picture of what could happen. The important question, of course, is what is likely to happen. While few are so bold as to answer that question, knowledge of the factors that have affected population growth should bring us closer to determining how much of the "population problem" is real, and how much is spurious.

INDUSTRIALIZATION AND POPULATION GROWTH IN EUROPE. The essential ingredients in population growth are the birth rate and the death rate. In the preindustrial West, the interplay of these factors produced but a modest population growth. Fertility was high, but so also was mortality. The industrial revolution allowed man to produce his means of subsistence with a dramatic efficiency, and this, in turn, released some men for other pursuits. New knowledge in various fields began to be amassed, and man became better and better equipped to cope with his environment.

It is not difficult to understand why man in his humanity or his vanity began to devote more attention to preserving life and increasing longevity. Following the industrial revolution, the nations of the West began to experience a pronounced drop in their death rates. More lives were preserved at all ages, and in particular the infant mortality rate was drastically reduced. With the pronounced drop in death rate, the stage was set for a rapid population growth.

For a time, the birth rate of Western nations continued at its pre-industrial high level. The combination of a high birth rate and a low death rate, of course, spells rapid population growth, and indeed the Western nations did experience a population upsurge in this early industrial period. The potentially explosive features of the population growth were noted by Malthus, who quite correctly pointed out that the then current increase in numbers could not go on indefinitely.[2] Before long, he posited, man's ability to reproduce would outstrip his means of subsistence, and misery, want, and famine would be the plight of the masses.

The great population growth in the West was almost entirely due to the lower death rates that accompanied industrialization. For a time the birth rate remained unaffected. One might expect that after man learned to produce more efficiently he would see in this newfound knowledge a means of allowing him to have more and more children. But the effects of industrialization on the birth rate were otherwise. For a number of reasons, not all of them understood even in retrospect, industrialization eventually produced a lowered birth rate.

While we cannot pursue the matter at length, it is well to indicate the features of industrialization thought responsible for the decrease in births. Industrialization implies urbanization, and small families are more compatible with city living than are large families. A child in an agricultural society is an economic asset in that he is able to help produce the means of subsistence for his family, the more so as he becomes older. But the child in an industrial society is an economic burden, perhaps even a luxury; rarely can he contribute any substantial amount to the productive economy of a family. Finally, industrialization changes the role of women, making it desirable and possible for them to work outside the home. Fewer children obviously are more compatible with working outside the home than are more children.

When it became apparent that industrialization was having a depressing effect on the birth rate, it appeared that the fears of Malthus were unfounded. Reasoning that the death rate could not possibly drop much lower, but that the fertility rate could and probably would drop, the forecasters then saw a declining population. The birth rates of the 1930s suggested that much of Europe was soon to reach its population peak and, thereafter, would decline. It was predicted that the United States would show an increase until it reached about 165 million in 1990 and then it, too, would settle down to a lower but stable population. Of course, things did not work out that way. Nevertheless, the current birth rates of Europe and America are nowhere near their potential high. Industrialization continues to have a depressing effect on the birth rate, but not nearly as much as was supposed

[2] Thomas R. Malthus, *First Essay On Population,* 1798. (London: Macmillan & Company, Ltd., 1926), a facsimile reprint.

in the thirties. For the most part, the nations of the West are growing at a modest rate.

INDUSTRIALIZATION AND POPULATION GROWTH IN ASIA. More than half of the people in the world live in Asia where the population picture is quite different from that in the West. The two largest nations in the world— China with almost 700 million people and India with about 400 million— are in the very early stages of industrialization.[3] But unlike the European countries at a corresponding stage of economic development, India, China, and other Asian nations have a tumbling death rate even before industrialization is off to a good start. The reason, of course, is that medical and technical knowledge, accumulated over a century or more in the West, is borrowed and quickly put to work saving and prolonging lives. Meanwhile, fertility remains high. The result is a population increase that is coming at the "wrong" time in the industrial development cycle. The early stage of industrialization in Europe was a painful experience, with the industries unable to provide new jobs as fast as millions were released from the old ones. But at least those countries were not faced with a rapidly growing population. When the expansion did come, the nations of the West were better prepared to cope with it, and immigration to the New World provided a temporary outlet for the excess population.

Table 13   Population and Population Growth by Continents, 1930–1959

Area	Number of people (in millions)				Annual percentage increase		
	1930	1940	1950	1959	1930–1940	1940–1950	1950–1959
World	2013	2246	2476	2905	1.1	0.9	1.7
Africa	155	172	199	236	1.0	1.4	1.9
North America	135	146	168	196	0.7	1.4	1.8
Central America	34	41	51	65	1.9	2.2	2.7
South America	74	90	111	137	2.0	2.1	2.3
Southwest Asia	48	54	61	76	1.1	1.2	2.5
South central Asia	362	410	466	546	1.2	1.2	1.8
Southeast Asia	128	155	172	208	1.9	1.0	2.1
East Asia	535	594	679	794	1.0	1.3	1.8
Europe	355	380	393	421	0.6	0.3	0.8
Oceania	10	11	13	16	0.8	1.5	2.4
USSR	176	192	—	210	0.8	—	—

SOURCE: Data from and computed from United Nations, *Statistical Yearbook,* New York, 1960.

[3] For simplicity we will deal mostly with the developing countries of Asia. The problems are similar in other parts of the world, notably Central America, South America, and parts of Africa.

The industrializing countries of Asia, by contrast, are facing not only the "normal" growing pains of industrialization but are compounding these with an unprecedented upsurge in their populations. What is more, by an accident of history this is occurring at a time when there are no more "new worlds" eager to receive people and, thus, temporarily to ease the population pressures in the developing countries.

For both the West and the East, therefore, the population curves are taking a different course than was once expected. The nations of the industrial West are not declining in numbers. Their populations rise steadily and no "peak" or "leveling off" is forecast for the immediate future. The developing nations of the East are experiencing a mushrooming population growth, earlier and greater than expected and not complemented by a decline in other parts of the world. Leaving aside for the moment the immediate effects of population expansion in the underdeveloped nations, for how long can a total world increase in population continue?

The World's Population Capacity

Estimates concerning the total population the world could support have ranged from 3 billion to 30 billion—in other words, from about as many people as there are now living to ten times the present number. Most of the reason for this range of difference lies in the failure to specify the conditions under which the hypothetical populations would be living.

In the long run, the total carrying power of the earth is limited by the availability of land and other resources, by man's knowledge of how to use whatever is available, and by the standard of living that is desired.

NATURAL RESOURCES. The limits imposed by the availability of land and other resources are broad and will not be reached for a long, long time. No matter what rate of population growth is assumed, it will be many centuries before we run out of land on which to live, to produce crops, and house our factories. To be sure, the world is exhausting some of its resources at a regular rate and some will be completely gone in the foreseeable future. This simply challenges man's ingenuity to devise ways of getting along without that which becomes scarce. Of course, in an ultimate sense even if not in the foreseeable future, the availability of land and resources do set an upper limit to the world's population. In other words, taking into account only the availability of land and natural resources, the current population growth can go on for some time, but not indefinitely.

TECHNICAL KNOWLEDGE. Some see reason to doubt whether man's technical knowledge can keep pace with his increasing numbers. They question whether human ingenuity and inventiveness can be developed as fast as need for them arises. A more optimistic view holds that scientific knowledge and technical ability are almost boundless and, furthermore, that man can acquire whatever degree of "know-how" an increased population may demand of him. Not to be overlooked, however, is the fact that *during any given era* man's lack of knowledge may effectively limit the number of people the world can support. Moreover, when dealing with the world's population, it is necessary that the knowledge and techniques be applied where they are needed, and that various other sorts of assistance be rendered to those nations in which the population pressures are the severest. But this may be unacceptable to those who can give the assistance, to those who need it, or to both. For the present, then, man's ability to acquire the technical knowledge to manipulate his natural resources and to apply it wherever it is needed may be considered as setting a limit to the number of people that the world can support.

LEVEL OF LIVING. The third factor influencing the population capacity of the world is the level of living that one assumes or specifies. To take a simple example, the United States with its present agricultural and industrial output could support twice as many people if their average level of living were half of what prevails today. There is a fairly broad range, furthermore, between a bare subsistence level of living and the high level found in our own country, with the result that estimates of the capacity of the world fluctuate widely depending on the level of living that is desired. The higher the level of living that is specified, the lower will be the limit of the earth's population capacity.

There is room for personal differences regarding the *desirable* size of the world's population, and there is room for differences among population experts concerning the *feasible* population capacity of the world. The experts agree that the present rate of growth cannot go on indefinitely. Assuming that the present rate of growth continues, they disagree over the timing of the arrival of acute, global population pressures, but in the long run, a quibble over even a century or two may be irrelevant.

Western demographers seem to be in agreement that, for reasons previously indicated, the *rate* of population growth in the developing nations is too rapid to permit orderly, democratic modernization with a minimum of human suffering. Marxists, in principle, believe otherwise, but Communist China already has made one bold attempt to cut its birth rate.

THE UNITED STATES AND WORLD POPULATION PROBLEMS

In an oversimplified manner it can be said that the world has two sorts of population problems, the one having to do with the uncomfortable rate of population growth in the underdeveloped countries, the other a longer-term problem of the ability of our planet to provide for the total population increase. Whether we care to admit it or not, both of these world problems are very much American problems as well.

One basic clash of values exists over the definition of America's responsibility in the world population crisis. Probably the majority of Americans do not see it as *their* problem. They see the population explosion in the developing countries as a problem for those countries, and if the people in such places seem bent on multiplying themselves to suffocation, then it is their own concern. To be sure, many temper such a conclusion with a hope and a wish that the underdeveloped countries will somehow manage to escape continued starvation, disease, and poverty. These humanitarian sentiments, however admirable, are simply modifications of the basic premise that the world's population growth and the rapid increase on the other side of the globe are of no real concern to Americans. But the weight of the evidence suggests otherwise.

It is a dangerous illusion for Americans to imagine that the world's population growth is none of their concern. After all, the population capacity of the world, whatever it may be and whenever it may be reached, exists for all humanity and not just for a few nations. As this limit is actually approached, or even if it is wrongly assumed the limit is being approached, crowded and starving people will not contentedly ignore the presence of less-populated parts of the world where people are living in abundance. A starving man finds it easy to justify stealing food from his neighbor, perhaps the more so if his neighbor had it in his power to help him but refused to do so. Americans should not find it difficult to understand this general point, for it was only a few hundred years ago that their ancestors felt morally justified in taking over a large part of a continent from inhabitants who were weaker, sparsely settled, and not utilizing the natural resources to their fullest advantage.

Long before maximum population is reached it is likely that Americans will be affected by the rapid population growth in the underdeveloped countries. The underdeveloped countries will, sooner or later and in one way or another, become industrialized. Americans should be particularly concerned over *how* the one third of the world that is uncommitted to capitalism or communism chooses to complete its economic development. Will India, Indonesia, Pakistan, and the countries of South America follow the lead of Communist China, which offers a method for even an overpopulated country to industrialize, or will they adopt the ways of the West? This choice will be critical.

Today, of course, the underdeveloped countries are no threat to the Western world. However, a confederation of Communist, industrial nations holding the bulk of the world's population could well be expected to wield the bulk of the world's power. Ideologically and economically separated from the powerful nations of the world, what then will become of America and its way of life? Perhaps this is proof enough that the world's population problem is indeed an American social problem.

POSSIBILITIES FOR REDUCING THE WORLD POPULATION PROBLEM

Among the probable minority of citizens who feel that America cannot escape some responsibility for world population affairs, there is sharp disagreement as to what this country should do. With regard to the pressures in underdeveloped countries, population experts recommend a two-pronged attack, the one upon economic development, the other upon population growth.

Obstacles to Economic Development Assistance

Ideally, from the standpoint of America and the West, the underdeveloped, overpopulated countries should be encouraged to industrialize rapidly, but in such a way that the social costs will not be so great that the people turn to totalitarian communism in a desperate hope for a faster or better method. For America to assist in the industrialization of underdeveloped countries would require a great investment of talent and manpower, an outlay of money far surpassing the total of our "aid programs" of today, and all in all a full commitment to the idea that such assistance was desirable and important. Highways at home may have to be judged less important than schools and technical institutes abroad. Scientific and technical manpower may have to be diverted from glamorous space-age pursuits to problems of better agricultural practices, the development of industries in keeping with the technical talent and needs of the countries, and the discovery of new industrial or food uses for native resources. How many Americans, one wonders, would be willing to see our proposed moon landing postponed indefinitely or even for ten years in order that we could assist a foreign nation to industrialize without too great a toll in human misery?

The ramifications of full commitment to assisting in the economic development of underdeveloped countries are seemingly endless. Surely our import and export practices would have to be changed and our tariffs modified, and this could affect the jobs of workers at home. As every specific feature of a total program is touched upon, it is evident that some cherished value of some Americans would come into conflict with the value of wholehearted assistance in the economic development of other nations.

Obstacles to Population Control Assistance

The problem of moving rapidly from an agricultural economy to one that is capable of supporting great masses of people at a decent level of living is extremely complicated at best. The difficulties are compounded when the masses increase at such a rate that modest technological improvements are offset by the population growth. It seems clear enough that the countries modernizing today would find their task less difficult if they could keep their numbers from growing at so rapid a rate. Not everyone accepts this position, but even among those who do there is often sharp disagreement as to the means that should be used.

For humanitarian reasons, almost all Americans immediately would reject the proposal that we allow or encourage the underdeveloped countries to return to a stage of high death rates. Proposals quite close to this, however, have been advanced, as when it is suggested that medical assistance be withheld from countries that are not inclined to "cooperate" with the United States. Opening our doors to immigrants might ease the problem of developing nations somewhat, but it is doubtful if immigration could be practiced on a large enough scale for its effect to be noticed. The only feasible and acceptable plan for controlling population growth in the underdeveloped countries, therefore, is assisting in lowering their birth rates.

Not all methods of lowering birth rates are acceptable to the industrializing nations or to Americans. Unless they can see a reason for doing so, for example, it is unlikely that delayed marriage will be found acceptable in the developing countries. The great majority of Americans probably would object to abortion as a means of controlling fertility, large numbers would object to sterilization, and the Catholic minority of our population would object to both of these methods and to mechanical or medicinal contraceptives as well.

Reaching agreement on a suitable means of birth control is a serious obstacle to providing help for developing nations to control their fertility, but probably not an insurmountable one. The Protestant Episcopal Bishop James A. Pike, for example, has urged that our National Institute of Health conduct research to make the "rhythm method" of birth control, the only acceptable method from the Catholic viewpoint, more reliable.[4] Bishop Pike was commended for his "admirable gesture of friendliness and good will" by the Catholic theologian, Rev. John A. O'Brien.[5] The same Catholic theologian spoke of the substantial agreement among Catholics, Protestants, and Jews on the objectives of family planning and has reminded Catholics of their obligation to respect the rights of conscience and of religious freedom of all people.[6] It would be naïve to conclude that the conflict of values between Protestants and Catholics is no longer an obstacle to providing birth control assistance to other nations, but it would be equally naïve to conclude that it is the only obstacle.

Any birth control program for developing nations would be tre-

[4] Reported in William H. Draper, Jr., "Birth Control: The Problem We Fear to Face," *Look* (December 5, 1961).

[5] Rev. John A. O'Brien, "Let's Take Birth Control Out of Politics," *Look* (October 10, 1961).

[6] *Ibid.*

mendously expensive and would require a great number of doctors, nurses, and medical facilities. But medical personnel and facilities are in extremely short supply in such nations and to divert their medical efforts from saving lives to preventing new lives may be asking too much. In addition, a great educational campaign would be needed before the people themselves would see the value of family planning. But how many educators can be spared for birth control education in nations where illiteracy is the rule? In a word, the underdeveloped countries are simply not equipped to embark on a birth control program that would effectively reach their masses at any reasonably rapid rate.

There is ample indication that Americans are not willing to extend massive fertility control assistance to the developing nations. The fundamental value conflict seems to be between those who feel that the birth rates around the world should be of concern to Americans, and those who do not accept this. Value conflicts over birth control methods and over other aspects of a fertility control program are evident even among those who feel *something* must be done. Meanwhile, the developing nations annually add millions to the world's population.

POPULATION PROBLEMS: THE DOMESTIC SCENE

In some ways the population problems in the United States fade into insignificance beside those of the world. Whether we carelessly reproduce or carefully control our numbers, it will scarcely be noticed in the short-run world population growth. The long run, of course, is another matter. It is true, too, that many Americans find it easier to grasp the population situation in their own country than in the world; they find it easier to imagine what a significant increase or decrease in numbers would mean in their lives, as well as to become intellectually and emotionally involved in the "population question."

The population problem with which we will deal concerns our numbers and their growth. This is not the only current population problem, nor necessarily the most important one. Problems associated with the age make-up of our population are dealt with in the chapters on Old Age and Education, and some of the effects of the movement of people toward urban centers are considered with problems of The City.

United States Population Growth

As a background for the problems of population growth in the United States, we shall review briefly the growth pattern over approximately the last century and a half, and we shall indicate what the population specialists believe will happen in the next twenty-five to fifty years.

Table 14 shows the population of the United States from 1790 to 1960 and the percentage increase from each decennial census year to the next. For seventy years, each census counted about a third more people than the census ten years previous to it. Then, beginning in 1870, the *rate* of growth began to fall dramatically and consistently. The nation continued to grow in numbers, but at a decreasing rate. The census of 1940 discovered that there were just 7 percent more people than there were in 1930. Unexpectedly, the *rate* of population doubled over the following ten years, and was up even higher by 1960.

**Table 14   Population Growth in the United States,
1790–1960**

Year	Number of people	Percent increase over preceding census
1790	3,929,214	—
1800	5,308,483	35.1
1810	7,239,881	36.4
1820	9,638,453	33.1
1830	12,866,020	33.5
1840	17,069,453	32.7
1850	23,191,876	35.9
1860	31,443,321	35.6
1870	39,818,449	26.6
1880	50,155,783	26.0
1890	62,947,714	25.5
1900	75,994,575	20.7
1910	91,972,266	21.0
1920	105,710,620	14.9
1930	122,775,046	16.1
1940	131,669,275	7.2
1950	150,697,361	14.5
1960	178,464,236	18.4

SOURCE: U.S. Bureau of the Census, *Statistical Abstract of the United States: 1962,* Washington, D.C., 1962, p. 5.

One way to appreciate the significance of the declining rate of population growth from about 1870 to 1940 is to consider what would have happened if the early growth rate had continued to the present. Beginning in 1790, the population doubled in numbers every twenty-five years for a hundred years. If this had continued for another seventy-five years, until 1965, the population of the United States would then be over 500 million, instead of its approximately 190 million.

Until World War II, then, population growth in the United States followed the general pattern of the industrializing West. As industrialization began, fertility remained high but the death rate decreased, making for a substantial rate of growth in total numbers. Thereafter, the birth rate also declined, producing a less rapid rate of growth. But instead of the continued decline in births, and an ultimate "leveling off" of the total population, we have had an upsurge in births since World War II. What, then, can we say of the future?

The Future Population of the United States

In the United States, knowledge of how to prevent conception has been diffused more and more generally throughout the society. More important even is the fact that the *idea of family planning* is extremely widespread. By the idea of family planning we mean simply the value position that it is right, good, or necessary for married couples to decide how many children they want and when they want to have them. Not only do Americans essentially agree on the principle of family planning, but most couples are able to keep the actual number of their children reasonably close to the number they desire.[7] To be sure, some couples desiring children find that they are unable to have them, in some families the first child comes sooner than planned, and in others the children are a little closer together than expected. Some families have more children than they planned, but even here it is usually a matter of one or two more children and not the six to ten more potentially possible.

The willingness and ability of American couples to control the size of their families makes for difficult forecasting. So much depends on what the people want to do. Past experience suggests that economic and social conditions do have an effect on the birth rate, with people altering their family size quickly and ably in response to what they feel is called for in the new situation.

Using present family size values and practices as a starting point, we can arrive at estimates of the future population of our country. By 1980 our numbers are expected to reach between about 230 to 272 million. Twenty years later the total population would be over 300 million. It has been estimated that if the three-child family prevails from now on, by 2050 the population of the United States will be 600 million![8]

There can be no doubt that the United States could support a vastly increased population. As early as 1944 the United States Department of Agriculture estimated, for example, that the nation's agricultural capacity

[7] Ronald Freedman *et al., Family Planning, Sterility, and Population Growth* (New York: McGraw-Hill Book Company, 1959), pp. 401ff.

[8] *Ibid.,* pp. 404–405.

would allow us to feed 380 million people.[9] Of course, our agricultural technology has been further improved since that estimate. For the population sizes forecast until the turn of the century at least, it is not a matter of how many people our country can support, but how many people we want. The fundamental value clash is over the desirability of our present rate of growth and the changes it will produce within the next fifty years.

Value Conflicts over Continued Growth

There are serious-minded people who contend that it is good for our nation to grow at something approaching its current rate. They point out that our whole economy is geared to expansion. We seem to have enough trouble with unemployment even when each year we need to produce more homes, more automobiles, and more goods and services of all sorts just to provide for the additional people. What, then, would happen if our numbers were not increasing as fast as they are at present? It is, thus, felt that a healthy economy can best be obtained by continuing an adequate population increase.

It is further contended that America's position of world leadership and perhaps even its survival can best be assured by maintaining a good rate of population growth. Among industrially mature nations, it is held, people mean power. The tremendous production increase during World War II is used as an example of the almost unbelievable capacity of an industrialized nation to produce goods, provided it has enough workers. Our phenomenal industrial output during the war, of course, was accomplished without the help of a sizable proportion of the nation's able-bodied males. Could not America's industrial genius be used to the benefit of the world? In America a worker could produce many times what is needed for an adequate level of living for himself and his family, so the more people there are in the labor force, the greater our national "surplus."

Just as vehemently, others argue that our situation at home and abroad is jeopardized by our present values concerning family size and the population increase thereby produced. They point to our congested cities and suburbs, our city streets clogged with automobiles and our highways that are nearly so. Parks, schools, hospitals, recreational facilities—no matter what one considers seems to be overcrowded. Obviously, it is contended, we are not now able to take care of our present rate of population increase. If the rate continues, it is held that each generation will have to accept an increasingly lower standard of living. Unless something is done to check our growth, our congestion will become worse and our overcrowded conditions unbearable.

[9] W. S. Woytinsky and E. S. Woytinsky, *World Population and Production* (New York: The Twentieth Century Fund, 1953), p. 535.

Proponents of slowing down our population increase further point out that world leadership is not a matter of numbers but ability, both technical and moral. A nation suffering under the weight of self-induced population pressures would be in no position, economic or otherwise, to help others. Finally, it is argued that our technological breakthroughs—especially automation—expand production without the need for a larger workforce.

It must be admitted that on both sides of the population issue are the idealists and the realists, the altruistic and the selfish. Undoubtedly at the root of some of the fears of a population explosion in the United States is the nagging thought that those who have will be asked to share with those who have not. But others have a deep respect for their fellow men, so much so that they would like to see them living decently and avoiding by self-control the less attractive controls of famine and disease. Some who favor a continuation of our birth rates likewise love their fellows, believing that all men should be as rich as they want to be, but believing also that a man with eight children is richer than a man with two by precisely six children. But there are selfish reasons for wanting continued expansion; some are simply blinded by their own personal values and would like to impose these values on the entire society. Others refuse to accept any responsibility for the future, believing that if this generation takes care of itself it has done enough.

The fertility pattern of the current generation of Americans will have an effect that will last longer than the next fifty years. It is a matter of arithmetic that our present population growth cannot go on indefinitely. Something, sometime, will check it. With regard to longer-run population growth in our country, the conflict seems to center on how its ultimate stabilization will be accomplished. Perhaps here again the division is between the optimists and the pessimists. The most optimistic view is that Americans voluntarily will control their fertility when it becomes necessary, and meanwhile science will provide. Perhaps interplanetary migration will be feasible, or maybe something else yet unknown to man will alleviate his population problem or even make him thankful for a densely populated nation—or globe. Others dismiss this kind of reasoning as idle and even dangerous fantasy. They further fear that before Americans get around to applying the brakes voluntarily it will be too late. The result will be that future American couples will have to be subjected to drastic restrictions and harsh living, all because their forefathers did not realize what they were doing as they reproduced with abandon.

The population issue is an intensely emotional one, with antagonists not only holding opposing values but also frequently disagreeing on the facts. An overcrowded country or world is not a very pleasant thought. One might suppose that rational men of good will could determine the facts and agree upon a policy. Perhaps this is too much to expect when the major nations on earth vie with one another in amassing arsenals of horrendous destruction. Needless to say, if those arsenals are ever used, the forecasts and predictions in this chapter will be of the utmost irrelevance.

SUGGESTED READINGS

FREEDMAN, RONALD, PASCAL K. WHELPTON, and ARTHUR A. CAMPBELL, *Family Planning, Sterility, and Population Growth*. New York, McGraw-Hill Book Company, Inc., 1959.

GRABILL, WILSON H., CLYDE V. KISER, and PASCAL K. WHELPTON, *The Fertility of American Women*. New York, John Wiley & Sons, Inc., 1958.

HAUSER, PHILIP M., ed., *Population and World Politics*. New York, The Free Press of Glencoe, 1958.

HILL, REUBEN, J. MAYONE STYCOS, and KURT W. BACK, *The Family and Population Control*. Chapel Hill, N.C., University of North Carolina Press, 1959.

Marriage and Family Living. 25 (February 1963). [Special issue, "Family Planning in Modernizing Societies."]

MEIR, RICHARD L., *Modern Science and the Human Fertility Problem*. New York, John Wiley & Sons, Inc., 1959.

ORGANSKI, KATHERINE, and A. F. K. ORGANSKI, *Population and World Power*. New York, Alfred A. Knopf, 1961.

PETERSEN, WILLIAM, *Population*. New York, The Macmillan Company, 1961.

SAUVY, ALFRED, *Fertility and Survival*. New York, Criterion Books, 1961.

MARRIAGE

8

It is not difficult to establish the existence and general recognition of many and fundamental problems in the area of sex, marriage, and the family. It will prove much more difficult, however, to unravel the complex fabric of social relationships for the purposes of isolating significant, basic social problems in this area and of charting the various proposals designed to cope with these problems.

Even were there no other obstacle, the student would experience unusual difficulty in this area of study because of his lack of training in objective thinking along these lines. Our emotions are so deeply invested in our concepts of what marriage is and ought to be, our own personalities have been so strongly fashioned by the kind of family system within which we were nurtured, and the basic components of domestic life are so inextricably interwoven with religious ideologies that objective thinking will encounter numerous and serious emotional blocks. This is usually so not because the proposed changes in the sex, marriage, and family area of life are so radical, but because the allegiance of most people to the stereotypes of the past is so steadfast that even minor alterations in the domestic way of life seem to be difficult, unnecessary—if not even dangerous—and sinful. Thus, if one has had a happy childhood in a family in which the mother devoted her entire time and attention to the care of children and the duties of homemaking, and in which the father "ruled the roost with a firm but gentle hand," it usually proves difficult to grasp quickly the logic of careers for married women and of democracy in family rule. The difficulty is not that we do not wish to be what we call progressive or that we do not espouse humanitarian values, but that we are so rooted in emotionally buttressed habits of thought and action that different ways seem ill advised, if not impossible of successful observance.

THE AMERICAN FAMILY TRADITION

Before we can thoughtfully consider the nature of present-day family problems and the changes, if any, that are being advocated, it is well to consider the kind of sex, marriage, and family system in which our society had its origins. The roots of the family system in America can be conceived, at the risk of possible oversimplification, largely in terms of three concepts: rurality, patriarchy, and sacredness.

Rurality

As we have pointed out at numerous points in this book, the over-all traditions of America are rural traditions. This nation is only just emerging from a society in which rural occupations, rural ways, and rural thinking constituted the basic motif of "the American way." During the last fifty to seventy-five years the great growth of urban centers has reconverted the basic structure of American life so that now we are predominantly an urban people with city ways gradually but certainly becoming ascendant. But our thinking has not been reconverted as quickly or as completely as our dwellings, our occupations, and our daily schedules.

In traditional rural society the family is the basic, central social unit. The family is the unit of production as well as the unit of consumption. There is work for every member of the family from the incredibly early age at which a child gathers the eggs, feeds the baby chicks, and picks strawberries. No one person makes the family living or spends it. The family's finances are a joint enterprise. Moreover, the farm family produces for itself many of the goods and services that the urban family has to buy. It is not the cost or the buying, however, that constitutes the real difference; the real difference is psychological, the necessary sharing of responsibility among the family members in the production of the goods to supply the family's needs from grandmother with the spinning wheel to grandchild garnering the strawberries. It is not difficult to nurture a "we" feeling when the every activity and every need of everyone are as closely interlaced as they were in the rural farm family.

Patriarchy

The rural family was rooted in the patriarchal tradition. It was taken for granted by virtually everyone that major decisions were to be made by the father and, that although one might disagree with his decisions, there was no escaping from them. One is not to infer that patriarchal rule necessarily meant tyranny because there is no necessary connection between the possession of power and the misuse of it. The point is simply that patriarchal government was the rule. Few doubted seriously that it was the only rule ordained of God, for after all, God too was masculine, a kind of super-father, firm and authoritarian but never unjust or to be questioned.

Sacredness

The traditional family also had a philosophical-religious logic which helped to hold it together and served as the frame of reference for inducting the young into it: First, marriage was "ordained by God in the Garden of Eden." That gave marriage supernatural sanction; it was no man-made institution to be tampered with by mortals, who somehow were not quite to be trusted in such matters anyway. Moreover, Jesus Christ spoke uncompromisingly against divorce. It was said by Him to be a sin, and that was that. Finally, reproduction carried a sacred aura. Except for a few very obvious and elementary facts, the biology and psychology of sex were mostly unknown and tended to be regarded as unknowable. Large families were held in high regard by virtue of the Jewish-Christian tradition that a man should be fruitful so that "his seed might inherit the earth." No one was especially concerned if a woman bore so many children or had them so close together that she died a premature death. She merely "passed on to her reward" earlier; there were some tears, of course, and the mourning husband soon went about finding another mate to take over the responsibilities left unfinished by his deceased spouse. No one talked much—except perhaps the poets—about happiness, whether or not the husband and wife "still loved each other," or whether the mental health of the third eldest son was secure. Somehow such matters were taken for granted. This was the way of life, and it worked *reasonably well most* of the time. If there were many who doubted the all-sufficiency of this scheme of things, they were not very numerous and certainly not very vocal.

The Modern Setting

As we have pointed out in Chapter 1, most Americans now live in the context of the mass society. And even those who reside on the fringes of it cannot escape many of its impacts. Looking at this mass society closely, a number of insights relevant to marriage and the family result.

1. TWO ORDERS OF REALITY: *De Facto and De Jure.* Law, religion, and informal influence converge to present a monolithic image of what sex, marriage, and family life *ought* to be. The specifications of this blueprint for the good life are well known to almost everyone: young people should be chaste before marriage, should marry for a combination

of love and "sensible reasons," should be self-supporting when they marry, should have children; women should have their first loyalty to child bearing and rearing, and should stay married; couples should so order their personal lives as to present a public image of solidarity, togetherness, and marital fidelity. This package of values is largely codified in law, supported by the sacred dogma of all churches and in innumerable ways by informal public opinion and the well-publicized preachments of the mass media. A visitor from Mars could easily get the impression that we live in a logically consistent and traditional system with little deviation, and that what deviation exists results in ready punishment of the contrite wrongdoers. This is the *de jure* order. It is uniform regardless of class or race, individual desire or need. It is *the* monolithic order.

By the time he is adolescent almost everyone learns that there is a second reality—a *de facto* order, the way things "really are," as distinct from what they are supposed to be. For example, according to the most accurate statistical information we have, premarital chastity is honored more in the breach than in the observance; many, if not a majority of young people do not wait until they are financially responsible before they launch into marriage and parenthood; at least a quarter of the people who marry become divorced, and substantial other numbers terminate marriages by desertion or other private arrangements. Millions of women who have children do not in fact take care of them themselves, preferring instead to subcontract their parenthood while they pursue other endeavors. And, while we do not know the exact percentages, reliable studies have indicated that substantial numbers of married pairs do not in fact live their lives in the monogamous state. Kinsey pointed out, for example, that if present laws dealing with sexual conditions were strictly enforced, over a majority of American males would be required to serve penitentiary sentences for sexual misconduct! Every state forbids abortion and yet several millions of abortions are known to occur every year. This listing could go on and on, but enough has been written to indicate that as a matter of *fact,* vast proportions and sometimes even majorities either ignore or clearly violate the behavioral proscriptions of law and ecclesiastical requirement. These deviants, if they can be so called, are not the poor and the uneducated. They are a cross section of the society, and some of the "deviations" are apparently more prevalent among the more educated, more successful, and socially prominent classes.

In view of the foregoing, it is exceedingly difficult to know where and whether to use a term like "deviant." Which is the deviant, the majority that is premaritally unchaste or the minority that remains chaste? Putting the matter academically: Is the person who deviates from the *de jure* order the deviant? Or the one who departs from the *de facto* order? To the holder of moralistic values, the deviant is, of course, the person who violates the legal-ecclesiastical-idealistic code. But to the more realistic person, one who is acquainted with *actual* behavior as well as the current preachments about behavior, it often becomes clear that the moralist's exemplar is really in the minority.

To adjudicate an issue of this sort is probably impossible. All the objective realist can do is to acknowledge—and in some measure to act upon—the fact that these two orders of reality exist in our society at this time. Not everyone, to be sure, actually manifests this duality. There are some people, probably a minority, who actually live in accordance with all of the *de jure* expectations; at the other extreme there is another minority who make no effort and no claim to do so. In between is the vast majority of Americans, however, who seem to "believe in" a monolithic value structure and in some measure approximate it in reality, but who also live by pluralistic modes that vary markedly from one another, apparently as adaptations to special circumstances of occupation, education, income, local life styles, and individual situation.

Almost anyone can demonstrate to himself how these two orders co-exist by asking any forthright contemporary several questions about his beliefs about sex, marriage, and family and then examining the conduct and the judgments of others, when clear violations of the ideals have been acknowledged. It is as if we live in two worlds, the one containing the preachments we accept and the other containing the practices that depart therefrom. Or perhaps one could say that we really live in a third world— a world of pretense where publicly, and to some extent privately, we make believe that practice and preachment are in fairly close harmony, even though we know that they are not.

2. ATOMIZATION. One of the traditional idealizations is that husbands, wives, and children ought to have their lives tied together closely in a web of interdependence and mutual help in meeting life's problems. In the rural family system this ideal was to a considerable extent realized. In modern mass society it is an almost impossible objective. The husband's world of employment is, in most instances, not only physically separated but also shut off psychologically from home and family, with only the vaguest understanding by the man's family of what that world is really like. Meanwhile, the society has set up specialized educational, recreational, and also religious programs dividing the siblings by sex and age, and their parents too, with the net result that there is exceedingly little time, energy, or interest for the "togetherness" that the family is admonished to practice. It would take genuine ingenuity to do so in the face of competing demands by a whole host of institutions, agencies, and organizations, at few of whose functions more than one person from the family is normally in attendance. The problem here is not simply a matter of time. It runs deeper. Each activity carries with it points of view, loyalties, and sometimes even values

that may or may not be shared by other members of the family. Even those families that make conscientious and intelligent efforts to share and keep abreast of the intricate maze of group activities of the various members face a Herculean task.

3. DEFUNCTIONALIZATION. Almost every historical treatment of the family institution makes the point that the family of the last century provided many functions for its members that are now provided by outside, special institutions. Today almost every community contains a whole galaxy of agencies that are designed to do for families, or for particular family members, things that in another time the family did for itself, and the members for each other. In a majority of homes, aged and indigent family members are not even any longer present. They are in nursing homes, or sanitariums, in "villages for senior citizens"—anywhere but the three-generational family. Education is chiefly carried on outside the home—by schools, summer camps, Boy Scouts, Girl Scouts, even night schools for father or mother if they are so inclined. Even churches seem no longer content to provide only family worship services—almost every night of the week some special age or sex group meets but seldom the total family group. Recreation is further fragmentized; there is open complaint in many a household that one or two television sets are not enough, because the adolescent wishes to watch an adolescent show, mother a woman's show, and father a sports event.

This is not to deny that many specialized agencies and institutions can do many of the things formerly done by the family in a technically superior way. Undoubtedly diapers come back from the diaper service more sanitary, possibly the T-V packaged dinner may be better balanced, and the televised major league ball game more brilliant than the sandlot game of old. The big difference is in the psychological focus. The family member of today looks *out* from the family to find his world of participation—work or play—while the traditional family member looked *in* to the family for his. It is quite possible that the discrepancy between the *de jure* and the *de facto* orders may be significantly related to this defunctionalization. The *de jure* order has not fundamentally changed for centuries but the *de facto* life modes have changed radically.

4. A SENSE OF MALADAPTATION. For whatever reasons, it is not difficult to demonstrate that there is a pervasive sense of unhappiness, of maladjustment, if not hopelessness, on the part of large numbers of Americans where their marital and family lives are concerned. A plethora of books, serious articles, and, more recently, national television shows have been devoted to depicting this condition and attempting to understand it. Phrases like "the entrapped housewife" have become household words. Any number of serious studies document the fact that disillusionment in one form or another is general; high divorce rates, informal desertions, and couples

who "stay together" despite acknowledged unhappiness, present a disturbing picture of domestic life. The high incidence of alcoholism, particularly among married women, adds to the sorry picture. In the face of these facts, the lucky ones, the insensitive ones, the innocent ones, and the simple moralists like to point out that people ought not to be this way, that the objective conditions of their lives are not so bad, that there should be a return to more austere life values, that a reaffirmation of religious faith or simple "togetherness" will cure what ails them. But this has been said for a long, long time, more recently even with full benefit of Madison Avenue techniques, and the condition does not abate. There is some reason to think that it is even accentuated. The hard realist cannot escape the fact that, for whatever reasons, there are symptoms of widespread maladaptation consciously acknowledged by large numbers and visibly manifest to the careful observer in many more cases.

Quite obviously, the foregoing paragraphs do not apply to everyone. Moreover, they may not apply at one point in life, but may apply conspicuously at another. Looking at the society collectively, however, at any point in time there are impressive numbers of people, acknowledgedly or otherwise, who are caught up in conspicuous man-woman unhappiness and maladaptation. Some of these persons are able to work out some "do-it-yourself" solutions to correct, or more likely simply to meliorate, the harder realities. But many lack the ingenuity or the luck to pull off the needed bootstrap operation.

It is quite possible that there are no real solutions for the present sex, marriage, and family problems and dilemmas. They may inhere in the social fabric in which we live. They seem to be individual problems because our focus is individual. Our friend Jane is observed drinking too much; her husband is running around; they are considering a divorce because, while they were once close, since he has moved up so rapidly in the company, he seems like a stranger to her and she seems so incorrigibly dull to him. Immediately our attention turns to Jane and her husband and their problem. But looked at in a broader context there is nothing unique about their problems. There are thousands, if not millions, caught in the same or very similar circumstances. Conditions so general must have causes also more general than the uniqueness and idiosyncracies of particular people.

The plight of Jane and Joe, and many other standard configurations like theirs, are part of the standard equipment of man-woman living in the twentieth century—at least in the mass society. Actuarially it is a great deal like the automobile accident rate. The high incidence is regrettable; it is always easy to second-guess an individual instance and show how it might have been averted, and undoubtedly numerous other possible catastrophes have been successfully averted. But no one seriously can doubt that so long as we have automobiles, driven at conventional speeds, with the kinds of driving skills which we now have, there is going to be a continued high incidence of death and maiming on the highways. Following the automobile accident analogy, much the same can be shown for problems in the domestic realm. Marked class changes due to education and job success, value differences between couples at the time of marriage, unrealistic hopes and anticipations pertaining to spouses and children, mass media presenting unreal, romantic, ever-youthful images of home and family, these and other conditions are part of the human mélange of our time. Some persons, like the especially careful driver, may come through unscathed, but even they are not immune. Others are lucky. Yet the realistic observer is forced to the conclusion that no solution will be dramatically successful, because the causal factors in the situation are numerous, enigmatic, and, as we have said so many times before, part and parcel of the way we live.

Specific Problem Areas

Not everyone by any means sees the problem as holistically as the above paragraphs have tried to present it. There is a pronounced tendency in our society to see problems, here as elsewhere, in more atomistic purview. This is evidenced by the way in which many people, even some experts, completely separate in classification and treatment such closely linked problems as divorce, the role of women, sexual morality, and the like. It is thus more as a bow to convention than as professional conviction, that we shall treat these separately in the following pages. To do so is often to distort reality seriously. In numerous instances the divorce problem, improper marriage education, the role of women, and morality are all tied together in an inextricable complex which any careful analysis will usually reveal as a close interrelationship. Nonetheless, there may be some merit in a separate focus, provided we recall the larger interrelationships as we proceed.

Monogamy and Rising Divorce

"Whomsoever God hath joined together let no man put asunder," is a familiar line from a standard marriage ceremony. It expresses the value of lasting monogamy. It carries the sanction of the Divine Being and admonishes the mortals to stay married. But let us look at the facts. Currently one marriage out of each four that are contracted ends in divorce. This is somewhat lower than the postwar peak, often quoted, at which time nearer to one out of three marriages resulted in divorce. Few would deny, however, that this rate is "too high."

The folk wisdom that we have inherited from an early age interprets the high divorce rate as simply a reflection of the defects of character and intelligence of the parties to the broken marriages. We are told that if marriage were more difficult to enter into, if people "thought twice," if people "observed the God-given codes," if mates were more "patient" and "less selfish," then the divorce rate would shrink. Young people are currently being reminded that in the good old days when people "took their marriage vows more seriously" divorce was almost nonexistent, the implication being very clear that present divorce rates are high because people do not take their vows seriously. No one knows, of course, whether the seriousness with which people regard their marriage vows is important or unimportant in the high rate of marriage failure, or for that matter whether it is even true that people regard their vows as any less binding than they formerly did.

Less moralistic interpreters see the problem of marriage instability in the nature of modern marriage rather than in terms of individual character. Modern life is different in its tempo, its objectives, and its needs. Marriage is not a thing apart from the general life, and thus it reflects the insecurities and tensions and rapid change of the whole society. Problems of inadequate income, poor mental health, impaired physical health, ideological difference, race, class, and occupational maladjustment all converge and leave their impact upon the families of the people upon whom the problems impinge. Wars and depressions set forces in motion that remake the family as surely as they remake governments. The impact of social change and problems is complicated further by the deep emotional and sentimental ties that people have toward marriage—ties which are rooted both in the religious heritage and in secular custom. Thus many people expect satisfactions that marriage does not, and possibly cannot, bring. Much strain is brought upon marriage also by unrealistic expectations and naïve underestimation of problems. Love, however important, is not enough to marry on, for example, and even the love that promises great security may be so misunderstood that it becomes a problem itself. All these and other factors are involved, irrespective of the moral integrity of the persons involved; the institution itself imposes the strain upon the person. This is not to imply that character is not important to successful marriage; the point is that character is not enough. Moreover, the forces that encroach upon the person frequently destroy in time the faithful adherence of many to high ideals.

Here we have a basic value clash with respect to the interpretation of the cardinal social fact that a smaller and smaller proportion of the people who get married stay married. One school of thought sees the causes largely in defects of character and other personal traits; the other school sees the chief source as a general societal one, tied up inextricably with the problems and changes of the entire society. There is probably validity to both views of the matter, but it seems certain that more attention must be given to the societal forces that shape the over-all pattern of living.

The Role of Women

Traditionally women have been homemakers and childbearers. They have largely fulfilled the function of perpetuating the race, finding no doubt much happiness in that role. But now women are said to have become "emancipated," by which is usually meant that they are free to substitute out-of-home occupations for part or all of their working time.

Today about one out of four married women take advantage of this freedom, and, for the first time in our history, there are actually more married than single women in the labor force. And many married women who pass up the opportunity for out-of-home work say that they have done so with much regret, indecision, and ambivalence. If a woman is happier with a career than with the traditional role of mother of a large family, then, say some, why should she not do so? Meanwhile other observers are extremely critical of her for shirking her duties, for mimicking men, and for denying their birthright to her unborn children. Actually the society has not made up its mind as to what the functions of the women should be, not even to the extent of granting to the individual woman the democratic right to make up her mind which way she wants to handle her life.

Sexual Morality

At one time in our history society was fairly well in agreement regarding the rightness and wrongness of sexual intercourse outside of marriage. All such behavior was "taboo" and that was that. Transgressors of the rigid code were found, to be sure, but they were apparently few, and from all reports they were dealt with swiftly and severely.

Today, from all indications, society cannot make up its mind on numerous matters of sexual morality. Almost anyone who has grown up in our society recognizes that the "underlying theme" of our sexual code is to relegate sexual intercourse to marriage and marriage alone. Premarital chastity is fostered as an ideal, and well entrenched in our stated ideals is the idea that it is somehow even more important that a married person engage in sexual relations with no one other than his or her spouse. At the same time, any American who reads his newspaper or merely listens to those around him knows full well that our stated sex codes are rather openly violated. He knows too, that there is a fairly widespread acceptance of the idea that the sexual code is open to discussion and interpretation.

What has emerged, then, is a rather confused morality. The individual is frequently forced to decide many issues for himself, and many find the task anything but easy. The moralistic restraints of the past no longer seem to "square" with his observations, and the older additional restraints of fear of "conception, infection, and detection" do not seem to carry the force that once they did. And even the "modern" emphasis on premarital chastity as a means of helping to assure a happy marriage is dismissed by some as but a more sophisticated kind of threat dressed up in subtle psychological garb.

A large part of the difficulty with the present state of our sexual morality, then, seems to be the divergence between societal ideals and tolerated practices and the general lack of consensus on the morality of premarital and extramarital sexual conduct. Precise facts are hard to get, but what samples and inferences we have seem to show that a wide variety of standards of conduct are currently being followed by substantial numbers of American people. Confusion, indecision, regret, guilt, deception, and disillusionment with both self and others are very common in this confused state of affairs. It is not difficult to find people—even among the philosophers—who will support almost any morality, but the difficulty is that a dozen other moralities which are inconsistent are sanctioned too.

Societal Frustrations

Even after one has decided upon what values he thinks the family ought to foster for him, he frequently finds that serious problems are still faced because of the nature of the society. He may, for example, think that early marriage and large families are good—but if he cannot get a house to live in and cannot secure an income large enough to support even a moderate-sized family, his good judgment in following the ways of his fathers can bring him little but disappointment. If a war interrupts his education for five years, then he must face the fact that he is five years retarded in his plan for the realization of marriage and family living. These five years can be troublesome years morally, physically, if not even spiritually.

Not only a person's personal virtues but the "high standards" of the society may also frustrate him. For example, America is notorious for its high standard of living. Color advertisements, attractive show windows, and his more opulent friends may stimulate in him a burning desire to participate in the high standard, but other societal realities such as the wage scale in his occupation or his own ability level or his poor fortune may prevent the high standard of living from being anything more than a tantalizing fantasy to him.

There are, of course, other sources of problems in the area of sex, marriage, and the family than those which we have treated, but we have discussed the major ones. In this treatment, emphasis has been placed upon the great diversity of value judgment among the various cultures in our society. We do not know precisely how much of the appalling amount of maladjustment and unhappiness in marriage stems from societal or how much from individual confusion. Very probably the dichotomy of individual and social is a very poor one, since the forces in the individual get there through social experience. Either way one looks at the matter, however, he is impressed with the sharp contrast in judgment concerning almost every objectively describable condition of the family in America. If the pessimists are right that this is a "lost generation," it is not difficult to see how a person could become lost in this morass of value confusion.

PROPOSALS FOR TREATING THE PROBLEMS OF SEX, MARRIAGE, AND THE FAMILY

Legislative Approach

Some persons and groups believe that the problems that we have been discussing can be solved by changes in the laws pertaining to marriage and family life. Others believe that the forces creating these problems are inherent in the social system, and that changes in law will have very little to do with the solution of them or may even make the problem conditions much worse than they now are. Meanwhile, there is a third, somewhat middle-of-the-road, school of thought that takes the position that there are certain legal approaches to the problems of marriage and family life which might assist at least some of the people to make better adjustments more of the time than is now the case.

LIMITATIONS. From the objective point of view the weight of accumulated evidence tends to support the somewhat middle-of-the-road position. Our experience with legislative reform in the field of the family indicates that there are serious limitations upon what can be accomplished by the passing of laws, by prohibiting this or that practice, or requiring that something be done under penalty of legal punishment. "You cannot legislate morality" is an adage in which there is considerable scientific truth. It means that even though it is possible to pass laws regulating the intimate conduct of people, it often is difficult, if not impossible, to enforce the laws if the people are not in sympathy. For example, we have laws on the statute books in most American states making it a felony for unmarried persons to indulge in sexual intercourse. It is common knowledge that such laws are frequently and flagrantly violated. Prosecutions of such offenses are almost nonexistent for adults, even though the law enforcement officers have knowledge of the violations. Numerous states grant divorces for adultery, but in cases where the accused has been found guilty of adultery, or where he admits his guilt, he is not then prosecuted for the felony of "fornication," "illegal cohabitation," or however it is termed in the laws of the state in question. Similarly, in cases of admitted or proved illegal paternity (bastardy), the couple is practically never prosecuted for the legal offense of illicit sex relations as a result of which the illegitimate child is conceived. Legal action is almost always limited to determining the correct paternity and the amount of the man's financial liability for the support of the child.

Of a somewhat different nature are the subterfuges that occur when persons desire strongly to behave in ways contrary to the provisions of law. This occurs thousands of times each year in almost every state in the union with respect to divorce. The laws stipulate that divorces may be granted when certain conditions, such as adultery, nonsupport, or cruelty have occurred. The injured party may then petition the court to dissolve the marriage, and, if the charges are sustained by the evidence, the court has no recourse but to grant the divorce. It frequently occurs, however, that couples desire divorce simply because they are mismated, no longer "in love," or have incompatible personalities. In other words, they desire divorce but have committed none of the overt acts for which divorces are granted in their state. This leaves the couple to choose from at least three legal subterfuges for securing the divorce anyway. (1) If they have the money, they may migrate to another state and establish a fictional, though technical, residence and secure the divorce there. (2) One mate may charge the other with such legal offense as desertion, even though it has not occurred, and the mate, in order to expedite the divorce, will offer no defense, thus implying his guilt of an act that he never committed. (3) After the couple decide they want a divorce, and it is impossible for financial or other reasons to go to an "easy" state, one or the other may deliberately perform some act such as adultery, for which reason, then, the court grants the other mate a divorce. The latter two procedures constitute, of course, "collusion," and the laws of most states require that if collusion exists the case should be dismissed by the court. Most divorce court judges realize that collusion, even perjury, exists in the majority of cases that they hear, but realize that it is practically futile to dismiss the case, because in most instances it will be brought up again under another pretext.

ROLE OF LEGAL REFORM. In numerous other ways it could be shown that prohibitory laws, even with strict enforcement, are of little value so long as they do not have the support of the people whose behavior they are intended to regulate. The foregoing is not intended to deny, however, that laws do have their place in the treatment of family problems. Legal reforms do have a legitimate role to play. What is that role? And what guiding principles exist for discharging the legal role? The following suggestions have been repeatedly offered as valid criteria.

1. Marriage and family laws should be democratically based—that is, they should embody the real wishes (values) of the majority of the

people. Many existing laws embody the prejudices of some crusading minority who long ago pressured a legislature into enacting legislation that, whatever its virtues at that time, does not now have the respect or support of the majority of the people. The laws centering around marriage, divorce, contraception, and other phases of family life are certainly in need of reexamination in the light of present needs and present wishes of the majority of the people.

2. The enforcement of democratically derived laws should be consistent and as completely effective as possible. Strict law enforcement is essential if any law is to accomplish its purpose. If we are to have laws, for example, that require that no persons under twenty years of age can legally marry, then there should be diligent enforcement at the time of granting licenses so that age falsifications are held to a minimum.

3. Laws should be uniform, or as nearly so as possible. The United States is notoriously vulnerable to criticism in this respect. Within continental United States there are fifty separate jurisdictions with fifty separate codes of marriage, divorce, and related laws. One student of the problem points out that

> the marital status of a man may change with kaleidoscopic swiftness as he crosses state borders. A present instance is found in three adjoining states; the same man by merely traveling across these states may be a legally married man, a single man, and a bigamist in turn, all within a distance of 15 miles.[1]

Startling as these revelations may be, they constitute only a beginning. Until recently the state of South Carolina did not allow divorce for any reason whatsoever. Among the various states divorce may be obtained for reasons that vary in number from one to twenty![2] Certainly if discrepancies such as these exist, they can contribute only to the cynical conclusion that laws cannot be very rational or important anyway, else they would have to be more consistent.

Some people believe that the solution to the problem of uniformity lies in a federal marriage and divorce law. While such a law would eliminate the confusion caused by the widely differing state laws and the possibilities of law evasion by removal from one state to another, it would create numerous difficulties. In the first place, if Congress did pass such a

---

[1] By permission from Ray E. Baber, *Marriage and the Family,* p. 75. Copyright 1953 by McGraw-Hill Book Company.

[2] In New York state, for example, divorce can be granted only for adultery. In Arizona a divorce can be secured for any of the following reasons: adultery, cruelty, desertion, alcoholism, felony conviction, felony before marriage, neglect to provide, pregnancy at marriage, bigamy, separation, indignities, drug addiction, violence, fraudulent contract, crime against nature, husband a vagrant, infamous crime, loathsome disease, or relationship within prohibited degree.

law—which is very doubtful—it well might be declared unconstitutional by the Supreme Court of the United States on the grounds that authority over marriage and divorce has not been delegated to the federal government by the several states. Secondly, if Congress did pass a uniform marriage and divorce law that was upheld by the Supreme Court, the law would constitute "an artificial *legal* uniformity of practice where there is no natural *social* uniformity of thought and need." [3] In other words, how should the uniform divorce law be written? Should it reflect the philosophy of New York, where adultery is the only recognized reason for divorce, or of Arizona where the law recognizes some nineteen different grounds? How could we possibly be equally fair to the wishes of people of varying viewpoint? To be sure it is probable that the thinking of the rank and file of people of New York and Arizona is not as dissimilar as one might assume from an examination of the laws of these two states, but nevertheless there are important regional differences in viewpoint. It is thus quite possible that a uniform marriage and divorce law "might increase direct violation, for a law is frequently unenforceable in sections where the prevailing sentiment is strongly against it. The clash would engender bitterness and strife." [4]

Thus, while we recognize the desirability of legal uniformity, we must also recognize the practical difficulties involved in achieving it, especially in the short run. It seems that we must work toward it as an ideal, striving to get individual states whose laws are the extremes to make such modifications as will gradually bring them more in line not only with the thinking of their own people but of their neighboring states as well.

4. Legal machinery should become less formal. Perhaps the best constructive example is provided by the juvenile courts and by the courts of domestic relations in some (too few) cities. Instead of handling domestic relation matters in the forbidding formality of the traditional courtroom with judge, jury, and contentious lawyers, and with galleries filled with curious persons who have no legitimate interest in the case, juvenile and some domestic relations courts are informal. There is a more or less diligent search for solutions that will be equitable rather than merely legal, and the judge has considerable discretionary power. He surrounds himself with technical experts on human behavior, such as psychiatrists and sociologists, who help him to arrive at the kind of decision that will best meet the needs of the persons before him. There is great need for an individualizing of judicial practice so that the law may assist people to work out humane and sound solutions of their marital problems based upon their own peculiar needs and circumstances. We must, it is argued, get away from the idea that a person should have endured a certain uniform accumulation of

[3] Baber, *op. cit.,* p. 76.
[4] *Ibid.*

humiliations and pain before he can secure respite from an intolerable marriage; we must emancipate ourselves from the notion that courts are primarily punitive agencies with jurisdiction over shameful wrongdoers. Gradually we have learned that through the courts adults and children may receive assistance in solving their problems, provided that the courts have legal freedom to do what is needed, and are staffed by people who can recognize human needs and who know how to meet them. We have only begun to make this transition, but the trend is clearly apparent.

Even at best, however, the legal approach leaves the more crucial phase of marriage problems largely untouched. Laws do not make couples incompatible, courts usually do not abuse children, and law-enforcement officers do not cause illicit sex conduct. At best the laws and law-enforcement systems can only serve as regulatory agencies, as umpires, so to speak, of the great enigma. For a more fundamental treatment of solutions that strike deeper at the root of marriage-related problems, we must turn to another approach.

Mental Hygiene Approaches

We now know, through the use of reliable research procedures, that there is much mental-emotional maladjustment among so-called normal or near-normal people. And, more important for the present discussion, we now have considerable evidence to show that family life has great influence upon mental-emotional health. It would be as accurate, of course, to say that the mental-emotional health of the persons involved has a great deal to do with family life. In other words, persons whose mental hygiene is poor introduce a serious strain on their personal relationships in marriage, with the result that there is much unhappiness and maladjustment and, in many cases, estrangement or divorce. On the other hand, poor mental health grows out of family and especially childhood unhappiness. Here, then, is the vicious circle: Unhappy families breed maladjusted children; maladjusted children grow up to make unhappy marriages. This is, of course, the general principle—that is, the above statement is true in terms of probabilities in the great majority of cases but may be incorrect so far as some specific case is concerned. Since our purpose in this book is to discuss social problems in the aggregate, we must be concerned primarily with the propositions that are true in general.

How, then, can we break into the vicious circle of personal-marital maladjustment? It is believed by most specialists in mental hygiene (psychologists, sociologists, psychiatrists, and others) that it is possible, though not easy, to break into the circle at several crucial points. (1) It is possible to some extent to teach parents, even though they themselves are not entirely well adjusted, enough about practical mental hygiene so that their children will grow up without too serious mental maladjustments. In other words, the amount or degree of maladjustment and unhappiness may be reduced, even though not entirely eliminated, in this way. (2) There is some reason to believe that the proper kind of education in preparation for marriage may have a beneficial effect in increasing the marital adjustment of the marriage partners, thus facilitating their happiness and contributing to the better adjustment of their children. (3) Through the treatment of individual cases by marriage counselors and other clinicians, some degree of improvement in personal adjustment can often be worked out.

MARRIAGE EDUCATION. Most colleges and universities now offer some kind of instruction designed to prepare the student for successful marriage and family living. The content of such education varies with the amount and kind of the teacher's professional training, the instructor's freedom to handle such "touchy" questions as sex and contraception, and the amount of time devoted to the course. A few high schools today offer some form of premarriage instruction, and the movement seems to be gaining momentum. YMCAs and YWCAs in some cities give instruction to young men and women whose formal education stopped before college. Likewise, some churches sponsor courses, study groups, and lectures in preparation for marriage.

The effectiveness, if not the very honesty, of these attempts is exceedingly irregular. Probably the chief handicap is a lack of sufficiently trained personnel to serve as teachers, lecturers, and discussion leaders. There is a strong tendency to use "safe" persons—that is, persons who will take sufficiently innocuous positions on most vital issues so that no one will be offended—and the result is that nothing very vital is taught. There is also a tendency to rely too much upon the common-sense qualifications of a teacher or discussion leader instead of insisting upon training in the sciences of human behavior. Eventually we must get rid of the notion that a man who has "set a good example to the community" by avoiding divorce or a woman whose children have escaped suspicion of delinquency can necessarily contribute wise counsel to a group of people seeking guidance in marriage. These achievements no more qualify a person to serve as a marriage authority than a lifetime of good health qualifies a man to serve as a physician. Until this is recognized, many of the people who try to get marriage education from so-called marriage courses will continue to receive the unprofessional instruction which is all too prevalent today.

A second limitation on marriage education, of course, is public apathy and public opposition. In almost every community there are a few powerful persons and minority groups who conceive as their righteous role the prevention of the young from receiving realistic information which might conceivably help to make their marriages more stable and happy. Of course this is not the avowed objective of these "purists." They usually contend that their real motives are to guard the "eternal moralities" and give other high-sounding and sometimes sincere purposes. But their effect is still unfortunate, since they accomplish the dubious purpose of closing the doors of scientific enlightenment to the people who need it most. It seems most unfortunate that the studies which our society makes through costly and time-consuming research are so often withheld from the people who could use them to make their own lives more happy and their children better-adjusted human beings. Opposition of this sort is fortunately diminishing in most parts of the United States but is still a serious deterrent in many communities.

PARENT EDUCATION. Most of the principles we have discussed in connection with marriage education apply also to parent education. The need is great. There is growing interest and diminishing community resistance. The serious bottlenecks are the lack of trained personnel and a preoccupation on the part of parents with quick and easy solutions to daily problems instead of with a real and vital concern for the long-run mental health needs of children. Courses are varied in content; probably also in effectiveness. Many of the sources of trouble in the adjustment of children are such that they cannot readily be controlled by parents, however well informed. In spite of all of these handicaps and limitations, the parent education movement is spreading, and there is some basis for the hope that it may result in an improvement in the mental-emotional health of some children at least.

MARRIAGE COUNSELING. Group education, no matter how thorough, cannot do the entire job for everyone. Individuals, pairs, and families also require special attention from time to time when their marital-adjustment problems become too difficult to handle by their own ingenuity. Often they need professional assistance to find what the problems are. This need has given rise to an emerging profession, known variously as marriage counseling, domestic relation consultation, family guidance, and the like.

Marriage counseling shows great promise but also has its limitations. First, there is an insufficient number of trained persons to serve as counselors. Second, the public, generally speaking, does not know when to consult a marriage counselor and how to distinguish a qualified counselor from a quack. The present-day problems of the marriage-counseling profession are very much like the problems of the medical profession seventy years ago. There is reason to believe, however, that the marriage-counseling profession will improve its qualifications and that the public will soon better understand what the values and limitations of marriage counseling are. The American Association of Marriage Counselors is working on both problems at present, and the outlook is somewhat hopeful.

Other Proposals

There are, of course, other value positions with respect to the conservation of the family. These cover a wide range. There are various movements to "strengthen the economic foundations" of the family by such diverse procedures as consumer cooperatives and efforts to secure more substantial income tax deductions for families with more children. Other reformers emphasize the need for a "return to religion." Still others advocate such radical departures from our traditions as free love and trial marriage. It will be obvious, even to the casual student, that such sweeping proposals are likely to encounter rabid opposition and to present such practical limitations that they hardly warrant lengthy attention in a book as general in scope as this one.

CONCLUSION

The societal roots of most family problems grow out of the inconsistencies between our older family traditions which were based upon rural life, patriarchal rule, and the conception of marriage as sacred, on the one hand, and the present milieu which is based upon urbanization, the democratic ideology, and a predominantly secular conception of life, on the other hand. As we have seen in so many areas of social problems, much of the difficulty stems from our attempts to maintain values based on a past social system and to use them in a modern system which is basically different.

We have discussed the main proposed attacks on the problems of sex, marriage, and the family under two captions: the legislative approach and the mental hygiene approach. The legislative approach, in spite of its serious limitations, appears to have some possibilities of limited scope and value. So long as forthcoming laws are democratically based, consistently enforced, reasonably uniform, and their application individualized, at least some amelioration of some of these problems may be anticipated.

Our major emphasis, however, has been upon proposals to improve persons' mental hygiene. This seems justified because of the close connection between the emotional adjustment of the person and his ability to function in the various roles which sex, marriage, and family norms require of him. We have examined the cycle of mental ill health as a basic factor in family breakdown and family breakdown as the basic factor in mental ill health, and have pointed out that this cycle is vulnerable to some measure of control through at least three channels: marriage education, parent education, and marriage counseling. We have assayed the strengths and weaknesses of each of these approaches. Together they should at least ameliorate some of the social problems of sex, marriage, and family and might possibly eliminate them.

SUGGESTED READINGS

BERNARD, JESSIE, *Remarriage: A Study of Marriage*. New York, Holt, Rinehart and Winston, Inc., 1956.

CUBER, JOHN F. and PEGGY B. HARROFF, "The More Total View: Relationships Among Men and Women of the Upper Middle Class," *Marriage and Family Living*, XXV:2 (May 1963).

GOODE, WILLIAM J., *After Divorce*. New York, The Macmillan Company, 1956.

KENKEL, WILLIAM F., *The Family in Perspective*. New York, Appleton-Century-Crofts, 1960.

KINSEY, ALFRED C., *et al., Sexual Behavior in the Human Male*. Philadelphia, W. B. Saunders Company, 1948.

KINSLEY, ALFRED C., *et al., Sexual Behavior in the Human Female*. Philadedphia, W. B. Saunders Company, 1953.

REISS, IRA L., *Premarital Sexual Standards in America: A Sociological Investigation of the Relative Social and Cultural Integration of American Sexual Standards*. New York, The Macmillan Company, 1960.

SPIRO, MELFORD E., with AUDREY G. SPIRO, *Children of the Kibbutz*. Cambridge, Mass., Harvard University Press, 1958.

EDUCATION 9

Generally speaking Americans are proud of their system of mass education and profess great faith in its eventual contribution to the evolution of a better social world. In view of this general consensus regarding its efficacy and our high utilization of it, it may seem unusual to find "education" included in a discussion of social *problems*. But there are some strong value conflicts in this area. Most of the societal conflicts tend to center not around whether education itself is good or bad but rather around the *nature of education* and the *kinds of teaching that are desirable*.

There is, to be sure, considerable belief that many American communities are penurious in their expenditures for education and that our loudly voiced respect for education is not very effectively translated into better school buildings, adequate salaries for teachers, and support of newer educational programs which now are known to be good but somewhat more costly than traditional ones. Comparative statistics have from time to time been compiled to show that our "gigantic educational structure" is not as imposing as it might at first seem to be. One statistician has calculated that the nation spends more money per year for liquor than it does for education. Others have made similar startling comparisons. It has been pointed out that our expenditures for education are shamefully low; not only do other nations exceed us in educational outlay but we, a wealthy nation, could well afford to support education more liberally than we actually do. Nevertheless, as compared to the other nations of the world, the American educational system now touches more people for a longer period of time than any other comparable system.

154

WHO CONTROLS THE SCHOOLS?

We hear much about the allegedly "free" character of American schools. The student learns in studying American history how the traditions of education were formed during the gradual emancipation of our schools from church and state domination. All too often the incorrect implication is drawn that American education is entirely free, in the sense that no one except the teaching profession dictates what shall be taught or tries to use the school as a propagandizing agency. The truth is, of course, to the contrary.

Pressure Groups

Educational administrators are constantly harassed by this group or that which wishes to use the schools for the purpose of indoctrinating children in the community with some point of view regarded as desirable. In Chicago, for example, during "Big Bill" Thompson's regime in the twenties, political pressure was brought upon the schools to teach American history in such a way as to perpetuate what historians had demonstrated were untruths about our history. Pressure has from time to time been brought to bear by "conservative interests" against the use of certain textbooks. Accusations vary in intensity from the outright charge that the books "strive to inculcate communistic attitudes in children" to the more moderate charges that the books advocate social change of which the complainants disapprove. Controversies over religious and moral questions are likewise numerous. One pressure group attempts to force the schools to disseminate propaganda against consumption of liquor and tobacco; another is devoted to putting pressure upon the schools so that Bible reading may become a required part of the curriculum; a third is currently attempting to encourage the school to give instruction on problems of marriage, while still another group bitterly opposes such educational training for high school students.

For What Does the School Exist?

The conflicting demands of these several groups are no mere quibbles over technique or course content: they are fundamental issues vitally affecting the very nature of education itself. The significant question which all of these demands repeatedly pose is: *Should the educational system of the society be the creature or agent of pressure groups or should it be a semiautonomous part of society, free to determine its policies on the basis of the professional judgments of teachers and administrators?* In short, there is reason to doubt whether Americans mean what they say when they praise the "freedom" of American education, for so many of them are members of pressure groups that spend considerable time and money trying to induce the schools *not* to be free and impartial.

Domination of Schools and
the Democratic Process

It should not be inferred that the task of maintaining a free school system is an easy one. The problem of domination by extraeducational "interests" inheres in the nature of the American system. If the schools are to be run "democratically," then they ought presumably to implement the wishes of the people. Hence, if the people wish to use their own schools as indoctrinating agencies, it is difficult to rationalize opposing their exercise of democratic rights. On the other hand, it is very doubtful whether the various pressure groups that perennially try to use the schools as indoctrinating agencies represent any significant portion of the total population; on the contrary, they are relatively small but powerfully organized special-interest groups with purposes that are difficult to justify as "in the interest of the public welfare." To be sure, attempts are usually made to "sell" pressure-group sponsored ideas to the public in the name of "Americanism," "character formation" or "proper respect for God," but closer examination usually reveals that the programs can be reduced to the simple terms of indoctrination in the mundane cause that the sponsoring group represents. This simply shows that the ideals of objectivity, openmindedness, and fair play that the schools have tried to observe on social issues are difficult to maintain in the practical situation.

There are even those persons who contend that it is a mistake for the school system to be neutral on social issues, that the teacher should throw the weight of his prestige and effort in one direction or another for the purpose of guiding the attitudes and ideas of the future citizens of the nation. Such a point of view is tantamount to saying that the school is a creature of the power groups of a society and that it exists as the propaganda agency for such groups.

Are the Schools "Communist Dominated"?

While it may not be as common a complaint as some others, probably the most serious charge against modern educators is that they are purposefully attempting to condition their students for life in a collectivistic type of society. The attacks range all the way from rather loose talk about "Socialistic leanings" of school teachers to the out-and-out charge that the schools are "Communist dominated." Generally speaking, the more specific the charge of this nature, the easier it is to demonstrate its utter falsity. It is simply a matter of record, for example, that very, very few teachers, at all levels, have been found to be members of the Communist party. Two Senate investigating committees, as a matter of fact, were able to discover only a handful of college instructors (42, to be exact, or less than three-hundredths of 1 percent of all college professors and instructors) who declined to affirm that they were not members of the Communist party.[1] The bulk of these, it appears, were motivated in their refusals to comment by reasons other than their guilt of subversion. The National Education Association, the professional society of elementary and secondary school teachers, has taken a strong stand on communism. Members of the Communist party are barred from membership in the NEA, and the organization has passed a resolution that members of the Communist party should not be allowed to teach in public schools. But still the allegations persist, and emotionally charged pamphlets filled with unsubstantiated generalizations continue to make their appearance. For example, one such pamphlet titled, "How Red is the Little Red School House?" [2] pictured on its cover a foreign soldier injecting a needle labeled Organized Communist Propaganda into the little red school house. Others, by innuendo, suggestion, or downright accusation, link any new idea with political radicalism, political radicalism, in turn, with socialism, and socialism with totalitarian communism, to "prove" that a teacher with an up-to-date educational outlook is therefore indoctrinating along Communistic lines!

It is probably little comfort to educators to realize that attacks directed at them are no recent matter. We can go back at least as far as 399 B.C. when the courts found the Athenian teacher, Socrates, guilty of corrupting the youth of his day. And, in a little different framework, another teacher of admittedly "radical" ideas was rewarded with crucifixion.

What Is the Purpose of Education?

There is a basic theoretical issue of educational philosophy that is implicit in the perennial squabbles over control of the policies of educational institutions. Stated in somewhat extreme form, the present value judgments seem to embody three distinct conceptions:

(1) That education should be concerned solely with the *indoctrination of the young into the culture of the group* that controls the educational system—that is, that the schools should teach each new generation to be

---

[1] Reported in an analysis of the hearings of the House of Representatives Committee on Un-American Activities and the Senate Sub-Committee on Internal Security in *Christian Science Monitor* (July 21, 1953).

[2] Published by Employers Association of Chicago, Chicago, Ill.

precisely like its predecessor in as many ways as possible. This we may call the "function of indoctrination."

(2) That the function of education is not merely to perpetuate the existing culture without bias, but to *evaluate* it—that is, to analyze it, to raise questions concerning the relative worth of things, and to *consider various proposals for the perpetuation or modification of the society* in which the students lives (more or less as we are doing in this book).

(3) That it is the function of education to *direct social change* along lines that appear to be desirable and in the interest of public welfare—that is, the schools should take the initiative in remaking society by shaping the attitudes and skills of children so as to facilitate an emerging but different society. This, too, is a type of indoctrination, but it is a dynamic rather than a static orientation. It warrants the term indoctrination, however, because the emphasis is placed upon teaching people what they ought to think, rather than simply training them to be critical, analytical, and open-minded about social issues.

If one examines carefully his own conception of education, he will probably find that he holds in some measure with all three of these somewhat distinct philosophies. He will probably maintain the school's right to teach reading, writing, and arithmetic, the social graces, and a respect for American traditions and culture. To this extent, then, he wants the schools to indoctrinate with the time-honored ways of thought and action which we have mentioned. But, like most people, he will also claim to desire that children be taught "to think," to analyze new ideas and learn to be critical, to learn not to accept blindly the accumulated errors of the past as if they represented eternal verities. Finally, he will probably doubt that it is possible for the world to remain changeless, will want his children prepared to live in the kind of future world that they are likely to encounter, because he wishes them to adapt as painlessly as possible to the requirements of new times.

So long as we state educational philosophy in such general terms as the above, not much controversy occurs. But when we specifically implement these broad principles, it is easy for controversies to ensue. Imagine the business-class parent who wants his child to "think clearly on social issues" when his son announces during the Christmas holiday that as a result of his economics studies, he is sympathetic with the cause of labor and has decided to become a union organizer. Had Junior decided to be a corporation lawyer as a result of "viewing all sides of the problem," Father might very well be pleased with the "liberalism" of his son's college. This not wholly hypothetical anecdote calls attention to the fact that differences in social philosophy and vested interests tend naturally to be carried over into one's educational philosophy, at least for some people in this society at this time.

CONTEMPORARY ISSUES IN AMERICAN EDUCATION

Ever since Russia launched its first successful space satellite, Sputnik, American education has been the focus of an inordinate amount of attention. While a few informed people have known for a long time that the Russian educational system has made great strides in certain aspects of education, namely science, mathematics, and engineering, the dramatic event of Sputnik opened the eyes of many to the fact that smug assumptions concerning the supremacy of American education were due for a reappraisal. Since that time (1958) American educational institutions have been the object of a great deal of criticism, some careful, responsible, and factually based, and some careless, irresponsible, and based on practically no evidence at all. In other words, American education has assumed the status of a generally acknowledged "social problem."

In terms of our already familiar frame of reference, this means that there is now a debate and to some extent practical political struggle concerning the reevaluation and reorganization of American education on all levels. To some extent old issues and value disagreements continue to rage, and such questions as whether education should be primarily "practical" or more "theoretical," and the extent to which laymen's opinion ought to enter into the determination of professional practices, remain issues. But the debate has gone far beyond the older questions. New questions, fresh proposals, and some basic rethinking have occurred. Meanwhile staunch defenders of the status quo and of the older traditions have been vocal too. Thus, the debate centers around the three familiar conflicts.

(1) Is there a problem, or rather problems, in our educational practices? Is it safe to say that prevailing opinion is in agreement, that all is not well and that something or other in the way of change is in order?

(2) *Can* anything be done about it? Again there seems to be agreement that whatever the problems are, they are amenable to treatment, by someone or other, in some way or other.

(3) What, specifically, *ought* to be done? Here the counsel is so varied, so numerous, that a near bedlam of voices is heard. It is the purpose of the following paragraphs to sort out some of the specific problems identified and to describe some of the solutions which have been offered to correct them. Few, if any, of these problems or solutions have reached the state, so far as can be determined, of clear majority support, yet most of the

minority evaluations are large enough, well enough organized, and force-fully enough presented to have brought about some modifications of 1950 modes of operation.

Reaffirmation of the Importance
of "Content" [3]

Under the impetus of a somewhat modified "progressive education" philosophy, apparent since the 1930s, it is alleged that a marked deprecia-tion of the importance of academic mastery of basic subjects has occurred. Standard, traditional subjects, like mathematics, science, and basic Eng-lish, have been played down, while new emphases, as on automobile driv-ing, social adjustment, and music appreciation, have been placed. The Uni-versity of Chicago's President Robert Maynard Hutchins once characterized American public schools as "one gigantic playpen," and Inez Robb, na-tionally syndicated columnist, added her bit about "the philosophy of the sandbox" which had taken over American education. These colorful epithets may have been exaggerated, but a large and responsible opinion maintains that they have not been wholly wrong. Books like Rudolf Flesch's *Why Can't Johnny Read?* became best sellers, and Admiral Rickover has sky-rocketed into a "national authority" on contemporary American education. Doubtless some of the criticism has been overstated, but the judgment is general that in the pursuit of such laudable efforts at creating "well-adjusted" and "well-rounded" personalities and making education a thor-oughly pleasant activity, we have reached the point where we do not educate very much.

It is difficult to determine how much influence the barrage of criticism has had. Selected cases can be marshaled to demonstrate that particular schools have reworked their curriculums, raised their standards, and seem in general to mean business about toughening up the educational experience of their students. There is some evidence from testing programs, where com-parable measures have been used over a period of ten years or so, that high school students' basic literacy and basic scientific and mathematics knowl-edge has been somewhat improved. There is now a countervailing criticism to the effect that schools and colleges have reacted too selectively to the criticism, that is, that they have envisaged the problem as primarily one of improving the teaching of science and mathematics and have tended to ig-nore comparably glaring deficiencies in the quality of education in the social sciences and the humanities. A strong case has been made by some critics for the fact that however shocking may be the scientific and mathematical

[3] The following several pages constitute a restatement and paraphrased summary of a similar discussion by the senior author in his *Sociology: A Synopsis of Principles,* 5th ed., chap. 28.

inadequacies of present-day students, their basic illiteracy in the broader purposes of education may be far more ominous for their own competency and the national security in the long run.

To isolate a problem is one thing; to solve it may be quite another. There seems to be far less unanimity concerning the implementation of programs to correct content weaknesses in education than in the identification of the weakness itself. Hard realists, both among professional educators and among the informed citizenry, insist that we have not made as much progress as we seem to have. Part of the difficulty, for example, grows out of the personal and professional inadequacies of large numbers of experienced teachers whose personal and educational roots go back to an earlier, more lackadaisical period. These, regardless of efforts by curriculum administrators, can only teach what they know and by ways to which they are already habituated. Until appreciable numbers of freshly selected and newly trained teachers join the ranks of the teaching staffs, it may be naïve to expect marked improvement in the content competency of the graduates.

The Need for a New "Discipline"

It is charged that schools have failed to require enough and *hard enough* work, especially for the superior students. This has had the twin effects, it is claimed, of inculcating bad work habits and being satisfied with much too minimal levels of accomplishment. Students are said never to have really learned the importance of hard work and the necessity for working under unpleasant circumstances in order to achieve acceptance. The net effect, it is claimed, is to ill prepare the student both for his maximal achievement and for his social responsibility. This does not mean that students do not currently work, and even sometimes work hard; the point is that they chiefly work for extrinsic rewards—grades, eligibility for athletic teams or other extracurricular activities, or to maintain their allowances from parents. What is lacking, it is charged, is any deep, internalized concept of the importance of the learning process per se, or commitment to personal competency and mastery of a field. These intrinsic rewards, it is claimed, are largely unknown to all but a few students. The status system of the school, and frequently of the teachers too, makes little provision for appreciating and rewarding this kind of excellence.

Accent on "Fads and Frills"

For several decades some educational theorists have stressed the objective of "well-rounded personality." It was insisted that the personality got "rounded" not by intellectual accomplishment but by participation in extracurricular activities, physical education programs, and just about everything except book learning. On balance, it would seem that the original idea was a good one, but that it had become perverted to the point where parents as well as students came to think of high school chiefly as an institution for the development of drum majorettes and football talents, and as a kind of social finishing school where young adults learned how to wear formals and buy corsages. Meanwhile, the A-student is more than a little suspect to teachers as well as students for being a "little odd" because he prefers to read a book rather than attend a football rally. In a sense, this line of criticism raises the same general issues as does the complaint about the lack of solid content. Content went out because these other things came in.

Athletic "Overemphasis"

A special case of extracurricular overemphasis centers around athletic competitions, particularly interscholastic football and basketball. The issue here does not concern intramural physical education participated in by all members of the student body. The concern is with the public exhibition aspect and all of its attendant diversions. In many communities there is more public interest on the part of parents as well as students in having a winning football team than in having a decent library, a well-equipped laboratory, or a competent science program. On the college level, the scramble for the recruitment of athletic talent gives the coaches, the administration, and more importantly the players, vivid lessons in duplicity in connection with recruitment practices outlawed by the conferences but nevertheless still practiced. Even school architecture is said to be dominated by athletic requirements. Numerous school plants would strike a visitor from another culture as magnificent and costly gymnasiums to which are attached a collection of substandard class rooms, libraries, and laboratories. This at a time when educational costs are running higher than many communities can safely afford. So runs the criticism.

It seems doubtful, despite these criticisms, that any change will take place in this phase of scholastic endeavor. A number of colleges, to be sure, have deemphasized intercollegiate spectaculars and a smaller number have abandoned them altogether. A still smaller proportion of high schools have done this too. This is counterbalanced, however, by those institutions that have reemphasized the athletic exhibition and come to rely upon it as an important public relations device.

It is difficult to assess responsibility for the emergence of the athletic preoccupation. Students obviously enjoy it, but are as a rule not in a position to bring about the condition. A certain kind of almuni mentality and a very widespread concept of community pride in this form of achievement seem to lie at the root of the matter. These influences are not readily amenable to control by the institution, certainly not by professional educators themselves, and it is for this reason chiefly that not much change is to be expected in the near future.

Antiintellectualism

By antiintellectualism is meant that the total impact of public school, and to some extent college, education has come to have the effect of depreciating intellectual pursuits in favor of other values. The popular term "egghead" came into existence about 1950 and, while not related directly to education at that time, expressed a widely held contempt for the man of learning and for intellectual pursuits generally.

Antiintellectualism, nevertheless, is a subtle component of formal education. Certainly no one openly advocates that students not be intellectual, not learn, or not seek intellectual development. Instead, to the extent antiintellectualism pervades education, intellectual pursuits are crowded out by other values, such as facilitating the life adjustment of the student, assisting him to develop his physical potentials, supplying him with sex education, providing him with "meaningful life experiences," and so on. During recent decades the exponents of such objectives have effectively demonstrated their merits. No one, it seems, has been successful in selling either all the students or the entire community, or, for that matter, even many in the teaching profession itself, on the merits of learning as established in the liberal arts tradition.

Studies of the attitudes of college students indicate that antiintellectualism survives through the college years, that insofar as college students work hard in their academic pursuits, most of them do so for nonintellectual reasons. Instead, they do so to enter a profession or occupation, or, more immediately, getting into a fraternity or sorority and remaining in one, or remaining eligible for some extracurricular interest which requires certain scholastic levels. The popular courses on most college campuses are usually not those in which the students are held to high intellectual achievement. The numbers of students among whom truly intellectual pursuits hold a high priority are few, and such students are often not highly placed in the status structure of the campus community.

Some critics have even charged that antiintellectualism has become prevalent among the teachers themselves, particularly in the public schools. A disproportionate part of a teacher's training period is said to go into methods of teaching, "understanding" of children, and the practical management of the school plant. This leaves little time for, and often less interest in, the development of the teacher as an educated person in the sense that he is conversant with significant ideas, truly and intellectually curious. Obviously these criticisms, if true, apply very unequally to the teaching profession. The disturbing thing to many people is that they should apply to *any* teachers whatsoever. Critics have been more articulate in their statement of this criticism than in their presentation of any practicable means for correcting it.

SOME TROUBLESOME TRADITIONS

Class Bias in the School System

Ostensibly the American school system is democratic. Apparently it was the intention, in establishing a free (that is, tax-supported) educational system, to make the benefits of education available to everyone, irrespective of class position, wealth, or income. The compulsory feature in school attendance was intended to further the over-all coverage of educational benefits. With the exception of a relatively few children who attend nonparochial, private schools catering mainly to the wealthy, there is considerable democracy in American schools. But it is a democracy more apparent than real. Studies of the interactions of school children show without doubt that the social class characteristics of the outside community also operate in the classroom where racial and religious prejudice, cliques, pecuniary rivalries, and other conditions inimical to the operation of true educational democracy are very evident and interfere with the attainment of the best possible educational experience for all of the children. More important, perhaps, in a practical way, is the fact that educational facilities are not used proportionately by the children of different economic levels.

Our so-called free education is not actually free beyond the elementary grades. It is true that often no high school tuition is imposed and that the children of rich and poor are legally equally free to attend, but books and clothes and miscellaneous expenses which must be borne by the parents of the child constitute a great, and often an impossible, financial burden for the parents to bear, with the result that high schools and especially colleges are virtually closed to children of low-income families. It is argued that this results in an appreciable loss of talent to a society and that, therefore, "something should be done" to stop it. To this end it is advocated that we develop some form of complete subsidization which would make it possible for all children to get as much educational training as they have the ability to absorb, irrespective of their families' abilities to pay. Obviously this is a costly proposal—at least it can be made to appear so by its opponents.

In another sense, the educational system is class-biased. It is charged that there is insufficient attention to the life needs of the lower-income people. There is said to be insufficient attention given, for example, to the vocational needs of the working classes. To some extent, of course, the vocational school is a step in this direction, but it is thought to be an insufficient step because in many communities there are no vocational schools and those that exist are often not supported by comparable funds and imaginative programs.

Segregated Schools

When we turn to a comparison of schools that are segregated on the basis of race it seems that the quality of our "free" education differs according to the skin color of the students pursuing it. At least that is the inference that can be derived from many of the available objective data. Statistics lend support to our remarks in Chapter 12 that school systems operating on the "separate but equal" doctrine are infrequently equal. And although the Supreme Court has ruled that such practices are unconstitutional, it seems that the segregated school system will, for a time at least, remain in some of the states. This particular issue in American education obviously is more than a "school problem."

Special Educational Needs

Most educational programs have been set up in terms of the needs of the more or less average child. There is, of course, a wide range of individual variation in the personalities of children, and hence there is considerable maladjustment of many children to the school system or of the school system to the children, whichever way one may care to state it. The child who learns more slowly than the average or who learns more rapidly than the average, the child who is hard of hearing, the child with emotional problems, the child with defective eyesight, and the child with peculiar interests and disinterests—all pose special problems for schools and teachers.

THE TRADITIONAL APPROACH. The older ideology simply attempted to coerce every child into conformity with the general pattern of education, and those who failed to measure up were required to repeat grades and endure humiliations of one sort or another designed to stimulate greater effort— the dunce cap, staying after school, extra "home work," and the like. Those children who were unable to fulfill the requirements of minimum conformity were, after more or less humiliation and concomitant mental-emotional damage, dropped from the educational process somewhere along the line. There are still many people, mostly laymen, who adhere to this conception of education. There is growing recognition, however, that the special needs of children, whether the result of extremes of intelligence, variations of emotional make-up, special abilities, disabilities, interests and apathies, require and deserve somewhat unique kinds of instruction and learning experience.

SPECIAL CLASSES. Two educational emphases, quite distinct in character, have grown out of this recognition of the great importance of individual difference. The earlier adjustment consisted of the formation of special schools and special classes for such categories of children as the hard of hearing, the slow learners, the fast learners, and "problem children." The chief difficulty with this segregated form of education is in the highly artificial nature of the educational experience of the child in the "special" class; he tends to lose touch with the larger community of more or less normal people. Thus, participation in these specialized classes fosters and accentuates uniqueness and maladjustment rather than teaching the necessary techniques for adjustment to the world of more nearly normal people in which the child will eventually have to live. Another difficulty with special schools and classes is the realization on the part of children and their parents that they are "different" from other people. In many communities great stigma becomes attached to a child's placement in a special class, particularly when the uniqueness in his personality is not especially conspicuous to the layman, and his assignment to a special group is deeply resented.

INDIVIDUALIZED TREATMENT. In order, then, to give such children a more nearly normal educational experience and to protect them from the stigma of low-status placement, considerable emphasis has come to be placed upon an educational system which does not segregate special groups. Instead it adapts itself to specialized needs and disabilities by the somewhat variable treatment of each child. Many educational experts allow greater and greater individual leeway in school work requirements, and justify the wide variations in type and amount of learning experience by mental hygiene criteria rather than by those of formal education.

Considerable public resistance has been encountered to this individualization of educational programs. The critics, better versed in the philosophies and rationalizations of the older education than in the newly discovered mental hygiene needs of children, have attacked the new education. They have cited such arguments as the "depreciation of academic standings," ensuing "lack of discipline," and the "unfortunate" result that many children now seem to enjoy their educational experience rather than to detest it. The implication is all too clear among many critics that, if the children like the new education, if some variation in curriculum for different students is allowed, and if clever and slow-witted students are allowed the same privileges, the system is per se "not sound." Many of the issues between professional educators and the communities they serve would be reduced or eliminated if a better job of interpretation of the objectives and values of the new education were diffused among the lay elements of the population. As the matter now stands, disagreements are common because there is often no real meeting of the minds between professional educators and laymen as to the values which the educational system is striving to implement.

Educational Services to Adult, Part-Time Students

As we have pointed out in innumerable places in this book, ours is a rapidly changing society. Changes occur so frequently and the individual's position in the social web is dependent upon so many different and intricate forces, that more or less continuous education is necessary to enable even the better-informed citizen to "keep up" with the ongoing process. Increasing numbers of people seem to understand the need for continuous education, not only to keep them apace of changing events in their professions and occupations but to keep them at least minimally intelligent with respect to the accumulated scientific and other knowledge which is of great practical importance in their daily lives.

The prevailing educational organization and ideologies, however, are not well adjusted to this obvious need. Many people still think of schools in terms of children, or at least of the relatively young, and it is not at all uncommon to hear even fairly well-informed people define "education" and "life" as though neither had much to do with the other.

TEACHING PROBLEMS. The existing educational system is not well suited to making the kinds of adjustment necessary to meet the educational needs of adult students. One of the problems of a large midwestern university which operates a night school for adults is the selection of a staff suited to the instruction of adults; another is to convince administrative and faculty committees that somewhat different educational procedures for adult students are not per se inferior merely because they are different. Some adult students have despaired of their attempt at further education because their instructors persisted in treating them as adolescents and pursued teaching practices better suited to juveniles than to their parents. Some of the more honest and introspective teachers have also been frank to admit that they feel ill at ease with more mature students and frustrated because techniques that are effective with adolescents seem not to be so effective with more adult personalities.

In the area of adult education we again see a familiar and fundamental ideological difficulty which is involved in so many other social problems: *Social change brings about new conditions and new needs for people, but we encounter ideological obstacles when we attempt to meet the new needs.* So often the personalities and the institutions upon whom new responsibilities fall are so bound in old ways and empty traditions that they operate at relatively low efficiency and high degrees of confusion.

New Roles for Educational Personnel

Traditionally the teacher has been thought of as a peculiar kind of virtuous and unreal personality, akin to the clergyman. One wag has said that there are three sexes in America: men, women, and school teachers. In the past the teacher was "to set a good example" to the children and to some extent to all of the community. She was not allowed to participate in many of the more or less tolerated diversions and recreations which other people found pleasant and inviting. Almost everything from her mode of dress and manner of speech to her morals was subject to public censure on the basis of standards of propriety appreciably higher than those to which the rest of the community was required or willing to conform.

Now we are confronted with a growing number of teachers, well trained and skillful in their handling of children, who refuse to be cowed by the tradition that a teacher is in any significant sense a peculiar personality type. To what extent this new group of teachers is the product of new modes in teacher training, to what extent it expresses an unconscious reaction to the extreme repressions imposed upon teachers in the past, and to what extent it simply embodies the extension of secular ideas to the teaching profession, we do not now know. But the fact of change is reasonably clear. Teachers today are permitted far greater personal freedom than in the past. They dress like other people, are free in growing numbers of communities to join unions, and insist on elimination or nonenforcement of those clauses in their contracts restricting personal conduct. Although it might be difficult to prove by strict statistical evidence, the generalization seems defensible that present-day teachers in America from the kindergarten to the university are becoming a much more nearly normal group in appearance, personal conduct, interests, and ambitions.

The lay community has by no means wholly approved this change, but despite the opposition that has occurred, the "new teacher" is as much here to stay as the "new family" or the "new government." He is the product, apparently, of social forces, and there is increasing recognition that the fates which brought him about were probably kind fates after all.

New Roles for Students

Not only has the role of the teacher changed, but the role of the student has changed as well. It is difficult to describe all of the changes and their true extent, but a few can be enumerated. There is growing recognition of the fact that students are human beings. Of course, it was never explicitly denied that children were human beings, but the traditional school tended to treat them as if they were at least some strange order to humankind, to be heard only on permission, to have their wishes and ideas always subject to the superior wisdom and censure of adults, their interests presumed not to be quite trusted, and their knowledge necessarily inferior. By contrast the present educational philosophy allows the student many new roles. Student government, for example, which is permitted to some degree, at least, in many schools and to great degree in a few, illustrates the change. Instead of always being told precisely what to do in the school situation, the modern student, at least from junior high school on, is allowed to make many decisions for himself. In consultation with his fellows he is permitted considerable voice, especially in the conduct of so-called extracurricular affairs and increasingly even in such curricular matters as what shall be studied, for how long, and when.

There seems still to be considerable opposition to the concepts of teacher-student curricular planning and to student courts for handling infractions of school rules, but both practices are spreading. Probably the chief reason for the opposition of many laymen to new teacher and student roles again grows out of values associated with older educational thinking in which the personal "example" of the teacher and the child's "respect" for the teacher and "discipline" were important concepts. These days many are more concerned with the *outcome* of the educational process, with the mental-emotional make-up that the child acquires and the social ideals that are developed, than they are with the empty luxury of such amenities as "respect" for teachers, formalized "discipline," and "example."

WHY ARE THE PROBLEMS "PROBLEMS"?

The obvious answer to the above question is, of course, because values differ. Let us, however, attempt to go beyond this obvious but important consideration. *Why* do the values differ?

Here, as elsewhere, values differ for a number of reasons. Typically reasons underlying values are not made explicit, because the person with the values may not have articulated them to himself, may be quite innocent of what values he holds, or may be ashamed of the values he holds. He may have vested interests which he feels require him to hold values of a certain sort. In the following paragraphs we will attempt to make concrete how some of these configurations operate.

1. In evaluating education many people, including some professional educators, have not thought through the implications of their own positions. This is evidenced by the fact that they say contradictory things, sometimes in the same paragraph, as, for example, insisting that the school should teach students "to think for themselves" and then surrounding the teacher with forms of censorship which can have the effect only of limiting the students' capacity to think by limiting the materials from which thinking

comes. On a cruder level, is the person who objects strongly to increasing the school budget for general operating expenses but who will support the expenditure of thousands of dollars to modernize the stadium and install lighting for night games. Examples of similar contradictions will readily occur to almost anyone who thinks realistically about the matter.

2. The specific assessment of a school program may be based on a set of unconscious values; this may have important implications for what the evaluator sees, whether he likes it or dislikes it, and what changes, if any, he would like to have made. The roots of antiintellectualism often lie here. Many adult citizens acknowledge that they did not like school very well. Their most vivid memories are of pranks committed, disciplinary action escaped, the oddities of this or that teacher, almost anything except of a sense of intellectual excitement and accomplishment and of personal intellectual growth. The school, like the policeman and the clergyman, somehow symbolizes restraint imposed at a time when freedom and not much else was cherished. Obviously these same persons did learn a great deal in school and in a general way they acknowledge this, but chiefly they think of the "value" of school in terms of vocational advantages—getting a better job, mastering skills that facilitated promotion, and the like. This conception of education gets through to children at a very early age. No amount of pious preachment about the importance of general intellectual growth or of bribes for getting better grades quite convinces many children that there really is any great adventure in it for them.

A special case of this same unconscious value influence is to be found in the general ambivalence toward the teacher, particularly the more learned teacher. In the eyes of many successful people, a teacher is a more or less good fellow who could not quite make it in the practical world of affairs. "Those who can, do; those who can't, teach." This is reflected in the penurious attitude of many people toward teachers' salaries. Low salaries, in turn, tend to cause the more capable people who would like to teach, to turn to other activities that pay more. In addition there is the constant surveillance of teachers lest they instruct children in ways that parents do not approve. Teachers have been embarrassed and even discharged for such "subversive" activities as assigning *The Scarlet Letter,* Hawthorne's American classic, for reading in a senior English class. And vigilante groups on a nationwide scale have recently sought to remove Robin Hood from grade school books because his efforts sounded to them Communistic.

3. Sometimes the underlying values are quite well understood by the value holder, but because he realizes that they are not defensible, he conceals them. A case in point is the property owner, particularly one of substantial real estate holdings, who opposes an adequate school budget simply because, his own children having now grown up, he wishes to escape with the smallest possible tax burden. Or the childless couple may hold a similar conception of citizenship. But financial considerations are not the only selfish

value positions that may be held. There are substantial numbers of contemporaries who want education to function purely and simply as an indoctrinating enterprise, and of highly reactionary ideas at that. To say so
openly would, of course, invite uncomplimentary attack. Better, therefore,
to conceal the real reason and carp at the real or alleged "subversion" of
some teacher, the "socialistic tendencies" in the textbook, or the "immoral
books" on the library shelf. These are no isolated or exaggerated occurrences. Any seasoned administrator, if he attempts a solidly educational
enterprise, remembers painfully a great many such skirmishes.

FEDERAL AID TO EDUCATION

One of the most explosive current issues centers around so-called federal aid to education. Actually, of course, we have had federal aid to education for many years. In 1960, 4.4 percent of public school education
came from federal funds in this country (see Figure 5). In addition $2.5
billion more of federal money were spent in assisting education on the

FIGURE 5   SOURCES OF PUBLIC SCHOOL FINANCE, 1960

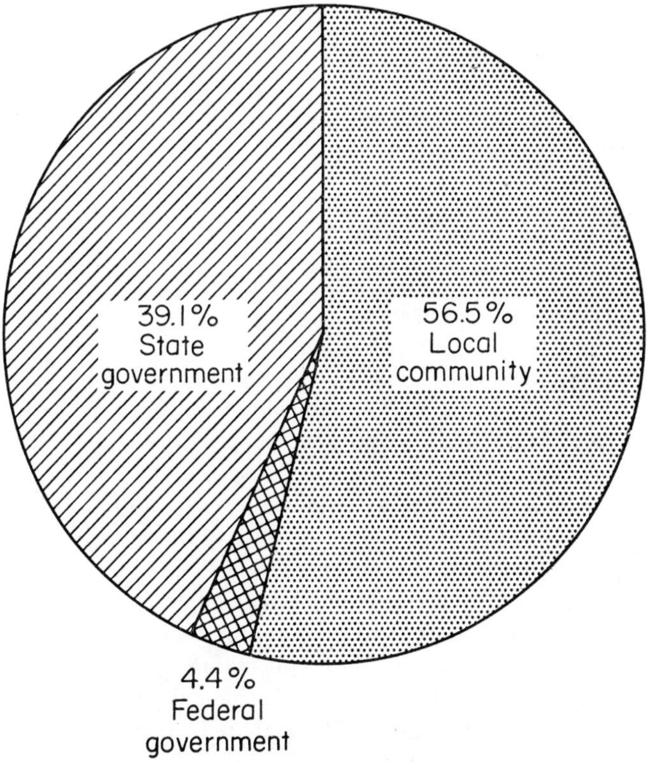

39.1%
State
government

56.5%
Local
community

4.4%
Federal
government

SOURCE: National Education Association, 1963.

college and university level. (See Table 15.) The issue, then, is not whether there should or should not be federal aid to education, but rather whether there should be more or less of it than now exists and what forms it shall take.

Table 15 Federal Government Funds for Education, 1959–1960

Program	Amount in thousands
Elementary-secondary education	*$1,131,412*
National Defense Education Act	80,129
Vocational education	30,235
Federally affected school areas	233,500
School lunch	305,511
Revenue from public lands—sales and leases	83,492
Indian education	47,133
Education of dependents of military personnel	34,150
Surplus property	252,405
Science education—National Science Foundation	4,463
School aid in special areas—District of Columbia, Canal Zone, territories and dependencies, Atomic Energy Commission facilities	20,745
Teacher training programs	39,480
Other	169
Higher education	*$1,209,052*
Traineeships and training grants	64,363
Fellowships and grants	53,265
Research grants and contracts	448,012
Loans: student loans of the National Defense Education Act and college housing loans	259,619

SOURCE: U.S. Office of Education, 1963.

The opposition to federal aid to education stems from a basic American value, namely, "local control" of education. How, then, did federal aid to education ever begin, and why do some people feel that it is necessary.

Obviously, the federal government has not given attention to public education because it had a surplus of money to get rid of. The federal government became involved in education because of the inability or unwillingness of local communities to support their educational programs on an adequate level. (State involvement in public education has sprung from the same condition.) Most federal expenditures for precollege education have gone to communities with substandard educational programs, chiefly communities with a property base insufficient to finance education adequately themselves. In other instances, the federal and state governments have financed programs that the local communities had not seen fit to establish, again usually because of the cost. The historical fact to be noted, however, is that if local support of education had been adequate, the federal government would not have needed to get involved.

Federal aid to colleges and universities is of several varieties, one of which goes back to the Land Grant Act from which most of the larger agricultural colleges and universities have been developed. Through grants-in-aid to the states, the federal government heavily subsidizes the Agricultural Extension Service and the Agriculture Experiment Stations throughout the United States, operating both through the land grant colleges. In recent years the federal government has supported hundreds of millions of dollars of research done by faculty and students in the large universities in such varied fields as military science and public health. Finally, the National Merit Scholarship system provides the most widespread program of college scholarships for students of outstanding merit. This by no means exhausts the kind or extent of federal involvement but gives some idea of the existing enterprises.

Most of the opposition to federal aid to education stems from a fear that local control of the school system will be weakened in proportion as federal and state assistance grow. Obviously materialization of this fear would constitute a serious problem, since in various ways the controller of the purse strings is in a position to control policies. In fact, however, numerous illustrations of dictatorial policies by federal agencies administering educational funds would be hard, indeed, to find. This does not, of course, disprove the fact that in the future federal domination might become a reality. A case in point affects states having segregated schools. There is complaint that federal funds are being and will be withheld from communities unconstitutionally maintaining segregated schools. On the surface this seems like a "threat to local autonomy." Yet the federal government could hardly do otherwise than refuse to support activities that are unconstitutional.

It is one thing to raise the bogy of federal interference in local school programs and policies and quite another to prove that such interference might in many cases be harmful. It is equally difficult for those who favor federal aid to prove that their proposals provide the answer to our educational deficiencies. Certainly there are many substandard educational practices, policies, and programs in many local schools throughout the land. The fact that they have local support seems hardly to their credit, if the local support cannot result in something better than is now offered. It is quite possible that part of the opposition to federal aid to education may be cynical —the real basis for the opposition is that a more forward looking and efficient school system is not really desired; the mediocre status quo is simpler and more comfortable to maintain. Proponents of more federal aid stress the fact that children and the nation in general are entitled to a better quality of educational program than many local communities up to now have been willing or able to provide, and they see federal aid as the best means of achieving this program.

CONCLUSION

In this chapter we have first treated the over-all problem of education —namely, the extent to which the educational system is and will be allowed to be free from domination by the rest of the society. Value clashes are frequent with respect both to the facts of the matter and to the desirability of a truly "free" and autonomous educational system. Generally speaking, there is a strong tendency toward trying to make the schools subservient to one cause or another, causes that are tied up conspicuously with the ideologies of various social classes. Apparently the various sides consider it important to win friends for themselves at the juvenile level. Many observers fear that an unfree educational system may already be in the making and are apprehensive about each new evidence that freedom is being lost. Despite the ease with which we can unmistakably demonstrate that very, very few teachers, at all levels, are members of the Communist party, the charges still persist that the schools are "Communist dominated." Under the guise of "fighting communism" a few groups have actually fought educational freedom.

Throughout this discussion it has been emphasized that the crux of our problems is the attempts of many people to meet new situations by the application of outworn and obsolete ideologies and practices, by which we do not necessarily mean that they were unsuited to a bygone day but that they are incompatible with present-day ideas, values, and material culture.

Throughout this chapter we have implied that the "problems of the school system" are not actually or uniquely the problems of the school system alone; they are, instead, the problems of the whole society *reflected in* the program of the school and in the changing roles of teachers and their students.

SUGGESTED READINGS

BEREDAY, GEORGE Z. F., WILLIAM W. BRICKMAN, and GERALD READ, with the assistance of INA SCHLESINGER, eds., *The Changing Soviet School*. The Comparative Education Society Field Study in the USSR. Boston, Houghton Mifflin Company, 1960.

BESTOR, ARTHUR E., *Educational Wastelands*. Urbana, University of Illinois Press, 1953.

HULBURD, DAVID, *This Happened in Pasadena.* New York, The Macmillan Company, 1951.

JEWETT, ROBERT E., "Why the Able Public School Teacher is Dissatisfied," *Educational Research Bulletin,* 36 (October 1957), pp. 223–234.

MELBY, ERNEST O., and MORTON PUNER, *Freedom and Public Education.* New York, Frederick A. Praeger, 1953.

RIESMAN, DAVID, *Constraint and Variety in American Education.* Lincoln, University of Nebraska Press, 1956.

RYANS, DAVID G., *Characteristics of Teachers: Their Description, Comparison, and Appraisal.* A Research Study. Washington, D.C., American Council on Education, 1960.

STEWART, GEORGE R., *The Year of the Oath.* New York, Doubleday & Company, Inc., 1950.

RELIGION 10

It is doubtful whether most laymen would include religion among America's more pressing social problems. Nevertheless, when the matter is viewed objectively, it is readily seen that religion in America intensifies, or in some instances creates, value conflicts out of which social problems arise. Partly this is due to the great complexities and diversities of values that are collected under the headings of "religion" and "the church." Some portion of that 65 percent of the population listed as members of some church are claimed by 250 religious denominations with great varieties of beliefs and practices. Other reasons why religion is credited with value conflicts lie in the fact of its espousal of some measures of social change, on the one hand, and its resistance, on the other, to some attempts at social change in the secular society. It is our purpose, therefore, to analyze the value conflicts and problem situations associated with religion rather than to embark on a survey or discussion of theological differences among religions.

THE CHURCH AND THE STATE

Government and religion are more thoroughly separated in the United States than in any other major country. The opening words of the first amendment to the Constitution specify that "Congress shall make no law respecting an establishment of religion, or prohibiting the free exercise thereof." Interpretations of the bearing of the first amendment upon specific laws and practices of government, however, have varied. Some have argued that any law that in *principle* makes possible an interlocking relationship of church and state is unconstitutional and a threat to the religious freedom of the American people. Presidents Grant and Garfield, for example, contended that government should not even aid the church to the extent of exempting its property from taxation because this prevented the divorce of church and state from being absolute.

Many churchmen, on the other hand, demand support of the church by the state far beyond tax-exemption of property. Especially in relation to education, church representatives argue that present policies in state-supported education actually operate to handicap religious education and indirectly to support secularization in education.

Parochial School Issues

The Roman Catholic church has taken the position that children who attend its parochial schools should be given the same aids that the state provides children who attend the public schools. At the present writing a bill to provide federal aids to public schools is blocked in Congress, in part by strong Catholic opposition because the bill does not provide similar aids to parochial schools.[1] Non-Catholic opposition is just as strong against including such assistance to church-sponsored schools.

THE CATHOLIC POSITION. Catholic spokesmen insist that a democratic state should recognize the right of parochial schools to give a civil education which conforms to legal standards together with a religious education which satisfies the desires of the parents and the church. When only public schools receive state support, it is held, an injustice is done to all non-public schools which by the states' own standards perform the same services (in nonreligious areas) for citizens of the state. Separation of church and state is said to require governmental "neutrality," by which is meant that the government should not favor secularized education over that which provides religious training in addition to secular instruction. It is argued that if the state withholds from these parochial schools privileges that are extended to public schools, it is thus putting pressure on parents to withdraw their children from Catholic schools and to send them to schools where either Protestantism or godlessness is taught.

This Catholic point of view has expressed itself in various specific issues throughout the country involving free transportation, books, and school lunches. In most of the legal testings of such issues, the courts have upheld the Catholic position. However, in one attempt to incorporate a parochial school into the tax-supported educational system of a community (North College Hill, a Cincinnati suburb), the court rebuffed the Catholic majority of the school board who had made this attempt.

THE NON-CATHOLIC POSITION. Those who oppose state-aided parochial

[1] The perennial nature of this problem is striking. The sentence that is footnoted was first written fifteen years ago and is equally true today!

schools argue that such aid would be the first step toward breaking down the barrier between church and state. If the Catholic church is permitted to obtain public funds for parochial schools, it is contended, it will then proceed to seize more and more power in its movement toward the alleged goal of becoming the one state-supported church. Since the public schools are open to Catholics as well as to non-Catholics, those parents who cannot afford to send their children to parochial schools are still free to indoctrinate their children at home and through the church. Public funds, it is argued, should not be turned over to schools where teaching is under ecclesiastical rather than public control.

The issuance of free textbooks to parochial schools is frequently cited as an example of the practical consequences to the public school system if state aid to nonpublic schools is once begun. In some of the states where free textbooks have been issued to parochial schools, the schools then began to exert pressure to assure that only "proper" textbooks were issued. Again, what may start out as a provision to allow parochial school children transportation on publicly financed school buses along regular routes may end up with the establishment of publicly supported routes designed especially to serve the parochial school children. In other words, once the principle of separation of church and state is violated by allotting *some* public funds to parochial schools, it becomes difficult to determine just where to "draw the line."

Protestant-Sponsored Religious Education

The earliest major attempts to bring about or keep religion in the public schools were largely made by Protestants. These attempts centered around the daily reading of a Bible passage, the singing of hymns, and the recitation of the Lord's Prayer. At the turn of the century and in the early 1900s, court cases in the separation-of-church-and-school area usually involved Catholics and Jews protesting against their children's compulsory attendance at Bible readings in the public schools, compulsory memorization of passages from the King James Bible, and the like. Nevertheless, there is still some type of Bible reading in the public schools of the majority of our states. Both Catholics and Jews continue to protest on what seems to be the indisputable basis that there is no such thing as a nonsectarian Bible. Passages selected, emphases and interpretations in reading, and other factors would inherently be affected by the prejudices of the teacher.

Another attempt upon the part of Protestants to bring religion into the schools was the released-time educational plan. As first developed in Gary, Indiana, in 1913, it meant releasing students before the end of the school day to attend religious education classes in their churches, but numerous variations have developed. It has been estimated that in 1948 (the year of one adverse decision of the Supreme Court) about 2 million children in over 2000 communities were participating in some type of released-time program for religious instruction. Protestant, Catholic, and Jewish leaders have provided instruction for their groups but, generally, the released-time plan has not been favorably accepted by Catholics and Jews. The reason for Catholic objections is not clear, but the Jewish authorities have been the most consistent of any religious groups in maintaining that religious education is a private matter that is the concern of parents and churches, and that public schools are for secular education exclusively.

Many Protestants further contend that the answer to the conflict over religion in the public schools is to provide a nonsectarian religion in which all the major faiths may find a common meeting ground. This likewise has met with the opposition not only of the nonreligious or nonaffiliated portions of the population, but also of most Catholics and Jews. Advocates of teaching universal religious truths, it is contended, are deluded by strivings toward unity within Protestant churches into believing that unity of the three major faiths is likewise possible. Such teachings, opponents of the nonsectarian program further suggest, would even more thoroughly convey the prejudices of the sponsors of the program than do the Bible-reading procedures.

In 1947 and 1948 (*Everson v. Board of Education* and *McCollum v. Board of Education*) the United States Supreme Court spoke out strongly against the use of public school buildings, facilities, or personnel in the support of any or all religious faiths or sects in the dissemination of their doctrines and ideals. The Court also contended (*McCollum* case) that such a position could not be legitimately interpreted as hostility to religion, but rather as the conviction that both religion and government flourish best when rigidly separated. A secular public school, according to the Court, is the means of reconciling freedom in general with religious freedom.

At this writing there is much discussion of two Supreme Court decisions of 1962 and 1963 that, in nontechnical terms, appear to mean that public schools may not sponsor public prayers, even if voluntary. Some prominent churchmen have agreed with the Court on the ground that the church should not enlist governmental authority to attempt to accomplish what the church itself is not able to do.

Various legal problems remain unsolved, and numerous educational and religious values continue in conflict. Desires upon the part of leaders of churches to strengthen their membership lead them to seek in differing ways the support of the educational institutions. The pursual of this value of greater security and growth for their particular religious beliefs brings them into conflict with the constitutionally embodied value of religious freedom as based on the rigid separation of church and state. All three major faiths have become alarmed in recent decades with the apparent growth of values that they consider unethical and immoral. They have tended to blame such social developments as divorce, crime, delinquency, mental illness, and alcoholism on the "godless public schools." Since their values include, however, varying degrees of disbelief in and distrust of the values of competing faiths, they cannot unite on the common value of getting the "godlessness" out of public-sponsored education.

Other Church-State Value Clashes

It must not be concluded that the only difficulties that have arisen over the principle of separation of church and state have had their locus in the schools. There are cases on record, although not many in number, in which the putting into practice of religious teachings clearly conflicts with laws of the state. For example, members of some organized religions, such as the Society of Friends, simply cannot continue to practice their religion and comply with legislation that requires them to bear arms. Using a stricter and more literal interpretation of the Commandment "Thou shalt not kill" than other Americans are wont to apply, some men have refused to be taken into military service, for even if they themselves did no killing, membership in the armed forces in time of war would seem to involve a certain amount of help and support for those who did kill. This particular issue eventually was resolved in favor of religion. A man who for religious reasons cannot enter military service does not now have to do so, although he is often required to perform some other service, such as serving as a mental hospital attendant, for a similar period of time.

One other example of a basic conflict between the laws of the state and the teachings of a minor-sect religion will perhaps suffice. The Church of Jesus Christ of the Latter Day Saints, or the Mormon church as it is better known, at one time openly taught that it was right and even good for a man to have more than one wife at the same time. It was not a matter of convenience or personal desire but that, according to this religion, men's and women's chances of reaching the hereafter were substantially increased under such an arrangement and that polygamy was considered right in the eyes of God. Although the major divisions of the Mormon church no longer encourage their members to practice polygamy, a few small subdivisions do so instruct their members, who have been discovered putting this religious doctrine into practice.[2] One such group was recently found in Short Creek, Arizona. Although they were living unto themselves in a remote section of the desert, the collective conscience of the rest of the state was sufficiently wounded to suggest that "something be done" about the situation. The re-

[2] In 1890 the president of the Mormon church issued a formal proclamation to members to refrain from polygamous marriages. From this date to the present the main body of the Mormon church has upheld monogamous marriage.

sult was that the husbands and fathers were arrested and the children were forcibly separated from their families.[3] Some serious thinking Americans, even though not believing in polygamy themselves, began to ask if this was not an open prohibition of the free exercise of religion.

The cases concerning the religions that teach nonviolence and the Mormon belief in polygamy illustrate that serious difficulties can arise when the principle of the separation of church and state is put into practice. For how indeed can the two remain separate if the teachings of one's religion result in his violation of state laws, or if his compliance with legal prescriptions necessitates his falling into disfavor with his church?

CENSORSHIP OR "THOUGHT CONTROL"

Organized religion has a long tradition of practice as well as an almost undebatable logic to support its position that censorship is both right and necessary. This breaks sharply, of course, with several other American traditions, notably free discussion of all ideas in all communication forms and, of course, the separation of church and state. The juxtaposition of these widely and firmly held traditions makes the subject of censorship a continuing and lively one. Specific issues change from time to time but the basic principles are enduring, the conflict almost incessant.

There is no escaping the historical fact that organized religion has in fact practiced thought control for centuries. It was official church spokesmen who decided that Galileo and Copernicus were peddling false doctrines about the universe. History abounds with other examples. To large numbers of people it seems altogether legitimate that the omniscience and supernatural sanction of the church's action should be binding upon their own thinking and upon the thinking of others. Millions of people in this country and elsewhere in the world see no value problem whatsoever in the insistence of organized religion that its leaders know better than they what they should and should not read, what kinds of scientific endeavor are appropriate and inappropriate, and even whether or not to accept the truth as the truth is currently known by the leading scholars and scientists of the time. The logic of the church's value position is thus convincing to many. Through apostolic succession one's contemporary churchmen operate not only as highly educated and wise shepherds of the flock, they carry out this function with divine sanction as God's representatives on earth. Who is to say such authority nay?

Of course, there are those who question the church's adequacy and legitimacy in determining the content of mind. There are two main di-

[3] This is by no means the strongest attack on the Mormon church. For a report of the conflicts throughout much of the church's history, see Kimball Young, *Isn't One Wife Enough?* (New York: Holt, Rinehart and Winston, Inc., 1954).

visions to this challenge. First, the Protestant challenge to the older Catholic tradition, the nub of which is that Protestants are theoretically unwilling to grant exclusive revelation to the Catholic church, or any other body. They feel they have a right to honor the way in which divinity is made manifest to the individual person, layman or cleric. They resent the monopolistic implications of the Catholic position, although some of them tend to make the same assumption themselves. When it comes to details, however, many Protestants and Catholics find little difficulty in agreeing on many specific ideas and expressions that they feel justified in censoring—so-called obscenity in movies and literature, atheistic teaching in the public schools or in the mass media, and so on.

Second, the most clear-cut challenge, however, has a constitutional basis—the separation of church and state, with the strong implication that spokesmen for the church are categorically no better prepared to decide what kinds of influences should be withheld or played down than is any other source of opinion. Finally, there is a rather extreme position that denies to either church or state the right to withhold information, points of view, artistic productions, political or moral philosophies, or any other intellectual creation from anyone. It is argued that there should be a completely free and open market for the exchange of ideas and cultural products, with the individual completely free to make up his own mind on what he wishes to read or see and what he wishes to think and feel about what he reads and sees.

It is in the context of value conflicts such as we have just described that specific censorship and thought control issues present themselves as recurring social problems in contemporary America. It is not possible to make a complete list of specific issues because they change from time to time, although there are a number of perennial problems, such as attempts on the part of religious organizations, or official spokesmen for them, to ban the exhibition of certain movies or to delete from them certain passages, scenes, or words that are deemed inappropriate for people to see or hear. Sometimes the censorship applies to all people and at other times only to the young. A second recurring problem concerns books and magazines, both with respect to their public sale and also to their availability in libraries, and especially public school libraries. Almost every classic in Western literature from Chaucer to Rabelais and from Shakespeare to Hawthorne to Orwell has somewhere or other been the object of an attempt on the part of church groups in the name of decency, morality, and piety to prevent its sale or library distribution. Sex information, even under the auspices of established professional authority, is frequently censored in one form or another. Particularly strenuous have been censorship efforts to prevent dissemination of information about contraception—in some instances only certain kinds of *effective* contraception.

(It would be a mistake to assume that all censorship springs from ecclesiastical sources. Much of the most blatant, extreme, and effective censorship in contemporary American society has a secular rather than a religious source. Various secular organizations, usually with alleged patriotic intent, also impose censorship chiefly upon public schools and colleges in an effort to prevent students from learning about political philosophies or socioeconomic programs which are considered inappropriate for them to know about. We are not in this chapter, however, concerned with this kind of censorship—only with thought control that derives from ecclesiastical authority.)

Special problems, quite apart from general philosophical questions of censorship, have presented themselves, two of which should be discussed specifically because of their importance and because of the necessary refinement of value positions which they involve.

The first of these issues centers around the legitimacy of censorship by religious authorities over persons not their own communicants. Thus, for example, it is argued that the Catholic church may have a clear right to prevent its own members from reading literature concerning contraception, but another more serious question arises when this censorship is extended by political means to non-Catholics over whose private lives the church has no legitimate authority. In a certain sense the issue becomes one of protection of the socially weak against the abuse of power by the socially strong. The problem is particularly acute in parts of the country where Catholic populations are large enough to exert strong political control over non-Catholics. In 1964 a test case in Connecticut is in the courts to determine whether a non-Catholic physician has the legal right to advise a non-Catholic patient concerning contraception. The current law in that state, originally sponsored by Protestant bodies but now backed by the Catholic church, clearly forbids him to do such. The important legal and moral question, however, is whether such a law is constitutional and whether it is "right." In many other communities, perhaps in less serious ways, the same issue presents itself.

A second special case raises a different aspect of the conflict with democratic ideology. Individuals and small groups frequently act as if they speak officially for large and powerful religious institutions when as a matter of fact they do not. People in all religious faiths vary appreciably from one another on many value questions. They interpret broad universalist principles quite differently. Some are very literalist and strict. Others allow more scope to discretion, judgment, and the spirit rather than the letter of the law. Booksellers have pointed out, for example, that whether or not they may stock a controversial book without reprimand from the local clergy depends upon which clergyman happens to be assigned to the local parish at the time. To clergyman A, *The Tropic of Cancer* is an inappropriate book to be sold in the community. He is succeeded by another clergyman who is disinclined to object to this book. What, then, is the position of "the church"?

An interesting and perhaps more significant illustration occurred many years ago in the United States in connection with the teaching of evolution. Several American Catholic bishops issued strong statements during the 1920s making it manifestly clear that the doctrine of evolution was inacceptable, instructed parish priests to so advise their parishioners, and in various ways tried to prevent schools and colleges from teaching this scientific view. Meanwhile the doctrine of evolution was being taught in a number of distinguished Catholic universities in Europe and the United States, and a great many Catholics do not know to this day that the mother church at Rome never officially took an antievolution stand. In other words, minorities large and small, in the church and out, aspire to become the media for censorship in the name of religious bodies, both Catholic and Protestant. Often much stricter thought control is attempted than the organization in whose name these groups claim to function would attempt to justify. Quite often the community is forced to deal in censorship issues with the more authoritarian minds, the more doctrinaire individuals, who often do not reflect the general religious denomination for which they appoint themselves as spokesmen. (This is equally true of secularly based censorship.)

Censorship has long been an effective tool for totalitarian regimes past and present, religious or secular. If one can control the intellect, he holds a mastery over the man. There is a strong temptation therefore to control by censorship ideas held to be unpalatable by the controller. In practice, however, no censorship system ever has been completely effective, although high efficiency has been achieved in many parts of the world.

Censorship has by and large faced rather "tough going" in the United States, with some glaring exceptions to be sure, for several apparent reasons. First, the Constitution of the United States sets forth certain guarantees in the Bill of Rights, which if observed would keep us relatively free. The Constitution in this respect is, of course, frequently circumvented, sometimes by legal subterfuge and at other times by vigilante violation. There is actually much more censorship than many people are aware of, and it must also by pointed out, many people are quite content to have it this way. They are unaware of the extent to which they are being "brainwashed," and even when this is pointed out seem quite content to submit to what they regard as a wiser authority than themselves.

Aside from constitutional guarantees, however, there is a basic view of human rights that censorship violates. This philosophy maintains that human dignity is deeply offended by the intrusion of any third party, sacred or secular, between a man's mind and the creative products of other men's minds, and that the right to choose among ideas, literary experiences, and courses of action is impossible unless all of the alternatives are available for consideration. For example, there would not be much sense in holding an election if only certain of the candidates were permitted to have their say. In much the same way it is impossible to be educated, much less wise, if someone else is to judge what information is permissible and with what points of view one is to be familiar. Each act of censorship, it is argued, enforces ignorance; the resulting intellectual vacuums make it impossible to be fully informed and capable of the wisest possible action.

The cogency of the various values notwithstanding, the censorship fight will undoubtedly continue. There are many careful observers of the American scene who feel that basic freedoms of access to ideas are slowly but surely being eroded. They point out that the total net effect of protecting the young, setting a good moral example for all, and protecting the nation from subversion, is to create a type of mentality that has growing areas of innocence and ignorance. They suspect that back of much censorship is a thinly disguised intention to preserve the censoring institution first of all, and they deeply resent therefore making people pawns in a manipulative game to protect monolithic tradition for its own sake.

Many who support censorship, however, reject the preceding implications and feel justified in their efforts for very specific and often quite plausible reasons. They do not want the minds of the young contaminated by false doctrines, immoral images, and dangerous heresies. They feel that even adults would find it easier to pursue the good life if they do not encounter influences tempting them to sin, immorality, and wrong thinking. To others, as we have said, this is an insulting condescension. It implies that some people know better than others what they should do. It smacks strongly of authoritarianism and paternalism, which go against the American grain, at least for some. Censorship issues take ever new forms, and probably no community is either immune from the problem or likely to long escape the insidious issues.

RELIGION AND SOCIAL ACTION

Traditionally, religious organizations have aligned themselves with reactionary forces in our society. Churches have often feared that alterations in the status quo would remove some of their existing benefits. In addition, strong advocacy of certain social reforms could well bring the withdrawal of financial support of the church by wealthy conservative members. Increasingly in recent decades, however, the leaders of the three major faiths have issued social pronouncements that commit religious organizations to changes in various aspects of the existing order. Many times these social creeds seem to represent a minority conviction attempting to achieve majority status, and many times action fails to follow pronouncement. Very few white parishes, for example, have attempted actually to bring in and fully accept Negroes in all church activities even though officially their churches are on record in favor of complete racial nondiscrimination. Nevertheless, at least from the standpoint of their efforts to educate their own members, many churches may no longer be accused of offering a religion that is the "opiate of the people."

Apocalyptic Churches

Many of the smaller sects, the new evangelical movements, and fundamentalist divisions in the older denominations continue to preach an other-worldliness that diverts its members from the problems of their society and constitutes an obstacle to social action. Jehovah's Witnesses, for example, teach that the course of history has been toward degradation, that it is close to its lowest depths, and that nothing in this world is worth attempting to salvage. With divine intervention momentarily expected, it behooves the member of an apocalyptic religion to concentrate on the saving of his own soul and the possible conversion of others to the select minority of the saved and to disregard the evils of the world about him. The financial success of numerous evangelical preachers of many varieties of "old-fashioned religion" is testimony to the continuing escapist appeal of apocalyptic teachings to large sections of the population.

Social Gospel Churches

During the past half century, most of the major religious denominations have become more and more concerned with the advancement of social causes. They have reacted against the emotional and personal-salvation values of the apocalyptic faiths and have come to concentrate on social issues such as race relations, crime and delinquency, international relations, and world peace. The social gospel advocates have contended that the old type of religion was occupied with "snatching brands from the burning." The church, they insist, must be concerned with the circumstances in which people live and must deal with society as a whole and the basic factors therein which produce sinful living.

WORLD PEACE. In the interim between World Wars I and II, strong peace movements were initiated or supported by many of the major churches. During the course of World War II, church leaders led all other educational forces in recommending a study of the terms for peace and the development of a world organization to maintain the peace. Most churches also supported the right of conscientious objectors to refuse military service and were instrumental in obtaining governmental recognition of this right in selective service legislation.

Many church leaders likewise protested the atomic bombings of Hiroshima and Nagasaki and have worked for international control of atomic bombs and reduction of armaments. They constitute the core of several movements to bring about world government, and offer their churches as meeting places for peace groups of all kinds.

Although at this writing current efforts toward world peace and world government do not look much more promising than the more naïve peace attempts made between the two World Wars, many churches deserve much of the credit for such social action as has been undertaken toward the realization of these values to which most of the population verbally subscribes.

RACE RELATIONS. While all major churches have frequently spoken out against racial discriminations of all types, most continue to operate along lines of racial segregation. Some of the most liberal churches in the north actually welcome Negroes for worship in predominantly white churches, but the majority merely profess belief in, and fail to practice, such "brotherhood." There is still truth in the assertion that eleven to twelve o'clock on Sunday morning is the most segregated time in America.

Not only within their own churches but for the most part in the rest of the community, the majority of church members are content to let the status quo continue in race relations. For the removal of discriminatory practices that has been achieved to date, minority groups owe much more thanks to the courts than to the churches. However, some credit for improvements in the treatment of minority groups should probably be given to the educational activities of religious organizations.

CAPITAL AND LABOR. Although traditionally affiliated with the objectives of business and finance, the three major faiths have issued denouncements of the exploitation of labor by capital. They have asked for controls on speculation and the profit motive, a wider and fairer distribution of wealth, social security, improvement of working conditions and reduction of hours, the right of collective bargaining, and abolition of child labor. While the gains of labor in such areas as these may have come more directly from other pressure-group techniques, and from legislation the support of many of the churches in labor's struggle for social justice has been of educational service. The church's support of some of labor's causes has lent "respectability" to labor's aims.

CRIME AND DELINQUENCY. The churches have contributed educationally to reforms in various public institutions, including those dealing with criminals and delinquents. Church leaders have often spearheaded movements in communities that have ended abuses and injustices in police departments and aroused the public to demand more adequate criminological and penological practices. Some of the improvements in probation and parole practices and in the development of juvenile courts may be credited to church activity.

It may be argued, on the other hand, that "do-good" activities of church people have actually contributed to the maintenance and spread of some forms of crime and vice. Religious zealots sometimes launch reform actions with little understanding of the problems or the values of the people involved in the problems. The church-sponsored Eighteenth Amendment is the most notable example of the enhancement of crime and vice by misguided reform. Prostitution, illegitimacy, gambling, and homosexuality are often merely diffused and made less subject to enlightened social control by reforming religionists. Social gospel religion is sometimes no more intelligently directed than apocalyptic religion in bringing about a better society.

Reaction

Direct attack on social evils advocated by the social gospel religionists has brought protests and countermovements in most denominations. These critics maintain that the proponents of action have, in their attempt to reform society, forgotten that the fundamental purpose of Christian religion is to "save the individual sinner." Some of the critics favor a complete return to the old revivalism, an emotional appeal to the individual sinner to be saved. Others, while favoring greater concentration of the church's attention on the salvation of individual souls, make their main point that the church's social role should be confined strictly to education rather than including coercive action. They point out that the church is competent to function only in relation to social ideals and motives, and that it should leave social action to government officials, social workers, and others who are presumably better qualified to conduct reforms.

THE IMPACT OF RELIGIOUS VALUES

Recently there has been a noticeable increase in membership of most of the organized churches in the United States. But religious leaders of all denominations are not altogether satisfied that the so-called mid-century spiritual renaissance is real, sincere, or likely to be lasting. Too many, it is said, are hopefully viewing religion as simply a pragmatic mechanism for accomplishing worldly goals that science and politics have been unable to accomplish. If religion works, so much the better; if not, try something else. Others see the recent upsurge in church membership as a reflection of the anxiety-laden atmosphere of our times. Religion is said to have become but a new type of personal therapy overlaid with appropriate scriptural references. Whether or not this "religious revival" is a revival of "real religion" and whether or not participants in it are "sincere" quite obviously depends on how and by whom these terms are defined. And since we are still so close to it, time alone will tell whether the growth in church membership is a temporary or lasting phenomenon. Nevertheless, we can attempt to investigate the more objective evidence concerning the impact of present-day churches on the American scene.

Influence of the Churches: Religion or Religiosity

Just how important is organized religion in contemporary American society? Roughly 65 percent of the population holds membership in a church, and probably half of these actively participate in some part of their church's program. If these estimates are correct (and they must be guesses because no fully reliable data are available on either membership or attendance), approximately two Americans out of every three do not directly participate in organized religious activities. But membership and attendance are only outward forms. What evidence is there that the teachings of the church are being taken seriously as guides to actual living? The evidence is very discouraging to serious churchmen of *all* faiths.[4]

Dr. George H. Gallup, director of the American Institute of Public Opinion, conducted a nation-wide poll consisting of ten simple questions on the Bible and religion.[5] The results seem to indicate that many, many Americans, church members included, are completely ignorant of basic religious concepts and have little factual knowledge of either the Old or New Testaments of the Bible. Only about one third of the adults, for example, knew who delivered the Sermon on the Mount, only 40 percent could give a reasonably accurate definition of the Holy Trinity, while just 21 percent could name even *one* prophet mentioned in the Old Testament. All in all, a mere 4 percent of the sample were able to answer nine of the ten questions correctly and only one in a hundred could give correct answers to all of the questions.

Finally, we need no study to document the fact that behavioral standards prescribed by churches are not adhered to by large numbers of persons who consider themselves members. Those in control of the churches know that their prescriptions are ignored or unheeded, but they retain the erring ones as members in good standing.

Are the churches, then, ineffective? The answer to this question depends, of course, upon what is meant by a church's being effective. We know that no church influences a majority of Americans to follow its chief teachings regarding beliefs, attitudes, and practices. There is likewise strong

---

[4] Glenn M. Vernon and Robert L. Stewart, "Is American Religiosity Real?", *The Humanist,* XIX: 1 (January–February, 1959), p. 14.

[5] Results released to press by American Institute of Public Opinion on December 19, 1954.

reason to suspect that most churches do not even so influence a majority of their own members. Perhaps it is justifiable to state that the churches are not impressively effective in the realization of their stated objectives. Indirectly, but to a degree very difficult to gauge, churches probably have socially desirable influences upon even some segments of society that never receive their teachings. Some of these positive values are briefly described in the following paragraphs.

AGENTS OF REFORM. We have already discussed in an earlier portion of the chapter the influence of the social gospel churches in achieving such reforms as more humane treatment of criminals, reduction of child labor, and improvement of the status of labor in general, and in education against racial discrimination and attempts to establish peace and world government. To the churches, too, must go some credit for the abolishment of slavery and the emancipation of women. Even some humanistic reformers who have denounced organized religion have unconsciously borrowed many of their social justice platforms from representatives of the church. Furthermore such a basic religious tenet as the dignity and worth of the individual has permeated the secular philosophy of democracy. These influences may not be measurable but are nonetheless significant.

PHILANTHROPIC AGENCIES. Until basic social reforms are achieved, individuals and groups who suffer under existing conditions have need of help, and the churches and church-initiated social agencies continue to provide much assistance. Even most of the social security and social assistance programs now sponsored by the government had their beginnings in organized religion. A withdrawal of church financing and church-affiliated personnel from the private social agencies that still do a significant portion of present-day philanthropic work would bring chaos to their activities.

INSTRUMENTS OF SOCIAL CONTROL. Although the conservative influence of the churches has sometimes frustrated scientific inquiry and delayed needed social improvements, it also functions as a barrier to undesirable changes or to transitions that are too rapid for social adjustment. When the pendulums of other aspects of the culture oscillate rapidly, slow-moving religious institutions preserve certain values. At least some of these values will probably be desired by succeeding generations of men to fit somehow into the culture patterns of their times.

SOURCES OF SECURITY. It is in this very conservatism of the churches that many people apparently find security. Even though many of the beliefs and practices of a particular religion may not bear rational examination, their relatively unchanging obscurantism in a rapidly changing world which emphasizes rationality brings solace to some individuals. Some future social order may be composed of individuals who need no such comfort, but the absence of such a need seems not to be the nature of at least a sizable minority of contemporary American citizens. And there is reason to suspect that, in times of crises, many Americans who are not affiliated with churches draw comfort from the beliefs and feelings and practices that these churches sponsor.

Putting the matter tersely, then, religion should be considered in a textbook on social problems for three important reasons:

(1) Through the diverse teachings and activities of its many component churches, American religion intensifies and in some instances *creates value conflicts* out of which social problems arise.

(2) Through its *resistance to changes* in secular society and its frequent opposition to the spread of new values, a large portion of organized religion may be further credited with *intensifying value conflicts* and accompanying social problems.

(3) Through its active *espousal of other social changes,* various reforms in the status quo, some portion of organized religion may be credited with *further intensification of value conflicts.*

Although there is justification for questioning the extent of the influence of the churches in some of their expressed objectives, little question can be raised regarding the significance of religion's influences in the foregoing relationships to the problems of American society.

Diversity and Conflict

Value diversity, in religion as elsewhere, need not mean value conflict. A certain kind of evidence is presented by the fact that this book has been revised by two authors, one of whom is an active Catholic and the other an inactive Protestant, yet not one question of consequence arose between them on these so-called explosive issues. Many, if not most, of the so-called value clashes between and within the several faiths are not really religious differences at all—they are the more fundamental consequences of ignorance versus information, charity toward diverse views versus arrogance and dogmatism, in short, the authoritarian intellect over against the mind with democratic, humanistic commitment.

SUGGESTED READINGS

CURTISS, JOHN SHELTON, "Religion as a Social Problem in Soviet Russia." *Social Problems,* 7 (Spring 1960), pp. 328–339.

DEDMAN, JEAN, "The Relationship Between Religious Attitude and Attitude Toward Premarital Sex Relations." *Marriage and Family Living,* 21 (May 1959), pp. 171–176.

GORDIS, ROBERT, *et al., Religion and the Schools.* New York, Fund for The Republic, Inc., 1959.

KANE, JOHN J., "Protestant-Catholic Tensions." *American Sociological Review,* 16 (October 1951), pp. 663–672.

KRAMER, ALFRED, "Racial Integration in Three Protestant Denominations." *Journal of Educational Sociology,* 28 (October 1954), pp. 59–68.

MUELDER, WALTER G., *Religion and Economic Responsibility.* New York, Charles Scribner's Sons, 1953.

PFEFFER, LEO, *Creeds in Competition.* New York, Harper & Row, Publishers, 1958.

ROSTEN, LEO, ed., *The Religions of America.* New York, Simon and Schuster, Inc., 1955.

VERNON, GLENN M., and ROBERT L. STEWART, "Is American Religiosity Real?" *The Humanist,* XIX:1 (January–February, 1959), p. 14.

LEISURE AND RECREATION [ ] *11*

It has been said that the only thing man can do for eight hours a day is *work*. He cannot drink or eat for eight hours a day, neither can he make love for eight hours a day.

For the present, let us grant that work in its usual sense plays a positive role in the lives of most people. Yet at the same time men yearn to be free from toil, an ambition that more people are increasingly realizing. Indeed, not too many generations ago a workweek of forty hours was but an idle dream, and only the privileged few had leisure in any large amount. Now that great numbers of people have considerable leisure time, do they yearn once again for more work? Is the newfound leisure a meaningful freedom or merely a great emptiness to be filled in any way? What values do men seek in their leisure, and what values could or should men seek? Before turning to questions such as these, let us attempt to sketch the background of this modern-day social problem.

Leisure, as the term is commonly used, describes the time that people have free after they have attended to the practical necessities of life. Throughout human history probably all men have had some leisure, and some men have even had much leisure. For our own society, however, it is only recently that great masses of people have had considerable free time.

In 1850 farmers and laborers had an average workweek of about seventy-two hours. Fifty years later the workweek was down to sixty hours. It dropped to about forty-four hours by 1940 and then to forty hours by 1950. While there is disagreement as to how much more it will be reduced, it is evident that a five-day workweek with eight hours a day is not considered an irreducible standard. Already, some plants have gone to a thirty-five-hour workweek, the electricians' union in New York city established a twenty-five-hour week (after which overtime wage rates begin) in 1963.

Realistically, not all of the reduction in the typical workweek has resulted in more leisure. Traveling to and from work is certainly a necessary part of one's job, and this factor probably adds an average of five hours a week to the time that is not one's own to do with as he pleases. Then, too, at least some of the "do-it-yourself" work around the home is not done voluntarily or because it is enjoyable. When the high cost of labor would unduly strain the family budget, performing such work oneself comes close to being as necessary as going to the shop or office. But even when we subtract from the presumably available leisure time the time spent traveling to and from work and the time spent doing necessary work around the home, it is still true that the bulk of American workers have considerably more leisure than even fifty years ago.

Shorter working hours leave a period of time every day during which one is free to do as he pleases. In addition, the new leisure also is characterized by larger blocks of free time. The reduction of the workweek to five instead of six days results in a certain amount of "bulk time" that could be devoted to leisure pursuits. Before the turn of the century paid vacations were practically unknown, whereas now millions of workers have a two- or three-week yearly vacation as part of their employment contract. The existence of larger amounts of such bulk leisure time opens up whole new areas of leisure pursuits; camping trips, long distance traveling, or even major remodeling projects around the home are among the things that require bulk leisure. These and other leisure activities would not be possible only by a reduction in the number of hours worked each day.

It should be pointed out that all segments of society are not participating equally in the new leisure. Among working men, the blue-collar worker in the larger industries has been affected most, while professional men, managers, and some technical workers work as long as, or even longer, than ever before. Because of compulsory retirement and other factors, those over sixty-five years of age have considerably more free time than their counterparts of fifty years ago. Regular employment of those under eighteen years of age is infrequent and, what is more, the school day is not nearly as long as what was once the usual working day of children. Up to now, the young, the old, and the lesser skilled worker have received the fullest measure of the new leisure. Whether for any of these groups it is a bane or a blessing is another matter.

Any discussion of the change in women's leisure time is complicated by the existence of different roles for women in modern society. Homemakers in general certainly have been released from many of the tasks customarily performed by their mothers and grandmothers. What is more, of the homemaking tasks that remain most can be performed more quickly today because of the household machines and more efficient equipment. Mothers of young children may find themselves with little free time, but when the children are older, and particularly when they have left home, the same mothers should find themselves with a great deal more leisure.

Married women who are employed outside the home, particularly if they have children, would seem to be one of the more leisureless groups in our society. Considering that between eleven and twelve hours a day are required for sleep, personal care, and eating, and that another eight to nine hours are spent on the job and traveling, there remain but a few hours a day. Out of these, of course, must come some homemaking tasks and some child care activities, however either are reduced by outside help. Finally, only a small minority of older women work outside the home. The leisure time of women thus varies considerably by marital and parenthood status, by the age of the woman's children, her own age, and whether or not she is employed outside the home. Put differently, our society has produced a potential of more leisure for women, but the potential is realized differentially by various groups of women. Over the course of her lifetime, however, it is probably true that the woman of today has considerably more free time than her counterpart living fifty or a hundred years ago.

LEISURE VALUES: POTENTIAL AND ACHIEVED

It is not difficult to support the claim that some leisure is good for people. After all, if men everywhere spent all of their time procuring the necessities of life, it is difficult to imagine how the arts could have been developed, how religion could flourish, or how the niceties of civilized living could have come into being. Whatever one's preferred definition of it, "the good life" in part requires a certain measure of free time.

Even though the value of *some* leisure for society's members can be defended, it does not follow that *more* is necessarily desirable. Much of the worth of the increase in leisure time would depend on how it is used, and therefore, what the people of the society "get out" of it. Not only that, but in evaluating the change we would need to consider various features of the society at the times when it had less leisure and when it had more. For example, if the work of a hundred years ago was more satisfying, more meaningful, and more personally rewarding than that of today, it is possible that even though it was carried on for longer hours, there was more of the "good life" then than now. It is theoretically also possible that fewer hours of leisure spent in some ways are better than more hours of leisure spent in other ways. Sooner or later, then, we have to face the question of the *quality* of leisure-time pursuits, in addition to the quantity of time available for leisure. On what basis can we compare trips to the county fair and to Disneyland? A church social and a TV evening at home? Even if the activities are seemingly similar, we do not avoid the matter of quality as when we ask, for example, whether resting on a bench in the city park has the same meaning as resting on a suburban flagstone patio, or whether either are equivalent to resting under the big elm in the east pasture. Such a question ignores how much time people have for resting, but tries to get at what it means to them and what it does to them.

Inquiries into the *meaning* of work and the *meaning* of leisure cannot be shunted aside as "too philosophical" for study, for they are at the core of our leisure problem. To deal with such matters sociologically, however, it would seem best to shift the level of analysis to a determination of what values people today could be deriving from their leisure pursuits and how fully they are doing so. Such matters are not really "intangible," for basically they rest on what we know about our society, the human personality, and what people are saying, doing, or failing to do. Analysis of contemporary mass society and the stresses and strains to which most members of our society are subjected, should lead us to see some of the values held by large numbers of Americans that are not satisfied by vocations but could be by avocations.

PERCEPTION OF FREEDOM. Many people, apparently, have a strong desire for "freedom," in the sense of a period of time during which their obligations are minimal and their activities voluntary. This, of course, is the antithesis of work, for work involves commitment of time and a surrender of freedom. What is more, the nature of the work in our mass industrialized society seems increasingly to demand a greater surrender of personal choice and decision with regard to such things as how one performs his tasks, the order in which he performs them, when his working day should start and end, and even when he may have his midmorning "break." Thus, an important value to be achieved in the off-work hours is the *perception of freedom* by the person himself.

FULLER USE OF MIND AND BODY. Another important characteristic of the modern occupational scene is the growing technology. Machines have taken over many of the physical and some of the mental tasks formerly performed by persons and have transformed the vast majority of occupations so that they require very little mental or physical exertion. In short, the minds and bodies of many Americans are only fractionally employed by their work. What leisure existed for earlier generations could often best be used in rest and relaxation; many modern workers have relatively little from which to rest and relax. More active recreation, mentally and physically, is apparently needed. Psychological and manual skills, unmet by many occupations, must be provided by leisure-time pursuits. A second value to be met through leisure in modern society is *the providing of opportunity for a fuller use of mind and body.*

ESTHETIC CREATION AND APPRECIATION. Closely related to the foregoing are the values of esthetic participation and appreciation. Creation and enjoyment of beauty, though variously defined, are found in every culture and are probably universal needs of mankind. Yet for many Americans, both at their work and in their homes, this value is unfulfilled. A third value, then, which it is thought should be met by recreation in modern society *is the providing of opportunity for esthetic creation and appreciation.*

INTIMATE GROUP PARTICIPATION. One of the most prominent characteristics of life in our modern mass society is its individualistic nature. Primary groups like the neighborhood and family are weakened, and most of the individual's contacts with his fellow citizens are superficial, impersonal, nonintimate. Whether by training or by nature or by a combination of the two, persons desire intimate group experience. The nature of most occupations is such today that this experience is not provided for most individuals in their work. Hence, again, it must be found in their leisure. A fourth value to be met by recreation in modern society is *the providing of opportunity for full, intimate group participation.*

DIRECT CONTACT WITH NATURE. Another characteristic of modern urban living and its occupations is the complete removal of most individuals from direct contact with much of nature. While we shall refrain from any poetic exaggerations about the "beauties of the earth and its flora and fauna," the vacation and holiday treks of urban dwellers to the country, together with the unanimity of philosophical and social thinkers concerning the values to be derived from contact with nature, make legitimate our inclusion of it as a need for many Americans that is currently unsatisfied by urban living. Since the work of most Americans keeps them in the city, this value, too, must be satisfied during their leisure. A fifth value to be met by recreation in modern society is *the providing of opportunity for direct contact with nature.*

OCCUPATION OF TIME. One important occupational aspect of modern American culture has already been mentioned and is repeated so that in its very obviousness it will not be overlooked. We refer to the fact that on a yearly basis most people today spend less than half of their waking hours at their usual job. Accordingly, people need *something* to do in the remaining time. Ideally, of course, it would be hoped that the free time would be eagerly anticipated, enjoyably spent, and pleasantly recalled, and that some of the other values of leisure and recreation would be simultaneously achieved. Nevertheless, a sixth and fundamental value of life that must be met is the sheer *occupation of time.*

We do not contend that these are all the values that must be met by leisure-time activities in modern American society, nor that these values are held by all Americans. They are apparently values held by many Americans, however, that are not satisfied outside their leisure hours, and they may serve as a frame of reference for examining the present status of leisure and recreation in the United States.

EVALUATION OF CURRENT LEISURE USES

In the light of the foregoing potential values to be achieved in leisure time, we shall now examine the prevalent leisure pursuits in American society. Our discussion does not attempt to be exhaustive, but we shall try to deal particularly with those uses of leisure about which there seem to be a real clash of values.

The "Do-It-Yourself" Movement

For ages man has practiced various arts and crafts and has personally constructed his dwelling or repaired his equipment. The recent phenomenon that goes under the ungainly popular label of "do-it-yourself" is nevertheless something new and something distinct to our industrial society. "Do-it-yourself" describes two general types of activities which, from the standpoint of leisure uses, should be considered separately.

On the one hand, do-it-yourself refers to the practice of arts and crafts in the home, in short, "making things." There can be no doubt that this sort of activity has increased greatly. At first glance it would appear to satisfy various leisure values, particularly the occupation of time, fuller use of mind and body, and the need for esthetic creation. There are, however, several characteristics of the movement that temper the fulfillment of these values, or even make it questionable whether the values are being achieved at all.

Some of the major difficulties with the do-it-yourself trend are its related characteristics of commercialization, professionalization, and standardization. Without undue cynicism, it sometimes seems as if the whole point of the movement is the creation of a "do-it-yourself *market,*" so that more and more people can be sold complete woodworking shops, home kilns for baking more and more ceramic ash trays, and power equipment of various sorts. It could well be that the existence of so much expensive craft equipment is partially responsible for the stress on the expertness of the finished product, rather than on the satisfaction from the experience. There is, of course, no objection to high standards or to pride in accomplishment. The point is, rather, that one can expect a diminution of the creative value of an experience if the major emphasis is on the end product. It is really considered a compliment to say that a neighbor's do-it-yourself bookcase looks as if it were made in a factory. It does, of course, closely resemble thousands of other homemade bookcases because the same "do-it-yourself" pattern was meticulously followed.

The standardization of do-it-yourself activities finds more complete expression in the hundreds of different kinds of "kits" available, most with precut parts and all with detailed directions. Some go even further, as in the case of the "build-it-yourself" transistor radio that is advertised as "partially preassembled." By buying the proper kit, one can fill his home with pictures "painted-by-the-number," and one can assemble anything from a ceramic-top table, to moccasins, or even to a plastic cadaver. No doubt millions of people find some enjoyment in assembling standardized products. We have a right to ask, nevertheless, whether this is the best our society can provide by way of creative and meaningful recreational activities.

In a somewhat different vein, do-it-yourself is also applied to construction, repair, remodeling, and decorating activities around the house and yard. As any suburbanite knows, Saturday morning is a busy time at the lumber yard, with customers stocking up on wood, paint, asphalt tile, and similar products for the weekend's activities. In order to evaluate the activities implied in the use of these products, one would have to know how they are being used and, more importantly, why they are used. Is it done only to "save money"? Has it been entered into voluntarily? A husband and wife can spend enjoyable evenings together while they repaint the living room, or the same things can be "jobs" that they feel compelled to do because they cannot afford to hire someone to do them. In general, home remodeling and repair work has the potential for satisfying such leisure-time values as fuller and different employment of mind and body, occupation of time, creativity, and even freedom from rigid schedules. Many probably find such activities interesting, and the results satisfying. But apparently it is easy to subvert these values with undue concentration on getting the job done.

"Moonlighting"

An extension of doing one's own work around the home is the practice of "moonlighting"—taking a second job under the light of the moon. While this is obviously not recreation, it is a way in which an estimated 3 million workers use the time that could be available as leisure time. Having achieved a shorter workweek on their primary job, millions then choose to spend the time in more work, adding an average of about twelve hours to their workweek.

Why is moonlighting so prevalent? One obvious explanation is that people need money. In general, however, it is among the better-paid industries that the workweek is the shortest, and thus that taking a second job is most feasible. Obviously, those engaged in it feel that the rewards of moonlighting are greater than the rewards of any alternative uses of their time of which they are aware. Unless the family is in obvious financial need, and unless this need cannot otherwise be remedied, it is an odd commentary on our newfound leisure that millions can find no better way to "use up" the time than by more work. Whatever the reasons for moonlighting, it is of course true that it results in a reduced period of time in which the values of leisure can be possibly achieved.

Commercial Recreation

For the most part people do what is easiest to do in their leisure, and the most universally accessible form of recreation for Americans of all ages is the commercially provided variety. The leading American "amusements" are movies, "beer joints," night clubs, reading, sports, television, and radio, both from the standpoint of amount of time spent and of the percentage of persons participating. Two important characteristics that all of these types of recreation have in common are (1) commercial domination and (2), largely, passiveness of roles. Even in sports, spectators vastly exceed active participants. An important football game, for example, will have upward of thirty-five active participants, some one hundred thousand spectators, and millions of radio listeners and newspaper readers. Similar millions of primary and secondary spectators center around two boxers and a referee. And so on with many other forms of recreation.

How well do commercial activities meet our six recreational values? Certainly they may be credited with successful fulfillment of the value of occupying time. The words and actions of many Americans testify to the point that they would "go crazy" if they were not able to "kill time" via movies, television, the radio, reading, and alcoholic drinking. The frequent use of the phrase, "kill time," gives us a clue to the doubtful satisfaction of many of the other desired values of living by commercial recreation.

The passive spectator nature of most commercial recreation is evidence of its failure to offer opportunity for "full use of mind and body." Listening to most radio programs, watching most television programs and movies, and reading most of the widest selling literature are little challenge to the intellect and none to the body. The same is true of the sports spectator and the "barfly." Sports participation, from the physical standpoint, is, of course, another matter, and popular sports that are commercially (in part) provided fulfill at least half of this value. For most Americans, however, the time and money spent in the passive commercial amusements far exceed the amount devoted to the active sports.

The values of esthetic creation and appreciation and of contact with nature are very limited in the major commercial recreations. The value of group participation is met in part by some of the "amusements," but usually in a superficial way. If commercial recreation fails so completely to meet important values of the American people, why does it remain so popular? One answer is that in most communities there are either no alternatives or no readily accessible alternatives. The widespread appeal of television is a case in point. Many, many Americans watch television programs every day, sometimes for hours at a time. On the surface it would seem that surely television must be meeting most of the important recreational values of its viewers. But at the same time many people frankly admit that television's chief advantage is that it gives them *"something* to do," some not unpleasant way of passing the time between the end of the workday and bedtime. Thus, various forms of commercial recreation may be resorted to not because of their own positive attraction, but simply because "there is nothing else to do."

Linked with this is the factor of "created demand"; commercial interests "whip up" appetites for their products by various techniques. Once people are lured into commercial recreational activities by various propaganda devices (and since there is "nothing else to do anyhow"), they tend to continue with them. "Low-level" recreation—that is, recreation failing to satisfy values defined as important by the society—is apparently habit forming. The person who begins attending insipid movies or reading only pulp magazines or watching television for many hours a day because he knows of no readily available alternatives, may soon reach a condition where he no longer consciously desires "anything better." At the same time, we are suggesting that many Americans at least unconsciously feel that much of their commercially derived recreation is a "waste of time." Somehow the promised "thrills" are never quite achieved, or the television programs begin to have such a degree of sameness that it is difficult to tell one from another or even the regular offerings from the summer reruns. Many people seem to have a growing feeling, sometimes more intense, sometimes more subdued, that despite their financial outlays for recreation "the good life" seems to be escaping them.

The popularity of commercial recreation continues and grows. A pertinent question is, What are the probabilities that commercial offerings will more adequately meet important social values?

The fundamental reason for the low quality of commercial recreation is profit. The kind of facilities, personnel, and space needed to provide the types of recreation giving opportunity for "full use of mind and body, esthetic creation and appreciation, full and intimate group participation, and contact with nature" are simply not in tune with the ring of the cash register. The probability that commercial offerings will alter appreciably to meet these values with any force is small indeed. Profit lies, to put it bluntly, in a small, low-rent "joint," with admission rates that "fit everybody's purse," and with a sufficiently brief and superficial type of entertainment to allow for a large "turnover."

Present Status of Private, Nonprofit Recreational Programs

Although the development of noncommercial recreation has been inadequate and much less impressive than the gigantic growth of commercial recreation, many public and private nonprofit agencies exist whose partial or full-time purpose is to provide leisure-time services. Private organizations recognized and began partially to meet the recreational needs of sections of the population prior to the acceptance of any public responsibility in this field. But their major concern in the recreational field has been with the leisure-time activities of youth.

COMPLEXITY OF PRIVATE RECREATIONAL OFFERINGS. It is not easy, however, even to gain a clear understanding of the recreational offerings for youth that are provided by the various private agencies. Some leisure organizations of youth are offshoots of adult organizations, such as youth church groups and youth groups affiliated with fraternal orders. Other youth organizations, although not affiliated with an adult organization, are led by adults. Then again, women's clubs, businessmen's clubs, and other adult organizations sometimes "sponsor" youth organizations by supplying facilities or encouraging the public to supply facilities, although they do not work directly with the young people. Finally, there are some organizations composed entirely of youth, directed by them, and not connected in any way with an adult organization. Some "Teen Clubs" fall into this category. Generally their resources for equipment and facilities are meager and they do not receive much community encouragement, probably because of their lack of adult influence.

The existence of such varied leisure-time youth groups makes it difficult to assess the recreational resources of a community. Many youth organizations, even those with recreation as a large part of their programs, tend to deemphasize their recreational objectives and accent such values as "character building," "personal adjustment," and "leadership training." This further complicates the job of evaluating the community recreational resources available to youth.

The same obscurity of recreational purpose characterizes the complex variety of organizations serving adults. Even lodges, fraternities, luncheon clubs, fellowship societies, athletic clubs, and the like, whose most obvious reason for being is the entertainment of their members, profess to high service, spiritual and other "uplifting" aims, and minimize, or even deny, their recreational functions. The idea that recreation in and of itself is a worthwhile goal is not widespread. Frequently recreation is rationalized as being necessary to promote health and well-being, to prevent boredom, to enable one to do his best on the job, and so on. For this reason, there are few community organizations with fulfillment of the recreational needs of adults as their avowed primary aim. Could it be that we still cling unconsciously to the notion held by our Puritan ancestors that "fun is sin"?

INADEQUACIES OF PRIVATELY SPONSORED RECREATION. Although the number of private organizations in the United States with varyingly covert recreational aims is large and their claimed memberships impressive, several glaring inadequacies appear in their recreational services. They are, first of all, primarily nonadult. The YMCA and YWCA and the settlement houses are exceptions with their adult recreational programs, but even these groups have activities directed principally toward youth and appeal to only a very small fraction of the adult population. Most of the other private organizations make no pretense of meeting adult needs. It is not suggested that the emphasis on the needs of youth should be reduced, for, as we shall presently observe, they, too, are inadequately served. We are merely pointing out that one deficiency of the recreational activities of private organizations is the lack of an adult program. (The adult services in fraternal and social orders, in general, have very limited programs for a very limited membership; or, as in the case of the large societies and veterans' organizations, largely duplicate commercial recreational offerings for their members' private consumption.)

In addition to inadequately serving adults, private organizations apparently fail in fulfilling the recreational needs of youth. Although the more than 100 national youth agencies have a steady and, for some, even an increasing membership, they actually reach but a small proportion of all youth. Apparently a large number of young people are attracted neither by the programs of such organizations nor by the personnel providing the program. Reasons often given by young people themselves for their lack of interest in these programs are that adults dominate the activities in such a way as to make full, intimate participation of the young people themselves unappealing or impossible, and that the activities themselves are designed to meet preconceived adult standards of what the young people "ought" to be interested in rather than what really interests them.

Even if we grant that some of these alleged deficiencies in the recreational programs of private organizations are exaggerated and unfair, it is obvious that we cannot expect these groups sufficiently to expand their programs to meet all of the unfulfilled recreational needs of all the old and young people in our society. For providing an area in which to experiment with new ideas on a small scale, for programs requiring individualized attention, for meeting needs of special groups, and for organizing efforts to secure community-wide recreational facilities, the private agencies are indispensable. But to bring adequate recreation to the whole community, the community must turn to itself.

Public Recreational Programs

Probably the first act of any government in the United States directed toward providing recreational facilities at public expense was the purchase of Central Park by New York city in 1853. The federal government purchased its first national park (Yellowstone) in 1872; one state had a park system prior to 1900. The public recreation movement is very young, and, considering its age, has reached impressive size.

GROWTH OF PUBLIC RECREATION. Beginning with the minimal notion of providing space for children's play and adults' rest, public recreation programs have gradually expanded the quantity and quality of their leisure-time provisions for all age groups in the community.

In communities with well-developed recreation programs, numerous facilities are available to people of all ages. In addition to the more usual playground and park facilities, some communities operate day camps, shooting ranges, bridle trails, outdoor theaters, and bowling greens. Winter sports and indoor recreation centers are being added as communities attempt to extend their program throughout the year.

At the state level we find increasing concern with recreation. Three states, North Carolina, California, and Vermont, have established separate governmental agencies giving full-time service to recreation and all fifty states have some type of recreation agency. Increased appropriations for recreation, making possible the steady acquisition of park lands and the improvement of existing facilities, point to the growth of recreation at the state level.

The federal government, through various of its departments and agencies, has long been interested in recreation. Recently the Federal Inter-Agency Committee on Recreation has been formed to coordinate the services of the many federal agencies concerned with recreation, to exchange information, and to do cooperative planning. Some see as the next step a separate federal agency devoted solely to recreation—a Federal Recreation Service.

This growth of public recreation at the community, state, and national levels has been sporadic and by no means easily won. Failure of public opinion to accept recreation as an important and inevitable part of life, noted in our discussion of private agencies, has been even a greater deterring factor for the development of an adequate public recreation program. "Hard-headed" taxpayers and their representatives have often been difficult to convince of the desirability of expending public funds so that people (especially adults) could "play."

SCHOOLS. One cannot travel far in our cities, towns, or rural areas without encountering a school. Furthermore, almost all schools have some outdoor play equipment, a hall or an auditorium suitable for larger groups, and all, of course, have the classrooms themselves. It would naturally be expected that the school would be the focus of much of our public recreation. As a matter of fact, considerable burden for local recreational leadership and for provision of some of the needed facilities has been placed upon the public schools. An increasing number of educators consider this a legitimate responsibility of the school for two reasons. First, the main activity for which the school needs to educate is the use of leisure. This is true both from the standpoint of the obvious ignorance of the creative use of leisure manifested by many Americans and from the standpoint of the large percentage of the individual's life that is now spent in leisure. Secondly, all leisure-time pursuits condition, or educate, the individual; it is to the school's advantage that the curricular and extracurricular types of education to which the individual is subjected be complementary rather than counteractive.

Although the conception of the complementary roles of education and recreation has gradually grown, it has by no means been unanimously adopted and acted upon by the schools. The notions still prevail, in practice if not in theory, that education is "preparation for life," something practical in which students start participating after leaving school, and that recreation is "fun here and now" and hence dispensable as a "frill" or justifiable only as a means of keeping students out of trouble after school hours. So long as these ideas are current in many communities, full cooperation of educators and the public in the use of school facilities and school leadership for recreational programs is not possible.

A related obstacle to the full use of the school in recreational programs is the traditional academic atmosphere that surrounds both its facilities and its personnel. Youngsters and adults alike have constructed the stereotype of teacher and school as something "stuffy" and displeasurable and, hence, not to be sought after in leisure hours. Like many stereotypes, truth is contained therein; many teachers bring to recreational activities a pedantic, instructional, "dignified" approach that is of doubtful value even in the classroom role.

Despite such difficulties, however, the schools in most communities have made contributions to recreation at least by encouraging extracurricular activities, by teaching an increasing number of subjects with leisure-time value, and by opening the school recreational facilities to some community-wide activities. A few school systems have organized and operated recreational programs for the whole community. Later, we shall have more to say about broader programs for leisure education.

LIBRARIES. Aside from schools, public libraries are the most universally available source of community recreation in America. Almost all cities over 10,000 population have public libraries, as do some smaller cities and towns. Libraries, particularly the larger and better financed ones, have increased their cultural offerings beyond the collection of books and other reading matter. Some have a weekly or more frequent "story telling hour" for children, conduct art exhibits, and have lending collections of art reproductions, films, and phonograph records. Still others seek to extend their services to persons in outlying areas by establishing branch libraries or traveling "bookmobiles." Since reading is probably the most frequent leisure-time activity, it is well that in many communities there is available a ready source of good reading material.

While the important contribution of the public library to the recreational life of the community is not to be minimized, the public library falls short of its potential service in a number of respects. Close to one fifth of the nation does not have ready access to libraries, and the libraries available to easily another third are inadequately supplied with books, staff, and other facilities. In the professional world, the poorly paid schoolteacher is ingloriously outshadowed by the poorly paid librarian. Just as the school suffers by failure to attract and hold competent persons for financial reasons, so does the library. While the competent faithfuls who stick by both institutions in the face of near poverty is impressive, a large number of incompetents is understandably found in each place. The skill of the good librarian is more than pulling the proper book off the shelf, just as the skill of the good teacher is more than masterly recitation of the multiplication tables. A competent librarian is one who not only knows books well, but is able to sense the needs and interests of her readers and skillfully guide them through a transition of tastes into new interests and new needs of which they were originally unaware. Such librarians plus an adequate supply of the best books in all fields plus comfortable and pleasant physical surroundings are essentials of a good public library. Such libraries are rare indeed, for most communities have not yet recognized the need to supply the funds that are prerequisite to this type of public educational-recreational service.

STATE AND NATIONAL RECREATION. There are many who feel that the total responsibility for public recreation cannot be left to the community alone. Many towns do not have the necessary resources, and in others the coordination of services is poor. Then too, there are certain types of facilities, such as extensive parklands, that most towns and cities cannot afford. State operation of recreational services, then, is one solution to the problem that faces the roughly four out of five Americans living in communities without a "reasonably adequate" recreation program.

Space does not permit a very full discussion of recreational services provided by the states and by the federal government. The main function of states in the recreational field at present is the provision of parks and forests. The program in most states was improved by federal assistance provided by the Civilian Conservation Corps during the depression years, but still more lands are required. Another important function now offered by a few states is a state recreation service which assists in appraising community resources, organizing local recreation systems, selecting and training leaders, and in obtaining funds for facilities and personnel.

Most of the extensive activities of the federal government in the field of recreation were temporary depression measures carried out by now deceased agencies like the Works Progress Administration, the Civilian Conservation Corps, and the National Youth Administration. Some permanent functions, however, continue under various federal auspices. The most notable of these are the National Park Service in the Department of the Interior and the Forest Service of the Department of Agriculture. Both of these services cooperate with local and state governments, schools, and private groups in providing recreational activities such as mountain climbing, pack and saddle trips, camping, fishing, hunting, picnicking, nature study, skiing, and the like. Valuable work in assisting and stimulating rural communities to provide adequate recreational opportunities for their population has been and continues to be provided by the Extension Service of the Department of Agriculture.

REMEDYING THE LEISURE PROBLEM

Education for Leisure

For some of the work in our society a great deal of education is required, and most of the work requires some education. Few, indeed, would dispute the necessity for education that is somehow related to preparation for life's work. But now we find that man has more time for leisure than he has for work. Surely this would suggest that we educate people for leisure pursuits as much as, or more than, we educate them for occupational pursuits.

It must be admitted, first of all, that people *are* being educated for leisure. What is lacking, it seems, is a general recognition of the need for education for leisure and a firm and wholehearted commitment to the position that such education is desirable. One fundamental clash of values in the social problem of leisure use, in other words, clearly occurs at the point of taking appropriate remedial action to deal with the problem.

While the issue is disputed, it seems that the evidence clearly shows that many, many people do not know how to use their leisure wisely. The aimless pursuits of teenagers, or the "excitement" they think up to escape from boredom, the hours spent at passive entertainment which fails to satisfy, and the search for "something to do" by people of all ages, all seem to attest to the need for leisure education. Nor is it farfetched to use as additional evidence the fact that an estimated 20 million Americans regularly use tranquilizing drugs, that millions need drugs in order to sleep at night, and so on. It is difficult to believe that such practices would be necessary if people really were "enjoying themselves" and finding satisfaction in the greater part of their days that are not spent at work.

One fear concerning leisure education is that it would rob the individual of his "free choice" in how to use his own leisure. After all, who are "they," the "experts," to say that a man should *not* spend evening after evening with his can of beer and his television if he so chooses? As we have indicated previously, this so-called free choice has illusionary qualities, for if someone knows of only one thing to do, he really has no choice at all! The more alternative ways of using his time that a man knows, and which are feasible for him, the more real choice he has.

Another criticism of leisure education, sometimes more a rumbling beneath the surface than an outright attack, is closely related to the matter of freedom of choice, but it deals more directly with the *evaluation* of different uses of leisure time. Here again we must state bluntly that one use of leisure is not "just as good" as another. In the light of what we know about the human personality and what we know about the potential values that leisure is capable of fulfilling, some uses of free time are better than others. Ultimately, of course, the individual should choose freely, but it simply does not follow that all personal choices will be good for the individual or his society.

Even if we were somehow to resolve the conflict of values concerning the need and worth of leisure education, there would still be serious problems attendant on producing quality leisure education for the masses. Ideally, education for leisure should be extremely broad in scope, embracing many types of learnings and suitable for people of all ages. Such education, furthermore, should deal directly with leisure attitudes and attempt to develop within the individual an appreciation of the range of values that can be achieved through leisure.

While the teaching of specific recreational skills is thought to be secondary to the developing of sound values, there is much that could be done, more or less immediately, better to equip the population with suitable skills for use in their leisure time. Most of the extracurricular activities of our schools, for example, cater to the presumed interests of only a minority of students, and those interests appear to be fleeting ones. Very few adults spend much of their leisure time playing football or basketball, yet these activities consume a large part of the resources for extracurricular activities in most schools. Even when the schools teach skills that have the possibility of "carryover" into the adult years, there seems to be more emphasis on expertness and near-professionalization here and now, than on opening the way for greater leisure enjoyment in the longer run.

The immediate proposals for improving existing leisure education and for expanding it to include people of all ages and in all walks of life, will, of course, take money. Salaries for recreational specialists may compete with those for teachers, policemen, and others whom communities tend to define as more necessary. While evidently there is some change going on in this area, proposals for increased budgets for leisure education frequently are met with more criticisms of "reckless expenditures" than praises for foresight and wisdom.

Research on Leisure

The same lack of firm commitment to the values of leisure that we noted with respect to leisure education also affects the quality and quantity of research on leisure. After all, competent people are attracted to fields that they consider important as well as "interesting"; similarly, money is made available through the federal government, the universities, and foundations for "important" research. In the light of our societal values, it is not surprising to find that relatively few people are engaging in research on leisure, that expenditures for this purpose are meager, and that the research output is correspondingly low.

It should be obvious that education for leisure and other proposals for ameliorating leisure problems should rest on sound knowledge. At present there seems to be a particular dearth of knowledge concerning the qualitative aspects of different uses of leisure time. We need to know, in other words, more about what happens to people as a result of alternative leisure uses, and not merely how people pass their leisure time. For the present it does not look too hopeful that the values of our society will permit sufficient research on leisure. It is, of course, on just such research that our best hopes rest for sound and effective treatment of our leisure problems.

Planning for Leisure

The final broad approach to remedying our leisure problem with which we shall deal is the planning that is needed at the community, state, and national levels. While the social machinery required for the needed planning may involve some expense, it is probable that greater deterrents are found in the threats to values some of the changes involve and the social inertia with regard to the leisure problem generally.

COMMUNITY PLANNING. Because of the complementary objectives of recreational and educational activities in a community, some sort of merging or coordination of these functions, rather than separate administration and policy making, is very much needed in all communities. This can perhaps be best accomplished, as the Educational Policies Committee of the National Education Association suggests, by a Public Education Authority (containing school, library, and public recreation administrations). A Public Education Authority should, for the coordination of the community's program, have a strong advisory relationship with private agencies carrying out leisure-time activities; such an advisory relationship should be mutual, with suggestions, assistance, pioneer efforts, and experimentation undertaken by private agencies in the field of leisure pursuits.

STATE PLANNING. Every state needs a planning agency with state-wide conceptions and authority in order to take a broad view of the leisure-time needs of its people and to see that these needs are met.

Most states have planning boards that could include a more active program of promoting and coordinating leisure-time functions and be delegated more authority for, and vitalization of, other aspects of their program. Essential parts of any state-wide planning for the use of leisure would seem to be the duty of equalizing recreational opportunities, including the granting of financial aid to local governments that are not able themselves to maintain costs of an adequate program; the provision of recreational services of a broader scope than local governments can furnish, including a more adequate park and forest service; and the rendering of advisory and promotion services for local communities.

A reorganization of state departments of education to secure broader and more progressive authority is also a need in most states, together with the coordination, through the state planning boards or some other medium, of revitalized educational and recreational programs.

More effective state library extension services could do much to reach persons for whom local public libraries are not now available, to help establish more libraries, and to assist existing local libraries in planning more adequate services in their communities.

NATIONAL PLANNING. Few educational and recreational leaders in our society feel any longer that it is possible to have adequate and fully consistent programs for the nation as a whole without some federal planning, promotion, and financial assistance. Strong public reaction against what is generally termed "federal interference" has been characteristic of the American people.

It is well to remember, in this respect, the words of Aristotle, "The state comes into existence, that man may live. It continues that man may live well." If as a society we are truly interested in living well, and if we take proper precautions against the granting of unbalanced authority to the federal government, our concern about too much participation by the federal government, as Lindeman points out, would seem to be unfounded.

What has to be taken into account in all planning under a federal system of government is the fact that every step in the growth of national power must be accompanied by a concurrent increase in local power. A federal system may be said to grow when the two foci of authority are convergent. I can see no fundamental inconsistency, for example, in the accelerated development of local recreation programs which are augmented by the national government. On the other hand, it seems to me thoroughly consistent with federal principles to assume that it is the function of a national democratic government to strive for an equalization of all elements comprising a good life. The function of a democratic government is to extend, not restrict privileges and opportunities, to give assurance, e.g., that if cultural leisure is good for the North and the East, it must also be good for the South and West. A government which cannot give such assurances will not long remain democratic.

When I contend for participation of the national government in developing a program for the people's leisure, I am often confronted by critics who insist that they recognize the strategic importance of recreation but they fear that a program such as I am advocating will open the door to politics. There are two appropriate responses to be made to criticism of this type: (*a*) there already exists a great deal of politics in almost every recreation department of every municipality in America; and (*b*) high politics is better than low politics. I have seen enough of low politics in the sphere of poor relief administered wholly by local authorities to know that the political process does not purify itself automatically by merely becoming petty.[1]

Planning on the national level must include research into the leisure-time needs of the whole society, coordination of federal, state, local, and private recreational services, and the promotion and (where necessary) partial financing of needed recreational services throughout the country. While recreation is to be thought of as an essential part of life itself and not as a means of solving problems in other areas of living, it is closely interrelated with many other activities about which government concerns itself. Coordination at the national level, therefore, should include more than strictly recreational functions and should especially take into account the interfunctioning of recreation with education, health, housing, labor conditions, and similar matters.

[1] Eduard C. Lindeman, *Leisure—A National Issue* (New York: Association Press, 1939), pp. 59–60. Used by permission.

SUGGESTED READINGS

AMERICAN ASSOCIATION FOR HEALTH, PHYSICAL EDUCATION, AND RECREATION, *Leisure and the Schools*. Washington, D.C., National Education Association, 1961.

ANDERSON, NELS, *Work and Leisure*. New York, The Fress Press of Glencoe, 1962.

FRIEDMANN, GEORGES, *The Anatomy of Work*. New York, The Free Press of Glencoe, 1962.

KAPLAN, MARY, *Leisure in America: A Social Inquiry*. New York, John Wiley & Sons, Inc., 1960.

KLEEMEIER, ROBERT W., *Aging and Leisure*. New York, Oxford University Press, 1961.

LARRABEE, ERIC, and ROLF MEYERSOHN, eds., *Mass Leisure*. New York, The Free Press of Glencoe, 1958.

MILLER, NORMAN P., and DUANE M. ROBINSON, *The Leisure Age: Its Challenge to Recreation*. Belmont, Calif., Wadsworth Publishing Co., 1963.

SCHRAMM, WILBUR, JACK LYLE, and EDWIN B. PARKER, *Television in the Lives of Our Children*. Stanford, Calif., Stanford University Press, 1961.

SOULE, GEORGE, *Time for Living*. New York, Viking Press, 1955.

RACE □ *12*

Disturbingly enough, most civilized people in the world know that America has a "race problem." Most Americans admit it. Studies of other societies show that racial difficulties, while sometimes found, are *not* an inevitable outcome of intergroup living. It is a strange irony that race problems tend to persist in a society that prides itself on its scientific search for knowledge and which is desirous of spreading its values and approach to life to other peoples of the world.

Intertwined in what frequently passes for "common knowledge" about race, is a conglomeration of facts, values, myths, and wishful thinking. Our first task, accordingly, is to try to sort these out and to determine what is known about race and racial differences. We need, following that, to face up squarely to what really is going on in our society in the area of race relations, and we need also to evaluate the remedial action that is proposed or attempted.

THE CONCEPT OF RACE

What Is Race?

It may, at first, seem absurd to raise the question, "What *is* race?" Surely it might be contended, everyone knows what a race is, and everyone knows full well to which race he and other people belong. But does he?

Race is usually defined as "a grouping of human beings distinguishable by the possession of similar combinations of anatomical features due to common heredity." Such a definition may imply a certain amount of preciseness, but in reality the concept race is far from precise. Indeed, the lack of clarity in the concept race causes more difficulty than at first might be imagined when it comes to determining who belongs to which race.

DIFFICULTIES IN CLASSIFYING GROUPS. Since the bases of racial classification are certain anatomical characteristics of humans, the study of race in and of itself is, strictly speaking, in the province of physical anthropology. Anthropologists have evidenced great difficulty in agreeing upon criteria acceptable for racial classification. Singly and in combination, many standards have been used—shape of head, skin pigmentation, shape of the hair in cross section, stature, color of the eyes and hair, amount of body hair, shape of nose, and others. The results of using such bases for the determination of race have consisted of contradictory classifications. For example, the most commonly employed classification is skin color, but there is no logical or scientific defense for the employment of this particular criterion. Millions of dark-skinned Hindus are thus visibly different from Caucasians in one respect, skin color, but they are also visibly different from Negroes with respect to hair texture, shape of nose, shape of lips, and so on. To which race do these millions of people belong?

There are other groups of people who cannot be classified as belonging to the Negro, Caucasian, or Mongolian race. Such are the Ainu of northern Japan with their light-to-dusky skins, their "Caucasian noses," and some Mongolian features. The aborigines of Australia and the Polynesians present a similar problem. When such difficulty is experienced in classifying entire groups of people in various parts of the world, the meaningfulness of the concept race certainly can be questioned.

DIFFICULTIES IN CLASSIFYING INDIVIDUALS. A somewhat related difficulty arises with regard to how to classify the offspring of parents of different races. A person with one Negro and one Caucasian parent is called a "mulatto," but does the mulatto belong to the white or Negro race? While probably in most places in the United States he will be treated *as if* he is a Negro, it is clear that he received half of his biological inheritance from his Caucasian parent. It is interesting that the expression "quadroon," referring to a person who is one-quarter Negro, emphasizes what a person is *not*. Anthropologically speaking, of course, the quadroon is mostly white.

In some of our states, finally, a person with seven-eighth's white and one-eighth Negro ancestry is defined as a Negro. But a legal definition of race must not be confused with an anthropological one, for clearly in those cases where the quadroon and octoroon are considered Negroes, the law ignores the larger measure of biological inheritance and rests its definition on the smaller. Another problem with the legal definition of race arises from the fact that a man can change his legal race merely by moving from state to state! To which race does a person belong who is defined as a Negro in some parts of the country but not so in others?

In the preceding paragraphs we have seen that there is a certain fuzziness to the concept race and that difficulties arise when we attempt to apply the usual criteria of race in classifying specific people or groups of people. From the sociological point of view, even more serious difficulties inhere in the nature and kind of standards that are used for classifying people as being meaningfully different from the rest of mankind. Put differently, how important or relevant, from the standpoint of social living, are the criteria for racial classification?

IMPORTANCE OF RACIAL CRITERIA. If for many, many generations a group were cut off from all others and consequently married only within itself, it is entirely likely that in time some of the inherited characteristics of its members would be noticeably different from those of other peoples of the world. It may even be that these differences would be "important," from some reasonably objective standpoint. If, for example, the individuals all inherited a tendency toward a stronger, healthier, longer-lasting cardio-vascular system than others, then this would seem to be important.

Most people would probably agree that intelligence is an important human characteristic, and that so are physical vigor, longevity, and perhaps an inherited immunity to certain diseases. However, it is truly startling to compare a list of important human characteristics with those inherited traits that serve as the bases for distinguishing among races. If we were able to approach the matter with objectivity, it would indeed be difficult to contend that the shape of one's eyes is important, so long as it does not influence ability to see. In a similar manner, there would seem to be no possible biological basis for concluding that the texture of his hair, the shape of his nose, or the color of his skin makes a person an inherently better or poorer example of the human species. The so-called racial characteristics would seem to be really trivial matters when compared with health, vigor, and intelligence.

Undoubtedly it is because of the triviality of racial characteristics that we experience difficulty in classifying a group, like the Hindu, who exhibit some characteristics of one race and some of another. We cannot decide whether nose shape is more or less important than skin color; whether hair texture takes precedence over eye shape, because, in the words of one student of the subject, "they are all empty things, and we have the impossible task of arranging them in some order—empty, emptier, emptiest." [1]

RACE AS A MYTH. The various difficulties with the concept race are enough to make us question whether race is a scientific reality or a myth. One authority on race has seriously suggested that "Races are fictions —the modern counterparts of witches, ghosts, and goblins—existing only in our minds. . . ." [2] The analogy with witches does seem to be a useful

[1] Brewton Berry, "The Concept of Race in Sociology Textbooks," *Social Forces,* 18: 3 (March 1940), p. 416.

[2] Brewton Berry, "A Southerner Learns About Race," *Common Ground,* II: 3 (Spring 1942), p. 89.

one. After all, at one stage of our history people "knew" that there were witches. Such creatures had a crescent-shaped mole or some other unmistakable "mark of the devil," and their twitching, jerky, bodily movements, their manner of speech, and other characteristics were quite observable. What is more, some people even admitted that they were witches. No one is suggesting that our ancestors did not really see the moles, observe the behavior, or hear the confessions of the witches. Today, however, we see and hear the same things but either we do not consider them important or we ascribe a different meaning to them. A crescent mole is considered a trivial blemish, and the "weird, jerky movements" are diagnosed as epilepsy or some other disease. In a similar manner, the biological trivia we now use to determine racial classification could lose their significance. While still observable, they could in time cease to be defined as important or noteworthy characteristics.

Because "race" does not seem to be a scientific reality from a physical anthropological standpoint does not mean that the concept is of no social significance. Mistaken ideas are as real as accurate ones to the person who believes them and, through his actions, to people who do not believe them. "Ghosts" and "witches" are not scientifically demonstrable entities. If a person or group believes in ghosts or witches and these imagined spirits influence his behavior, they become a factor that must be taken into account in understanding the behavior of the "believers" and also of the "nonbelievers" with whom they interact. The delusions and hallucinations of a mentally ill person, by way of another illustration, are "real" to him in his reactions to his environment, even though his physician can demonstrate that "in fact" they lack objective reality. While the delusions and hallucinations of the deranged individual are not directly experienced by his friends and family, these mistaken ideas and sensations become part of the social reality of these persons in their dealings with the ill person. In like manner, the erroneous subjective nature of the concept "race" does not render it *socially* insignificant. Many people act as if "race" were a scientific reality. Race attitudes, conflicts, discriminations, and inequalities are very real and very significant aspects of our problem society.

It is for this reason that we can, and really must, use conventional race terminology in our discussion of racial differences and race problems.

RACIAL ATTITUDES AND PRACTICES

Most people have heard the terms "prejudice" and "discrimination" as they are applied to racial or other minority groups. Since these concepts are basic to any discussion of our race problem and its amelioration, it is necessary to investigate their meaning, their sources, and their relationship to one another.

Racial Prejudice

Literally, prejudice means a prejudgment. One is prejudiced, therefore, if he has preconceived ideas or beliefs that are not based on knowledge. When it refers to attitudes toward minority groups, the term, prejudice, bears the meaning of incorrect and unfavorable opinions about the characteristics of the minority group members. Where prejudice exists, an entire group is prejudged in the sense that undesirable qualities are attributed to all members of the group. Usually included in the concept prejudice are the hostile emotions, the hate, the desire to maintain social distance, and other "negative feelings" toward the group against which one is prejudiced. Prejudice is thus a cognitive and emotive concept. It refers to beliefs and opinions about a group, and feelings toward the group.

Racial Discrimination

Discrimination, by contrast, is an action concept. It refers to unequal and unfair treatment and denial of rights on a group basis. If women, otherwise qualified, are denied jobs because they are women, they are being discriminated against. Discrimination thus involves differential treatment that is applied on a categorical basis to members of a group. Preventing group members from buying homes in a certain area, denying them the right to vote, forcing them to use separate washrooms, and other forms of overt action toward members of a minority group are properly referred to as discrimination.

As might be imagined, there is a relationship between prejudice and discrimination. But the terms are not synonymous. Before investigating the relationship between the two concepts, it is necessary to explore more fully the nature of prejudice. We shall turn, first, to the substance of racial prejudice in the United States, that is, the common beliefs, attitudes, and stereotypes about the Negro in our society.

Racial Prejudice and Race Facts

A system of certain extreme beliefs and attitudes concerning race is commonly designated as racism, and he who holds to this system of belief is spoken of as a racist. The essence of racism can be summarized as follows: [3]

1. The several races evolved from lower anthropoids at different stages in human history. Specifically, it is held that the Negro was the last to evolve; this accounts for his "apelike" characteristics.

[3] Arnold Rose, "Race and Ethnic Relations," in Robert K. Merton and Robert A. Nisbet, eds., *Contemporary Social Problems* (New York: Harcourt, Brace & World, 1961), p. 356.

2. As a result of differential evolution, there are meaningful intellectual differences among the races so that it is possible to speak of a superior race (white) and an inferior race (Negro).

3. By virtue of its innate superiority, the higher race has produced a superior culture; it is beyond the capability of the lower race both to participate fully in this superior culture and to transmit it.

4. Mixture of the races would result in biological deterioration of the superior race and the eventual deterioration of the superior culture it has produced.

Put bluntly, the typical white racist believes that the white race is superior to others biologically, psychologically, and culturally. Since such beliefs are common and persistent in America, there is a need to look at the kind of evidence that is used to support them.

BIOLOGICAL EVIDENCE ON RACIAL SUPERIORITY. Biological scientists now hold that man as a species evolved but once. It was long after this single evolution that noticeable differences within the species, that is, races, came into being as a result of movements to different parts of the world and long-continued virtual isolation of groups. This widely accepted position is clearly at odds with the racist belief that the Negro is closer to the ancestral anthropoid stock and represents an inferior, more "apelike" species than does the Caucasian stock. A discussion of theories of evolution could be an almost endless task. We can get at the root of the matter, however, by examining the characteristics of the races with respect to their resemblance to analogous characteristics of lower anthropoids.

Since the customary distinctions between the Caucasian and Negro "races" break down under close scrutiny, such a comparison runs into difficulty at the outset. Even if we accept the customary classification, however, the stereotyped Negro resembles the anthropoid less in some respects than do either the Caucasian or the Mongolian stereotypes. The wide flat nose and the long arms of some Negroes, for example, may be more "apelike," but their characteristically thick everted lips and smaller amount of body hair are least "apelike." With respect to thickness of lips, the thin-lipped Mongolians are closest to animals, followed by Caucasians, since apes have very thin or practically no lips. With respect to body hair the Caucasian is clearly the most "apelike." Careful anthropological studies indicate that there is an approximately equal number of anthropoid characteristics in the three traditional races and that none of these characteristics has demonstrable correlation with social or psychological factors.[4] Yet not a few members of our society continue to react to the "reality" of the "apelike nature of the Negro."

[4] Juan Comas, "Racial Myths," in United Nations Educational, Scientific, and Cultural Organization, *The Race Question in Modern Science* (New York: William Morrow and Company, 1956), p. 29.

Arguments closely related to the foregoing are often based on the "fact" that biological differences between the races "naturally must" be correlated with physiological and psychological differences. For reasons unexplained, it is argued that "superior" characteristics occur only in the "white race." No facts, however, are available to substantiate this belief in the superiority of "white" people. Logically we should expect to find none, for the best biological inference, based on a mass of empirically derived data, is that skin color and other similar gross anatomical characteristics are a product of natural selection acting upon mutations. The probabilities are high that this form of natural selection would have absolutely no social or psychological significance.[5] The burden of proof, in any case, is with those who contend such significance, and proponents of the hypothesis of relationship between such anatomical characteristics as skin color, on the one hand, and such psychological attributes as mental ability, on the other, have yet adequately to shoulder this burden of proof.

PSYCHOLOGICAL EVIDENCE OF RACIAL SUPERIORITY. While it is apparent that physical features do not cause psychological inferiority, we need to focus more specifically on the racist belief in the intellectual superiority of the white race. The high incidence of illiteracy among Negro groups, the relatively small number of Negroes who have attained educational and scientific distinction, and the poorer average performance of Negroes on a number of "intelligence tests" are all cited as "objective evidence" of their native intellectual inferiority. In regard to "intelligence test" results, the earlier contentions of psychologists that such examinations were a measurement of "native intelligence" have more recently been recanted. Environmental factors have been proved to be of considerable significance in determining test performance,[6] so it is only when environmental differences are absent, or at least negligible, that we can legitimately compare the intelligence-test scores of races or other groups.

In a white-dominated society, environmental differences are not "absent or negligible" for the American Negro. He is not given the same educational opportunities in many American communities, and even where the school facilities and personnel for the Negro are comparable to those provided the white child, comparisons of the two groups are not thereby justified. The preschool and out-of-school experiences of a child greatly affect his school performance. Evidence abounds that the social and economic conditions of many Negro homes are not conducive to the development of alert and interested "scholars."

Regardless of whether it is eventually established that Negroes are as

[5] *Cf.* Ashley Montagu, *Race, Science and Humanity* (Princeton, N.J.: D. Van Nostrand Company, 1963), p. 177.

[6] *Cf.* Raymond W. Mack, *Race, Class and Power* (New York, American Book Company, 1963), pp. 61–62.

intelligent, more intelligent, or less intelligent than whites, it must be remembered that it would be on *a group basis*. In a cross-section sampling of any physical type, wide variations of performance on intelligence tests or any other kind of psychological scale are always found. In *any* of the above three cases, then, it would still be true that many Negroes would be superior to many whites. And, of course, the less intelligent a white person is, the greater would be the number of Negroes who would have an intelligence superior to his. Perhaps it is this thought that prompts some to cling to the presently untenable position that "all Negroes are inferior."

CULTURAL EVIDENCE OF RACIAL SUPERIORITY. If there is no evidence that the white race is higher on the evolutionary scale than other races, and if there is no evidence that the white race is the intellectually superior one, why has the white man advanced so much further than any other race? This question, or some variation of it, is frequently advanced in the form of "irrefutable" argument in favor of white supremacy and superiority. Let us examine the reasoning underlying this argument.

First of all, on what criteria do we base our judgment of the "further advancement" of the white man? Obviously we take our own particular type of cultural achievements and judge other civilizations in terms of these achievements. To evaluate the civilizations of the Chinese or Indian or African peoples on standards derived from Euro-American culture is somewhat analogous to judging the competence of lawyers or ministers or engineers on criteria set up for members of the medical profession. The Western white man's particular type of cultural achievements focalize in his mechanical ingenuity and skill and in his conquest of physical nature, but the overwhelming evidence of the "problem nature" of his society is testimony enough to his failure to date to develop a generally successful formula for living. An impressive case can be made for the greater success of other cultures in developing such a formula. Long ago, for example, the "lowly Eskimo" had achieved one of the primary goals toward which Western man is still striving—the absence of warfare, full "peace on earth." If we take almost any other criterion than sheer bulk of material "progress," we can find other cultures with more convincing achievements than those of Western civilization. There is no universal standard that we may employ to rate one culture superior to another.

In the second place, historical perspective is needed in any attempted judgment of the superiority of one culture over another. Even if we were to grant the superiority of Western culture at this point in history (which, as we have just seen, is an unwarranted assumption), we may not legitimately argue from a temporary to a permanent superiority, based on biological factors. Western culture at the time of Columbus, for example, did not even compare favorably on materialistic grounds alone with such civilizations as the Chinese and East Indian. Much of the activity of Western nations in the fifteenth and sixteenth centuries was directed toward acquiring some of the "superior" material comforts and conveniences of Eastern societies. Not a little of the material progress of Western culture, in fact, may be traced to the borrowing of ideas and material inventions of non-Western, nonwhite peoples.

Thirdly, any close relationship between race and culture may be questioned on the grounds of "impurity" of any racial stock in a specific culture and of variability in the cultural achievements of any specified race. Western culture, for example, is the product of nonwhite as well as white peoples. The most "primitive" tribes of Siberia are of the same racial stock as the most "cultured" Chinese. American Negroes are thought to be "naturally musical," and yet ethnologists report that many tribes in Africa have little or no music. Any alleged "cultural superiority" of a designated "race" breaks down under examination of either the whole culture or the whole race.

Sources of Racial Prejudice

Whether it is of the admittedly extreme racist type or a somewhat milder variety, race prejudice is obviously rampant in our society. But how does such prejudice originally develop? Where do we get our attitudes and feelings about race?

Various hypotheses have been advanced to account for the development of race prejudice. None is fully proved or seems to cover all possibilities; some lack plausibility in the light of modern knowledge of attitude formation. Several of the more common attempts to explain the formation of race prejudice are discussed in the following paragraphs.

IS PREJUDICE INNATE? It has often been contended that each individual is born with some kind of biological mechanism that causes him "instinctively to prefer his own kind" and to recoil from other races. The best indication that "dislike of the unlike" is not innate in human beings is the research revelation that children, especially very young children, do not show race prejudice. Their likes and dislikes for other children are based upon criteria other than physical appearance. As children get older, of course, and learn more of the adult evaluations, they take on the characteristic race prejudices of their groups.

Further evidence against any innate basis for race prejudice is the wide cultural variability of race attitudes. American Negro soldiers, for example, were as generally welcomed during World War II in the various activities of the English and French societies as were American white soldiers. Even within our own society we find so many variations in the nature of prejudice that any hereditary basis appears ridiculous. In the South, where race prejudice is regarded as most categorical, many white parents refuse to permit their children to attend the same school as Negro children. Many persons in the North do not object to their children attending the same school with Negro children, but do object to having Negroes living in their neighborhood. But Southern families not only have Negroes in the same neighborhood, but permanently living within their own homes and entrusted with such intimate matters as the preparation of food and care of children. If there were an innate basis for race prejudice, such intimate physical contact could hardly be tolerated.

Finally, there is no evidence whatsoever that an attitude pattern, like race prejudice, can come to a person through the germ plasm. All patterns of evaluation, like other attitudinal phenomena, are learned through the real or vicarious experience of the person.

It is probably seldom a deliberate, formal, teaching and learning situation, but prejudice is nevertheless learned. As it is expressed in a less publicized verse from *South Pacific,* "You've got to be taught to hate and fear . . . You've got to be *carefully taught."*

What are the true reasons for race prejudice which underlie the rationalizations submitted by the prejudiced? The extreme lengths to which some white members of our society will go, often at great inconvenience to themselves, to "keep the Negro in his place" indicate that *race prejudice must serve some purpose for the prejudiced.*

ECONOMIC SOURCES OF PREJUDICE. The primary motive seems to be an economic one. Throughout history we find numerous examples of the exploitation of minority groups for the fruits of their labor. The ancient Romans and Greeks justified their use of other peoples as slaves on the basis of innate superiority over these groups; the medieval lord was, by birth, a superior brand of human being compared to his serfs; the Nazis, as members of a superior Aryan race, were justified in their own minds in appropriating the property of groups they considered inferior; and so with hundreds of other possible examples. In these instances, just as with the American white and Negro, the dominant group found distinct economic advantage in its prejudice against the dominated group. Physical characteristics, such as the skin color of the Negro, serve as very convenient marks of distinctions between the two groups. Dark skin indicates at once in American society an individual who can be economically exploited with impunity. By virtue of its prejudice, the dominant white group in America may appropriate for itself the best jobs, the greatest wealth, and the resulting "better things of life."

PSYCHOLOGICAL SOURCES OF PREJUDICE. Another reason for the development of race prejudice is the sense of security and self-confidence derived by the least successful members of the dominant group from feeling superior to another group. It has often been observed that the lower economic classes among the whites frequently manifest the most intense prejudice against Negroes. Studies have shown further that individuals who are frustrated in various of their life goals are likely to find in a disfavored minority group a convenient "scapegoat" for their troubles. It does not solve one's problems to see in "the Negroes," "the Jews," or for that matter one's boss or one's wife, the cause of his frustrations, but it reduces the need for self-blame.

PERPETUATION OF RACE PREJUDICE. Although race prejudice serves a purpose for the prejudiced, there may be an unawareness on their parts of such a purpose and an honest belief that their attitudes are merely the reflection of "obvious facts." It requires considerable intellectual effort, together with some knowledge of the results of scientific investigations, to arrive at an understanding of the myths involved in the "facts." It is so much easier to go on believing what one was conditioned to believe early in life. Even when intellectual understanding of the false basis of race prejudice is achieved, very often the emotions, the real "stuff" of prejudice, remain unaltered.

Once a prejudice has become ingrained in a people, then, it is hard to root out. One contributing cause of the persistence of prejudice is that the bias itself deprives the group against whom it is directed of opportunities necessary for them to acquire the type of behavior patterns considered desirable by the dominant group. The operation of prejudice becomes "self-feeding"; since the minority group is kept "unequal" to the dominant group, it is forced to have the "inferior" attributes against which the majority group is prejudiced. It is a "vicious circle" somewhat comparable to a parent's prohibiting a child from attending school and then being "prejudiced" against this same child because he does not know how to read.

Racial Discrimination

As we observed earlier, racial discrimination refers to differential treatment of individuals on the basis of their presumed race membership. There are, of course, many types of discriminatory practices. In the paragraphs that follow, we shall strive to summarize the present status of discrimination in the economic, housing, educational, political, and social areas of life. While our chief concern is to indicate the amount of discrimination that now exists, we shall also try to indicate the direction in which we are moving and what we can expect in the immediate future.

DISCRIMINATION: ECONOMIC. Any unequal treatment of the races that more or less directly affects the members' ability to secure a livelihood can be thought of as economic discrimination. Included under economic discrimination would be discrimination in hiring and firing, in pay rates, and other aspects of employment. But also included would be the difficulties in securing a business loan if one is a Negro, or, if he operates a small business, the necessity in many cases of limiting his sale of goods or services to members of his race. Difficulties in buying land and becoming a member of a trade union would be other examples of economic discrimination.

The most visible type of economic discrimination is that which has to do with the employment of Negro workers. In recent years the fight for occupational equality has focalized in legislation under the name of "Fair Employment Practices."

The federal Fair Employment Practice Committee was established in 1941 to insure representation of minority manpower in war industries, but it went out of existence in 1946 with the end of the presidential wartime emergency powers.[7] The federal FEPC owed its existence to the combined effects of the wartime manpower shortage, the existence of the necessary legal mechanisms, and a favorably disposed administration. Filibuster by some Southern senators and other measures have defeated attempts to secure permanent federal legislation requiring employers who hire large numbers of workmen to employ Negroes or other racial groups in approximate proportion to their numbers in the total population of the community from which the industry draws its employees and requiring employers to pay Negroes the same wages which are paid to whites *for the same kind and amount of work.*

At present, a minority of the states, of which New York was the first, have passed Fair Employment Practice laws. Most of the laws are patterned after that of New York, which forbids discrimination in hiring, firing, wages, working conditions, and promotions.

Even if current efforts to secure Fair Employment Practice laws for the nation as a whole are successful, job and wage discrimination against Negroes will not be totally solved. Public opinion in many communities would find ways of circumventing the laws; prejudices against Negroes on the parts of supervisors and fellow workers would still find ways of expressing themselves to the Negro workers' disadvantage; and a number of types of employment would not be covered by the laws. Negro physicians, for example, are often not "invited" to join the staffs of the large, modern hospitals in most communities. Negro lawyers frequently find that prejudice against them on the parts of legal colleagues, judges, and juries renders effective functioning in court very difficult. Although officially Negroes are not prevented from becoming physicians and lawyers and from "freely" practicing in these professions, they are so handicapped in their roles that many Negro citizens feel the need for employing white persons in these professions in order to obtain the best available legal and medical services.

DISCRIMINATION: HOUSING. The second large area of value conflict

---

[7] For a comprehensive discussion of the federal FEPC and state Fair Employment Practice laws see Louis Ruchames, *Race, Jobs, and Politics* (New York: Columbia University Press, 1953).

concerns housing segregation, the requirement that Negroes live in areas set aside partly by law and mostly by illegal and unconstitutional tradition as "Negro areas." The battle of the "restricted covenant" (which specifies that only white persons may live in designated real estate) has become a focal point of value clash second only to equality of jobs and wages. Small sections of the community are specified "Negro sections"; the rest of the community, presently occupied and projected into the future, is for "whites only." Not only are large numbers of Negroes crowded into an amount of space that is far too small for decent living, but rents run higher than for comparable white quarters and community facilities—police and fire protection, parks and playgrounds, sanitation provisions, and the like—are almost invariably poorer.

The problem of segregated housing areas for Negroes becomes increasingly acute, for the designated "Negro areas" fail to grow at the same pace as the community as a whole or as the Negro proportion of the population in the large Northern cities (to which there has been heavy Negro migration beginning about 1900). Expansion of Negro sections is vigorously fought by white persons who live in parts of a city that would be "taken over." And yet we cannot go on indefinitely packing Negroes into sections of cities that already house several times the numbers for which they were originally designed. Either a peaceful breakdown of "restricted covenants" must be achieved or we must expect increasing tension and conflict in our large cities of the type that we have had in Detroit, Chicago, and New York.

DISCRIMINATION: EDUCATIONAL. Another area of value conflict concerns the segregation of the races in the nation's public schools. As late as the beginning of 1954 seventeen states and the District of Columbia had laws requiring racial segregation in their schools, and in four other states racial segregation was permissible. It was generally held by such states that their citizens would receive their constitutional guarantee of "equal protection of the laws" if Negroes and whites were provided with separate school facilities—the so-called separate-but-equal doctrine. Many members of both races, however, questioned both the practice of segregation and the doctrine of "separate but equal." In the first place, practical application of the doctrine over many years revealed that the races were certainly separated but that the schools provided for the Negro were frequently not equal to those provided whites. The evidence regarding average expenditure per pupil in Negro and white schools, the amount spent for textbooks, and the like leaves little doubt concerning the general lack of equality of separate schools.

Even more important, however, was the charge that "separate but equal" is an impossibility, logically and otherwise. Can we label equality a situation in which some American citizens are prohibited by law from associating with other citizens in the course of pursuing something that is required by law? Finally, there was the argument that segregation denied the segregated students their chance of exchanging views with some other students and that by its very nature it impaired the personality development of pupils in the lower ranking of the segregated groups.

The clash of values over segregated schools has been disputed legally, editorially, and in other ways for a number of years. On May 17, 1954, the Supreme Court of the United States declared certain legal aspects of the battle over—segregation of the races in public schools is illegal. The following excerpt from the Supreme Court decision indicates some of the reasons on which the decision was based:

> We come then to the question presented: Does segregation of the children in public schools solely on the basis of race, even though the physical facilities and other "tangible" factors may be equal, deprive the children of the minority group of equal educational opportunities? We believe that it does.
>
> Such considerations apply with added force to children in grade and high schools. To separate them from others of similar age and qualifications solely because of their race generates a feeling of inferiority as to their status in the community that may affect their hearts and minds in a way unlikely ever to be undone.
>
> We conclude that in the field of public education the doctrine of "separate but equal" has no place. Separate educational facilities are inherently unequal.[8]

In the ensuing decade we have seen that the rendering of a Supreme Court decision did not eliminate the clash of values over segregated schools. But caution is required lest one overestimate or underestimate the value conflict that remains. On the one hand, the disturbances at Little Rock have to be seen in the light of the quiet school desegregations in Nashville, Greensboro, and Louisville. Many places in the South do seem to be moving toward desegregation with the "deliberate speed" specified by the Supreme Court, particularly if one does not have too rigid a definition of speed.

It must be remembered that residential segregation still exists, particularly in the North. The effect of this is that schools theoretically open to both races frequently are attended by just one. And sometimes great efforts are taken to construct or reconstruct school districts so that just this situation will prevail. Then, of course, we cannot ignore the prolonged evasion, in some places, of the Supreme Court decision and the attempts to circumvent it. All things considered, it appears that now, ten years after the decision, most Negroes are in all-Negro or predominantly Negro public schools.

[8] Cited in Public Affairs Pamphlet No. 209, "Segregation and the Schools" (New York: Public Affairs Committee, 1954).

DISCRIMINATION: POLITICAL AND LEGAL. In our mass society, there are many laws and regulations that, taken together, have a considerable effect on the daily lives of all of us. The right to influence these laws is a precious right indeed. It is exercised, of course, largely through one's ability to vote in local, state, and national elections. There is considerable evidence that the Negro in American society is discriminated against in his ability to influence the political decisions and legal processes of our society.

In the past the law itself was used to prevent Negroes from voting. Even recently there were, in the South, various regulations such as the poll tax, "grandfather clauses," and literacy and "Constitution knowledge" tests (often so administered that the Negro had no chance of passing). There can be no doubt that these regulations effectively reduced the Negro vote. For example, as late as 1961 the report of the federal Civil Rights Commission indicated that Negroes were prevented from voting in 100 counties in eight Southern states.[9]

Another example of how the law was used to prevent the Negro from having an influence on the laws that govern him occurred more recently in Tuskeegee, Alabama. In 1957 there were about 4700 adult Negroes and 2000 adult whites in Tuskeegee. Sensing that it would become increasingly more difficult to prevent the Negro from voting, steps were taken to remove him, politically speaking, from the city. Tuskeegee had a more or less rectangular shape; in 1957 it was gerrymandered into a twenty-six-sided affair that excluded the residences of all but ten Negro voters. Thus the Negro in Tuskeegee lost his right to influence matters in the community in which he lived.

Most people, finally, are well aware of the various extralegal ways that have been used, particularly in the South, to prevent the Negro from registering or from voting. To prevent them from voting, Negroes have been told that they would lose their jobs, they have been intimidated with threatening letters, and they have received warnings that physical harm would come to them.

In some cities in the North, the Negro vote is rendered ineffective by the more subtle method of so arranging districts that white persons outnumber Negroes and make it difficult or impossible for a Negro to be elected to an office. In general, then, the Negro wherever he lives is underrepresented in city, state, and federal government. He is thus prevented from using the machinery of government, in any appreciable amount, for bettering his lot and he has no real voice regarding the laws under which he must live.

DISCRIMINATION: SOCIAL AND PERSONAL. Part of the American social world is inaccessible to the Negro entirely, and other parts are extremely unlikely of attainment. In the recent past, various public facilities, such as parks, swimming pools, restaurants, theaters, and hotels, were operated on a

[9] Reported in Mack, *op. cit.*, p. 13.

racially segregated basis. This was done visibly in the South where signs with the words, *White Only,* openly admitted discrimination. In the North, however, more covert means were used to produce the same effect, even in states that had laws expressly forbidding discrimination in public facilities. For example, it was not until more than a dozen suits were brought against them that downtown restaurants in Columbus, Ohio, agreed to serve Negroes and thus abide by the state law that forbade racial discrimination in such circumstances.

Discriminatory practices in social relations involve a deliberate attempt to segregate the races in various public facilities or to prevent the association of people of different races. Removal of such discrimination, therefore, would result in greater personal freedom for all members of society. At the present time, of course, neither white nor Negro is really free to choose with whom he wants to associate, for strong social and extralegal pressures are exerted to force him to limit his personal associations to members of his own race.

Probably most Americans are aware that their freedom to choose a marriage partner is curtailed by the existence of laws against interracial marriage, or social pressures that make such marriages difficult. Twenty-seven states expressly prohibit Negro-white marriages. It is interesting to note, in this connection, that in 1948 the California Supreme Court declared that state's antimiscegenation law unconstitutional. The matter reached the courts when two Catholics, one white and one Negro, protested that the state of California was restricting their religious freedom by not allowing them to receive the sacrament of matrimony.

It is ironical that some of the strongest adherents of the racist position that people have a "natural preference" for members of their own race are the very ones to insist that we need laws to prevent intermarriage. No doubt many white racists would be insulted if it were contended that it is only the threat of legal punishment that keeps their fair-skinned daughters from the arms of Negro lovers. Judging from the intermarriage rates in states that allow Negro-white marriage, removal of discriminatory marriage laws probably would have little effect on the number of such marriages. The absence of discriminatory marriage laws would not, of course, prevent one from choosing a member of one's own race. On the other hand, laws against intermarriage seem to imply that one race is too inferior to the other to allow their members to marry if they wish.

The Costs of Racial Discrimination

There can be little doubt that the Negro minority pays a price for living in a society that practices racial discrimination. Certainly Negroes are harmed by the practices that work against them in securing a job, establishing a home, educating their children, and so on. Less apparent is the fact that the entire society is harmed, in fairly objective and demonstrable ways, and that it pays dearly for its discriminatory practices.[10]

Perhaps the cost to our society of discrimination that is easiest to see is the direct economic cost. In simple terms, it costs more money to operate two distinct school systems than one larger one, and it costs money to provide separate eating facilities in public places, separate washrooms and toilets, and separate drinking fountains. Employers lose money when they cannot hire and promote workers on the basis of their ability to perform the required work, but feel that they must take the race of the worker into account. Of course, the consumer also loses, for he is paying higher prices for his goods than if they were produced by the most efficient workers, regardless of race.

Less apparent, but equally real, economic costs of discrimination result from the chain reaction effect of some discriminatory practices. Higher disease rates, brought about partially by overcrowded housing conditions, create an unhealthy environment for all. Sometimes the diseases themselves must be fought at public expense, but even when this is not true they may result in costly job turnover or absentee rates.

It would be next to impossible to estimate how much it is costing our society because we fail to develop and utilize the talents of all of our members, regardless of race. It is hard even to imagine what our social, cultural, and economic development would be like if race were not a barrier to becoming educated, filling leadership positions, and otherwise making social contributions in keeping with one's ability.

A final area of economic waste includes the price we pay in dealing with racial problems and tensions. More work and money than is realized goes into such activities as preventing racial conflict, protecting Negroes from physical harm from whites, conducting court trials for those accused of breaking discriminatory laws, and testing the constitutionality of various laws and practices.

Whatever the sum total of the economic costs of racial discrimination and prejudice would be, it is quite possible that other social costs are greater still. Consider the effect on the mental hygiene of both the group against whom the prejudice and discrimination are directed and the group that is practicing the prejudice and discrimination. Certainly a price is exacted when as a society we encourage or merely tolerate practices that fill men's minds with suspicions, distrust, false beliefs, weird superstitions, and hatred toward their fellow men. People who harbor such feelings are expending psychological energy that could be utilized in better ways. It is a frightening thought that many Americans are not actually living in a real world with real people, but one populated with bogeymen of their own creation whom

---

[10] Lack of awareness of the costs of discrimination also can be considered as a source of discrimination. *Cf.* Arnold Rose, *The Roots of Prejudice* (Paris: United Nations Educational, Scientific, and Cultural Organization, 1951), pp. 19–24.

they feel it is proper to mistrust, to hate, and to discriminate against, so that they can be "kept in their place." Surely this does not bespeak good mental hygiene!

Another noneconomic cost of prejudice and discrimination is the effect these practices are having on the moral fiber of our society. It is difficult to retain complete confidence in the democratic process, full respect for the law and law enforcement, and an unshakeable belief in the dignity and worth of a human being when in our daily lives we act as if these principles do not hold, at least for all of the people, all of the time. Finally, we cannot ignore the effects of our racial problems on international goodwill. It is understandable that people of other nations find it hard to have full confidence and respect for "the American way of life" when, to them, it seems to include intolerable indignities.

AMELIORATION OF THE RACE PROBLEM

As Emerson has said, "The history of persecution is a history of endeavors to cheat nature, to make water run uphill, to twist a rope of sand." There are certain indications that the "rope of sand" in the United States is beginning to crumble. Increasingly there is evidence among whites, even among Southern whites, that there is growing awareness and sensitivity to some of the facts about race. Many are finding it more and more difficult to reconcile race discrimination with democratic and Christian ideals.

> . . . Even a poor and uneducated white person in some isolated and backward rural region of the Deep South, who is violently prejudiced against the Negro and intent upon depriving him of civic rights and human independence, has also a whole compartment in his valuation sphere housing the entire American Creed of liberty, equality, justice, and fair opportunity for everybody. He is actually also a good Christian and honestly devoted to the ideals of human brotherhood and the Golden Rule. And these more general valuations—more general in the sense that they refer to all human beings—are, to some extent, effective in shaping his behavior. Indeed, it would be impossible to understand why the Negro does not fare worse in some regions of America if it were not constantly kept in mind that behavior is the outcome of a compromise between valuations, among which the equalitarian ideal is one.[11]

The conflict of values inherent in race prejudice, on the one hand, with values inherent in the democratic ideology, on the other, cannot, then, be represented simply as the Negro fighting for his democratic rights versus the dominant white group consistently attempting to prevent his getting them.

---

[11] Gunnar Myrdal, *An American Dilemma* (vol. I; New York: Harper & Row, Publishers, 1944), p. xlviii. Used by permission.

That is only part of the problem. Another important part is the conflict of those same values running through every phase of society, making itself felt increasingly in the conscious and unconscious attitudes of a growing number of people: *the basic incompatibility of race discrimination and a democratic way of life.*

To be sure, not all people in our society now recognize or accept the essential incompatibility of our race relations practices with the major values of our society. But even among those who accept the idea that movement toward complete equality of the races is necessary and desirable, there is a strong clash of values concerning the best ways to deal with the present situation and to further the movement toward full equality. As we have seen earlier in our discussion, race prejudice and discrimination tend to be self-perpetuating. Because of our initial feelings and actions, many Negroes are unable to compete successfully in various spheres of life. Our prejudice thus continues to be directed against these "obviously inferior" people, and continues to justify further discrimination. There is evidence of value conflict concerning how to "break into" this vicious circle. One important issue comes down to the question, "Should we strive to reduce racial prejudice in order eventually to eliminate discrimination or should we legally prohibit discrimination and trust that a reduction in prejudice will follow?"

Reducing Prejudice

One common school of thought holds that the soundest approach is one that concentrates on changing the attitudes of the prejudiced. Not until people think and feel differently, it is held, will antidiscriminatory legislation or other measures for improving relations be truly effective. This approach is largely a matter of education, in its broadest sense. Its proponents admit that in the past this process has been slow and will probably continue to be so. The principle on which this approach rests was formulated by the early sociologist Sumner in the assertion that "stateways (laws) cannot change folkways." Proponents further point to the results of national prohibition as evidence that legislation contrary to majority opinion is unsuccessful.

It would seem "to make sense" that we cannot force people to think and feel democratically and to look on one another as fellow human beings. It is usually contended that education, and not coercion, is the proper way to reduce prejudice. Even so, there are problems. If the main attack on the race problem is to educate people as to the desirability of values contrary to their own and persuade them to give up their prejudices, who is going to do such educating and persuading, and what techniques should they use? And how do you get prejudiced people to submit themselves to an educational process that has as its avowed aim the destruction of their values?

There is no doubt that racial prejudice is a contributing factor to continued racial discrimination, and there is no doubt that attitudes and even strong values can be altered. But in view of the practical difficulties associated with such a process, and its general lack of success, there is reason to question whether education is the most effective and most efficient method of ameliorating our race problem.

Reducing Discrimination

An almost diametrically opposed approach is the one that sees antidiscriminatory legislation as the one way of reducing our racial problems. One argument is that the legal elimination of discrimination will allow the Negro to compete educationally, economically, and socially on a more equal level with whites. Following successful competition, it is held, whites will find that their stereotypes and prejudices can no longer be defended.

Supporters of this position further argue that the elimination of discrimination is a worthwhile goal in its own right, even if it does not seem to have any noticeable effect on prejudice. They would contend that in every area where it would seem feasible, discrimination should be removed just as soon as possible. If people choose to keep their personal hates and suspicions, at least they would be required by law to behave democratically.

It seems that as a society we have been slow to accept the approach that calls for an all-out attack on desegregation, possibly because underneath we have had the feeling that it *would* work. At any rate, there has been no dearth of rationalizations against this approach. But recent experiences have shown that people do not always react to the removal of discrimination in the way that they or others anticipate they will.[12]

The Future of Race Relations in America

As we have indicated, many of the steps that already have been taken in the removal of discriminatory practices seem irreversible. This does not mean that from now on we can expect quiet desegregation and, soon, complete equality of the races. On the contrary, in any social change that is as far reaching and as radical as that involved in complete equality of the races, we can expect a certain amount of conflict. Probably we should expect some regrouping and strengthening of the forces opposing desegregation and, now and then, some temporary setbacks.

It must be admitted that various delaying tactics and countermovements could, in the short run, drastically slow down the process of desegregation. The degree of a person's pessimism regarding the possibilities of

[12] For cases of anticipated and actual reaction to FEPC legislation see Ruchames, *op. cit.,* pp. 183–188.

bettering the race problem depends, to a considerable extent, on his beliefs concerning the strength of the democratic ideology in American culture. If the white American people can live comfortably by merely paying lip-service to democratic ideals, they are unlikely to make a forceful attack on the race problem because the conflict of values between these ideals and race discrimination is not likely to become sufficiently acute. If on the other hand, the democratic ideology is so powerful and fundamental a set of values in American social life that the dominant white group will be forced again and again to face the conflict of these values with the racial discrimination that remains, then progress toward complete and general racial equality can be expected.

SUGGESTED READINGS

ASHMORE, HARRY S., *An Epitaph for Dixie*. New York, W. W. Norton and Company, Inc., 1957.

DRAKE, ST. CLAIR, and HORACE R. CAYTON, *Black Metropolis*. Rev. ed., 2 vols. New York, Harper & Row, Publishers, 1962.

GARFINKEL, HERBERT, *When Negroes March*. New York, The Free Press of Glencoe, 1959.

GRIFFIN, JOHN HOWARD, *Black Like Me*. Boston, Houghton-Mifflin Company, 1961.

KING, MARTIN LUTHER, JR., *Stride Toward Freedom: The Montgomery Story*. New York, Harper and Row, Publishers, 1958.

MENDELSON, WALLACE, *Discrimination*. Englewood Cliffs, N.J., Prentice-Hall, 1962.

MONTAGU, ASHLEY, *Race, Science and Humanity*. Princeton, N.J., D. Van Nostrand Company, Inc., 1963.

MYRDAL, GUNNAR, *An American Dilemma*. New York, Harper & Row, Publishers, 1944.

ROWAN, CARL T., *Go South to Sorrow*. New York, Random House, 1957.

SIMPSON, GEORGE E., and J. MILTON YINGER, *Racial and Cultural Minorities*. Rev. ed. New York, Harper & Row, Publishers, 1958.

TUMIN, MELVIN M., *Desegregation: Resistance and Readiness*. Princeton, N.J., Princeton University Press, 1958.

ZANDEN, JAMES W., *American Minority Relations: The Sociology of Race and Ethnic Groups*. New York, Ronald Press, 1963.

PHYSICAL HEALTH □ 13

Enjoyment of the highest attainable standard of health is one of the fundamental rights of every human being without distinction of race, religion, political belief, economic or social condition. This statement represents neither a utopian vision nor a radical theory, or perhaps it represents both. It is taken from the constitution of the World Health Organization which has been ratified by some eighty nations, including our own. American society, then, has stated its health values in no uncertain terms—achievement of the highest attainable standard of health for all of its members. If everyone agreed on this goal and on methods of reaching the goal, then physical health would not be considered a social problem.

Our first task in this chapter will be to investigate the extent of physical illness in our society. By so doing and by paying particular attention to variations in rates of illness and disease within society, we shall see that the goal of achieving the highest standard of health for all society members is one that currently our society has not been able to reach. Our discussion of the social, as opposed to the medical, explanations for the physical health problem attempts to indicate the barriers that stand in the way of achieving the goal and the value conflicts that exist over effective methods for removing the barriers to better physical health for all people.

THE NATION'S HEALTH AND HEALTH NEEDS

There are many different ways of measuring and describing the health of a society's members and the health problems of a society. Certainly the death rate and the average age at death tell something about the society's health. The sheer number of people who are ill is an important consideration, especially if one is able to describe the length and severity of their illnesses, and the extent to which these interfere with the usual routines of people. Actually, good health is more than the absence of sickness or disease. A more positive approach would consider the extent to which people are "in good physical condition" and possess close to their highest potential level of strength, energy, endurance, sensory ability, and the like.

Rates of sickness and disease, therefore, provide one, but only one, indication of the health needs of a society. At the present time it is next to impossible to get reliable facts on needed improvement in health among those not technically ill, but ideally such a measure is desirable. To more nearly complete the picture of the health needs of a society, we would also need some indication of environmental health needs, for to the extent that the society is producing, or failing to correct, an environment that is harmful to the health of its members, that society has definite health needs. Basically, then, our discussion of the health needs of America deals with (1) the more obvious health needs of individuals and (2) the public health needs of the society.

Rates of Illness and Disease

Until recently it was difficult to obtain reliable estimates of the extent of illness in our society. Only sporadically was an adequate, large-scale study conducted. The recent federal law that established the National Health Survey did much to correct the situation, for it authorized the Public Health Service to operate a continuing study of the extent of illness and disability in the United States. Each year the National Health Survey conducts studies on different aspects of health and illness. Information is obtained by interviewing a large, nationwide probability sample of the civilian, noninstitutionalized population of the United States. With a reasonable degree of accuracy, therefore, the findings can be generalized for the entire country. The discussion that follows utilizes various studies of the National Health Survey.

CHRONIC ILLNESS. A physical illness or disorder generally is considered chronic if it exists for three months or longer. Using this definition a recent National Health Survey discovered that in a given year about 41 percent of the population reported a chronic condition.[1] Such conditions, as might be expected, were more prevalent among older people, but they were reported also by about 21 percent of children and young people under

[1] U.S. Public Health Service, *National Health Survey*, "Limitation of Activity and Mobility Due to Chronic Conditions," Series B, No. 11 (Washington, D.C.: Government Printing Office, 1959), p. 1. In the remainder of this chapter the abbreviated citation, *National Health Survey*, will be used for these reports.

twenty-five years of age and by about 48 percent of the people between the ages of twenty-five and forty-four. In a given year, an estimated 70 million people have one or more medical complaints or disorders that have lasted three months or longer.

Table 16   Extent of Chronic Illness in the United States

Age	Percent with any chronic condition during year	Percent with chronic condition which limited activity
0–24 years	21.0	2.2
25–44 years	47.5	7.4
45–64 years	59.9	16.4
65 years and over	77.3	42.3

SOURCE: U.S. Public Health Service, *Health Statistics from the U.S. National Health Survey,* "Selected Health Characteristics," Series C, No. 6, Washington, D.C., Government Printing Office, 1961.

ACUTE ILLNESS. An acute health condition is defined as one that lasts less than three months and which causes a person to seek medical attention or to restrict his usual activities. Many minor aches, pains, and complaints are, therefore, not included. Nevertheless, in a given year the nation as a whole reports about 368 million acute conditions, or an average of two acute conditions per person each year.[2] Some indication of the severity of the conditions can be obtained from the fact that in over 60 percent of the cases medical attention was sought.[3]

IMPAIRMENTS. Finally, in a typical year, the people of the United States report about 24 million impairments, considered as permanent or chronic physical defects that result from disease, injury, or congenital malformation.[4] About half of the impairments involve paralysis, absence of feet, hands, fingers, and other defects and abnormalities in the musculo-skeletal system. Among the sensory impairments there are almost 1 million cases of blindness, 6 million hearing defects, and over a million cases of speech defects. Presumably many of the impairments of the senses and in the body generally could have been prevented or could now be corrected.

DISABLING EFFECTS OF ILLNESS. The foregoing rates of the extent of illness and impairment do not in themselves indicate the extent to which the conditions interfere with the activities of people or prevent them from lead-

[2] *National Health Survey,* "Acute Conditions," Series B, No. 18, 1960, p. 3.
[3] *Ibid.*
[4] These and subsequent data on impairments from *National Health Survey,* "Impairments by Type, Sex and Age," Series B, No. 9, 1959.

ing a normal life. Some indication of the extent of disability is necessary to provide a more complete picture of the magnitude of the health needs in our society and of the importance of the physical health problems. The National Health Survey has made studies of two aspects of disability: in one it considers chronic or long-term inability to carry on one's usual activities, in the other, relatively short periods of restricted activity.

CHRONIC DISABILITY. During a typical year, an estimated 17 million Americans experience a period of chronic disability.[5] For the entire year or a large portion of it they were unable to carry on their normal work, school, housekeeping, or other routine. At least a million of those with a chronic disability were unable to leave their house, while an estimated 3.5 million had serious trouble in getting around alone.

As might be expected, the chronic disability rate increases with age, ranging from less than 1 percent among children and youth to about 32 percent among those sixty-five years of age and over.

Not generally recognized is the fact that long-term disability is inversely related to family income. Among those in families with incomes of $2000 or less, about 21 percent had some degree of chronic limitation of activity. The rate drops to about 11 percent in the group with incomes of $2000–$3999, 7 percent in the next highest group, and 6.7 percent for those in families with yearly incomes of $7000 or more. The same general pattern prevails for the more serious types of chronic disability, that is, a physical inability to get around by one's self. Mobility limitation was found among 8 percent of those in the lowest income brackets but only in 1 percent of those in families with incomes of $7000 or more.

SHORT-TERM DISABILITY. Short-term disability considers the number of days during a year that poor health forces people to restrict their usual activity, to spend the day in bed, or to lose the day from work, school, housekeeping, or other activity. On an average day, about 7.5 million are restricted in their usual activities because of illness or an injury.[6] Each person in the United States experiences an average of sixteen days a year of activity restriction, of which six days are spent in bed. The average worker misses almost eight days of work a year because of illness. On a typical work day, almost 2 million people are absent from work due to illness.

The extent of short-term and chronic disability and the rates of acute and chronic disorders should leave little doubt but that the health of American citizens could be improved. Certainly we are not now able to keep everyone from getting sick. Even at the present stage of medical knowledge, however, there is much that could be done to prevent illness, to cure it more

[5] Data on chronic disability from *National Health Survey,* "Limitation of Activity and Mobility Due to Chronic Conditions," Series B, No. 11, 1959.

[6] Data on short-term disability from *National Health Survey,* "Disability Days," Series B, No. 29, 1961.

rapidly, and to reduce the amount and intensity of disability associated with it. Particularly illuminating is the relatively low rate of serious disabilities among people in families with better incomes, for it suggests that the national rate could be drastically reduced.

PUBLIC HEALTH PROBLEMS

In a sense it is meaningless to distinguish between health problems of individuals and public health problems, and certainly it is true that people and not "the public" get sick. At the same time it is clear that the provision of sanitary facilities, the assurance that the water, food, and air are safe, and the prevention and control of epidemics must be handled on a societal rather than a private basis.

The past has seen violent battles in the field of public health. If a smallpox epidemic were to break out in one of our communities today, we would not only insist upon public control, but expect public enforcement of preventive methods through the use of vaccines and by other measures. But for many decades such procedures were forcibly resisted on professional, religious, economic, and political grounds. Physicians felt then that they were the only ones capable of dealing with disease and resented attempted enforcement of reports, quarantines, and the like. Many religious groups defied isolation and quarantine as interfering with the Divine plan, and commercial interests opposed them on the basis of interference with trade and closing of markets. Added to these professional, religious, and economic objections was the political philosophy of individual rights. If a man wanted to have smallpox in his home or place of business, it was his concern, and he did not want any snooping public health officials interfering with his God-granted individual rights.

In spite of the initial resistance to public health regulations, considerable progress has been made. The control of some epidemic diseases is a case in point. The mortality rates of diphtheria, typhoid fever, whooping cough, and measles have been reduced by more than half since the turn of the century. Epidemic diseases are no longer the major causes of death and industrial absenteeism. Of course, the dramatic reduction of crippling poliomyelitis is the most current example of the efficacy of better medical knowledge combined with a vigorous public health effort.

While many of the epidemic diseases have been brought under control, there are still problems in the broad area of environmental health. What is more, new problems are constantly arising. Very often these are social problems, and are not merely a matter of discovering and applying technical knowledge. All too often many are not even aware that a problem exists. Moreover, proposed and attempted programs to reduce the problem frequently meet with strong opposition from those who feel their vested interests are being threatened. The discussion of public health issues that follows will be limited to the extent of just a few of the problems in the area of environmental health. What is being done, and what can be done, to meet public health problems will be handled in a later section.

AIR POLLUTION. No one needs to be told that air is an important natural resource. Today, in metropolitan areas particularly, it must be recognized also as a *limited natural resource*. Considering the air we breathe as limited is a new, and perhaps frightening, concept.

A community's air supply is limited in the sense that it has only a certain capacity to dilute and disperse pollutants discharged into it. Beyond this capacity, various undesirable effects on the health and well-being of the people are evident. Air becomes polluted because daily we discharge into it various gases and particles, such as those found in the fuel we burn in our homes and factories, "exhaust" from automobiles, and in the chemical by-products of many industrial processes. Within a geographical area, increasing both the number of industrial processes and of people add to the pollutants in the air. According to a recent study, air resources in many of our metropolitan areas are now being used close to their capacity and in some cases the acceptable limit of pollutants in the air has already been passed.[7]

The division of air pollution of the U.S. Public Health Department has estimated that economic damage caused by air pollution is in excess of $7.5 billion annually.[8] It is likely that the true economic cost would be found to be even higher if we could measure accurately the damage to crops and livestock, the corrosion of materials and soiling of surfaces, interference with ground and air transportation, and effects on the health and productivity of the populace. With regard to the matter of health, the subcommittee on air pollution stated that "a growing body of circumstantial evidence testifies that long-term, low-level air pollution exposures can contribute to and aggravate chronic diseases which affect large numbers of our population." [9] What is more, a study of 103 cities and 28 nonurban places found that the level of carcinogens (agents thought to produce cancer) in the air was sixteen times higher in urban areas.[10]

At the present time, therefore, there is ample evidence that air pollution should be a matter of national concern. The continuing trend toward

[7] Public Health Service, *Report of the Committee on Environmental Health Problems to the Surgeon General* (Washington, D.C.: Government Printing Office, 1962), p. 17.

[8] *Ibid.*, p. 78.

[9] *Ibid.*, p. 17.

[10] *Ibid.*, p. 81.

urbanization and the growth of industrial processes, many of the latter involving the creation of synthetic materials with chemical residues, mean that the problem will become more serious in the future.

OTHER PUBLIC HEALTH PROBLEMS. It is neither feasible nor necessary to provide details on the many other public health problems. A mere enumeration of some of them will indicate that current standards of what constitutes a healthy environment are not now being met. The more traditional problem of assuring an adequate supply of good water is a case in point. Stream pollution is notorious, and the situation becomes worse all the time. The movement to the suburbs around our cities often has preceded sewer extensions, with the result that an estimated 24 million people, four times as many as in 1945, rely on a private septic tank. Frequently this results in serious pollution of ground waters that serve as a water supply for the same people.

Despite our past successes in controlling foodborne diseases, outbreaks still occur. With our present distribution of food products, moreover, people all over the country can be affected. In 1961, for example, outbreaks of food poisoning in California and Minnesota were traced to a hollandaise sauce manufactured in New York state.[11] New problems related to the provision of pure food continue to arise. Adequate checks and controls are needed to assure that the automatic vending of meals, and freezing, drying, and other food processing techniques do not impair the purity or nutritional value of the nation's food. These are but a few examples of the many, "modern-day" public health problems.

SOCIAL EXPLANATIONS OF THE PHYSICAL HEALTH PROBLEM

The data in the preceding section make it clear that we are not now achieving the goal of the highest attainable standard of health for all members of society. Our unmet health needs are of a serious magnitude, more so, as we have noted, in some groups than in others. Part of the problem, of course, is a technical medical one in that we need continually to improve knowledge of disease prevention and control. But better medical knowledge would be to no avail if it could not be applied to the people requiring medical attention.

What we describe as social explanations for the unmet health needs in our society can be envisioned as barriers that prevent people in need of medical services from receiving them. Up to a point, good health is purchasable. The cost of medical care, therefore, bears investigation as a social explanation for unmet health needs. Another factor that needs to be considered is the availability of physicians. While there exist other social ex-

[11] *Ibid.*, p. 147.

planations for society's health problems, such as the health attitudes of the population and the accessibility of hospitals, to name but two, our discussion will be restricted to the costs of medical care and the availability of physicians.

Costs of Medical Care

In recent years private expenses for medical services amounted to over $20 billion. About two thirds of this was paid to physicians, hospitals, and dentists; one fourth was spent on medicines and medical appliances; the remainder was spent for laboratory and nursing services, the service of paramedical personnel, such as chiropractors, naturopaths, chiropodists, and the like. Almost half of all families spend $200 per year or more for health services.

The costs of medical care to individuals has increased rapidly over the years, more so than the cost of many other items. For example, during the period 1939 to 1960, all items in the consumer price index increased by 113 percent; the cost of medical care services increased by about 131 percent. For the more recent period 1955 to 1960, the average increase of all items was 10.5 percent, while the increase for medical care services was 24 percent.[12] Whereas twenty years ago expenditures for medical services accounted for about 4 percent of all expenditures, today the proportion is 6 percent. In view of the total personal expenditures for medical care, and the willingness of Americans to devote an ever-higher portion of their income for such care, it would seem that as a nation we are spending enough money to buy adequate medical care.

Our purpose in investigating the costs of medical care is to see whether these costs are a partial explanation of the unmet health needs of the society. It could be argued that hospital costs, physicians' fees, and the like have risen so rapidly that people simply cannot afford the medical care that they need. Among those with a comfortable or better income, such an argument becomes difficult to defend, for the people at such income levels can afford various luxuries. At lower income levels it could be a quite different matter. The relationship between family income and medical costs and medical care bears investigation.

Great differences are noticed in the cost of medical care for different income groups. The cost for families with a total family income of less than $2000 a year is $165 per year; families earning $7500 or more spend an average of $411 for health services. The higher the income, the more money is spent for medical care. It is important to note that medical expenses take a far larger *share* of the income of the poor man than they do of

[12] Public Health Service, *Medical Care Financing and Utilization* (Washington, D.C.: Government Printing Office, 1962), p. 41.

those in better financial circumstances. As shown in Table 17, the proportion of the family income spent for health care *decreases* from 13 percent among those at the lowest income level to about 4 percent among families with an income of $7500 or more.

Table 17   Family Income and Family Health Expenses

Family income	Average family health expenses	Percent of family income
Under $2000	$165	13.0
$2000–$3499	226	8.4
$3500–$4999	287	6.4
$5000–$7499	336	5.4
Over $7500	411	3.9

SOURCE: U.S. Public Health Service, *Medical Care Financing and Utilization,* Washington, D.C., Government Printing Office, 1962, p. 56.

It has been argued that these figures simply indicate that "the rich" are charged a higher fee for basically the same medical care that the rest of the population receives at a more modest cost. It is a prevalent belief that any family, regardless of its income, can and does receive adequate medical care for its members. But let us examine the facts.

Over the years careful studies consistently have shown that the higher the family income, the greater is the use of physicians' services. This generalization is again borne out by the more recent National Health Survey. In this study of the entire civilian, noninstitutionalized population of the United States, information was obtained on the number of physician visits per family member in a year, and whether the visit was made at a doctor's office, home, hospital clinic, or other place. The lower income groups were more likely to visit a doctor at hospital clinics, many of which, of course, provide free service or charge only a small fee. When all doctor visits are totaled, regardless of where they occur, it is found that the higher income groups still had more visits per family member than the lower ones.

The difference in the use of physician services by income groups, while existing for all age groups, is more pronounced at some ages than others. For example, children in families with an income of $7000 or more average 7.6 visits to a doctor each year, as compared to the 4.2 visits of children in the lowest income group. The more affluent aged have an average of 8.7 doctor visits a year, while those over sixty-five whose family income is under $2000 average 6.5 visits. Women within the childbearing age have two or three more visits to a doctor a year if the family income is $7000

Table 18 Family Income and Number of Doctor Visits per Year

Family income	All ages	Average number of doctor visits per person per year					
		0–4 yrs.	5–14 yrs.	15–24 yrs.	25–44 yrs.	45–64 yrs.	65 +
Under $2000	4.6	4.2	2.3	4.0	3.9	5.1	6.5
$2000–$3999	4.6	5.4	2.5	4.4	4.6	5.4	6.6
$4000–$6999	5.1	6.6	3.9	4.8	4.9	5.4	6.9
Over $7000	5.7	7.6	4.9	4.8	5.7	5.6	8.7

SOURCE: U.S. Public Health Service, *Medical Care Financing and Utilization*, Washington, D.C., Government Printing Office, 1962, p. 223.

or more than if it is less than $2000.[13] The steady increase in the use of physician services by income can be seen by considering the women between twenty-five and thirty-four years of age. Those in families with less than $2000 a year averaged 4.6 doctor visits a year; with $2000–$3999, 5.6 visits; with $4000–$6999, 6.6 visits; and with $7000 or more income, 7.6 visits.

The same general relationship that prevails between income and use of physicians' services exists also for dental visits. People at the highest income levels average three times as many visits to a dentist as those at the lowest level. The proportion of persons with no visits to a dentist in a given year drops from 78 percent to 42 percent as income increases.[14] It should also be noted that the number of persons per thousand who have lost all of their natural teeth is three times higher in the lowest income groups than it is in the highest income group.[15]

Low income people, therefore, spend a higher proportion of their income for medical services, but have less to show for it in terms of visits to doctors and dentists. The total number of doctor visits, whether at hospital clinic, place of work, home, or doctor's office increases with increasing income.

Race is also related to the number of visits to doctors and dentists, but since many Negroes are at lowest economic levels this could be expected. It is nevertheless true that whites average two more visits to a doctor per year than Negroes, and this despite the greater use of free clinics by Negroes.[16] In a given year, about 80 percent of Negroes do not visit a dentist, as compared to 57 percent of whites.

[13] These and immediately subsequent data from *National Health Survey*, "Volume of Physician Visits," Series B, No. 19, 1960.

[14] *National Health Survey*, "Dental Care," Series B, No. 15, 1960.

[15] *National Health Survey*, "Loss of Teeth," Series B, No. 22, 1960.

[16] *National Health Survey*, "Volume of Physician Visits," Series B, No. 19, 1960.

Number and Distribution of Doctors

The number of doctors in a society has an obvious relationship to the health of the society's members. Other things being equal, it is reasonable to suppose that the more doctors available to the people, the lower will be the rate of unmet medical needs. The number and distribution of doctors in the United States can be thought of as a social explanation for the nation's unmet medical needs, for the supply of physicians is, within limits, flexible and it is affected by the values of the society. Altering the system of financing medical training, for example, more than likely would have an impact on the supply of doctors. Let us see first, however, how the present supply of physicians compares to needs and standards.

For many reasons it is difficult to define what constitutes an adequate number of physicians. Much would depend on whether we want full medical attention, including *prevention* of disease, or whether we would be content with something less than this. Does our society want to extend medical services to those not able to pay for them? If so, more doctors would be needed than if their services were utilized only by those who could afford them. If as a society we want to continue to encourage more doctors to engage full time in medical research, then the ratio of doctors to the general population should be higher than if all were in private practice. These difficulties notwithstanding, we can use the present physician-population ratio as a starting point.

In 1963 there were approximately 260,000 physicians, producing a ratio of about 141 doctors per 100,000 population. The ratio of physicians has been dropping and is now actually less favorable than it was in 1949. The country will need 330,000 doctors by 1975, *merely to maintain the ratio that exists today*. If the present rate of growth of medical school graduates continues, we would have an estimated 313,000 doctors in the United States by 1975, or a deficit of 27,000 by this standard.

In view of the underutilization of doctors by certain income and other groups, it seems safe to conclude that there is now a shortage of doctors. In view of the increasing number of older people in the population and the desirability of more doctors engaging in medical research, there is good reason to hold that in the immediate future the ratio of doctors should increase. But present trends indicate that by 1975 the shortage of physicians will be greater than it is today.

It is quite apparent that there are gross differences in the supply of doctors by state and by sections of the country. Washington, D.C., with its ratio of 290 consistently has had the highest doctor-population ratio. Some states, notably Mississippi, Alabama, North Dakota, and South Dakota, have a ratio of 75 or fewer doctors per 100,000 civilians. Actually, two thirds of the states have less than the national average ratio. The better supply of doctors in the heavily populated urban areas affects the national average and gives a somewhat unrealistic picture of the over-all supply of doctors.

In part, a low supply of doctors can be offset if those available work longer hours, see their patients for a shorter period of time, or do both. Thus, in the northeast area with its favorable supply of physicians, doctors have an average of 4400 patient visits per year. In the south, the comparable figure is 6200. Of course, patient load cannot be increased indefinitely without affecting the quality of the medical care.

The conclusions seem inescapable that today there is wide variation in the physician supply and that in many states the doctor-population ratio is too low for adequate medical care. The unmet medical needs of the nation partly can be explained by the facts that (1) there is a general shortage of doctors and (2) doctors are poorly and unequally distributed throughout the country. If present trends continue, both of these conditions will be more pronounced in the future.

VALUE ISSUES IN THE AMELIORATION OF PHYSICAL HEALTH PROBLEMS

Almost everyone would agree that sickness, disease, and other marks of poor health are undesirable. When new methods of meeting health problems are suggested, however, we frequently find anything but unanimity of opinion. In the preceding section we isolated the cost of medical care and the unavailability of an adequate number of doctors as two explanations for the continuing personal health needs of our society. These are both manipulatable causes in that it is within our knowledge and resources to remove them as obstacles to the goal of better personal health for the population. We will now look at the proposals for removing these obstacles and the value conflicts with which the proposals are met. The section concludes with a brief discussion of what would be involved if we were to remedy our public health problems.

Medical Costs and Payment Methods

As we have noted, one of the barriers to achieving adequate medical care is its cost. Obviously, then, one approach to reducing the problem, of assuring that more people get better medical attention, would be somehow to alter the method of paying for medical services so that cost would no longer operate to prevent those in need of medical attention from receiving it. Broadly speaking, there are three ways in which medical costs could be met: (1) they could be met privately, through current income, savings, or borrowing; (2) they could be met through privately purchased prepayment plans or health insurance; and (3) they could be met through a compulsory health insurance plan. Each of these broad methods presents serious problems, both with respect to the effectiveness of the system and with respect to the acceptability of the method to the people. Neither aspect can be ignored. If the system does not work, in the sense that it does not help more people to receive better medical care, then, of course, it is no solution to the problem. At the same time, if a payment system is unacceptable to the people, then even if it is potentially effective it probably will not be adopted.

PRIVATE PAYMENT METHOD. Apparently, the bulk of the American people have already rejected the completely private and individualistic system of meeting all medical costs. They are unwilling or unable to pay for all medical care as a need for it arises, meeting the bills through current income, from savings, or by assuming a debt that would be paid off through later income. The high cost of medical care and the sporadic and unpredictable nature of medical expenses presumably are some of the reasons that make this system unacceptable. For these same reasons, the private, individualistic system probably would not be an effective one today. If this were the only way of meeting all medical bills, even more people than now do so would be inclined to postpone or forgo needed medical attention because of the cost factor.

VOLUNTARY HEALTH INSURANCE. The essence of a health insurance plan is that it spreads the costs of some medical care over time and over a group of individuals. All people in the plan pay a fixed sum monthly or yearly and then are entitled to certain medical services should the need for them arise.

Most Americans find voluntary health insurance acceptable, or at least prefer it to meeting all medical costs through current income. Almost three fourths of the people have some form of hospitalization insurance, and over two thirds have insurance for surgical costs as well. Only a very small proportion of the people, on the other hand, have insurance that covers substantially complete physician's services.

A major criticism of voluntary health insurance is that it does not remove the barrier of cost that comes between the need for medical care and the attainment of it. A look at who *does not* have hospital and surgical insurance is quite illuminating. Two thirds of the people with incomes of less than $2000 do not have hospitalization insurance, as compared with but 15 percent of those with incomes of $7000 or more.[17] Almost half of the people sixty-five to seventy-four years of age have no hospital insurance and about 56 percent have no surgical insurance. At older ages the proportion *without* insurance jumps to over two thirds. The disabled are dis-

[17] Data on health insurance coverage from *National Health Survey,* "Interim Report on Health Insurance," Series B, No. 26, 1960.

tinctly less likely to have health insurance, and so are the unemployed. Thus, the poor, the aged, the infirm, and the jobless—those who would seem to need it most—have no medical insurance whatsoever.

The high cost of medical insurance, coupled with the minimum coverage of almost all plans, is cited as another indication that voluntary health insurance cannot effectively remove the cost barrier to medical care. The average plan that covers only hospitalization and surgical charges costs over $30 per person per year, or over $150 a year for a family with three children.[18] It has been estimated that this type of insurance covers, on the average, only about *one fourth* of the total medical and health expenses of insured families.[19]

It should be obvious that existing prepayment plans do not provide the final answer for financing the medical costs of the masses. In addition to the limitations mentioned earlier, it should be recognized that most of the insurance plans make no attempt to cover the cost of extended treatment in mental hospitals, tuberculosis sanatoriums, and the like. Diagnostic treatment in a hospital is almost universally excluded, and most plans do not pay for chronic or other conditions that existed before the contract was purchased. Finally, the waste and inefficiency involved in operating hundreds of different plans is cited as a weakness of the voluntary health insurance system.

The fact that almost three fourths of the people have some form of health insurance would seem to indicate that they find a private prepayment system the best alternative *currently available* for meeting some of their medical costs. That the remainder cannot or do not purchase such insurance, coupled with the criticisms of existing plans, presents the other side of the picture.

COMPULSORY HEALTH INSURANCE. Another method of removing the cost barrier to adequate medical attention would be to require that all people be covered by health insurance administered or controlled by the federal government. The costs of medical services would be paid from a fund derived from the wages of employed persons in much the same fashion as unemployment compensation or old-age insurance operates today. The "compulsory" aspect of the medical insurance is based on the calculation that only in that way could a sufficiently large fund be accumulated at sufficiently low cost per worker to be practicable for the low-income groups in our population. It would be similar in principle to existing nonprofit group health insurance plans in that the costs of the insurance would not be based on how much medical care an individual received, but the rate would be based on the average cost of the medical care received by all

[18] *Medical Care Financing*, p. 83.

[19] Herman M. Somers and Anne R. Somers, *Doctors, Patients, and Health Insurance* (Washington, D.C.: The Brookings Institution, 1961), p. 11.

group members. With a national compulsory health insurance plan, of course, the costs of medical care would be "averaged out" over all of the people.

A compulsory medical insurance program could be as comprehensive as the people desired. That is, it could, like most voluntary plans, merely cover some of the hospital and surgical costs; on the other hand, it could cover these costs completely and could cover also visits to doctors for treatment or diagnosis, periodic health examinations, and the like. Of course, the more comprehensive the plan, the more completely would it allow people to receive the medical care they need, regardless of their ability to pay for it.

There can be little doubt that compulsory health insurance has a potential for removing financial blocks to seeking medical attention. Major criticisms of the plan include the charges (1) that it would be an inefficient method for financing medical care, and (2) that in providing medical care for all, the quality of medical care would be reduced.

While it is admitted that the existence of many, duplicative voluntary private health insurance programs results in waste and inefficiency, it is feared by some that a federally controlled single system would be subject to so many "bureaucratic entanglements" that it would be even more inefficient and wasteful. Since the compulsory insurance plan has not been tried in this country, its efficiency from an economic standpoint could only be estimated, and even this would require a great deal of study. More to the point, many claim that efficiency should be of less concern than effectiveness, that is, whether the system actually would result in better medical care for more people.

There seems to be general agreement in American society that the method of paying for medical service has some influence on the quality of the service received. There is a sharp difference of opinion, however, on whether compulsory insurance would have a positive or negative influence on the quality of medical care. The medical profession traditionally has favored the "fee-for-service" principle according to which the individual physician has the right to set his own fees for his professional services. It is felt that a major deviation from this principle would reduce the physician's incentive to strive for excellence in the service he renders. Others, in a diametrically opposing manner, hold that only when the physician is protected from having a financial interest in his patient can he make his decisions on treatment solely on what is medically indicated. Where one group contends that tampering with the "fee-for-service" principle would destroy the doctor-patient relationship, the other believes just as strongly that the relationship would be improved.

As in any area of sharp value conflict, epithets are hurled at those advocating compulsory medical insurance. The most effective "bad name" attached to compulsory medical insurance has been that of "socialized medicine." Since many Americans are automatically opposed to anything social-istic, this technique has been successful thus far in arousing much opposi-tion to the proposed legislation.

Proponents of compulsory medical insurance have likewise not been consistently above name calling and imputation of undesirable motives on the part of their opponents. Some of them have said that certain physicians not only lack genuine interest in the health of the American people, but that as "unscrupulous businessmen" rather than true "servants of the peo-ple," they fear a system that would prevent them from charging fees out of proportion to services rendered.

Because of the intense value conflict, it appears unlikely that com-pulsory medical insurance soon will be deemed by most people as an ac-ceptable method of removing the cost barrier to better health. Probably the immediate future will see some action to remedy the medical cost situation for those whose plight is the most serious, such as the aged and the very poor. The intensity of the value conflict suggests that even for these groups the issue will be bitterly fought and, realistically, the result will be some-thing far less than a complete medical care program.

Number and Distribution of Physicians

If as a society we are truly interested in better personal health for more people, it is necessary that we increase the number of physicians. The var-ious methods of doing so are fraught with value implications.

If an adequate supply of physicians is to be available in the future, something approaching a "crash program" is necessary. Many more med-ical schools would need to be built, equipped, and staffed, and many more young men and women would have to seek a career in medicine. Federal funds could be used, and probably would be necessary, both for construct-ing the medical colleges and for providing full subsidization of the education of medical students. Such "federal interference" is decried by the medical profession and by others who feel that it is undesirable. Yet private re-sources are apparently inadequate to bring about the increase in the supply of doctors that is now needed and that will be needed to keep up with the growing population. Of course, if financial considerations were not effec-tively keeping the demand for medical services below the level otherwise required, the present and future supply of medical personnel would have to be even larger than that which is indicated by today's utilization rate.

Until and unless opposing factions can reach agreement on the im-portance of increasing the supply of medical personnel, and can reach agree-ment on methods to bring about the increase, we can expect no real attack on the problem. Meanwhile, physicians and probably a significant group of laymen in sympathy with them will continue to interpret the ameliorative efforts of others as unwarranted attacks on the medical profession and their time-honored values. Just as surely will other groups see in the resistance to programs that would greatly increase the number of doctors an unscrupulous attempt by physicians to keep their wages high by keeping their numbers scarce. And so the clash of values continues, and with it there also continues a shortage of medical personnel.

Meeting Public Health Problems

While the idea of public health regulation is now well rooted in American society, it is doubtful whether most Americans are prepared to accept the magnitude and scope of an up-to-date public health program. Part of the difficulty, it seems, is an apathy born of ignorance. It is unlikely, for example, that our urban citizens have accepted polluted air as a necessary feature of city living. More likely, they seem not to care because they simply are not aware of the problem. But increasing the people's awareness of this and other public health issues would still not resolve the problem, for the nature and scope of the public health problem are such that forceful and presumably unpalatable action is necessary.

Granted that the scope of public health regulation is greatly increased, just what would be needed to develop *adequate* public health services commensurate with today's needs? We would need more money, a great deal more money, than we now appropriate for such purposes. Is this money readily available? Certainly not in many of our small, poor, rural counties where current public health services are most inadequate. Should states provide the funds to poor counties? Here we step on some political "value toes." When the states provide funds to counties for any purpose, they demand that certain standards be met in the use of those funds. State-dictated standards are not always identical with the standards of county politicians, and even where there is no sharp disagreement as to standards, the "dictation" process itself is often resented and brings about conflict. Furthermore, many states indicate that they cannot or will not markedly increase expenditures for public health. In these states there could be no other alternative than supplementation of state financing by federal funds, with resultant conflict even greater than at the county level.

Whether funds were derived from city, county, state, or federal sources, there would be a necessary increase in taxation. Here the taxpayer who is "all for improved public health services" would find his ardor for the program cooling and his public health values in conflict with other values contingent on lighter taxation. Even with money forthcoming, many a politician at our various governmental levels would find it difficult not to attempt to divert some of the funds into channels that would seem of greater immediate political worth than an "adequate public health program."

Organized medicine would not find itself free of all conflict in regard to really *adequate* public health services. Many physicians would have to choose between a radical altering of their type of private practice or a joining of the public health staffs. Young graduates of medical colleges (most of whom indicate a preference for private practice in large urban centers) would also find their values disturbed, for a large number would be needed in small communities and rural areas where public health services are now least adequate. The very organization of our medical colleges would probably need to be radically revised, for it is extremely doubtful that present medical school facilities could be stretched to meet the demands for an *adequate* public health service staff for the whole nation.

Many a value of certain business interests would be crushed by adequate public health services, for not a few of our industrial structures and processes and our business-operated dwellings are not conducive to optimum public health.

Values such as "my home is my castle" would have to tumble for a large number of our "average citizens." Obviously an adequate public health program could not succeed with every person's continuing with the sort of life, however unsanitary and unhealthful, he pleased within "his own four walls."

And so, almost infinitely, are major changes necessary in our society in order to provide *adequate* public health services. Everyone agrees the goal is a desirable one, but the methods necessary for achieving the goal bring numerous values into conflict.

SUGGESTED READINGS

APPLE, DORRIAN, ed., *Sociological Studies of Health and Sickness.* New York, McGraw-Hill Book Company, Inc., 1960.

SMITH, RALPH LEE, *The Health Hucksters.* New York, Thomas Y. Crowell Company, 1960.

SMOLENSKY, JACK, and FRANKLIN B. HAAR, *Principles of Community Health.* Philadelphia, W. B. Saunders Company, 1961.

SOMERS, HERMAN MILES, and ANNE RAMSAY SOMERS, *Doctors, Patients, and Health Insurance.* Washington, D.C., The Brookings Institution, 1961.

U.S. PUBLIC HEALTH SERVICE, *Medical Care Financing and Utilization.* Washington, D.C., Government Printing Office, 1962.

U.S. PUBLIC HEALTH SERVICE, *National Health Survey.* (See specific series and reports under this title.)

U.S. PUBLIC HEALTH SERVICE, *Report of the Committee on Environmental Health Problems to the Surgeon General.* Washington, D.C., Government Printing Office, 1962.

U.S. SOCIAL SECURITY ADMINISTRATION, *The Health Care of the Aged,* Washington, D.C., Government Printing Office, 1962.

MENTAL HEALTH 14

Before mental disease there were demons, and before medicine there was magic. The world of primitive man is peopled by witches and evil spirits who have the terrifying power of driving men mad. These malevolent, supernatural beings are all around him. They live in his forests and in his streams, and their awesome ability to affect men's minds can only be stayed by appropriate countermagic.

As late as the eighteenth century in colonial America, a common explanation of bizarre behavior, strange or incoherent utterings, and uncontrollable shrieks and cries was that the person was a witch or bewitched. Or, the deranged person was simply labeled mad. For the most part, madness was considered incurable, and the person so afflicted was destined to live out his life in a prison. The history of mental disorders as types of illnesses that can be prevented, treated, and cured is a short one indeed. It is prefaced by a far longer history of ignorance and superstition.

Even today there is much ignorance regarding mental health. Many still think in terms of a strict dichotomy between the sick and the well, not realizing that the absence of a serious, chronic, or disabling mental illness is not the same as a state of good mental health. Many are ignorant, too, of the extent of severe mental disorders, of their nature and causes, and of the curative and preventive treatments that already are possible.

One result of the accumulated ignorance on mental health is that there is a clash of values regarding whether or not a problem actually exists. Probably everyone realizes that there are mentally ill in our hospitals, but beyond this many lay people clash quite severely with professional judgment over the dimensions and proportions of our mental health problem. Where many laymen see only the severely ill, the professional sees much additional evidence that bears on the state of our nation's mental health. As a result of this initial and basic clash of values over whether or not we even have a mental health problem, we find additional value conflicts over what constitutes a necessary remedy for the situation.

The differential awareness of the mental health problem should become more apparent as we look at the evidence, or symptoms, that professionals observe in our society, and how these same symptoms frequently are either not noticed or are misinterpreted by laymen.

EXTENT OF EMOTIONAL PROBLEMS AND POOR MENTAL HEALTH

Although the clashes of values continue to be largely in the area of gaining general social recognition of the existence of a major social problem of mental health, it is not at all difficult for even an untrained observer to find evidence, if he will admit of it, that many Americans are mentally and emotionally unwell. If one were asked to choose a single word for characterizing many Americans both individually and in their relationships with one another, considerable justification could be made for the selection of the term "maladjusted." Many persons in our society seem tense, anxious, unhappy, dissatisfied, fearful, skeptical, cynical, pessimistic, and depressed. Not very many Americans indicate that they have found entirely comfortable roles in life and are satisfied with them. The observer finds it difficult to discover more than a few people who are not complaining about one or another aspect, or the totality, of their estate in life. Anxiety seems to pervade the personalities of many members of our society, and tension seems to characterize their interrelationships.

We do not, however, need to rely on such a subjective impression to have evidence of mental health difficulties in American society. More objective symptoms of maladjustment, tension, and distress are available, and it is to an examination of some of these that we now turn.

The Mental Health of Americans: A Self-Portrait

Much can be learned about the mental health of a society by determining how the people see themselves. Do the people feel troubled or worried? What, in their opinion, bothers them? Do they consider themselves happy most of the time in their marriages and in other areas of life? A study designed to answer these sorts of questions has recently been reported under the title, *Americans View Their Mental Health.*[1] Almost 2500 people

[1] Gerald Gurin, Joseph Veroff, and Sheila Feld, *Americans View Their Mental Health* (New York: Basic Books, Inc., 1960).

were interviewed, and the sample was so drawn that it is reasonable to think of the interviewed group as a cross section of the adult, noninstitutionalized population of the United States. The study deals with "normal" men and women of various ages and in all walks of life.

The findings that follow give some idea of how the people see themselves: [2]

(1) About one fourth of the men and over a third of the women claimed that they worry a lot or all the time; another 7 percent of both sexes indicated they worried sometimes.

(2) About 10 percent of the people answered that generally speaking they are "not too happy"; at the other extreme, about a third said they are "very happy." The not too enthusiastic response, "pretty happy," was given by slightly over half of the men and women.

(3) Twelve percent of the men and 25 percent of the women stated that at some time they had felt they were going to have a nervous breakdown.

(4) Professional help for a personal problem had, at some time in the past, been sought by 14 percent of the people; another 9 percent stated that they had had a problem for which professional help would have been useful but that they had not sought such help.

(5) Over one third of the sample reported that they had marriage problems; about a third rated the happiness of their marriage as average or below average.

(6) Over 10 percent of the married people said that they frequently or often felt inadequate as a marriage partner; many more, over 40 percent, said that they felt this way once in awhile.

Most people, probably, would agree that the study in which the above findings are reported was well executed and that it objectively reports how the people said they feel. We would expect no such agreement, however, on the *interpretation* of the findings. Specifically, there is good reason to believe that many people do not take such results seriously, claiming that "everybody has problems" or that the people could rid themselves of their woes if only they "tried harder." Standing in opposition to this point of view would be many professionals and a few laymen who would be deeply concerned with the fact that a sizable minority of Americans are worried, unhappy, feel inadequate, or have thought that they were on the verge of a nervous breakdown. They would see in such symptoms evidence that the mental health level of our society is not all it should be. The differing interpretations of the same set of facts on the people's self-assessment of their mental health is, of course, an indication that a clash of values exists be-

[2] Adapted from Gurin, *op. cit.,* pp. 22, 38, 42, and 102.

tween those who believe and those who do not believe that our society has a
fairly serious mental health problem.

Divorce

It is in the marriage institution that we have the most highly publicized
evidence of personal and interpersonal unhappiness. Numerous studies have
established the fact that a large percentage of husbands and wives are unhappy in their marriages, and, although the divorce rate has declined somewhat from its postwar peak, the long-term divorce trend continues upward.
While there is no scientific evidence on which to base an assertion that
Americans in the earlier periods of lower divorce rates were correspondingly
happier in their marriages, it is clear that many present-day Americans *are*
unhappy in their marriages.

Whatever the alleged causes of divorce or the moral implications of a
rising divorce rate, they need not here concern us. Regardless of the particular factors contributing to increased divorces in the United States, the
generalization that a growing number of Americans are openly dissatisfied
with the marital phase of their lives would appear inescapable. Whatever
else it does or does not represent, the rising divorce rate may be taken as
symptomatic of widespread tension in one important area of modern social
living. Some, of course, fail to see in the rates of marital unhappiness any
indication of personality difficulties among the people who cannot get along
with a mate that they themselves have chosen.

Juvenile Delinquency

Other statistical symptoms of tension and maladjustment in American
society are the misbehavior and legal transgressions of youth that are customarily lumped together under the heading of juvenile delinquency. While
crime and delinquency rate comparisons in time and place may not be considered highly reliable (see Chapter 16), the consensus is that juvenile
delinquency is on the increase. Just as in the case of divorce, we need infer
nothing about the specific causes of delinquency to regard it as symptomatic
of personal adjustment. Since, by definition, the delinquent is a person who
behaves contrary to established rules, delinquency may be considered as
another evidence of tension between the individual and his society. Although the individual delinquent, like the individual divorcé, is not necessarily a victim of serious mental illness, a rising rate of delinquency
demonstrates growing dissatisfaction among young people with traditionally approved ways of life.

Psychosomatic Disorders

Still another significant evidence of the extent of mental health problems is found in the growing research in the field of psychosomatic medicine. Actually, as Dr. Rowe puts it, ". . . in a broad sense, all illness is 'psychosomatic' since most emotional illnesses have physical components and most organic illnesses have emotional aspects." [3] The term, "psychosomatic disorder," customarily is reserved for those instances in which it is reasonably clear that the cause of the physical symptom or disease was initially emotional. There are four general types of illness where psychological expressions using bodily systems have been most frequently observed by internists: cardiovascular (the heart and its system); gastrointestinal (stomach, intestines, and related organs); the whole group of cephalalgias, arthralgias, and myalgias (aches and pains in the head, joints, muscles, eyes, and the like); and the allergies.

Much more research is needed in the field of psychosomatic medicine before any completely indisputable statistics may be presented on the extent to which various bodily pathologies are influenced by and stem from mental and emotional maladjustments. The foregoing material, however, is illustrative of information that has already accumulated in sufficient amount and reliability to indicate that personality difficulties of various types play a tremendously important role in contributing to health problems traditionally considered in strictly "physical" terms.

Occupational Maladjustment

Occupational unrest is another symptom of tensions in personal mental hygiene and in interpersonal relationships. Turnover and absenteeism are two major problems in many of the vocations in modern American life. While other factors contribute to these conditions, mental hygiene difficulties are significant causal agents. Failure to get along with fellow workers or "bosses," home worries, general life dissatisfactions or unhappiness, specific distaste for the type of work, alcoholism, illness, and related reasons frequently appear on reports as reasons for absence or separation from employment, and all of these factors contain, in full or in part, evidence of personality difficulties that fall into the general category of mental health problems.

Even many workers who are seldom or never included in statistics on absenteeism or turnover indicate in numerous ways their varying degrees of

[3] Clarence J. Rowe, M.D., *An Outline of Psychiatry* (3d ed., Dubuque, Iowa: Wm. C. Brown Company, 1959), p. 18.

occupational maladjustment. The extent to which major industrial and commercial establishments are turning to psychiatrists, psychologists, and sociologists for assistance in constructing "worker surveys" and "worker guidance programs" is in itself testimony to the growing seriousness of morale problems in many occupations. And many of the surveys instituted by management, labor unions, and various agencies of the government add still further weight to the generalization that a high percentage of Americans are unhappy in their work.

Escapist Activities

When people consistently try to escape from reality, it is reasonable to conclude that their experiences in the "real world" are unsatisfactory. There is evidence that, in greater or lesser degrees, many in our society find the "real world" so harsh, so troublesome, or so boring that they feel the need to get beyond it, at least temporarily.

The most common form of escape, of course, is daydreaming. In itself daydreaming does not bespeak poor mental health, but if carried to extremes and particularly if one's major satisfactions come in the dream world of his fancy, it is an indication of an inability to adjust to life as it really is.

There are other ways to escape from life and its problems. One can flee reality by using narcotics. The most consumed drug is, of course, alcohol. All recent studies indicate that not only are more men and women using alcoholic beverages but that the number of "heavy, escape drinkers" and chronic alcoholics is growing. Although exact statistics on the extent of alcoholism in previous generations are not available, the proportion of alcoholics, especially among women, probably exceeds that of any previous period in our history. In like manner, an increasing number of persons apparently need some sort of sedative all or part of the time in order to sleep. Because the sale, purchase, or use of most other types of narcotics (such as opium, morphine, and marihuana) is illegal, any accurate estimate of the number of users is impossible to determine, but most everyone realizes that the number of users is significant.

Not to be ignored is the amazing response of people to tranquilizers, even to the point of borrowing prescriptions for such drugs from friends, supporting a brisk and profitable trade in bogus, ineffective drugs, and giving rise to a "black market" where the drugs can be purchased without a prescription. Millions of Americans regularly depend on tranquilizers. In some cases, these drugs have proved quite beneficial for the severely mentally ill in hospitals and they have been prescribed for other patients, but the therapeutic value of the drugs under such conditions is not here the question. The point is that when masses of people turn so readily to a pill that promises tranquillity, there is good reason to suspect that there is something wrong with them, with their world, or with the world as they see it.

Severe Mental Illness Rates

Most obvious evidence of all that the mental health of the American people is a matter of grave concern is the number of persons who become so acutely ill that they require attention at a mental hospital. It has been estimated that one person in twenty will, in the course of his lifetime, require hospitalization for mental illness. On a given day there are over 600,000 patients in hospitals for mental disease. Another 100,000 mentally ill people are cared for in other settings. Each year close to 200,000 new patients are admitted to mental hospitals, and 100,000 former patients are readmitted. This means that, on the average, over 800 people enter a mental hospital each and every day of the year.

Table 19   Patients in Mental Hospitals, 1935–1960

Year	Number of mental patients	Number per 100,000 population
1935	421,446	331.2
1940	483,448	367.2
1945	519,593	407.3
1950	578,130	384.9
1955	631,503	389.1
1960	609,795	342.3

SOURCE: U.S. Bureau of the Census, *Statistical Abstract of the United States: 1962,* Washington, D.C., 1962, p. 83.

Within the last ten years or so several of the tranquilizing drugs have been found to be effective in the treatment of the severely mentally ill, and thus to result in the earlier release of patients from mental hospitals. For example, the use of drugs and intensified treatment of patients resulted in 23 percent more patients being released each year from New York state hospitals.[4] Such results are indeed impressive, but they should not lead to unwarranted conclusions concerning the efficacy of newer treatments for all of the mentally ill. In the last decade, as indicated in Table 19, the number of patients in mental hospitals, as well as the rate per 100,000 population, have decreased. While the national trend is encouraging, the number and rate of hospitalized mental patients is still quite high. Were it

[4] Annual Message to the Legislature (New York, 1958).

not for the newer treatments, of course, the rate of mental hospital patients undoubtedly would have continued to grow as it had until about 1955.

These are some of the basic facts about the prevalence of *severe* mental disorders. When we add the somewhat less emphatic, but equally tangible, indications brought out in the foregoing paragraphs, further apologia of the subject seem superfluous.

A Classification of Personality Disorders

It is unnecessary to be an expert on the medical aspects of mental illness in order to deal with the phenomenon as a social problem. At the same time, it is useful to have some conception of the nature of mental disorders and the types of behavior frequently exhibited by the mentally ill. Such an understanding not only corrects possible misconceptions of mental illness but also enables one better to appreciate explanations of the mental health problem and recommendations for reducing it. For this reason, let us turn our attention to a classification of personality disorders.

We have yet to see a classification about which no valid objections could be raised, and this certainly applies here. Indeed, psychiatrists have come to concentrate more on the source and symptoms of, and most effective therapy for, the individual patient's difficulties and to be less concerned about placing this patient in a "textbook" category. It is useful, however, in order to have an understanding of the immense range of personality disorders, to attempt some classification. The student, then, should realize that the following is offered as a rough guide to the varieties of mental illness and not as a precise classificatory device for the diagnostician. Three main categories of personality disorders will be discussed under the headings of (1) psychosis, (2) psychoneurosis, and (3) psychopathic personalities.

Psychosis

The most severe and readily discernible form of mental illness is psychosis, which is roughly synonymous with what in lay and legal terminology is referred to as "insanity" or *"non compos mentis."* Psychoses are usually roughly classified into two main subdivisions: organic and functional. A person suffering from a psychotic condition is generally quite noticeably out of touch with reality. He often manifests what psychiatrists term hallucinations, delusions, and illusions; he indicates by his words or his actions that his ideas, emotions, sense perceptions, or memory differ considerably from what his society designates as "normal."

ORGANIC PSYCHOSIS. An organic psychosis is one in which the principal source of the condition is a structural pathology of the brain or central nervous system. The most frequently occurring organic psychosis is paresis, which is caused by spirochetes' (syphilis germs') lodging in brain tissue. Meningitis (inflammation of the meninges or membranes covering the brain) and encephalitis (inflammation of the brain, popularly known as sleeping sickness) are two other examples of brain infection that may produce psychotic conditions. Some of the many other types of organic psychoses may result from brain trauma (injury); disturbances of the circulatory system (most familiar of which is cerebral arteriosclerosis, or hardening of the brain arteries); prolonged, severe, and frequent epileptic seizures; brain tumors; and toxic conditions (external, such as alcohol, morphine, or an industrial poison; internal, such as diabetes, uremia, and pellegra).

FUNCTIONAL PSYCHOSIS. Functional psychosis is a severe mental disorder for which no structural basis has been discovered. No brain lesions nor biochemical irregularities can be found that are demonstrably causal factors for the psychotic condition; or, said more simply, there seems to be no organic source of the mental illness.

The leading functional psychosis is schizophrenia. Approximately 20 percent of all first admissions and one half of the patients resident in mental institutions are diagnosed as having this type of psychosis. Schizophrenia, meaning "split mind," is an appropriate term in two respects: (1) the patient has divorced himself from effective contact with the physical and social environment, has "withdrawn into a world of his own"; and (2) the patient manifests a "split" between his thoughts and his feelings, has emotional behavior that is incongruous with his ideational processes (may laugh uproariously, for example, when stating that his mother has died).

Schizophrenics can and do recover from their illness. Although there is little consensus on the exact recovery rate, there is good agreement that many patients originally diagnosed as suffering from schizophrenia have returned to useful lives in their communities.

The cause or causes of schizophrenia are largely unknown. Studies of identical twins and investigations of family histories seem to indicate that for *some* patients inherited characteristics cannot be ruled out. Many other schizophrenics are "recruited" from the mass of apparently normal families. For this reason, attention is more frequently turned to the stresses and strains of life and other environmental factors that seem to suggest to some that it is better to forsake the complicated world of reality for one of their own creation.

The second most common of the extreme functional disorders is manic-depressive psychosis. Patients with this disorder constitute about 10 percent of first admissions to mental hospitals and about 12 percent of the resident hospital population. Characteristically the patient demonstrates extreme shifts of mood from extreme elation, excitement, and activity (manic stage) to extreme despondency, melancholia, and stuporous depression (depressive stage). Some patients do not go through the mania-to-depression (or vice versa) cycle, but exhibit the symptoms of only one phase.

Manic-depressive psychosis has a higher recovery rate than schizophrenia. Two thirds or more of all patients recover, and in more than half of the cases there is no recurrence of the disease. In some cases, a recovered patient has another attack, just as some heart patients apparently recover completely while others suffer repeated attacks. Hereditary factors are stressed a bit more for this disorder than for some others, but the results are far from conclusive. One authority found that in addition to partly dominant, "manic-depressive" genes, other genes plus emotional stresses or environmental factors must be present in order for the disease to be manifest.[5] Despite repeated investigations of patient's body chemistry, glandular functions, and the like, little really is known about the causes of this illness.

Psychoneurosis

The psychoneurotic individual, unlike the psychotic, maintains considerable contact with reality. He is often able to adjust for long periods of time to many aspects of his environment, and his mental illness may become apparent to the untrained observer only in what, for the patient, constitutes a crisis situation. Numerous categories of neuroses have been proposed; the four most frequently found in the more recent literature are (1) anxiety states, (2) conversion hysteria, (3) neurasthenia, and (4) obsessive-compulsive reactions.

ANXIETY STATES. It is probable that anxiety lies at the root of all psychoneurotic conditions. Some neurotic patients, however, have a chronic sense of apprehension as their outstanding symptom, and it is this group of patients who are placed in the present category.

Anxiety differs from "normal fear" in at least two fundamental respects. Anxiety, first of all, unlike fear, appears either with no observable stimulus or to a degree that is out of proportion with the stimulus. If, for example, one's life is being threatened by an armed gangster, to turn pale, perspire, experience palpitations of the heart, feel gastronomic disturbances, and develop a tremor would be "normal" fear reactions. To experience comparable responses daily upon boarding a streetcar, however, would constitute an "abnormal" anxiety state. In the first example, the psychosomatic reactions were in harmony with the external danger stimulus; in the second illustration, the same kind of reactions were disproportionate to the stimulus. Fear is predominantly rational, and anxiety is predominantly irrational in respect to the stimulus.

A second way that "normal" fear differs from "abnormal" anxiety is

[5] Amram Scheinfeld, *The Human Heredity Handbook* (New York: J. B. Lippincott Company, 1956), p. 133.

that the source of anxiety tends to be largely unknown to the person experiencing the fear. The source of the anxiety is "hidden in his unconscious mind." In the foregoing example of the person experiencing extreme psychosomatic reactions upon boarding a streetcar, he cannot give an adequate explanation of why he feels as he does. The real source of his anxiety stems from conditions "buried" in his past experiences. The person experiencing fear can consciously account for his reactions on the basis of the immediate stimuli in his environment.

It should be noted at this juncture that so-called normal people are not free from unreasonable fears or anxieties. The panic reactions into which not a few persons are thrown by the presence of mice, by the need for handling worms or garter snakes, by a walk through a cemetery at night, and the like, are of the same species as the anxieties of a psychoneurotic. The difference between a "normal" person's anxieties and those of a neurotic is largely a matter of intensity of reactions, frequency and persistence of responses, and the degree of social maladjustment resulting from the specific nature of the anxieties.

CONVERSION HYSTERIA. It was pointed out that a person suffering from an anxiety neurosis is generally unaware of the real source of his "fears." He is, however, acutely aware of the anxiety reactions themselves. In hysteria, on the other hand, the source of the neurotic condition has been repressed so deeply into the unconscious mind that the individual denies the very existence of anxiety or of any type of mental or emotional conflict. The hysteria type of neurosis does not express itself in consciously recognizable anxiety reactions, but takes the subtler forms of symptoms of bodily disease or physical disability. The mental conflict is "converted" into a physical complaint; thus, the patient is no longer aware of conflict or anxiety, but merely aware of his apparent disease or disability.

The simplest explanation of conversion hysteria is that the psychoneurotic unconsciously seizes upon a physical disease or disability as a means of escaping his anxieties and conflicts. By developing physical illness he not only excuses himself from the necessity of solving his difficulties, but he accomplishes this result by a method for which he is apparently not responsible. He has escaped his conflicts (at the conscious level) and, at the same time, developed a condition for which he is likely to receive sympathy and special conveniences from his associates.

The student must remember, however, that this process just described (in overly simple terms to make it understandable) takes place *below the level of consciousness* of the person developing a conversion hysteria. He does not consciously decide to become ill or disabled; it happens to him, is beyond his conscious control. In like manner, he cannot will to get well. A patient who is suffering from hysterical blindness, for example, is just as unable to see by consciously wanting to do so as he would be were both his eyes removed. Only psychiatric treatment, on the one hand, or some particular type of crisis situation, on the other, can restore his ability to see. The hysteria patient is an *ill* person, not a malingerer.

NEURASTHENIA. Neurasthenia more nearly resembles the anxiety neurosis than hysteria in that the anxieties and conflicts of the patient are nearer the conscious level. Unlike the anxiety conditions, however, neurasthenic illness is manifested more in chronic fatigue than in fear reactions. The term "neurasthenia" means "nervous exhaustion"; the exhaustion, however, is not the fatigue of physical tiring but derives from the conflict of emotions. The patient is characteristically struggling to solve problems he does not clearly comprehend and the sources of which are unknown to him. The complete neurasthenic state (popularly, the "nervous breakdown") appears at the climax of frustration where the patient unconsciously "gives up" the battle with these ghostlike emotional adversaries.

A frequent accompaniment of neurasthenia (and one that links neurasthenia more closely with the anxiety neurosis) is hypochondria, which is defined as a "morbid anxiety about one's health." The neurasthenic, baffled by his constant fatigue, is apt to begin imagining he has all kinds of physical illnesses. He hears or reads of the prevalence of tuberculosis, anxiously reads up on the disease, and decides that he has it. His anxiety about his health readily shifts focus. Today he is worried about tuberculosis, tomorrow cancer, the next day brain tumor, and still another day heart disease. The hypochrondriac is one of the chief "headaches" of the physician and one of the main sources of income for the quack and nostrum peddler.

OBSESSIVE-COMPULSIVE REACTIONS. In the final category of psychoneurosis that we shall briefly discuss are the obsessions and the compulsions. An "obsession" is an idea over which the person has lost control; a "compulsion" is an overt action over which the person has lost control. Many laymen have heard of compulsions such as kleptomania, the compulsion to steal, and pyromania, the compulsion to start fires, but almost any type of behavior can be compulsive for someone. In some cases, a person exhibits both obsessive and compulsive reactions, as in the case of the patient who was obsessed with the idea that she was infecting herself and others by the germs on her hands, and felt compelled, therefore, to wash her hands almost continually and to avoid touching doors and other objects that people before her had touched.

Most normal people have some obsessions and compulsions. Observe, for instance, the number of persons who become uncomfortable if prevented from lifting back the lid of a mailbox after having deposited a letter; they feel *compelled* to do so. Other examples are frequent checkings that doors are locked, pictures are straight, gas fires are extinguished, hands are washed, and the like. Obsessions appear in similar fashion. We all have ideas to which we *must* cling, regardless of the proved illogic or inconvenience of holding to them.

It is when the number and intensity of, or social maladjustment associated with, these obsessions and compulsions become patent in the life of the individual that he may be diagnosed as having an obsessive-compulsive neurosis. It is, in short, when his obsessions and compulsions "take over" his thoughts and actions to a sufficient degree to render him obviously inefficient or "abnormal" in various social situations that he is clearly neurotic.

Psychopathic Personalities

Our third principal division of personality disorders is most frequently referred to as the psychopathic personalities. Professional difference of opinion is greater in regard to the nature and origin of psychopathic personalities than in relation to the major psychoses and psychoneuroses. Some psychiatrists feel that many persons described as psychopaths are actually psychotic; others lay great stress on the *constitutional* nature of the illness—meaning that the environment can make the psychopath neither better nor worse.

Amid these and many other differences of opinion, however, a fairly clear clinical picture emerges. The psychopathic personality is characterized more by a moral than a mental defect. His is a character illness. Although psychopaths demonstrate *intellectual* understanding of right and wrong, they indicate incapacity for *feeling* the moral implications of their acts.

> . . . they exhibit a seeming pathological inability to be mindful of routine obligations and sensitive to the rights of others. It is as if they lacked the capacity to appreciate the ethical implications of conduct problems. The word *appreciate* is used advisedly in this context; for with them it is not a question of not *knowing* the "difference between right and wrong," but of not being able to evaluate such a difference emotionally. In a purely cognitive manner they "know" that it is "wrong" to stab a child, to pour acid on a puppy, or to steal money from a blind newspaper vendor. However, they fail to experience the emotional revulsion which crimes of this character arouse in the average man. Such affective responsiveness is probably more necessary in determining ethical choices than abstract knowledge of legal codes. This was rendered quite evident during the prohibition era when vast numbers of "respectable" citizens violated the law because they "didn't *feel* it wrong to take a drink." [6]

[6] David B. Klein, *Mental Hygiene* (rev. ed.; New York: Holt, Rinehart and Winston, 1956), p. 132.

Another outstanding characteristic of the psychopathic personality is his apparent inability to learn from experience. His moral defect is as rigid as the mental defect of a feebleminded person. Pleading, psychiatric treatment, kindness, punishment, and so on, all fail to touch him. At the first opportunity, he reverts to his lying, cheating, stealing, debauching, or whatever other channels in which his psychopathic behavior customarily expresses itself.

EXPLANATIONS OF THE MENTAL
HEALTH PROBLEM

As we have already indicated, not too much is known about the precise causes of most mental disorders. Scientists in such fields as neurology, genetics, endocrinology, and biochemistry continue to do research in their specialties that could lead to more definitive knowledge about the causes of mental illness. These types of research rest on the assumption that it is something *within the individual* that makes him succumb to a mental disease. Meanwhile, social scientists also have been conducting research on the theory that factors *external to the individual,* that is, features in his social environment, are important contributing factors to mental illness. The two theories are not really contradictory. It could turn out, for example, that some people have a strong predisposition to a certain type of mental illness which only becomes a manifest disorder if they are subjected to certain patterns of family tensions or other unfavorable social situations. To further complicate matters, it could likewise be true that the best treatment for such an afflicted individual would consist of drugs that acted on one of his endocrine glands.

The student of the *social problem of mental illness* need not be aware of all of the theories on the causes of mental disease. He should be aware of the social factors associated with mental illness, for to the extent that characteristics of our society or features of social living contribute to mental breakdown, the society itself can be considered a "cause" of mental illness.

Some sociological studies of the social problem of mental illness have been focused on the society as a whole in an effort to discover whether certain features of the culture of American society are related to the prevalence of mental disorders. Sociologists also have investigated the differential proneness to mental illness, attempting in this instance to discover whether certain groups or types of people within the society are more likely than others to become mentally ill. Both types of emphasis, of course, can tell us much about mental illness and both may lead in time to more effective preventive programs.

Cultural Characteristics and
Personality Disorders

The theories that follow attempt to explain the mental health problem in terms of general features of our culture thought to be capable of producing a significant number of personality disturbances in the society. The theories rest, on the one hand, on what is already known about the cultural organization of this society and, on the other, on varying rates and types of mental disturbances in our own and other societies. The theories are addressed to explanations for the functional psychoses, the neuroses, and other symptoms of tension, rather than the organic psychoses.

Societal Complexity Theory

Most students of human behavior believe that the increasing complexity of society contributes to the growing mental health problem. This would seem to be true in two important respects. First, the number and variety of demands for adjustment placed on the members of our complex society greatly exceed those patterns of behavior exacted from members of simpler societies. The life of modern man is a mass of intertwined institutional exactings; he is obliged to relate himself to many other human beings, most of whom are absolute or relative strangers, in complicated economic, governmental, educational, recreational, and religious settings. His predominantly agricultural forefathers, on the other hand, had most of their relationships confined to the less demanding and far simpler environments of their own families and of neighbors known for a lifetime.

The physical environment of members of simpler societies is characteristically the same plot of land on which they were born (or a very similar one), the old and familiar home and barn, and the livestock; their lives consist, to a great extent, of relating themselves simply to land, home, barn, and livestock. Modern man's physical environment is a gigantic mechanism whose operation is dependent upon complicated cooperation with impersonal laws. He is forced to adjust to many powers and gadgets from income taxes to automatically operated elevators, from traffic signals to juke boxes, from fire departments to subways.

Relative to modern man premodern man was little challenged to modify his behavior. If he once "made the grade" of his society, he could be very secure in his remaining years with the adjustment achieved. Social change was, relative to modern "progress," so slow that it was scarcely perceptible in the longest of lifetimes; there were very few "new things under the sun" in an individual life span. The increasing tempo of change in modern society is too patent to merit illustration. Suffice it to say, by way of further warning of the urgency of mental health problems, that all indications point to increasingly rapid and radical alterations of our behavior patterns that will probably make the period between the beginning of the industrial revolution and the onset of this "atomic age" seem, by contrast, a stable one.

Another way that the increasing complexity of society appears pertinent to an understanding of the rising prominence of mental health problems is through its revealing of maladjustments that would have gone unobserved in a simpler society. The rising incidence of mental illness may be more apparent than real. Rather than *producing* new tension states, in many instances, modern societal situations may merely *expose* tension states that would have passed unnoticed, or at least unreported, in a simpler environment. All sorts of eccentricities that would be considered a "man's own business" in a rural setting, for example, could become highly inconvenient or even dangerous in a complex urban environment. Add to this that one of the increases in societal complexity is advanced skill in recognizing and diagnosing mental and emotional difficulties, and you have the essentials of the "exposure" aspect of the societal complexity theory.

In so far as this second point is true, of course, it reduces the validity of the societal complexity theory as an explanation of the "cause" of increased mental illness, for it calls into question the whole proposition that mental illness is *actually* greater in a complex than in a simple society. The exact amount of truth in either the causal or exposure propositions cannot be demonstrated beyond question. If a man "breaks down" in a complex societal situation, who can state definitely what he would or would not have done had conditions been different at that exact moment in his life? Most observers hold that the truth lies somewhere between "cause" and "exposure," with the weight perhaps more on the latter.

"Schizoid Culture" Theory

Another hypothesis in relation to the "cause" of increased mental illness also places the "blame" on modern society, but emphasizes the inconsistency rather than the sheer complexity of contemporary behavior patterns. The "schizoid culture" theory postulates that modern man is confused not by the number and variety of the demands made upon him, but by the unresolvable conflicts that occur between some of these demands. He becomes unhappy, filled with anxiety, neurotic, psychopathic, psychotic, and so on, not, for example, because both the economic and religious institutions require many things of him, but because some of the things required by his religion cannot be harmonized with some of the adjustments necessitated by his economic system. Such conflicts need not be interinstitutional but may occur within the same institution. In government, by way of illustration, full subscription to the principles of democracy exists side by side with machine politics, graft, manipulation of votes, exclusion of Negroes from participation, and the like.

As in the case of the societal complexity theory, conclusive proof or disproof of the "schizoid culture" theory cannot be mustered. That our culture is inconsistent or "split" cannot be denied; that these conflicts between various aspects of our culture "cause" individual mental and emotional maladjustments does not, however, necessarily follow. It could be just as plausibly argued that mentally ill individuals have produced or "caused" this "schizoid culture." Trite though it be, again it is probably correct that "the truth lies somewhere in between." The sociological principle that individuals are molded by their culture and, in turn, mold that culture probably applies as fully to abnormal as to normal behavioral manifestations.

Differential Proneness to Mental Illness

Epidemiology is the study of the distribution of disease. This approach to learning more about the nature of diseases, and eventually bringing them under control, has been used for some time in the field of physical medicine. The results have been fruitful. More recently, the same general approach has been applied to mental illnesses.

Epidemiological studies have made it quite clear that mental illness is not distributed evenly within our society. The rate varies according to certain already discovered social factors and social conditions. In other words, by virtue of possessing or being affected by these social factors, some groups of people within our society are more prone to mental illness than are others.

Sociological studies consistently have discovered a linkage between social class and mental illness: the lower the social class the higher the rate of psychosis. A careful study in the New Haven area, for example, found that while schizophrenia was the most common psychosis at all social levels, its rate was nearly eight times as high in the lowest social class as it was in the two highest classes.[7] The other psychoses also were related inversely to social class. With some, the rate was two to three times higher in the lower classes, while the relationship of the organic psychoses to social class was far stronger even than it is for schizophrenia. Statistically speaking, the conclusion is inescapable that the lower one's social class position the greater are his chances of contracting a severe mental illness.

Marital status is also linked to mental illness. Divorced people contribute more than their share to the rolls of the mentally ill. Next highest rates are found for the single, the widowed, and the married, in that order. In a similar manner, it has been found that rural areas have lower mental

[7] August B. Hollingshead and Fredrick C. Redlich, *Social Class and Mental Illness* (New York: John Wiley & Sons, 1958), p. 232.

illness rates than urban areas, and that within the cities the rate decreases with increasing distance from the center of the city.

The discovery of differential rates of mental illness within society brings us closer to understanding the causes of these diseases. The next research step is to attempt to identify the specific social conditions experienced by the high-risk groups that constitute an unhealthy environment. What is it, in other words, about lower class living or urban living that makes people more prone to mental illness? Why are the divorced more susceptible to a mental disorder than the married? Already some research has been done in these areas. It has been found, for example, that certain family relationship patterns which prevail in the lower class are related to the development of a mental disorder.[8] Much more research needs to be done, however, before it can be said that the social factors that make for a psychologically unhealthy environment have been isolated.

VALUE ISSUES IN THE AMELIORATION OF THE MENTAL HEALTH PROBLEM

Presumably no one stands to gain by our high rate of mental illness. It would not be difficult to gain consensus on the point that, if possible, those now ill should be returned to a useful life, or that it would be better if people were less troubled, were happier, and were altogether in better mental health. But when it comes to taking actual steps toward improving the treatment of the mentally sick, developing methods of prevention, or otherwise doing something about a situation that presumably no one wants, we are likely to meet with apathy or downright objections.

Part of the trouble, it seems, is that many of the proposals for doing something about the problem cost money. The alternative of doing nothing also costs money, probably much more than most people realize. Our approach to the treatment of the social problem of mental illness accordingly will be organized in terms of the costs of the broad alternatives. Both with regard to the present expenditures and with regard to proposals for reducing the problem we will provide some of the details of how the money is, or could be, spent. In this manner it will be seen that an important stumbling block in reducing the problem is the clash of values over the nature and size of society's expenditures for mental illness.

The Present Costs of Mental Illness

A little reflection makes it apparent that it is extremely difficult to compute what mental illness is costing our society. A recent study in this

[8] Jerome K. Myers and Bertram H. Roberts, *Family and Class Dynamics in Mental Illness* (New York: John Wiley & Sons, 1959), especially Chap. 4.

area found it desirable to separate the *direct costs* and the *indirect costs* of mental illness.[9] The direct costs of mental illness include the actual dollars we spend caring for patients in all public and private hospitals, the money that is spent on outpatient treatment whether by psychiatrists in private practice or through mental health clinics, and the pensions and compensations that are paid for psychiatric disabilities. It is estimated that these direct costs alone amount to $1.7 billion each year.[10] This figure does not include such direct costs as expenditures for new buildings, depreciation allowances on existing structures, or the dollar value of mental health lectures or the time spent by clergymen counseling those with emotional problems. Almost anyone can think of other costs that should be included if the figure for the direct costs of mental ill-health was to be complete.

The indirect cost of mental illness is an estimate of what the people suffering from mental illness would have contributed to the economy were they not sick. The most obvious way to measure this is in terms of the earnings lost by people who are not working because they are in a mental hospital. Using average wage rates, it was recently estimated that people in mental institutions lost $700 million in one year.[11] Of course, every year many patients are discharged and some die, while an approximately equal number of new patients are admitted. Thus the loss of $700 million goes on and on.

Based on the prevailing discharge and death rates, it has been further estimated that the group of patients admitted to a mental hospital for the first time in a given year will in the course of their lifetime lose over 500,000 years of work because of their hospitalization for mental illness.[12] To the indirect costs of mental illness already mentioned, we should add, of course, the costs of lower productivity by the emotionally disturbed who remain on the job. Some attempt also should be made to attach a dollar value to the homemaking services that are lost while wives and mothers are in mental institutions.

When we add the yearly indirect costs of $700 million and the yearly direct cost of $1.7 billion we discover that mental illness is costing us close to $2.5 billion annually. As we have indicated, this is a low estimate because it does not include various direct and indirect costs that are difficult to measure. Finally, it should be firmly kept in mind that we have been dealing only with *financial costs*. From a humanitarian point of view there are certainly other types of "costs," such as the suffering that is endured by the mentally sick and by those deprived of their loved ones.

[9] Rashi Fein, *Economics of Mental Illness* (New York: Basic Books, Inc., 1958).
[10] *Ibid.*, p. 47.
[11] *Ibid.*, p. 87.
[12] *Ibid.*

Proposals for Better Treatment

The present financial costs of mental illness to our society give some indication of the enormity of our mental health problem. Efforts for ameliorating the problem can be broken down into two types: (1) those directed at treating and returning to a useful life as many of the mentally ill as possible, and (2) those aimed at preventing others from joining the ranks of the mentally ill. Conflicts in value are much in evidence regarding the specific recommendations in both types of programs. A more general conflict of values also exists over whether or not we really need ameliorative programs of major proportions. We will be in a better position to understand these value clashes after we have investigated the nature and scope of treatment and preventive programs that have been proposed.

Despite the slight decrease in the number of mental patients, hospitalization of the severely ill will continue to be necessary and even desirable. Most psychotics are unable to cope with the complex problems of life and must, therefore, be removed from their usual social environment. Placed in an adequate mental hospital, chances for recovery are good. Personnel and equipment are available for his treatment, the routine of institutional life eliminates the need for much difficult decision making, and the patient is assured adequate diet and rest. For the occasional psychotic, removal from society is further necessary to assure that he will not harm himself or others. Thus, the adequacy of treatment of the severely mentally ill largely depends on the adequacy of our mental hospitals.

It is easily demonstrated that our mental hospitals are far from adequate. Overcrowding is quite common, the doctor-patient ratio is too low to allow optimum psychiatric treatment, and physical conditions and facilities are poor. All too frequently this means that the patient can receive little more than custodial care while supposedly undergoing treatment for his illness. The indictment against the people would not be so severe if, as a nation, we did not "know any better." But psychiatric knowledge has advanced rapidly in the last decades and recommendations repeatedly are made concerning the treatment of hospitalized psychotics necessary to insure their recovery or improvement.

To operate a scientifically modern mental hospital takes a great deal of money—much more money than the people and the legislatures of most states have indicated that they are willing to spend for this purpose. Modern buildings and equipment are expensive, and so are the best qualified personnel to staff the institution. To lure psychiatrists and psychiatric social workers and nurses into arduous institutional work, salaries must be paid that are somewhat commensurate to those obtained with private agencies and in private practice. Likewise wages providing a comfortable standard of living rather than current "starvation wages" must be paid to secure high quality personnel in the psychologically important roles of attendants. Until the necessary amount of finances is provided for adequate buildings, equipment, and personnel, all the "horror stories" and "public exposures" are not likely to alter significantly the facts about which they are written.

Table 20   Ratio of Mental Patients to Personnel in Public Mental Hospitals

	1940	1945	1950	1955	1959
Ratio of patients to					
Physicians	274.8	384.3	247.7	199.6	135.3
Graduate nurses	94.0	166.8	101.1	80.8	62.8
Other nurses; attendants	10.3	13.0	8.1	6.9	5.7
Social workers	1144.9	1050.6	612.4	409.0	297.6

SOURCE: U.S. Bureau of the Census, *Statistical Abstract of the United States: 1962,* Washington, D.C., 1962, p. 83.

The ratio of psychiatric personnel to patients has been improving. Even so, as shown in Table 20, the recent ratio of 1 doctor for about 135 patients is far from adequate for effective treatment. With more patients treated in outpatient clinics and in private practice, new needs are growing much more rapidly than the new supply of psychiatrists. Even if a sufficient number of properly qualified persons can be persuaded to undertake psychiatric training, it will be at least a decade before the need will be met, for a minimum of five years' training following the receipt of an M.D. degree is necessary to produce a fully qualified psychiatrist. There continues also a shortage of psychiatric nurses, social workers, and qualified attendants.

There are various ways of alleviating the shortage of psychiatric personnel, most of them involving the expenditure of money and most also involving an intense clash of values. The federal government, for example, could underwrite the training of psychiatrists, psychiatric nurses, and psychiatric social workers. This could involve not only providing free education but also granting a subsistence allowance for the students. It is well recognized that many young people of ability cannot afford a college education, let alone the costs of additional training. It is reasonable to assume that from the totality of those who cannot afford higher education and those who are now paying their own way a sizable number would be persuaded to enter the psychiatric professions if they could obtain full scholarships and adequate subsistence allowances. This seemingly "radical" idea is approximated, of course, with regard to the training of military experts.

Preventive Measures

There is a certain amount of overlap between programs designed for treating those presently ill and measures for preventing mental illness. For example, personnel are needed for both sorts of programs. Most of the psychiatric training of these people can best proceed in mental hospitals, so that better equipped, less crowded hospitals would improve both the treatment of patients and the training of personnel for preventive work.

The recommendations for preventing mental ill health that shortly follow are immediately available points of attack within our present social structure. Fundamental preventive attack indisputably would require radical changes. It would mean removal of the related problems of poor physical health, malnutrition, inadequate housing, and unemployment. It would mean more effective general education, occupational guidance, education for marriage and parenthood, and so forth, all of which is to say that mental health problems are closely interrelated with other social problems and will not be solved apart from them.

PROVISION OF MENTAL HYGIENE CLINICS IN LOCAL COMMUNITIES. It is ridiculous to talk about preventing mental illness so long as most communities do not at the present time have competent psychiatric services available even for the minority of the population that can afford to pay private fees. Even in the relatively well-staffed metropolitan areas, most psychiatrists are able to handle only the cases most severely in need of assistance. And the great mass of the people cannot pay the fees demanded by private psychiatric practitioners.

The only practical answer to the problem of meeting the needs of the majority of persons in the local communities is the mental hygiene clinic or guidance center. Again we run into difficulties of finances and insufficient personnel. The latter must come by the means already indicated, and the former must be derived from a combination of governmental and philanthropic sources. But, until the "normal" person has a reliable place to take his worries and fears and maladjustments, talk of preventing "abnormalities" is rather meaningless.

PROVISION OF COMPETENT COUNSELING SERVICES IN THE SCHOOLS. While it is rather fantastic at the present time to think of providing actual psychiatric service in most public schools, it is quite feasible to inaugurate more and better educational programs for training counselors. These persons would be able to treat minor personality difficulties among school children and to recognize more serious difficulties for referral to the community mental hygiene clinic. This would be a most significant aspect of prevention, for it would catch most mental illnesses in their initial stages when psychotherapy would be most effective and efficient.

EXTENSION OF ON-THE-JOB COUNSELING SERVICES. A number of the more progressive industrial and commercial establishments now provide counselors for their workers. It is a service that should be made available in all establishments hiring more than a few workers and could be linked to the mental hygiene clinics of the community in much the same fashion as suggested for counseling in the schools. Many workers have personal problems with which competent counselors could assist; some of these problems, without counseling help being available (as it generally is not at present), grow into serious mental health difficulties. Even when personal problems remain relatively small ones, they greatly reduce the efficiency and happiness of workers. From a strictly business point of view, management has found that a counseling service more than "pays for itself." Furthermore, potentially serious personality maladjustments in some workers may early be detected and referred to the mental hygiene clinic for effective psychiatric treatment.

MORE FUNDS FOR PSYCHIATRIC RESEARCH. With many physical illnesses, basic research has uncovered sufficient knowledge about the nature and functioning of the disease so that methods of controlling it become possible. There is every reason to believe that the same approach can work equally as well with regard to mental diseases. In the long run, therefore, probably the best preventive measure is more psychiatric research. It is true that our society is now spending a lot of money on psychiatric research, and it is also true that this has "paid off" in the sense of greater knowledge about mental disorders. In order to increase our knowledge to the state where mental disorders can be prevented, much more research is needed. Whatever is the proper amount of money and effort that should be devoted to such research, it is clear that research on mental diseases is not now in proportion to the seriousness or extent of the problem. We have already pointed out that about one half of all hospital patients are mentally ill. It might be supposed, then, that funds for mental health research would approach those for all other medical research combined. But government and private grants for mental research account for between 5 and 10 percent of all medical research grants. While money spent is not the sole criterion, modern research in any field cannot proceed adequately without considerable funds being made available.

THE BASIC CLASH OF VALUES: WHICH COSTS SHALL WE HAVE?

It should be obvious that the various foregoing proposals for more effective treatment of those presently mentally ill and for better prevention of these illnesses would be expensive. Not to adopt such measures is also expensive. As indicated in our discussion of the direct and indirect costs of severe mental illness, our society is already paying dearly for its mentally ill. Can we afford to, or *should* we spend more in this area?

When thinking of long-range effects, probably we should ask not whether we can afford to spend more on mental health but whether we can afford not to spend more money. It is quite likely, in other words, that increased expenditures can be justified *from a strictly economic point of view.* For example, increased costs of treatment may very well be offset by the additional earnings of patients made possible by their earlier release from the hospital. The provision of mental hygiene clinics where the emotionally disturbed could be treated in early stages of their illnesses could, in the long run, be cheaper than allowing people to become so sick that they both must cease working and must be treated in a mental hospital. Providing more psychiatrists, psychiatric nurses, and social workers may, again in the long run, not decrease but *increase* the number of other workers who are actively and efficiently in the labor force.

Not everyone, of course, accepts the position that long-term benefits will accrue from immediate expenses, even when the benefits are restricted to financial ones. Among the probable minority who do accept the position, there are those who believe we cannot afford the immediate expenditures regardless of their eventual value. Of course, all that it would take to increase mental health research grants, provide better hospital equipment, and the like, would be to spend less elsewhere. Ultimately, then, it becomes a question of values, a question of what should we do rather than what can we do. Should the federal government's defense budget be reduced so that its current budget for mental health could be increased? Should states build better highways or hospitals? Should schools hire more teachers or guidance experts? While we must avoid overemphasizing the competitive nature of allocations for these purposes, it is probable that in the short run if we spent more on mental health we would need to spend less on something else.

It seems clear that today the opposing value positions with regard to mental health do not have anything like an equal number of adherents. More people believe that nothing needs to be done than believe that something should be done. Many feel that not much more can be done than we are doing, while few believe otherwise. Many are indifferent and few are concerned. To be sure, there is some increase in the societal recognition of mental health as a problem. But until the distribution of the "many and the few" is reversed or radically altered, the possibilities for great strides in the reduction of the problem are not great.

SUGGESTED READINGS

BETTELHEIM, BRUNO, *The Informed Heart: Autonomy in a Mass Age.* New York, The Free Press of Glencoe, 1961.

FREEMAN, HOWARD E., and OZZIE G. SIMMONS, *The Mental Patient Comes Home.* New York, John Wiley & Sons, Inc., 1963.

GURIN, GERALD, JOSEPH VEROFF, and SHEILA FELD, *Americans View Their Mental Health.* New York, Basic Books, Inc., 1960.

HOLLINGSHEAD, AUGUST B., and FREDRICK C. REDLICH, *Social Class and Mental Illness.* New York, John Wiley & Sons, Inc., 1958.

JACO, E. GARTLY, *The Social Epidemiology of Mental Disorders.* New York, Russell Sage Foundation, 1960.

JOSEPHSON, ERIC, and MARY JOSEPHSON, *Man Alone: Alienation in Modern Society.* New York, Dell Publishing Co., 1962.

MACIVER, JOYCE (pseud.), *The Frog Pond.* New York, G. Braziller, 1961.

MYERS, JEROME K., and BERTRAM H. ROBERTS, *Family and Class Dynamics in Mental Illness.* New York, John Wiley & Sons, Inc., 1959.

SROLE, LEO, *et al., Mental Health in the Metropolis.* New York, McGraw-Hill Book Company, Inc., 1962.

OLD AGE ☐ 15

To most people, life is precious. Dreams of magic elixirs that would somehow stay the inevitable forces of time are legion, and a great deal of human effort has been spent on maintaining and prolonging life. It is paradoxical to find that now that more and more people are living longer we consider old age a "problem."

Why does man's ancient quest for longevity, now reaching some measure of success, constitute a "problem"? In what sense is old age a problem of society, rather than a physical condition of individual old people? What are the essential features of this social problem? These are among the questions we will attempt to answer in this chapter. Since societal concern with old age is of relatively recent origin, we will begin with some basic information relevant to aging and the aged.

Life Span and Life Expectancy

The span of life refers to the length of time that members of a species have the biological capacity for living. Within the animal kingdom, there is, of course, great variation in the life span of the various species. The life span of the fruit fly, for example, is measured in hours, while the giant tortoise has a span of hundreds of years. No one knows exactly what is the life span of the human being, but it has been estimated at about 100 years. The number of years that the human organism can survive, in other words, seems to be close to a hundred. As far as can be determined, the life span of the human being is today the same as it has been for a long, long time.

Life expectation is an actuarial concept. For a group of people born in the same year it is possible to estimate, on the basis of past experience, the number that will survive the first year of life, the number that will survive for five years, ten years, and so on. With some living a shorter time and some longer, the *average* number of years that the group of people will live can be computed. If of a hypothetical group of people born at the same time half died within the first year and the remainder lived to the century mark, the *average life expectancy* for the group would be fifty years. Life expectancy averages also can be obtained for a group of people at any given age, and not just at time of birth. In each case, the figure would relate to the average number of additional years that the group of people at the specific age will live.

At the turn of the century, the average life expectancy at birth was about forty-eight years for men, and about fifty-one years for women. As noted in Table 21, by 1960 about twenty years had been added to the average life expectancy at birth. On the other hand, those who were sixty-five years old in 1900 could expect to live an average of twelve additional years. Men of this age in 1960 had an average life expectancy of about thirteen years, and women an average of fifteen and a half years. At age seventy-five, men and women now live on the average of about one more year than their counterparts in 1900.[1]

Table 21   Life Expectancy at Birth and Selected Ages, 1900–1960

	Average expectancy of life in years							
	At birth		At age 20		At age 40		At age 65	
Year	Male	Female	Male	Female	Male	Female	Male	Female
1900	48	51	42	44	28	29	11.5	12.2
1910	50	54	43	45	27	29	11.3	12.0
1920	56	59	46	47	30	31	12.2	12.8
1930	59	63	46	49	29	32	11.8	12.8
1940	63	67	48	51	30	33	12.1	13.6
1950	66	72	50	55	31	36	12.8	15.0
1960	67	74	50	56	32	37	12.7	15.6

SOURCE: Adapted from annual reports, U.S. Department of Health, Education, and Welfare, *Vital Statistics of the United States.*

It is apparent that the dramatic increase in life expectancy at birth is due largely to the declining infant mortality rate and the death rate of children. It is nevertheless true that more people are living out a larger portion of the life span allotted to the species. The smaller increases in life

[1] Henry D. Sheldon, *The Older Population of the United States* (New York: John Wiley & Sons, Inc., 1958), p. 17.

expectancy at middle age and beyond mean that more and more people in our society are falling within the statistical category of "aged." And when we are dealing with millions of people approaching old age, and when this number itself is growing, even small increases in expectation of life can result in a numerically quite significant increase of older people.

Number and Growth of Aged

Before we can speak about the number of persons in the population falling into the old-age category, we must have a definition of what constitutes old age. Any chronological age that is selected as the beginning of old age is bound to be artificial. Some people are slow in thought and action, "worn out," at sixty; others proceed vigorously and efficiently with their daily lives at seventy-five. Since there is a growing tendency to retire employed persons at sixty-five, that age is often arbitrarily chosen as the beginning of the old-age period. For statistical purposes, then, we shall accept this customary definition of an aged person as anyone sixty-five years of age or older. We shall, however, take occasion later to discuss less arbitrary and more functional criteria that may be used in describing old age.

There is no doubt but that there has been a significant increase in the number of persons sixty-five years of age and older. In 1900 there were some 3 million people in this category. By 1930 their numbers had more than doubled, and then doubled again by 1950. In 1960 there were more than three times as many older people as there were at the turn of the century.

Table 22   Total Population and Population 65 and Over, 1900–1963

Year	Total population	Number of persons 65 and over	Percentage of persons 65 and over
1900	75,994,575	3,080,498	4.1
1910	91,972,266	3,949,524	4.3
1920	105,710,620	4,933,215	4.7
1930	122,775,046	6,333,805	5.4
1940	131,669,275	9,019,314	6.8
1950	150,697,361	12,271,178	8.1
1960	179,323,175	16,559,580	9.2
1963	188,844,000	17,562,492	9.3

SOURCE: Data assembled from reports of the Bureau of the Census.

The number of aged continues to increase at a rate of 300,000 to 400,-000 per year; in 1963 they numbered about 17.5 million. And we can predict with some accuracy how many aged there were will be in the future. All of the people, for example, who will be sixty-five or over in the year 2000 have already been born and already are almost thirty years of age. Barring some mass catastrophe that would affect the death rate of this age group, it can be estimated that there will be at least 28 million people age sixty-five and over by the year 2000. Regardless of the present and future growth of the rest of the population, we can expect to add about 10 million old people in the next thirty-five years. Just from the standpoint of the numbers involved, old age becomes an increasingly important matter of social concern.

Proportion of Aged in Total Population

The sheer number of old people in a society is important for various reasons. It makes a difference, for example, whether as a society we need to provide for the economic, health, recreation, and other needs of 9 million or 18 million old people. But it is also necessary to know what *proportion* of the population is sixty-five and over and what changes are taking place with regard to the growth of this segment *relative to the growth of the rest of the population.*

In 1850 only 2.6 percent of the population were sixty-five or older. In 1900 the percentage was 4.1; in 1950, 8.1; in 1960, 9.2; and in 1963, 9.3. The percentage of old people at some future date obviously is dependent both on how many old people there will be at that time and the total population size. We can be less precise with any prediction dependent on future birth rates. Current estimates place the proportion of older people at between 13 and 15 percent of the population at the next century turn.

It should be apparent that persons over sixty-five are now, and will continue to be, a "sizable minority." It is not too much to expect, in a democracy, that the wishes of this ever-growing segment of our population will have increasingly more impact on our economic, social, and other policies.

THE NATURE OF "OLD AGE"

Aging is generally a very gradual process. Various physical, psychological, and sociological traits come to characterize persons who are growing old. No one old person has all of these characteristics, but the traits are found among old people as a group.[2]

---

[2] In this section on the nature of old age the authors have drawn heavily upon material contained in Ruth Cavan, Ernest Burgess, Robert Havighurst, and Herbert Goldhamer, *Personal Adjustment in Old Age* (Chicago: Science Research Associates, 1949). Although no material is quoted, much is paraphrased, and the authors wish to express their indebtedness to this very thorough and careful research.

Physical Old Age

Not only is there a broad range of variation among individuals as to when a particular type of physical decline or deterioration will appear, but there is no one age in any specific individual when all functions begin to show a decline. Often, too, changes in physical functioning occur so slowly in later life that they are difficult to measure except over relatively long periods of time.

Some of the physical changes that will generally occur at some point in the period of old age (providing the person lives long enough for many of these things to occur) are general decline in physical strength and vitality, increased tendency toward fatigue, and a slowing down in reactions. These are often preceded, accompanied, or followed by some such organic deficiency as a failing in hearing or eyesight. The old person likewise becomes much more susceptible to chronic illnesses or incapacities resulting from specific diseases, falls and broken bones, or gradual failure of internal organs to function properly.

It should be emphasized again that there is considerable individual variation with respect to the presence of these physical marks of aging. Among the physically old will be found men as young as fifty, while others who are years their seniors will in some respects be "younger." And we are not talking about "youthful outlook" nor are we giving support to popular beliefs about maintaining one's youth by "thinking young." It is simply a fact that people exhibit the *physical* symptoms of old age at different chronological ages. From a practical standpoint, then, this means that in addition to earlier existing differences, old people of the same age differ in their physical ability to work, to read, to play, to drive automobiles, and so on. All too frequently our policies toward the aged ignore these differences.

A given individual, furthermore, does not exhibit each of the various indications of physical old age with the same intensity. His eyesight, for example, may begin to fail earlier or may fail more rapidly than his hearing, or both of these faculties may continue to be "good" long after his cardiovascular system has quite definitely "aged." For an individual, then, this lack in a uniform progression of the aging process may mean that he is "too old" to perform *his* job at sixty-five, sixty, or even younger, but that he is physically capable of performing other jobs. This applies too, of course, to types of recreation and anything else that requires use of one's physical faculties.

Psychological Old Age

The commencement of old age is a phenomenon that may first become apparent through mental rather than physical decline. Psychological deterioration is much more difficult to measure than physical decline. Criteria are less reliable and valid. Full cooperation of the subject is necessary for successful mental testing, and older people are often less familiar with and interested in psychological measurements than are younger people. Then, too, because of wide individual variations in all age categories, psychological test results would be needed on the same persons over many years in order to give an accurate picture of mental decline. Most tests, in addition, are based on the experiences of children, adolescents, and young adults, and frequently may not be applicable to the experience-world of an older person.

The chief data which are available, therefore, are based on observations, especially of psychiatrists who have older persons as patients, rather than upon systematically and statistically derived samplings of the older population. Presence of many of the following traits in intense form is characteristic of senile dementia. Most older people have a number of these characteristics to some degree, however, without bordering seriously on actual mental illness. The most common psychological deteriorations are loss of memory (especially regarding recent events), inability to concentrate over long periods of time, and difficulty in learning new skills. Other common mental developments are attitudes of suspicion, narrowing of interests, feeling of insecurity, of guilt, and of being unwanted, conservatism and inflexibility, a tendency to relive the past, worry (especially about money and health), garrulity, hoarding, and increased liking of quiescence and dislike of activity.

The standardized tests that have been administered to groups of older people indicate that the various types of mental skills apparently deteriorate at different rates. For example, performance on vocabulary, general information, and verbal comprehension tests has been found to show little or no decline until a very old age, while there is some indication of a more pronounced decline on the "reasoning" and "judgment" tests.[3] Much more research needs to be conducted in this area and with regard to attitudinal changes of the aged.

It should be clear that psychological characteristics of aging, like physical ones, do not occur in all individuals at the same chronological age and do not progress at the same rate for all persons. Some men may find it best to retire from work or to change jobs at sixty, while others may be psychologically equipped to continue their lifetime work to seventy-five or over.

Sociological Old Age

Furthermore, old age also constitutes a sociological phenomenon in that it implies that there is a position in society somehow different from that of adult, and that associated with this position of older person are responsibilities and privileges likewise different from those of the adult. In still

[3] Wilma T. Donahue, "Psychological Aspects of Aging," in T. Lynn Smith, ed., *Problems of America's Aging Population* (Gainesville: University of Florida Press, 1951), pp. 56–60.

another sense is old age a sociological phenomenon. The various physical and psychological characteristics of older people are defined by, evaluated by, and thus derive their full meaning from the society in which the older person is living. While, for example, a seventy-year-old person would not change his objective condition as he went from place to place, the part that he would be expected to play as an older person and the way in which his physical and psychological conditions were evaluated would most assuredly differ from society to society.

The usual adult in our society is expected to provide for his economic needs, to maintain an independent household, to have some sort of gainful or purposeful pursuit, and to manage without too much help from others his personal affairs. As an older person gradually relinquishes more and more aspects of the typical adult role he slips into the status of "aged." Often, for the man, the shift in status begins abruptly by his retirement from full-time employment. Women, usually less conspicuously and less abruptly, give up household management. At any rate, at about the time of a man's retirement, or shortly following his termination of employment, there is often a loss of the independent household. Or, in case the woman outlives her husband (as an increasing number of women are tending to do), the independent home may be given up shortly following her husband's death. Whenever it occurs, and almost whatever the new arrangement may be, giving up an independent home is an indication that one has relinquished one of the characteristics of the full adult and is entering the status of aged.

Large numbers of old people become economically dependent upon their children or upon society, and in so doing lose still another responsibility of the usual adult. In addition, this frequently puts the dependent older person in a position subordinate to adult children, social workers, or supervisors of a nursing or old people's home.

Finally, many old people come in time to require a great deal of assistance with their personal affairs or are unable to manage them at all. They are not able to get their own meals reliably, to manage whatever financial resources they have, or to protect themselves responsibly from the elements and traffic. In short, they cannot take care of themselves, as we expect the normal adult to be able to, and they require the supervision of others. When this stage is reached, the older person has clearly changed his status from that of full adult. Just as surely, the relinquishment of purposeful pursuits, the giving up of an independent household, and becoming financially dependent all represent significant steps toward the complete change of status.

We have said that old age is a sociological phenomenon in the sense that the symptoms and characteristics of older people take on meaning from the society of which the older person is a member. Perhaps a few examples can best illustrate this point.

Two common psychological characteristics of aging, as we have seen, are (1) the tendency for the memory of recent events to fade more quickly than the memory of early years, and, (2) an increase in garrulity or "talkativeness." When these traits are combined we have a person who will willingly talk for hours about the "old days," and who can describe in some detail the events, the problems, and the general way of life at the time of his youth. In our own fast-moving society, such abilities, frankly, seem to have little worth, and he who has them is found annoying or is merely tolerated. In many primitive societies where heavy emphasis is placed on tradition, the same qualities are considered valuable, for it is precisely in this way that the myths, legends, and history of the group are passed from generation to generation and that the traditional values of the group are reinforced.

If, to take another example, a society was so organized that several generations customarily lived in the same household, the increasing inability of an older woman to manage a household might almost go unnoticed. Gradually, the younger women would take on more duties, while the older one just as gradually relinquished hers. Perhaps never, or only near the close of her life, would it be clear to the older woman and her society that she had lost the status of full adult. The same objective, personal conditions that lessen ability for household management would not, as in our society, be a conspicuous indication that one of life's cultural milestones had been passed.

While old people everywhere may as human organisms show signs of the same degenerative processes at work, as members of different societies old people find that these signs and symptoms are variously interpreted and have varying effects on the part they can play in their group.

Need for Subcategories of Old Age

Confusion has arisen from terms such as "old age" or "the aged" to refer to all people who have had sixty-five birthdays. But the number of years that people can live beyond sixty-five is too great, and the individual variations in the aging processes are too varied to allow us to expect any real homogeneity in the sixty-five and over group. The serious suggestion for increasing the width of our doorways to enable the ready passage of the wheel chairs of our "aged" may not make much sense to the man who thinks of the aged in terms of his sixty-six-year-old, agile, and quick-witted mother and others like her. Again, the recreational needs of the seventy-one-year-old man who boasts of his ability to command "a day's pay for a day's work" are scarcely the same as those of one who is chronologically his junior but who has "aged" to the extent that residence in a nursing home seems advisable.

In order to avoid the confusion accompanying the use of the term "old age" to describe such a broad and varied period of man's life, one authority has suggested the division of the postadult years into three periods: early senescence, middle senescence, and later senescence.[4] The periods would be differentiated on the basis of the degree of deviation from adult standards. It is not yet possible, however, to measure such deviation precisely, but there would seem to be much merit in the use of subcategories of old age even if based on crude and approximate criteria.

PROBLEMS OF OLD AGE AND VALUE CONFLICTS

Like people at any stage of life, older people have problems. There are some conditions and situations that are more or less unique to old age and constitute problems for a great number of older people. The several major difficulties of old age that we will investigate are *social* problems, since added to the objective situation is a conflict of societal values that has helped to bring about the condition, has aggravated it, or perhaps has just hindered its amelioration. More than this, there seems to be an underlying clash of values of a major sort that permeates the various problem conditions of old age and is an expression of competing philosophies regarding old age generally. This underlying conflict concerns whether the role of the older person in our society shall be a relatively autonomous or a relatively passive one. After we investigate the nature of this basic conflict, we shall see how it is reflected in the more specific problems of old age.

Autonomous versus Dependent-Passive Role

There are two directions in which societies can go, and have gone, in developing a position in their group for older people.[5] We can think of these as polar opposites, although it would be rare to find either of the extreme types in practice. A society tending toward the one extreme would do everything possible to allow the older person to function as autonomously as he did in his middle years. He would be expected to be, and, if necessary, helped to be an independent agent, making his own decisions, retaining as many responsibilities as he could, and determining and caring for his own needs and wants. The older person would be as self-governing of his behavior and as self-controlling of his destiny as he was capable. The societal policy would be that the older person maintain as closely as feasible the degree of autonomy he had at the peak of adulthood.

[4] Cavan *et al., op cit.,* p. 8.
[5] We are indebted to Robert J. Havighurst for the distinction between the alternative social policies for old age. See Robert J. Havighurst, "Life Beyond Family and Work," in Ernest W. Burgess, ed., *Aging in Western Societies* (Chicago: The University of Chicago Press, 1960), pp. 299–353.

At the other extreme we have the value position that the part an older person plays in society should be a passive one. In general, this would mean that he should withdraw himself as completely as possible from the real and active world. He should relinquish, or be forced to relinquish, his control over life's forces. His family, his society, or some group within the society, would plan for him and see that his needs, as they felt them to be, were met. The older person would place himself in the hands of others who, in turn, would try to make his life as comfortable and enjoyable as possible. The older person would "take it easy," loaf, and rest, and would not have to worry much about the world around him.

As we look at our own society at the present time, it is apparent that we have loyal adherents to the policy of an autonomous role for the aged, and just as loyal adherents to the opposing policy of a passive-dependent role. Older people themselves generally prefer as much autonomy as society allows and of which they are capable. Many others are also in favor of a relatively autonomous role for the aged, feeling simply that it is good for man to be an independent agent and to look after himself, even though it may be difficult to do so. It is also felt that it is good for society to have as many of its citizens functioning autonomously for as long as possible.

Those advocating a more passive role for the aged are not without humanitarian feelings, nor do they have anything "against" older people. It is simply argued that our modern society is too complex for the older person to function in it autonomously. It is better, according to those advocating this policy, to admit that the older person cannot care for himself and to help him to relinquish his responsibilities and free himself of his obligations as graciously as possible. The policy of an autonomous role for old people is criticized, finally, as being quite unrealistic. The average person in our mass society, it is pointed out, has little real control over his job or his income, and increasingly his leisure is directed by professional leaders in entertainment fields. Under such circumstances can we really expect a person suddenly to become master of his destinies when he reaches age sixty-five?

It should be apparent that as a society we can scarcely endorse either a policy of complete autonomy or complete passivity for our older people. Not only must we reckon with individual differences among older people, but the same person can go through a period after age sixty-five when he *could be* relatively autonomous and, later, a shorter period when he is forced to be relatively dependent. Despite these difficulties, it would be possible to formulate a general policy regarding the direction in which we should be moving, and we could strive to implement this policy in as consistent a manner as possible. As we turn now to specific major problems of old age in our society, we shall see how the lack of consistency in this regard can aggravate an already serious problem or make difficult the acceptance of ameliorative action.

Economic Problems

In our relatively affluent society it would seem to be a reasonable goal to eliminate absolute poverty among the aged. No doubt we would approach consensus on the idea that those over sixty-five, those, in other words, who have labored forty or more years in our society, should not experience dire financial need in their declining years. At the same time, there is evidence that many are not aware of the true economic plight of older people. Our first task, then, is to take a hard look at the economic realities of life after sixty-five. Only then can we grapple with the various alternatives for dealing with the economic problems of older people.

After a series of studies in many different cities, the Bureau of Labor Statistics developed a budget for a couple over sixty-five years of age which would allow them a "modest but adequate" level of living.[6] The budget assumes that both husband and wife are in reasonably good health and are able to care for themselves. It would provide for a two- to three-room rented dwelling, food, and other goods necessary for a healthful existence, and for participation in community life. It does not provide for an automobile. In recent years the needed yearly budget has ranged between $2700 and $3300, with some variation by section of the country and size of city.

Table 23   Income of Older Persons and Families, 1961

Total yearly income	Percent of families, head over 65 years	Percent of unattached individuals over 65 years
Under $1000	8.5	45.2
$1000–$1999	22.3	33.7
$2000–$2999	18.8	10.8
$3000–$3999	13.4	4.4
$4000–$6999	19.8	4.0
$7000–$9999	8.8	.7
$10,000 and over	8.4	1.2

SOURCE: *Current Population Reports,* Series P-60, No. 39 (February 28, 1963), p. 17.

Some, of course, would claim that provision of only a "modest but adequate" level of living for older people is too low a goal for our society in its time of relative abundance. Surely, it would be contended, older people should be able to afford a few more of the luxuries of life, perhaps more extensive travel and home ownership, and surely some provisions should be made for those with more extensive health needs. The fact remains, as in-

[6] Mollie Orshansky, "Budget for an Elderly Couple; Interim Revision by the Bureau of Labor Statistics," *Social Security Bulletin,* 23 (December 1960), pp. 26–36.

dicated in Table 23, that we are still a long way from providing even a minimum adequate standard of living for millions of older people. While it is apparent that no one measure would "solve" the financial needs of the aged, the following are the basic means currently available for meeting these needs.

EMPLOYMENT. We must remember that well over a third of all people more than sixty-five years of age are between the ages of sixty-five and sixty-nine and that about half are less than seventy-two years old. For this earlier portion of what we think of as old age, therefore, employment would seem to be a reasonable alternative if the people themselves were able and willing to work and if society was able to find employment for them.

The idea of someday retiring from work seems generally and increasingly accepted in our society. It is not necessarily inconsistent to find, at the same time, that many older people would like to continue working or actively seek new employment after age sixty-five. For example, a study by the National Committee on Aging found that in companies without a fixed age for retirement policy about 60 percent of the sixty-four-year-old men desired to continue working.[7] Various other studies have discovered that large proportions of those approaching the usual retirement age would like to keep on working. Apparently, the prospect of retiring, *under today's conditions,* is not too attractive for those for whom it is an imminent possibility. A part, perhaps even a large part, of the unattractiveness of retirement is the radical decline in standard of living that goes with it. In other words, while probably a large proportion of Americans find nothing wrong with the idea of retirement, many feel that it is necessary to remain employed in order to secure a reasonable income.

Table 24   Proportion of Older Workers, 1900–1960

	Percent in labor force				
	1900	1920	1940	1950	1960
Males 65 years and older	68.3	60.1	45.0	45.8	31.8
Females 65 years and older	9.1	8.0	7.4	9.7	10.1

SOURCE: U.S. Bureau of Census reports.

During World War II, it was forcibly demonstrated that many older people were capable of taking an active role in the productive economy. Many studies since that time have found that placed in the right job, older workers have production and absentee records similar to those of younger workers.

[7] Quoted in Clark Tibbitts, ed., *Handbook of Social Gerontology* (Chicago: The University of Chicago Press, 1960), p. 366.

With many people over sixty-five needing to work for financial reasons, able to work, and wanting to work, what really is the problem? Why do not the older unemployed people simply find employment and thereby solve various of their difficulties? Some see our rapidly changing technology as the major difficulty in that the older worker inevitably finds himself with un-salable skills and abilities. Others shift the blame to "big business" and "management," pointing to the policies of compulsory retirement at a fixed age and to discriminatory practices in hiring older people. Others see "the unions" as the big culprit in that organized labor's efforts at securing com-pany pensions, unemployment compensation, and health insurance make it economically infeasible to hire older people.

It is difficult to believe that as a society we are simply too ignorant to meet the various problems said to prevent employment of those over sixty-five years of age. After all, a society capable of sending rockets to the far side of the moon could be expected to be able to find a way to retrain older workers and to solve the other difficulties associated with their em-ployment. It makes more sense to conclude that our society really does not want those over sixty-five to continue working, and particularly that it does not want to allow the individual himself to determine whether and for how long he should work after the arbitrary age of sixty-five. In this instance, therefore, we seem definitely to be favoring a passive-dependent role for the aged rather than an autonomous one. Today, at least, employment does not seem to be a feasible way for the bulk of older people to meet their financial needs, even if they are physically and psychologically able to work.

INSURANCE FOR OLD AGE. Even if our society tacitly approved or actively encouraged the employment of older people, it would be entirely unrealistic to expect that all of them could meet their financial needs through current employment. Sooner or later the inevitable forces of life take their toll, and the individual is unemployable because of the extent of his physical and psychological aging. This, of course, has always been true, for always there have been old people at that stage of life we have designated as later senescence. Until the mid-1930s, however, there was no general plan to provide pensions for the aged. Older people worked for as long as they could and then lived on their savings, were supported by their children, or lived out their remaining years at the state- or county-supported "poor farm." It was the occasional and progressive company only that provided for re-tirement income, and consequently the great bulk of workers did not have a guaranteed source of income for their postemployment years.

Spurred on by the high unemployment rates of the depression years and the increasing problem of how to care for people of all ages, the federal Social Security Act was passed in 1935. Originally, part of the act provided for monthly benefits for retired workers, thereby removing at least one group from the rolls of job seekers. Various successive amendments have considerably broadened the scope of the act so that the Old Age, Survivors, and Disability Insurance program (OASDI) as we know it now provides benefits for such categories of persons as the totally disabled worker between the ages of fifty and sixty-four, children of deceased, retired, or disabled workers, and wives and widows of eligible workers, in addition to the benefits for retired workers. The proportion of workers eligible for OASDI has also increased so that at present more than nine out of ten employed persons are covered by the program.

OASDI is an exclusively federal program supported at present by equal contributions from employer and employee. When a person reaches sixty-five and retires, or when he retires thereafter, he receives monthly benefits. Such benefits are payable to eligible individuals as a matter of right; regardless of need, eligible retired workers are entitled to them. While the amount of the monthly benefits is based on a person's earnings while he was employed, it is not on a strictly proportional basis. Low income workers receive retirement benefits closer to their previous earnings than those paid to higher income persons.

The minimum monthly benefit for a retired worker has risen from $10 in 1935 to $33, while the maximum has increased from $85 to $127, since the 1958 amendments. Today an eligible older couple can receive up to $190.50 per month. However, the average actually paid in recent years is $70 a month to aged male beneficiaries. Only about 2 percent were receiving close to maximum figure, while about one fourth were receiving less than $50 per month.

Obviously, older people cannot maintain themselves at a "modest but adequate" level of living by social security payments alone. For many older people, in fact, such benefits will provide less than half of what would be required.

It seemed to be the original intent of the Social Security Act that older beneficiaries should completely retire, thereby freeing jobs for younger workers. In the last ten to fifteen years there have been various changes, but the depression-minded philosophy prevails to the extent that OASDI benefits can be withheld if a person earns "too much" in a given period. Thus, the individual's "right" to OASDI benefits can only be exercised if he meets the "retirement test" and has more or less removed himself from the labor force.

If our society were interested in creating as fully autonomous a role for the aged as possible, it would seem that we would take steps to assure that each older person had as free a choice as was possible concerning his employment. If OASDI payments were an absolute right, instead of partially being a financial lure to retire, the decision-making power of the older person accordingly would be increased. Recent amendments to the Social

Security Act have allowed individuals to earn progressively more from employment without forfeiting their rights to OASDI benefits. What remains of the "retirement test" notion, however, suggests that we still prefer older people to play a passive-dependent role in society.

OLD-AGE ASSISTANCE. In recent years about 2.5 million people over age sixty-five have been helped to meet their financial needs through Old-age Assistance payments. Workers and employers do not contribute directly to this program; the funds are derived partly from the federal and partly from state governments. The Old-age Assistance (OAA) program recognizes the fact that probably there will always be some older people with financial needs that they are incapable of meeting themselves. In earlier years, of course, many workers were not covered by social security. But even today there are older people who have unique health needs, who have only meager savings, if any, or who are unable to supplement their OASDI payments through current employment. The OAA helps such older people to have an adequate standard of living, even if there are some difficulties with the current program.

Among possible improvements of the OAA program is, first of all, the size of the monthly payments to recipients. These are admittedly low, and in some cases woefully inadequate. Recently, the average monthly payment to Old-age Assistance recipients was $64.24 for the country as a whole, with a low of $29.19 in one of our states.[8] In about three fifths of the states the average OAA payments range from $50 to $80 per month.[9] Since some of the recipients are not covered by social security, and since all of the recipients, in order to be eligible at all, are in financial need, it would appear that the average payment for most of our states is too low.

Another problem of the Old-age Assistance program today is probably as much administrative as financial. As we have seen, the purpose of OAA is to help older people who are in financial need. Theoretically, therefore, the monthly payments should be based on how much the older person needs in order to have a decent living. In practice this has been difficult to accomplish and, in most of the states, there has developed the concept of the "average need" of older people. Thus, while there is still a flexibility in the amount of payments, older people *tend* to receive the same payment regardless of their actual needs. If the principle of need were the sole determinant, we would, of course, find some older people receiving OAA payments two, three, or four times as large as some other older people. What is more, it is not unlikely that some OAA recipients could have a higher monthly income than those under social security or those who have a part-time job. While there is nothing wrong with this in light of the concept of financial need, it is possible that it would cause some difficulties in

[8] *Ibid.*, p. 239.
[9] *Ibid.*

a society such as ours that is accustomed to thinking of income as a reward for personal effort.

Associated with the OAA program today are the conflicting values concerning the "relatives' responsibility requirement." The idea is prevalent in our society that public assistance should not be given to older people whose relatives, particularly children, have the financial ability to care for them. While the laws in our various states differ, about two thirds of the states do impose some kind of financial obligations on relatives of older people. Some defend the "relatives' responsibility requirement" on the basis that the general public should not have to support those older people who have economically capable relatives. They point out, furthermore, that failure to insist that relatives support "their own" will tend to weaken family ties in the United States. The opponents of the "relatives' responsibility requirement" are equally as vigorous in their arguments. In the first place, they point out that the cost and difficulty in collecting from the relatives may result in an actually small amount of savings to the taxpayer. They wonder, in addition, whether family ties are strengthened or weakened when it becomes necessary to force children to support their parents. Finally, there are the practical problems of determining the ability of the younger people to support their older relatives, of determining which of the younger relatives should support them, and so on.

It is clear that the present meaning of Old-age Assistance in our society has strong overtones of charity, if not being equated precisely with it. But it should be recognized that this is not the only meaning such a program *could have*. It is conceivable at least that a society could come to define such assistance as *a right*. That is, our society could say in effect that every older person has a right to minimum comforts in his old age, regardless of his own ability to provide for them. While this is a "radical" thought for today, there would seem to be some merit in it from the standpoint of the older person himself. Very few people really are completely comfortable about accepting "charity" of any sort, nor are the aged different in this respect. If Old-age Assistance were to lose its connotation of charity, it would seem to do much for the self-respect of the older person. As long as the payments continued to be based on need, the negative criticism that without the unsavory connotation of charity many more would apply for payments, is actually support for the change; it would simply demonstrate that just that many older people are in financial need. Realistically, it is unlikely that in the immediate future we will change dramatically the nature or meaning of Old-age Assistance. It is well to remember that the mere existence of the program means that we at least tacitly recognize societal responsibility for our older citizens.

INDUSTRIAL PENSIONS AND PRIVATE ANNUITIES. Two additional sources of income for some older people are pensions received from the company for which they worked and private insurance plans they may have purchased during their years of employment.

Actually, the first company to provide a pension for its employees was the American Express Company, which established its plan in 1875.[10] Despite this early start, only an insignificant number of workers were eligible for an industrial pension as late as the 1940s. Since that time more industries have responded to the strong union pressures for workers' benefits of various sorts. Today, it is estimated that about 18 million people are covered by some type of industrial pension; this represents less than 40 percent of all wage and salary workers however. As might be expected, company pensions are most frequently found in large organizations and in those where the workers belong to a strong union.

Company pension plans differ widely both with regard to the size of their payments and their eligibility requirements. A recent study of thirteen of the larger plans found that workers with thirty years' service and with monthly wages of about $350 would receive from $50 to $146 per month upon retirement.[11] Even for the less than half of all workers eligible for an industrial pension, the benefits received can be considered only as a supplement to other retirement income. Finally, only a very small portion of the nation's wage earners can afford to purchase an annuity from a commercial concern. A man of thirty, for example, would have to pay about $500 per year, or a total of over $17,000 before he is sixty-five, in order to receive a guaranteed yearly income of $2000 thereafter.

Income Sources and the Role of the Older Person

As we have seen there are only a few basic ways by which, either separately or together in some combination, the older person can satisfy his economic requirements. He may work full-time or part-time, he may draw social security benefits, he may request Old-age Assistance, he may be eligible for an industrial pension, or he may get support from relatives or friends. Only a small proportion of Americans are able to live in their later years on previously acquired savings. It is now necessary to relate the various sources of income for older people to what we have labeled the central problem of old age, that is, whether we are encouraging in our society a relatively autonomous or relatively passive-dependent role for the older person.

With regard to the employment of older people, we have seen that frequently the choice of whether or not to work does not really rest with the

[10] *Ibid.*, p. 243.
[11] *Ibid.*

individual. Increasingly, companies have a compulsory retirement age. In addition, the older person seeking employment frequently meets with discriminatory practices based on age. Retraining programs for the older worker whose skills have become obsolete or whose health suggests he enter a different type of employment are all too infrequent.

The Old-age, Survivors', and Disability Insurance program, at least as it functions at present, encourages the worker to retire, for most frequently it is only then that he can receive full benefits. Similarly, industrial pensions are paid only to those who leave their place of employment. Whether or not compulsory retirement is desirable in order to reduce unemployment in other segments of society is not here the issue. The point is, rather, that under current practices the worker is prompted to withdraw from the active world of employment and to accept what is frequently a less active role. In a very real sense, practices that strongly encourage retirement reduce the degree to which an older person can control his own destinies and order his own life.

Old-age Assistance, finally, casts the older person quite definitely into a passive-dependent role. He must, of course, demonstrate that he is in financial need. Most frequently he must also agree to the state's taking a lien on his property equal to the payments he will receive, thereby seemingly reducing his chances of again becoming solvent and independent. What is more, frequently he is still not eligible for assistance if he has relatives who can be persuaded to support him. The necessity for Old-age Assistance cannot be argued and, indeed, the merits of the program are many. It is nevertheless true that as presently construed and administered it favors a dependent role for the aged rather than an autonomous one.

Health Problems

It is paradoxical that while the growing number of older people is a reflection of health progress, yet some of the greatest inadequacies in health care are found among older people. A part of the aging process, as we have defined it, is the general loss of physical vigor and the decreased functioning of various physiological processes and organs. The existence of health needs among the aged is not in itself a social problem. The health needs of the aged become a social problem when there are societal factors that prevent or make difficult the meeting of these needs at a level consistent with our available knowledge. In addition, there should be social concern with the health needs of the aged inasmuch as health is almost bound to affect the role of the older person on the job, in his family, or in the community.

There are various indications that health needs and health problems increase with advancing age. One study concluded, for example, that of every 1000 persons who were well at age forty-five, about 10 percent would need medical attention within five years for a chronic disease or major impairment.[12] The ratios increase to about 25 percent at age sixty, 40 percent at age seventy, 57 percent at age eighty, and 90 percent at age ninety. Various studies have shown that older people have more frequent trips to physicians and have more hospital admissions.[13] What is more, older people are hospitalized on the average for about twice as long a period as younger ones.[14] With an average stay of eighteen days when hospitalized, this tends to be an expensive procedure.

Older people seem to have difficulty meeting the costs of the medical care that they can be expected to require. As we have already seen, many are operating on an extremely limited income. Coupled to this is the fact that, as a group, they are likely to need more costly medical attention than other age groups. But the person over sixty-five is decidedly less likely to have some kind of hospitalization insurance. Many profit-making health insurance concerns either charge higher rates for persons over sixty-five or simply refuse to insure those in this "higher risk" category.

How and how well the health needs of our older people are met have definite implications for various aspects of their lives. Certainly the older person in need of treatment he cannot afford is at a disadvantage in competing for a job and is less able to function well in his family and to participate in recreational pursuits or community affairs. Not to be overlooked is the manner in which medical attention is provided even to those older people fortunate enough to secure what they require. Forcing an older person to be a charity patient of a private physician, to take a bed in the charity ward of a hospital, or to apply for special medical "relief" is tantamount to foisting on him a dependent-passive role. On the other hand, were all older people able to obtain the medical attention they need, whether financed through private health insurance, current income, or government health insurance, not only would the health of older people be better, but they would also be helped to see themselves as nondependent, self-respecting, full-fledged members of society. Better health and certain methods of obtaining it go hand in hand with a more autonomous role for the aged. The dispute over medicare means either that we are unwilling to admit this relationship or that we have no real consensus on the desirability of more autonomy for older people, particularly if it threatens other values.

Lack of a Meaningful Role

Today we are an urban, industrial, rapidly changing society. The bulk of the labor force are working for a wage or salary, rather than being self-employed on the land or in their profession. As this trend was developing, workers lost the right to a job that once they had and were simply "laid off"

---

[12] *Ibid.,* p. 172.
[13] See p. 243.
[14] Tibbitts, *op. cit.,* p. 528.

as they grew older. Recently, as we have seen, federal laws and strong labor unions have made it possible for people to have a minimum of economic security in their old age. But the right to a social security check and a company pension have been bought at a dear price. The worker must give up his economic role and go into retirement.

The complaint of older people that they feel "useless" or that they have "nothing to do" cannot be dismissed as mass indulgence in self-pity. They are expressing a fundamental problem of our society, that is, the need to develop a personally satisfying and socially useful role for older people, particularly those who are retired. Whatever else their problems may be, the older people in general are searching for a meaningful role in society that will provide them with a sense of purpose in life. There is a certain intrinsic purpose to life when one's daily efforts are expended to provide a living for himself and his family. Life has an inherent meaning and significance, even if one is not completely satisfied with the nature of his work or the standard of living it allows.

The basic challenge in modern society, it seems, is to develop a role for the older person that will provide him the same degree of satisfaction, self-respect, and sense of participation in life that usually he experienced during his working life. Almost by definition, such a role must be a socially useful one, although this does not mean that the older person must "work" in the usual sense or that he must be paid for what he does. The search for a socially useful, personally rewarding role for the older person has begun, but at the present time our efforts in this direction have not been too successful.

In recent years there has been effort on the part of society to provide for the recreational and social needs of older people. Some have labeled the programs "superficial" and the activities "busy work" but, at any rate, there has been a real growth of organizations for and by the aged. In a few localities, civic and other organizations have provided club rooms or game centers where the older person can spend his time at shuffleboard or cards, or, as one such "club" boasts, where checkers, "both regular and Chinese," are available. It is undoubtedly true that some of the aged are able to spend their days more pleasantly and with less concern over "what to do" as a result of the existence of such centers. But life for the aged is still far from being purposeful and useful, and some oldsters complain that it more resembles "playing at living" than living itself. Others, perhaps the more cynical, charge that our society has not really prolonged life—it has simply postponed death.

A large part of the difficulty in finding a meaningful role for the aged in recreational pursuits is that traditionally the recreational role of the adult has been subordinate to his other roles. As a matter of fact, some have stressed the point that leisure pursuits should be considered valuable only for "re-creating" one's energies for his important life's work. It is true that play and fun and leisure are increasingly being accepted in our society as desirable ends in themselves. The older people of the present, of course, lived most of their lives before the advent of this "fun morality." It remains to be seen whether the present generation of young workers, when they are older, can find in full-time leisure pursuits satisfaction sufficiently close to what they experience in their work-plus-leisure pursuits today. At any rate, for the present and immediate future it would seem that we must go beyond a recreational role in our quest for a meaningful life for older people.

It is undoubtedly true that the family life of older people has the potential for allowing them to maintain their sense of worth, importance, and dignity. An older married person does not think his or her spouse replaceable even if society does. The "need to be needed" can find fulfillment to a certain degree. Life under such circumstances cannot be completely devoid of meaning, assuming, of course, that the marriage is a reasonably happy one. All too frequently, however, some admittedly cruel facts of life interfere with the potentially satisfying family life of the older couple. Their income may allow few comforts and maybe not even basic necessities. Perhaps the limited budget cannot be stretched to cover annoying chronic ailments. In such cases home and family can scarcely be expected to render the psychological comfort of which they are capable.

Then too, of course, many older people experience a significant period of widowhood. Home life for them tends to be an unsatisfactory one. It is a life alone with too little income. Or it is with children in a tense relationship. Or it is in a poor and cheerless old people's home with other unwanted aged. Disguised as they may be with the word "home" in their name, it is difficult to imagine that many regard such places as an adequate substitute for the more usual variety of home. The public-supported institution usually can furnish only a minimum of care and comfort, and some such "homes" lack basic necessities and have even been called veritable "firetraps." Private institutions usually offer better physical facilities and equipment, but many old people and their families cannot afford the costs of a private institution, even if some kind of nursing care seems necessary. Basically, institutional provisions for any group in the population tend to be inadequate substitutes for full and useful social functioning.

The lack of a useful role for our aged, whether in economic spheres, in community life, or in the home, is a very real phenomenon to many of the aged. It is not something, furthermore, that can be remedied by any simple measures, for it is intricately tied up with the other problems of older people. Perhaps the relationship among the various problems of the aged will become more evident as we turn to a discussion of suggestions for the amelioration of these problems.

AMELIORATIVE PROGRAMS

As suggested earlier, the problems of the aged have only appeared in the past decade or so because of the recent increase in the number of old people, and because value conflicts have tended to develop only as our society has become more and more urbanized. This has had the practical result that there are few specific remedies that can be judged, so that we are necessarily restricted to broad "plans of attack."

Research

A prerequisite to realistic planning is more extensive research into the sociological, psychological, and physical factors of old age. The research that has been done over the years has forced us to question some of our earlier notions regarding the aged and has indicated the nature and extent of their problems. Now there is need for research directed toward the amelioration of the problems that have been discovered. It has become apparent, for example, that there is lack of a purposeful social role for many of our aged. But what kind of a role can we substitute and how will this new role affect our general economic and social life? We have learned much about the physical processes involved in aging, but there is still much more to learn. What, for instance, are the *meaningful* criteria of physical aging and how can these accurately be measured? When, according to these criteria, does an individual become "too old" for gainful employment, or for *what kind of* gainful employment?

In order to obtain the answers to these and a host of other questions, there has to be a certain relocation of our values. Problems of old age will have to receive a more prominent place in the hierarchy of problems our society wishes to attempt to solve. Geriatrics will have to become as important a field of medical endeavor as pediatrics. Housing programs for the aged may compete with plans for superhighways, parks, or even schools. The value conflicts involved in devoting increasingly more attention to problems of the aged are not to be minimized.

Immediate Programs

Although the need for large-scale planning and research is urgent, there are some things that can be done today to lessen the problems of the present population of older people. Some of these are "stop-gap" measures designed to treat the symptoms of the difficulties rather than remove the difficulties. But to the 18 million old people now living they would represent a real improvement over present conditions. First of all, we could provide better for the financial needs of those older people in need of such assistance. The machinery for doing this is already in existence in the form of the federal OASDI and the federal-state OAA programs. Most states need to convert their county almshouses into nursing homes, which will take paying old people as well as the indigent. A few states have begun to address themselves to the psychological and social problems of the inhabitants of old people's homes as well as to the improvement of their physical well-being. But much more needs to be done, including the provision of occupational therapists, recreation specialists, and social workers for such homes.

Industry and other employers of large numbers of people can, with little expense, help prepare workers for retirement. Several large concerns already provide counseling and guidance programs that begin five years before retirement, but such programs are not as yet widespread. Finally, communities can provide recreational facilities geared to the capabilities and desires of older people and can add to their social welfare staffs counselors and social workers who are specifically trained to deal with the problems of the aged. Although all of these suggestions require the expenditure of some money, they would not be costly. To put them into effect, however, it is necessary that society recognize the existence of problems and become willing to do something about them.

Attitudinal Changes

The chances of securing many of the specific recommendations for temporary relief of problems of the aged, as well as the direction of research resources and long-range planning to problems of this age group, rest in a large part on the ability of society to develop new attitudes toward old age and its problems. Employers may have to change their minds regarding the employment of older workers, and retirement programs may have to be revamped. Older people themselves are faced with necessary changes in attitudes regarding what constitutes a useful role, and individually they need to prepare for shifts in roles. The rest of society must somehow accept or adjust to these role changes, whatever they may come to be. Such changes in attitudes will not be easy for a society that has defined usefulness as productivity, and in which youth is beauty, the new is perforce better than the old, and economic idleness is somehow indecent if not downright wrong. But various attitudinal changes that cut across our whole scheme of values, nevertheless, are necessary before large-scale ameliorative programs can be instituted. This is a problem that even the most selfish young adults should consider worth solving, for while they may fancy themselves as not intimately involved in some social problems, most of them will one day be old people.

SUGGESTED READINGS

BARRON, MILTON L., *The Aging American: An Introduction to Social Gerontology and Geriatrics*. New York, Thomas Y. Crowell Co., 1961.

BURGESS, ERNEST W., ed., *Aging in Western Societies*. Chicago, The University of Chicago Press, 1960.

CUMMING, ELAINE, and WILLIAM HENRY, *Growing Old: The Process of Disengagement*. New York, Basic Books, Inc., 1961.

KLEEMEIER, ROBERT W., ed., *Aging and Leisure*. New York, Oxford University Press, 1961.

REICHARD, SUZANNE, et al., *Aging and Personality*. New York, John Wiley & Sons, Inc., 1962.

TIBBITTS, CLARK, ed., *Handbook of Social Gerontology*. Chicago, University of Chicago Press, 1960.

TIBBITTS, CLARK, and WILMA DONAHUE, eds., *Social and Psychological Aspects of Aging*. New York, Columbia University Press, 1962.

VEDDER, CLYDE B., ed., *Gerontology: A Book of Readings*. Springfield, Ill., Charles C Thomas, 1963.

U.S. DEPARTMENT OF HEALTH, EDUCATION, AND WELFARE, *The Nation and Its Older People: Report of the White House Conference on Aging*. Washington, D.C., Government Printing Office, 1961.

CRIME AND THE CRIMINAL *16*

No one needs to be told that crime is a social problem, but several sophistications regarding various aspects of the matter should be spelled out. The common sense conception that crime is simply a violation of law, that the problem is solved when violators are punished, that "causes" of crime are known, and so on, may lead to an exceedingly naïve, unrealistic, and possibly dangerous disposition of a much more involved question.

Several problematic questions rest at the base of the larger question, notably the following:

(1) What acts should and what acts should not be prohibited by law? And why?
(2) How "serious," *really,* are certain traditionally "undesirable" acts, assuming even that there is agreement about the undesirability?
(3) How should the violator of law (criminal) be handled? For what purpose does the state take jurisdiction over him?

We turn now to a fuller treatment of these three encompassing value clashes.

"CRIME IS DEFINED BY THE LAW"

There are agreements as well as disagreements in American society, as elsewhere, concerning what acts are inimical to the public interest and ought, therefore, to be forbidden by law. It is important to distinguish carefully, first, between acts that are regarded as *undesirable* by overwhelming consensus and those which are actually *violations of law*. Common language is confusing at this point. A frugal housewife standing in the checkout line at the supermarket gasps at the luxury items in the basket ahead and righteously asserts, "It's a crime the way some people spend their money." Assuming that the shopper in question has spent his money unwisely and that there could be agreement to such an effect does not, of course, make his actions criminal. There is no law that stipulates what food a person may buy, and it is highly doubtful that any agreement could be reached that such a law would be desirable. Somewhat more specifically, the consumption of tobacco and liquor, particularly by persons of moderate means, raises this concept sharply. Possibly the majority opinion is that too much of the consumers' money goes into such purchases, but few would seriously suggest that there ought to be a law forbidding the moderate income person from spending money on liquor and tobacco. Thus, there is no necessary equation of undesirability and criminality, even though sometimes we indiscriminately use the word, "crime."

Similarly, the religious concept *sin,* is confused with law. Almost all Christian religions hold to this concept one way or another, and taboo certain acts and activities—and even thoughts—that are regarded as infractions of Divine decree. Some of these sins are, of course, also punished in law, like murder, theft, perjury, and the like. But there are many acts clearly regarded as sinful concerning which no laws are now in operation, or are seriously being contemplated. This is one of the disputed areas of public opinion, however, when one gets down to more specific cases. Some people believe, for example, that birth control is a divinely censured practice and that religious teachings against it should be reinforced by law. At least one state of the Union actually has and enforces such laws. Similarly, some religious groups have attempted to secure and enforce rather strict laws concerning the free expression of artistic talent, especially in theatres and movies, and to a lesser extent in books and magazines. The various states and local communities in the United States present a kaleidoscopic picture on this question, varying all the way from almost complete freedom on the one hand to very restrictive and oppressive policies on the other. Not all persons who favor such laws do so, of course, for religious reasons; some reason that the "bad example" set for children and less responsible adults is in itself a sufficient secular rationale for a censorship program.

With the foregoing in mind it may be helpful to differentiate at least three categories of acts concerning which there are laws and legal regulations, and highly varied judgments from person to person and group to group in our society.

1. First, society, through its legislative power, has reached almost unanimous judgment that certain acts are undesirable and has indicated that persons who commit them should be punished. In this category are the prohibition of murder, kidnaping, and the like. Society also requires obe-

dience to compulsory school attendance, compulsory military service for men, compulsory taxation, and many others. To be sure, in a few extreme special circumstances an occasional apparent exception is granted, but these are rare and for all practical purposes, one might designate this first category of taboos and requirements as almost *universally agreed upon,* codified into law, and usually enforced by the police power.

2. There is another large and important category of acts concerning which there is substantial agreement as to what people ought and ought not to do, but there is disagreement concerning *whether the law is or is not an appropriate way* to secure conformity to the public expectations. Many of these acts fall into the general area of what is loosely called morality. There is substantial agreement, for example, that the excessive consumption of alcoholic beverages is undesirable for a host of practical and humane reasons. But there is by no means any general agreement that conformity should be enforced by legal prohibition except in a few peripheral matters such as not allowing intoxicated persons to drive automobiles, forbidding the sale of alcohol to minors, or to anyone else on religious holidays. There is, however, a vociferous minority persistently working for very restrictive legislative action on this and related matters. Censorship, already discussed above, is a further illustration of this category. Opinions differ sharply concerning whether no restriction, limited restriction, or stricter regulations should be imposed, by whom enforced, and so on.

By no means all matters of morality are, however, so personal. Some are vested with the public interest and constitute a conception of morality accepted only by some people.

(a) Should we permit unlimited contributions to campaign funds by individuals or corporations, when it is possible, if not likely, that the officials receiving them will be in an important position to influence legislation in which the contributor has an important stake?

(b) Should persons responsible for assigning government contracts to competing corporations own stock in the companies to which the government business can be "thrown"?

(c) Should elected officials be permitted to place on the public payroll, members of their family, close business associates, and others who have prior and other relationships to the official?

(d) Should a union leader be permitted to invest the union's funds in business enterprises where he would stand to gain by such investment?

The list could be extended indefinitely, but the above examples represent recurring and troublesome problems. Again, opinions regarding such matters are very divided, laws vague, inconsistent, and irregularly enforced.

3. A third category involves acts that some people regard as socially undesirable, whether so defined by law or not, but that others consider

wholly within the individual's personal discretion. Examples of this category would be such "issues" as the use of birth control, the consumption of alcohol and tobacco, censorship, and the segregation of ethnic and racial groups. In a democratic society considerable effort is expended by groups and persons who often believe that they uphold noble causes in the attempt to convince, if not coerce, legislatures to pass laws designating that the acts that they disapprove should be forbidden to everyone. Sometimes such pressure groups speak for very small minorities and at other times for substantial ones. Occasionally they succeed in passing more restrictive laws than the majority of the population is later willing to conform to, and in such cases violations are rampant, enforcement is difficult, and in the end there is a great deal of confusion. Sometimes the laws are later repealed.

From the foregoing it should be apparent that the words "crime" and "criminal" stand for a multiplicity of individual and public interpretations. Crime is assuredly not equivalent to wrongdoing, nor does it refer to universally forbidden acts, nor does it represent necessarily unanimous, or for that matter even majority, judgment. The whole question of what is and what is not criminal, particularly in a democratic society, involves a maelstrom of differing opinions, differing religious and ethical traditions, and reflects changing conditions and circumstances. To say unqualifiedly that crime is simply a violation of law is to take comfort in a kind of simple-mindedness which in its naïvete covers up a tremendous variety and confusion in a continuing process of change and redefinition of human action.

"Seriousness"

Opinions on the seriousness of legal violations are as varied as are the judgments as to what actions are to be taboo. The question of "white-collar crime," to be discussed at length later in this chapter, raises some confusing issues. For the moment we shall define white-collar crime simply as violations of law that are committed in the ordinary course of practicing one's occupation and which usually involve violations of trust. The white-collar criminal, such as the embezzler, the giver or receiver of a bribe disguised as a business gift, the blackmailer who is paid in the form of business or professional favors, has as a rule not received the same kind of public attention and contempt as has the person who commits the more direct attack against individual property, such as the auto thief or the shoplifter. Yet the amounts of money and property involved have been staggering as compared to the kinds of "crimes against property" to which attention is ordinarily given.

Perhaps the more extreme instance of differential evaluation of human action concerns "the rackets," illegal practices carried out in the guise of legitimate business activities but closely tied up with illegal enterprises such as gambling, prostitution, and the drug traffic. Some in our society regard the rackets as simply a special kind of vaguely legitimate business; at the other extreme others view the rackets as unequivocally criminal and would like to see effective laws passed and strictly enforced in order to stamp them out. Other persons fall in between these two extremes—they disapprove some aspects of the rackets, wink at others, and may from time to time even benefit directly or indirectly from some aspects of them.

"Treatment"

Even where there is working agreement that certain acts are to be forbidden and an acknowledgment that violations are serious, there is a wide difference of opinion as to how the wrongdoer (criminal) should be handled. This is an enormously complicated question, involving at the outset such basic issues as what kind of and how much evidence is required before arrest can be made, before arraignment can be sustained, and finally before guilt can be determined. It is well known that even after guilt is determined, wide differences of opinion exist both among experts and among laymen concerning what ought to be done with, to, and for the criminal. This raises such familiar questions as to whether capital punishment is a justifiable disposition, for what reasons it is justifiable, and whether or not it is effective in achieving the stated objectives. To some people "treatment" simply means rehabilitation of the wrongdoer, by whatever means prove effective. Others complain that wrongdoers are not punished enough, are "coddled too much," and still others appear more concerned with making the criminal "pay" for his crimes than with making him, if possible, into the kind of person less likely to commit criminal acts again.

Thus, the larger questions about crime, its conception, its treatment, comprise an enormously complex matrix, complex because we have pluralistic ideas with respect to what is and what is not crime, highly varied judgments as to how serious various crimes should be regarded, and a plethora of theories, philosophies, and programs for the treatment of the criminal. The remainder of this chapter will be concerned with some of the important facts, judgments, and practices subsumed under the title of "Crime and the Criminal."

CHANGING CONCEPTIONS OF CRIME AND THE CRIMINAL

When we define crime as "a breach of the legal norm" and the criminal as "the individual who has committed such acts of breach," we have set up no categories of "universal" or "natural" or "unchanging" crimes. Just as there is wide variance in other social values, there is likewise much difference from time to time and place to place as to what constitutes criminality. The criminal code of our society not only differs in some respects from that of any other society, but is in a constant process of redefinition to meet our own changing social conditions and values.

The laws at any particular point in American history include two sources of norms of right and wrong conduct: the "age-old" mores and the more recent rationally formulated ideas. Thus, a "modern" criminal may have violated one or more of the legal norms long established in our social heritage, such as those pertaining to murder, rape, or theft (but it is to be noted that the legal definition of even these crimes varies from state to state and from time to time within the same state), or he may have committed a breach of recently defined legal norms relating to the manufacture, sale, or use of foods and drugs, to gambling, or to traffic regulations.

Crime as a Career

A considerable, but not precisely known, amount of crime in American society is committed by careerists. The term "recidivist" is used to refer to those criminals found guilty of second, third, fourth, or more offenses, and criminals are sometimes classified on a scale ranging from "one-time offenders" through "occasional offenders" through "habitual criminals" and "racketeers" to "professional criminals." Such categories obviously are not clear-cut and are subject to many errors arising from inefficiencies of arrest, conviction, incarceration, and reporting by police, courts, and prisons. A person classified as a one-time offender may, for example, be a professional criminal fortunate and clever enough to have been caught, convicted, and imprisoned only once!

Sufficient study has been made, however, of recidivists in crime so that the modern criminologist now knows some of the characteristics of a criminal career. The process whereby a person becomes a careerist in crime apparently does not differ fundamentally from the process whereby a person becomes a careerist in law, plumbing, medicine, business, carpentry, or baseball. The novitiate to crime passes through an apprenticeship in which he learns, through association with "experts," the skills, attitudes, terminology, and philosophy of the racketeer or of the professional criminal.[1] As with other types of careers, the individual becomes a professional criminal or a racketeer through association, training, and experience. Further-

---

[1] The stereotyped distinction between the "racketeer" and the "professional criminal" seems to have considerable validity. The former typically is a member of an organization operating in such activities as bootlegging, gambling, sponsoring of prostitution, and various "shakedown" activities; the latter, by contrast, tends to be a "smooth," quiet operator of confidence games, counterfeiting, forgery, and the like. The socialization of these two types of criminals differs in content and in personalities "selected," but seems to be similar in process.

more, in-group associations of criminals appear comparable to the unions and professional societies of other occupational groups. The noviate must be "taken under the wing" of one of the criminal groups and pass through a probationary period of "learning the ropes" before he can achieve the status of a professional.

"SCHOOLS FOR CRIME." The major recruiting stations for careerists in crime appear to be the reform schools, jails, prisons, and reformatories. There the first-time or occasional offender may make the "proper contacts" with professional criminals and racketeers for developing a criminal career. He not only establishes friendships with and learns skills and attitudes from professional criminals who are his fellow inmates, but he receives informal credentials to the "right people" in the criminal world outside the institution. For a criminal a short "stay in the stir" is almost a prerequisite to getting ahead in his chosen profession. Through the gradual acquisition of skills, attitudes, and contacts, the perpetrator of petty, unskilled offenses moves upward in the criminal profession to the status of one sufficiently skilled and sophisticated to commit a major, complicated crime.

CHOICE OF CAREER. What causes some persons to choose a criminal career? Despite many claims made as to positive knowledge of causes by various individuals and agencies in our society, specific answers to this question have not been validated. Increasing consensus among criminologists, however, is to the effect that the *causes of persons choosing criminal careers are as varied and as difficult to determine and classify as the causes of some persons becoming politicians, others dentists, and still others high school teachers.*

Relation of Crime to Changing Social Norms

As we have seen, crime is most clearly defined as an intentional act in violation of the criminal code. The provisions of the criminal code depend, obviously, upon what values the *controlling element* of a society decide should not, without punishment, be violated. Such values change in time and place and this change is reflected both in what is considered a crime and society's reaction to transgressors.

SOCIAL VALUES AND DEFINITION OF CRIME. A well-known criminologist reports that some years ago it was discovered that about three fourths of all inmates of state and federal prisons were there for committing acts that had not been crimes fifteen years earlier.[2] The many relatively new laws concerning business and occupational practices, employment of children, and conservation of natural resources, provide further evidence of the changes that have taken place with regard to what is and what is not

[2] Harry Elmer Barnes and Negley K. Teeters, *New Horizons in Criminology* (2d ed., New York: Prentice-Hall, 1951), p. 77.

allowable under the law. It has been estimated that since 1900 over 500,000 new state laws have been enacted.

The changing definitions of crime also operate to remove some acts from the category of criminal behavior. Prior to the repeal of the Prohibition Amendment, any person selling liquor anywhere in the United States under any circumstances and for any other than medicinal purposes, was upon arrest, conviction, and imposition of a penalty, a criminal. Today this is still true in a few states and in some counties of some other states, but in most places in the country is no longer true. Other laws in regard to the sale of liquor render other acts crimes, however. In Ohio, for example, to sell on Sunday any alcoholic beverage other than a certain percentage beer is a criminal offense. If this law is repealed, it will no longer be categorically criminal to sell stronger alcoholic beverages on Sunday.

SOCIAL VALUES AND REPORTING OF CRIMES. Social values affect the crime in a community in many other ways than through definition of an offense in the criminal code. Since the criminal in modern society, for all practical purposes, is the individual who is reported to the police, arrested, tried, found guilty, and sentenced, many *social values can intervene at any point in this sequence to render an act officially criminal or noncriminal.* In the matter or reporting the crime to the police, for example, there may be many blocks; *until the crime is so reported, it does not officially exist.* In America such crimes as homicide, theft, and rape are rather consistently reported, but other crimes such as blackmail, embezzlement, fraud, and abortion are not consistently reported. Social values of persons against whom the offense is committed, of friends and relatives of the offender, and of observers of the offense obviously will differentially affect the reporting of crime. If my house is burglarized, I am very likely to report it to the police; if I am being blackmailed, I am much less likely to do so. If my neighbor is a thief, I shall hasten to report the fact; if my neighbor confides that he has been "cheating" on his income tax, I may feel that it is "his business."

Social values not only affect the reporting of crimes differentially, but such values change as to what should be and should not be reported. Abortion, for example, is designated as criminal by our legal norms in essentially the same way that it was several generations ago, but judging from such evidence as is available concerning its increase, it is considered more lightly by a growing number of members of our society. Kinsey has pointed out that many, many American males and females, according to laws now on the books, could be placed in prison for various sex offenses. Many of these offenses are probably known to others who could report them to the police if they felt they "should" do so.

SOCIAL VALUES AND ARRESTS. Social values also affect arrests. Not all crimes reported to the police end in arrest of the offender even when he is apprehended. Aside from corruption of police by bribes (which is an appreciable factor in stopping the official process of justice at least at some times and in some communities), there are many reasons why the police may feel that arrest of the offender is not advisable and, hence, no crime gets on the books. As practically everyone realizes, prostitution is widely practiced in all large American communities and in most smaller ones. When a reform drive is in progress, many arrests of prostitutes are made; when "the heat is off," the prostitutes, not unknown always, at least, to the police, return to the community and resume their activities. The attitude of many Americans on the subject of prostitution seems to be that it is criminal and, when forced upon their attention, should be prosecuted, but that unofficially it is not undesirable and may be tolerated.

OTHER INFLUENCES OF SOCIAL VALUES ON CRIME. Trial, finding of guilt, and sentence or suspension of sentence are likewise influenced by social values and changing public sentiments. Public opinion, with no apparent rationality, varies from indignation to apathy in regard to various types of offenses officially defined as crimes, and the crime rate varies with it. Frequently a crime wave is undoubtedly nothing more than a change in social values, usually quite temporary, which influences reporting to police, arrests, trials, convictions, and sentences in such a way as to increase the number of "crimes."

Fallacy of Statistical Analysis of Crime

The student has probably realized from the foregoing section that statistics based on crimes reported to the police, arrests, indictments, and convictions are so influenced by social values currently existent that they do not afford highly reliable bases for comparing crime rates. Suppose, for example, that we wish to know whether a certain crime—say counterfeiting—has increased during the past decade in a specified community and how the rate in that community compares with the rate in another community. We immediately encounter numerous problems, of which the following would be typical. Is the enforcement of the law against counterfeiting more or less effective today than ten years ago? In Community A as compared with Community B? What are and were the strength of community sentiments against counterfeiting (and, hence, consistency of reporting to police) today and ten years ago in the two communities? If differences are thought to exist, how much allowance can we make for them in adjusting our statistics and how can we scientifically justify the degree of adjustment? What are current sentiments and policies in regard to arrest, trial, sentence, and imprisonment of known counterfeiters as compared with ten years ago, in Community A as compared with Community B? How do the activities of the federal government against counterfeiting compare in the two time periods and in the two communities? How do we interpret our statistics on these matters and how do we justify our interpretations?

SOCIAL CLASS AND CRIMINAL STATISTICS. Another differential affecting statistics of crime not yet touched upon is that of social class. The boy from a lower-class family who steals an automobile will almost invariably be reported to the police, arrested, tried, convicted, and sentenced. The boy from a family of means *may* go through the same procedure, but he is less likely to do so. The report of his "crime" is apt to get no further than his father, who is trusted by the person whose car has been stolen to deal properly with the matter. If the theft is reported to the police, they may deem it wise, because of the respectable reputation of the family, not to "book" the boy, but merely to warn him and his father. If the arrest takes place, the judge may dismiss charges upon assurances from the boy and his father that "it will never happen again." If the boy of means is tried and found guilty, sentence may be suspended. And so on with other differentials based on class privilege, including various legal loopholes available to the better-class boy through the employment of high paid and competent legal talent. Hence, crime statistics in the *same city* at the *same point in time* are not necessarily reliable indices of offenses committed.

LIMITED USE FOR CRIMINAL STATISTICS. Crime statistics are not totally useless in this connection. If used cautiously within narrow limits for a few crimes known to have wide public cooperation in reporting (of a very public nature and considered highly injurious to the public welfare, such as murder, rape, or robbery), statistics may give rough indices of volume of crime. But so far as being reliable and valid indications of general crime as a social problem, particularly in time and place, crime statistics are very nearly worthless.

Fallacy of Causation

Proposed "causes" of crime are probably more numerous than the suggested "causes" of any other societal phenomenon. Theories of causation have been so numerous that a mere listing of them would cover many pages; they fall into several main categories: geographical, hereditary, constitutional, psychological, and social.

WHAT IS A CAUSE? Rather than go into a detailed examination of the proposed causes of crime, it is advisable, first of all, for us to understand what we mean by a cause. Its popular usage is quite loose and unscientific. You may say that sitting in the draft or getting your feet wet or staying up too late was the "cause" of your catching cold. While such things may or may not be predisposing factors—that is, increase your likelihood of catching cold providing the causal agent is present—none of them "causes" the common cold. A cause of anything, in the scientific usage of the term, is the "sufficient and essential forerunner" of the specified result. Not only, to return to our example, do people sit in drafts, get wet feet, and sit up too late without necessarily catching cold, but people sometimes catch cold without undergoing any of these conditions. None of these things, therefore, can be considered the "cause" of your catching cold.

DIFFICULTIES OF ISOLATING CAUSES OF CRIME. When we turn to the proposed causes of crime, we find ourselves in a position very comparable to our foregoing example. Feeblemindedness, endocrine disturbances, psychopathic personality, insanity, social disorganization, slums, bad companions, broken homes, movies, alcoholism, economic depressions, and the like, have been suggested, both casually and by the process of laborious research, to be the "causes" of crime. And yet we not only find persons exposed to or falling into any one or any combination of these categories who do not become criminals, but we find criminals who fail to meet these causal requirements. There are, for example, criminals who come from broken homes, but noncriminals also come from broken homes, and all criminals do *not* come from broken homes. Broken homes, therefore, are not the "cause" of crime, for they are not the sufficient and essential forerunner of criminality. The same goes for any other suggested cause or combination of causal factors.

Since social conditions will probably never be sufficiently controllable to isolate causal factors in such complex behavior as criminality, the search for causes in crime will undoubtedly remain a fruitless one. As we shall observe later in this chapter, professional criminologists are increasingly turning their attention to more productive research. It is sufficient to observe here that knowledge of actual "causes" of crime is by no means necessary for progress to be made through empirical research regarding predictive, preventive, and control factors in crime. Scientifically based changes that effect crime reduction may be made in society without concern about whether or not ultimate causes of criminal conditions have been isolated.

POPULAR PROPOSALS FOR REDUCING CRIME

The search for causes of crime, however, appears as strict rationality and rigid science compared with proposals for "curing" the criminal and reducing or "wiping out" crime. It has become fashionable to claim that almost any public or private agency's request for funds will, if granted, bring about the reduction of crime and juvenile delinquency in the community and help "straighten out" young men and women who have already committed crimes. The recreational program of, for example, the YMCA or the local settlement house is not to be defended on its own merits alone; the subscriber is assured that his contribution will prevent crime and lead to the reform of criminals. Sex education is not to be thought of as desirable in itself; such education will prevent delinquency. With all respect for the sincerity of motives of such claimants, it is obvious that their hopes tend to influence their judgments, for they offer nothing approximating scientific evidence for their claims.

Stricter Penalties and Better Law Enforcement

More rigid enforcement of our criminal laws and more severe punishment of offenders are two of the most frequently recommended methods for reducing the amount of crime in our society. Better law enforcement in itself, it is interesting to note, would actually increase the crime rate, for as we have observed, the only totally practical definition of the criminal in our society is that of an offender who is arrested and proved guilty of the alleged offense. Hence, the more offenders caught, arrested, tried, and proved guilty, the higher the official crime rate. Obviously, then, the argument for more rigid law enforcement as a means of reducing crime depends upon what we do as a society with those who are officially proved to have committed crimes. Let us, therefore, examine the proposition of stricter penalties as a method of reducing crime.

STRICT PUNISHMENT AS A DETERRENT. The strictest penalty possible for a crime is, of course, death for the offender. Until about three centuries ago almost all crimes were punishable by hanging. Social justification for hanging was simply that the crime had injured society and that society not only deserved vengeance through the payment by the criminal with his life, but needed to show potential criminals that "they couldn't get away with that sort of thing." The evidence is fairly clear that the existence of the death penalty does not serve to deter people from committing crime. In eighteenth-century England, for example, public hangings of pickpockets had to be discontinued because too many people had their pockets picked while witnessing the hanging of pickpockets. A current study in the United States shows that the seven states without the death penalty all have "murder and nonnegligent manslaughter" rates lower than the national average. It has even been suggested that the death penalty actually may serve to increase the crimes for which it is stipulated. An early case in point is that of the English bankers in 1830 who petitioned for the abolishment of the death penalty for forgery since, because of the severity of the penalty, too few convictions could be secured.[3] More recently, a noted criminologist has pointed out that the Lindbergh Act, which makes kidnaping a capital offense when the victim is carried over a state line, may encourage a kidnaper to kill his victim rather than release him and risk the chance of exposure.[4] It is not to be construed from the foregoing illustrations that there is an in-

[3] *Ibid.*, p. 77.
[4] *Ibid.*, pp. 74–75.

verse relationship between crime and the severity of the punishment. Rather, they indicate that criminals are apparently not deterred by the realization that severe punishment awaits them if they are caught.

For most crimes in modern society the only forms of penalty that have public approval are imprisonment and fines or a combination of the two. Stricter penalties through a system of fines would have practicability for only a relatively small percentage of offenders, those in a financial position for paying heavy fines. Since a large percentage of at least the habitual offenders come from the lower economic classes in our society, stricter penalties through heavier fines would not seem to offer very fruitful crime-reducing possibilities. Even in those cases where the penalty for the crime is a fine, the alternative to payment (an alternative that many offenders are forced to take) is incarceration. In addition, there are many crimes for which the only penalty offered is imprisonment.

The argument for stricter penalties for crime seems to reduce itself, then, to longer prison sentences. The popular supposition that this would reduce crime finds no support among professional workers in the fields of criminology and penology. The "threat" of a long prison term does not seem to deter criminals, and a long sentence in a conventional prison does not seem to "reform" them. Even prison officials themselves, those whose livelihood depends upon the continuance of the prison system, have little to say in its support.

LIMITATIONS OF PUNISHMENT. After a thorough analysis of justifications for punishment and the data available in regard to the efficacy of current punitive usages, Reckless, one of the nation's outstanding criminologists and penologists, arrives at the following conclusions:

> It is already apparent that there are definite limitations to punishment, in spite of the generally accepted justifications for it. On the positive side, *i.e.,* from the standpoint of what it actually does to the offender, (1) it may make him cautious about concealing his activities; (2) it may stigmatize him and isolate him from the society to which he should be adjusted; (3) it may martyrize or heroize the culprit; (4) it may develop in him an anti-social grudge and a strong resentment of authority, not conducive to law-abiding existence. On the negative side, *i.e.,* from the standpoint of what it does not do, (5) it does not prevent crime in others or relapse into crime; (6) it does not repair damage to society; and (7) it does not reconstruct the personality of the offender.[5]

In speaking of the ineffectiveness of imprisonment as a method of reforming the criminal (and, hence, reducing crime), Sam A. Lewisohn, then president of the American Prison Association, stated:

[5] By permission from *Criminal Behavior,* p. 276, by Walter C. Reckless. Copyright 1940 by the McGraw-Hill Book Company, Inc., New York. It is noteworthy that Reckless' summary, made over twenty years ago, is equally true today, and yet so many retain a faith in the efficacy of punishment!

Too many of our citizens believe in the "cash register system of justice." When a man commits a crime, they feel a judge should press his finger on a key marked "burglary" or "robbery" or "larceny" or "felony," and presto! Out comes a piece of paper saying, "You owe society a debt of so many and so many years." And off the offender goes to prison to be punished.

But soon after that offender is given a number he hears the strange word "rehabilitation." He wonders—and so do I—if he can be punished and rehabilitated at the same time. And he is also confronted with a maze of inconsistencies.

Suppose he is rehabilitated long before the expiration of his term. He must still remain behind bars at a cost to the state of $500 a year. Suppose he does learn a trade. When he is released from prison, state laws prevent him from engaging in that trade. And too often he cannot even obtain a job because of his past indiscretions. Is it any wonder then, that so many offenders return to prison? [6]

With such evaluations of the effectiveness of our present punitive practices by experts it would hardly seem sound logic for us to subscribe to the hypothesis that more of the same, only worse, is a solution to the crime problem. There would seem to be no evidence that stricter penalties would reduce the amount of crime.

Education and Religion

Two of the most general of the popular proposals for reducing crime concern increasing the effectiveness of education and religion. So long as the proposals are kept at the general level of discussion, there is hardly room for dispute, but, likewise, there is nothing to be done to implement them. That is to say, one can scarcely deny that in some way through the institutions of education and religion noncriminal rather than criminal behavior patterns should be inculcated in the members of our society. It is when we come to examine the specific methods of changing the programs of the church and the school in order to prevent the development of criminal behavior patterns that we encounter difficulty. To say that the home and the church should prevent crime is one thing; to know how this is to be accomplished is quite a different matter.

ROLE OF THE CHURCH IN REDUCING CRIME. The role of the church in crime reduction is usually conceived in terms of increasing the church's effectiveness as an agent in equipping the individual with a system of morals that will lead him to resist and reject criminal behavior patterns. That is precisely what the church has been attempting to accomplish for centuries,

[6] Sam A. Lewisohn, "Presidential Address" given at the 76th Annual Congress of Correction, sponsored by the American Prison Association, Detroit, Mich., October 4, 1946. Sensitive and informed people *today* still must report the same deplorable failure.

and, although scientific proof is not available, to some extent probably has accomplished. Yet the church today fails to reach roughly half of the non-criminal population and seems at a loss as to methods of increasing its appeal. That criminals and potential criminals can be readily convinced of the desirability of their becoming active church participants (and, hence, be subject to whatever reformation program the church undertakes in their behalf) seems highly doubtful. Put differently, the church probably does not, for the most part, effectively reach the criminal and potentially criminal elements in our population and does not, to date, give indications of knowing how to reach them. Even granting that contemporary religious programs would divert persons from criminal patterns (which, in itself, is not an established fact), we seem at present ignorant as to means to induce criminals and potential criminals to participate in these programs.

PUBLIC SCHOOL VERSUS CRIME. With compulsory school attendance, the problem for education differs from that for religion. The school reaches, for a time at least, those who adopt criminal as well as noncriminal careers. But apparently many school programs are ineffective both for discovering the predelinquent and dealing with the already delinquent child.

Many school authorities recognize the school's ineffectiveness in dealing with predelinquency and delinquency and various remedial programs have been suggested. Most of the proposals involve some form of provision of clinical and social services. Child guidance clinics, mental hygiene clinics, and child welfare agencies have been suggested as additional services needed to make it possible to recognize, understand, and treat various categories of children requiring special help. Although such services would seem educationally desirable and very worthy of trial, there is still too little scientific evidence for substantiating the claims that crime and delinquency would thereby be reduced.

Even if we were to accept on faith the efficacy of recommended clinical and social services in the school, the economic wherewithal for the implementation of such programs on a wide scale would not seem to be readily forthcoming. As this is being written, communities throughout the nation are having difficulty meeting the economic needs of regular personnel without undertaking to provide what (to be effective, at least) would have to be a costly clinical and social program. Added to this is the current scarcity of personnel qualified to operate such a program. For the time being, therefore, these proposals would seem to lack widespread practicality.

Platitudes on Crime Reduction

Description of popular programs for reducing crime would not be complete without mentioning some of the many platitudes uttered on the subject.

BLAME ON THE HOME. One of the most frequently heard of the weak, empty remarks is that "the home is at fault." How this is believed to have meaning as a solution is difficult to understand, and yet many persons who believe that they are speaking quite seriously on the subject of crime utter similar sayings. That most of the basic aspects of personality are formed in the home environment few psychologists would deny, but application of such a general truth to the likely inception of criminal behavior patterns provides us with no specific program for the reduction of crime. Just what about some homes predispose some of the children in those homes to adopt criminal ways? And then knowing that, what specific programs of home change would be feasible? Facts resulting from specific research, rather than the pointing of a platitudinous finger at the home, may bring us a starting point in crime prevention at one of its likely general sources.

MENTAL ILLNESS. Another frequently encountered platitude in crime prevention is one to the effect that criminals "ain't right." Mental illness as a "cause" of criminality would seem to be implied in this statement. While the earlier criminological literature often gave a good deal of weight to mental disorders of various types, recent studies fail to back up these claims. Since a very small proportion of criminals have been adjudged feebleminded or insane, and since a very small proportion of the feebleminded and insane manifest criminal tendencies, neither mental condition may be considered a significant source of crime, much less a helpful lead to crime solution.

THE INDIVIDUAL HIMSELF. Another empty saying that is found among proposed solutions to crime as a social problem is that "it depends on the individual." As it stands, of course, the statement has no meaning. The vague notion, however, that often seems to underlie the platitude is a partially digested conception of modern education's emphasis on individual differences. Another implication sometimes apparently included is that the individual who has fallen into criminal patterns must by his own efforts extricate himself; little or nothing is said about how the criminally inclined individual is to be instilled with the motivation to effect his behavioral changes. Neither the implication that individuals differ nor that reform must come from within the individual helps us to formulate a program of crime prevention or control.

"BORN CRIMINALS." One of the most futile of the platitudes is that "criminals are born that way." Even if we were to assume hereditary sources of criminal behavior (and none of the many contentions made in this regard has been validated), no eugenical program for reducing the number of criminals in our population is considered practicable.

Our analysis of platitudes could go on for many more pages. It is hoped that the examples have been sufficient to caution the student to avoid the all too frequent tendency to seize a catchphrase, without analysis, and to present it as a solution to a complicated social problem.

PROFESSIONAL CONCLUSIONS ON SOURCES OF CRIMINALITY

As has been previously indicated, the "causes" of crime and the criminal are currently unknown and, to a considerable extent, probably unknowable. This does not mean, however, that criminologists have made no progress in the understanding and control of crime. In the remaining sections of this chapter we shall consider, first, professional conclusions regarding the sources of criminal behavior patterns and, secondly, professional recommendations for the reduction of crime as a social problem.

Differential Contagion and Risk Factors

Although studies of the sources of crime have produced no conclusive results concerning causation, they have pointed to various factors in both the individual and the environment that are correlated with the appearance of criminal patterns. These studies have further indicated that most criminal behavior is directly acquired from persons in the individual's association who already manifest the behavior. Such information has led to the use of such terms as "risk factors" and "differential contagion" to refer to the conditions conducive to the adoption of criminal behavior patterns. As the terms imply, the criminologist is placed in a position analogous to that of the physician dealing with a disease such as poliomyelitis (infantile paralysis). The causes of crime, like the causes of poliomyelitis, are not completely known, yet a number of helpful facts are known about both "diseases." Crime, like polio, is contagious, that is, caught from those who already carry the germs. In addition, contagion follows certain selective patterns, not all aspects of which are known, rather than indiscriminately affecting all persons exposed to the disease. Just as physicians have found that various factors such as age, time of year, lowering of resistance, and exposure in certain public places (such as swimming pools) increase the risk of the individual's contracting poliomyelitis, the criminologist has found such factors as age, sex, class, and exposure to certain residential areas increase the risk of the individual's "contracting" patterns of criminality.

PLACE OF RESIDENCE. It is generally true that the incidence of crime is higher in large cities than in small towns and rural areas. This is more true of the most prevalent crimes—theft, burglary, and auto theft—than it is of the less frequently occurring "crimes against the person." Large cities, of course, offer greater opportunities for gainful crime, for disposal of goods, and for secrecy. Certain types of criminals whose operations depend on large numbers of people, as the "bookie" and the "number writer," obviously work where large numbers of people are found. Furthermore, since more criminals are found in cities than rural areas, an urban child has more opportunities for first-hand experience with crime and criminals.

Many studies have been made to determine the relationship between crime and place of residence *within* the city. While some cities do not fall neatly into geographical patterns, it has been found, in general, that most forms of crime decrease progressively as we move from the center to the periphery of a city. Stated differently, these studies show that place of residence is one important risk factor in criminality, that criminal contagion is highest in the central core of the city and diminishes in amount in proportion to distance away from this center. Since these centers are characterized by much transiency and lack of community stability, they make possible easier rebellion against established law and order by the individual and also make more likely his "contagious contact" with criminals who thrive in the anonymity of these areas.

SOCIAL STATUS. Since there is a tendency for people living in the same section of the city to be of somewhat similar status, this factor is related to the foregoing one. Studies have repeatedly discovered, nevertheless, that the lower status person is more likely to "run afoul" of the law than the higher status person. As we have already indicated, this relationship is at least partially explained by differential crime reporting and differential treatment of persons suspected of committing crimes. From the point of view of "risks," however, it is nevertheless true that the odds favor the lower status person having his name recorded on a police blotter.[7]

(1) Persons in the young adult, just past adolescent ages are disproportionately the most criminal.

(2) Males are disproportionately more criminal than females. This is partly due to the fact that certain offenses are more characteristically male behavior: rape, assault, and certain traffic violations.

(3) Negroes and immigrants, probably because they occupy different class positions, commit more crimes for which they are apprehended than is the case for the rest of the population.[8]

A "Medieval Penology"

It has long been realized that one of the most important sources of crime is the very penology presumably designed to prevent and "cure" criminality. The very concept of penology is rooted in the idea of punishment for the criminal; the notion of reforming the criminal is a relatively recent one in our cultural history and has been superimposed upon the idea of

[7] Walter C. Reckless, *The Crime Problem* (3rd ed., New York: Appleton-Century-Crofts, 1961), pp. 34–37.

[8] For an extended up-to-date treatment, see Reckless, *op. cit.,* chap. 3.

punishment. Although reform of the criminal is the most frequently expressed purpose of our police, court, and prison practices, these practices have remained more nearly aligned with the punitive ideology of an earlier period than with modern theoretical pronouncements of intent to reform. There is increasing evidence that criminal punishment and criminal reform are irreconcilable social goals.

The "medieval penology" as it applies to our courts takes the form of punitive justice dispensed to individuals who fall into specified categories of violation of the criminal code. Legal justice is in harmony with the ideology of punishment: crime committed, price to society paid. It is not, however, in harmony with the ideology of reform, which must take into account the individualized background of the person leading up to the committing of the crime and the individualized needs present which must be met in order to help the person to divert his behavior into noncriminal channels.

In like manner, current practices of penal institutions are geared to the dispensing of justice in the form of punishment to the individual for having gone contrary to the criminal code, but are not designed to provide individualized treatment to the offender to help him achieve noncriminal methods of social functioning.

The revealed experiences of persons who have been subjected to the justice of our courts and the "reforming" of our reformatories add up to a weighty testimony that "justice" is much more likely to engender contempt for the law and desire for revenge than to stimulate motivation for reform and that penal institutions increase motivation, knowledge, and skill in criminal, rather than noncriminal, behavior patterns and render the inmate less acceptable for noncriminal roles upon his return to outer society.

It is not herein suggested that no sincere efforts have been made to improve court handling and penal treatment of criminals. Progress in the direction of individualized treatment has been made with the increasing use of probation and parole, the indeterminate sentence, lessening severity of punishment, development of dormitory-type, minimum-security institutions, attempted separation of first offenders from recidivists, and the like. But most of these attempts at individualized treatment of the offender have been piecemeal rather than thorough and consistent reformulations of court and penal practices. The basic tenets of punishment have remained, and relatively superficial tenets of reform have been added. Our courts still, for the most part, send violators of criminal codes to penal institutions to be punished, and, while there, many of these violators (both out of reaction to the court "justice" dispensed and the penal treatment received and out of contacts with more experienced criminals in the institutions) are processed into more thoroughgoing criminals than they were when they entered. It appears to some observers that the superimposed notions of reform have done little other than render the ideology of punishment less efficient. Be that as it may, it would seem undeniable that the persistence of a "medieval penology" must be reckoned with by modern society as one source of persisting criminality.

Inherent Problems of Institutionalization

Institutionalization of any type for the criminal constitutes a problem in his reform and must, in itself, continue to be a source of further criminality. To institutionalize a criminal is to remove him to a special social world where his chief contacts will be with other violators of the criminal code. It is to remove the criminal from the society to which you hope to stimulate his noncriminal adjustment, to accustom him to a process of special-world adjustments, and to return him, regardless of the special-world treatment, to an outer society in which he carries the label of "ex-convict." He is apt to find that this label lacks censure in only one section of outer society, namely, the criminal group. That there is relapse to criminality following the most "progressive" type of institutionalization should cause us small occasion for wonder.

While improved institutional practices are not only justifiable upon humane bases in themselves, but are likely to reduce the amount of crime breeding and crime entrenching within these institutions, any institutional program will probably continue to be a source of criminality.

PROFESSIONAL RECOMMENDATIONS FOR AMELIORATION OF THE CRIME PROBLEM

It is certainly apparent to the student by now that crime is a deeply entrenched social problem concerning which causes and full-blown solutions are unknown. To date our scientific knowledge of criminal behavior must be stated largely in negative terms, that is, that claims of such and such individuals and groups regarding causes and solutions to crime are unwarranted or unverified. The general summary of criminological investigation is that no panacea to eliminate crime either exists or is likely to be forthcoming. While in themselves programs of greater economic security, more and better education, better use of leisure time, better health, slum clearance, and the like, are certainly worthy social goals, their relation to crime prevention or reduction has not been demonstrated. Four specific proposals for crime reduction stemming from professional criminologists would seem to merit further consideration and experimentation.

Reducing Crime by Revising
the Criminal Code

One obvious way to reduce crime in a society is to reduce the number of offenses that are defined as criminal. This proposal is not so evasive and insipid as first thought might indicate. It would mean the discarding by society of many petty rules, the elimination of small penal sanctions, of which the greatest proportion of modern social offenses consist. It would permit society to concentrate its criminal code on those values deemed most thoroughly related to the general welfare and to free its police, its courts, its reforming institutions, its probation and parole officers, and the like, for full attention to these major violators and their reformation. Our juvenile courts and our juvenile and adult probation have already set precedent for the "excusing" of certain types of offenses under certain circumstances. But this has, again, been the superimposing of new rules designed for reformation upon old rules designed for punitive justice. Complete renovation of our criminal code to render it a relatively simple instrument defining crime as violations of major social values, rather than continued additions to the present mass of criminal laws, constitutes this proposal.

This implies, of course, that society is able to "make up its mind" on which are its major values. Gambling is a much publicized case in point. In some states it is now legal to bet on the outcome of a horserace provided the bet is placed at the track's parimutuel window. To make the same kind of bet through a "bookie" is illegal. Some contend that "people will always gamble" and suggest that much illegal behavior could be reduced if the public were provided with a legal, readily available outlet for its gambling urges. The gambling syndicates that stand to lose considerable revenue and those that feel gambling is categorically "wrong" obviously oppose "legalized gambling." The pros and cons of this particular issue are too numerous to present here, but it illustrates how value conflicts can and do interfere with the job of much needed renovation of our criminal code.

Guidance of the "Natural Leader"

Regardless of their specific sources, most criminal behavior has its inception in childhood and adolescent delinquency. This has long been recognized, and many youth agencies have claimed to have programs that "prevent and reduce juvenile delinquency." Since, until very recently, no controlled experiments have been conducted as part of the procedures of these agencies, there has been no verification of their claims and, on the contrary, some evidence for doubting them.

Probably the first approach to producing a program that, on the basis of control groups, could be shown to reduce delinquency in high delinquency rate areas was the Chicago Area Project. It was set up in such a way as to use natural instead of artificial groups and local instead of imported leaders. Further characteristics of the project follow: the program is determined locally rather than by following standardized procedures imposed from the outside; already existing neighborhood facilities and institutions are employed; trained personnel are kept in the background, but are constantly available for assistance to the "natural" leaders in improving operational effectiveness; data and records are accumulated whereby results may be frequently evaluated.

Comparison of the reduced number of arrests of persons in the experimental area with those in a carefully matched contiguous area (where no comparable program was in progress) has at least tentatively demonstrated the effectiveness of the "natural leadership" techniques employed in the Chicago Area Project. While further and more extensive experimentation is needed, the superiority of this type of guidance program for youth, rather than the standardized program superimposed on the community by out-group leadership, would seem to be indicated.

Improved Social Work Programs

A more general attack on crime, primarily through work with delinquents and predelinquents, consists of improving the services offered by casework and group-work agencies. A few of the many important proposals follow:

(1) Development by casework and group-work agencies of a program designed to inform their communities about the services they are prepared to give and the resources, both material and staff, they need to provide adequate services.

(2) Strengthening and extending of existing social services and creating of new ones to meet such needs as more and better casework services in the schools; special training for truant officers in casework techniques; development of more cooperative planning of leisure-time activities of schools and group-work agencies *with,* rather than *for,* youth; child guidance centers with psychiatric services; employment of additional qualified probation officers by juvenile courts; employment of social workers to do interviewing and referral by police departments or their juvenile aid bureaus; setting up of research programs for discovering new and additional needs in the field of juvenile delinquency and of more adequate educational programs for keeping the public informed of these needs and progress made in meeting them.

(3) More effective coordination and integration of private and public social services.

(4) Assuming of greater responsibility on the part of community leaders for establishing the structure and on the part of the staff for making continuous evaluations of both the quantity and quality of the social services in light of current needs of children and adults of the community.

(5) More effective efforts to attract competent college students to the field of social work.

(6) Further encouragement of and impetus to research in the field of juvenile delinquency and its prevention, and in ways of developing more effective social work techniques for meeting needs in the field.

Development of Predictive Devices

In our discussion of the sources of criminality we mentioned the study of risk factors related to the development of criminal behavior and the contemporary inadequacy of the results of this study. It seems very probable, however, that considerable hope for improvement of social controls over crime and the criminal will stem from the accumulation of more accurate data in regard to criminal risk or liability. Out of studies providing us with more accurate statistical information concerning various risk factors associated with criminal behavior, various predictive scales will be developed. Some progress in the development of predictive devices in the field of crime has already been made, but since they are based on inadequate knowledge of risk factors, they may be regarded only as crude beginnings.

The development of accurate predictive instruments regarding those likely to adopt delinquent or criminal patterns of behavior and of those likely to revert to such patterns following treatment would provide society with means to curtail futile expenditures of time, money, and energy in misdirected preventive and treatment programs and to concentrate full efforts where they would bring the desired results. Devices already developed, while crude according to the best scientific standards, are great improvements as bases, for example, for predicting success or failure on parole compared with the combinations of guesswork, "insight," and sentiment currently employed by most of our parole boards.

In conclusion, the student is cautioned to remember that while an overwhelming bulk of literature going under the name of "criminology" has accumulated for centuries, only recently have criminologists in large numbers begun to attack scientifically the very important social problem of crime. For those seeking swift cures for the problem, the present status of our knowledge is indeed discouraging; for those recognizing the complicated nature of social behavior generally, and of criminal behavior specifically, that we have come so far in so little time in the development of scientific methods for dealing with crime and the criminal should be amazing.

SUGGESTED READINGS

BEATTIE, RONALD H., "Criminal Statistics in the United States–1960," *Journal of Criminal Law, Criminology and Police Science,* 51:1 (May–June 1960), pp. 49–65.

CRESSEY, DONALD R., and JOHN IRWIN, "Thieves, Convicts and the Inmate Culture," *Social Problems,* 10:2 (Fall 1962), pp. 142–155.

DINITZ, SIMON, FRANK R. SCARPITTI, and WALTER C. RECKLESS, "Delinquency Vulnerability," *American Sociological Review,* 27:4 (August 1962), pp. 515–517.

GLUECK, SHELDON and ELEANOR, *Predicting Delinquency and Crime.* Cambridge, Mass., Harvard University Press, 1959.

NEWMAN, DONALD J., "White Collar Crime," *Law and Contemporary Problems,* 23:4 (1958), pp. 735–753.

PITTMAN, DAVID J., and WILLIAM F. HANDY, "Uniform Crime Reporting: Suggested Improvements," *Sociology and Social Research,* 46:2 (January 1962), pp. 135–143.

RECKLESS, WALTER C., *The Crime Problem,* 3d ed. New York, Appleton-Century-Crofts, 1961.

ROSE, ARNOLD M., "Some Suggestions for Research in the Sociology of Law," *Social Problems,* 9:3 (Winter 1962), pp. 281–283.

SCHWARTZ, RICHARD D., and JEROME H. SKOLNICK, "Two Studies of Legal Stigma," *Social Problems,* 10:2 (Fall 1962), pp. 133–142.

SPERGEL, IRVING, "Male Young Adult Criminality, Deviant Values, and Differential Opportunities in Two Lower Class Negro Neighborhoods," *Social Problems,* 10:3 (Winter 1963), pp. 237–250.

TAYLOR, R. S., "The Habitual Criminal," *British Journal of Criminology,* 1:1 (July 1960), pp. 21–31.

TRASLER, GORDON, *The Explanation of Criminality.* London, Routledge and Kegan Paul, Ltd., 1962. Distributed by the Humanities Press, New York.

JUVENILE DELINQUENCY 17

On the surface it would seem that juvenile delinquency is simply a special case of crime, the obvious differentiation being that delinquency is committed by subadults, eighteen years of age or less. But "delinquency" as ordinarily used refers to much more than simple legal violation. It includes acts and even attitudes that have no counterpart for the adult population. Thus, school truancy and even extreme maladaptation to school, keeping late hours in public places, refusal to obey parents, "noisiness and carousing" are typically regarded as "delinquency." Some kinds of delinquency are so defined merely because the behavior, while quite permissible for adults, is forbidden to subadults. Smoking and drinking alcoholic beverages are cases of this type.

The juvenile codes of most states are so inclusive that juvenile courts are frequently required to assume jurisdiction over certain children whose offenses are utterly trivial; in some instances the child himself has committed no offense at all but has merely been in the company of those who have. The net effect is one of utter confusion. Familiar and recurrent statistics on the dramatic rise of juvenile delinquency "rates" may reflect changes in acts defined as delinquent, or result from changes in the vigilance of police officers and public informers, or reflect innovations resulting from a different personal philosophy on the part of the presiding judge in the community in question. Obviously, doubling or trebling the police force can cause a "wave" of juvenile delinquency in almost any American city: since many of the acts more or less normally committed by adolescents are technically illegal, any change that increases the proportion who get caught will result in a sharp rise in the delinquency "rate" for the community.

The foregoing should not be taken as an attempt to minimize the gravity of the juvenile delinquency problem. Delinquency in connection with improper handling of motor vehicles alone constitutes a threat to life and property for almost every community, the potentials and sometimes the actual incidences of which are staggering. It is small comfort to a maimed person or the survivors of a dead one that some adolescent "hotrodder" had been abandoned by his parents, been mistreated by his teachers, and was simply enjoying a few moments of "outlet for deep frustration." And from the point of view of the juveniles themselves their delinquencies may affect personality structure so that normal adult roles are almost impossible to assume with competency. Sexual promiscuity, for example, and the alarming rise of venereal infection among teenagers in recent years augur lasting problems of phenomenal proportions. Other illustrations will readily occur to any thoughtful person.

Viewing the delinquency problem in the light of our familiar threefold value conflict structure, a terse formulation of the delinquency problem may be stated thus:

(1) There *is* general value agreement that various acts called juvenile delinquency are in fact problems.

(2) There is general agreement—more confidently among laymen than among professionals—that the juvenile delinquency problem can and should be controlled by collective measures.

(3) There is sharp value disagreement, in fact utter chaos, with respect to precisely *how* the alleged problem can and should be attacked. In almost every community there is a near bedlam of voices, confidently pronouncing that this or that program would, if carried out, solve or at least materially improve the condition. Part of this confusion stems from differing conceptions of what ought and what ought not be called delinquency, but most of it stems from differing conceptions of the effectiveness of this program or that. A sharp cleavage exists between professional and lay opinion and even the professionals show considerable variation with respect to their judgment and their familiarity with competent research on the subject.

The rest of this chapter will provide factual material amplifying and interpreting the above three general propositions.

BACKGROUND

Adolescence Is a Normal Stage of Normal Life

There is substantial agreement among professionals that a necessary preliminary to understanding delinquency is understanding the juvenile. Most juveniles, presumably, are not delinquent, certainly not officially so, and it does seem basic to attempt to understand the "psychosocial stuff" with which we are dealing.

It is difficult when talking with most adults to secure a dispassionate and consistent focus on adolescence or preadulthood per se. The tendency is to spring immediately into questions of evaluation, interpretation, explanation, and sometimes defensiveness. To be realistic, perhaps we, too, should begin at this same point.

Judging from the attention the adolescent receives, there can be little doubt that many Americans believe that there is "something wrong" with present-day youth. Parents of teenagers exchange knowing glances, shake their heads in despair, and try to convince one another that sooner or later their offspring will pass through this "stage." Some are not really convinced and seriously question whether the youth of today will ever become responsible and mature members of society. Whatever their specific reaction, many adults are aware that adolescence is a period of strain, for themselves as well as for their children.

Probably the chief value clash that gives rise to what is called "the adolescent problem" is between the vested interests of adults and the vested interests of adolescents. From the point of view of the adolescent, he is an adult. In a gadget-infested culture his adultness is clearly manifest to him, since he can do such things as drive an auto, even "soup it up" into "a hot rod" with frequently more success than can his father. Sexually he is grown up too, with a whole new world of adult-forbidden fulfillments before him. The adolescent wants to prove his "adulthood" by any and all devices available to him. It does not seem unreasonable to him to want to do so, and he champs at the bit when older adults admonish him to "grow up first," to "be a little more patient," to "get some more experience," and "not to be impulsive." The adolescent is in a real sense the sociological version of being "all dressed up with no place to go."

The older adult, on the other hand, sees the adolescent as an irresponsible, not yet *really* mature human being who shows great promise, if he will only stay childlike for a little longer, that is, if he will not do adult things or think in adult ways. It is entirely possible, moreover, that some of the superior skills of adolescents may threaten the superiority of older adults, more even than is easy to admit. If adolescents can only be kept "acting their age" a little longer, there may be more comfort for the status-threatened adult.

The basic viewpoint from which *we* shall attempt to see the problem of the adolescent is one of neutrality—of stepping aside and trying to understand what, characteristically, the adolescent wants and needs in terms of *his* personality, over against what the older adult wants and needs in terms of *his* personality and social position. Not very many people are capable of this kind of detached objectivity because they have become so ego-involved in *being* an adolescent or an older adult and therefore in *seeing* the social world largely, if not solely, from one age-status position. It is not so much that either adolescents or older adults do not *wish* to see the problems from the point of view of the other group, but rather that they find it almost impossible to free themselves sufficiently from themselves, and from their age-group concepts of the world, to permit more than an occasional glimpse into how the other conceives of reality. We shall attempt, nevertheless, to do precisely that—to assay the value perspectives of adolescents and adults with a view better to understand what each group wants and needs and to evaluate the proposals for accomplishing a better liaison between the two.

Biological Versus Sociological Maturity

The term "adolescent" is frequently used in such a way as to make it appear to be synonymous with the biological term, "puberty." A sharper distinction should be consistently held to. *Puberty* is a biological term and refers simply to that stage in the development of a person after which he *seems* to have become an adult in the sense that his sexual characteristics appear mature. Most humans, however, are sterile during the first two years or so of puberty. The organism, moreover, is not mature at puberty in that growth is not yet complete and physical vigor has not reached its apex. *Adolescence,* on the other hand, is a *social status* in which the human being finds himself just prior to being admitted into the society as a full-fledged adult member with all of the responsibilities and privileges which adults normally have. *Adolescence and puberty may coincide in time, or either may follow the other, depending upon the culture in which the person is reared.* In a given culture, moreover, little allowance is usually made for the fact that different persons attain puberty at different times, and adults tend to treat all of the young alike, as if they became pubertal at the same age. This means that prepubertal children may be treated as adolescents and postpubertal children as preadolescents. Needless to say, this may seriously aggravate for many children the problems of growing up.

An Intercultural View of Adolescence

In different societies adolescence (1) comes at markedly different times, (2) has markedly different duration, varying from an almost insignificant period to eight or ten years, and (3) is accompanied by unequal amounts of trauma or shock or difficulty.

In many primitive societies, for example, a person simply becomes an adult with the onset of puberty, although usually puberty is marked as a distinct period and is often accompanied by rites and ceremonies which publicly proclaim the fact that the boy or girl has become a man or a woman. Sometimes this period of transition comes immediately at the time of puberty and sometimes somewhat later. Being a sociological rather than a biological state, of course, considerable leeway is allowed, depending largely on the values of the culture in question.

In some societies adolescence is a very brief status. It may consist merely of a short, public ceremony. At the other extreme, adolescence stretches out over a period of eight or ten years. In our own society the average child becomes puberal at between ten and thirteen years but is not considered an adult, for many important purposes, until during the early twenties.

Most importantly of all, a cross-cultural view of adolescence reveals clearly that both the kinds and the amounts of shock or social disturbance which are supposed to accompany adolescence are highly variant. *In some societies adolescent trauma are practically nonexistent.* When children become adults they simply take on adult responsibilities, without fuss and turmoil and all of the many manifestations that adolescence so often has in American society.

We are forced, then, to the conclusion that adolescence becomes a problem in American society because we make it a problem. This does not mean, of course, that we contrive with diabolical sadism to invoke the scourge of adolescence upon our children. Rather, we have built the kind of society with the kind of values, material culture, and moral concepts that make adolescent trauma a by-product of modern living. *If,* for example, we did not have automobiles, and *if* we characteristically allowed children to go to work at full employment at any age at which they wished, and *if* we allowed "teenagers" to marry whenever they thought they had found the correct mate, *then* we would be without many of the characteristic problems that bring adolescent turmoil to plague both the adolescents and their elders. It is not meant to imply that we ought to make such changes in our present culture; we are simply stressing the fact that, *given* our particular value system and material culture, it is more or less inevitable that we have the problems between youth and age which we usually do.

Conditions Conducive to Adolescent Trauma

It is not necessary to restrict ourselves to vague generalizations concerning the conditions in our culture that contribute to making adolescence a period of "storm and strife." In any scientific treatment of the values of American society the cultural sore spots, as far as adolescent difficulty is concerned, are readily apparent. Some of these, as a matter of fact, were isolated years ago by the anthropologist Margaret Mead following her studies of adolescence in various societies.[1] The following are among the more sig-

---

[1] See especially her "Adolescence in Primitive and Modern Society," in V. F. Calverton and S. D. Schmalhausen, eds., *The New Generation* (New York: The Citadel Press, 1930).

nificant features of our culture largely responsible for adolescence constituting the kind of problem it does.

THE EXTENT OF CULTURAL ALTERNATIVES. In small, relatively homogeneous societies the "choices" available to a person embarking on adulthood are relatively limited. The paths that can be traversed are few, and the signposts are clearly marked. In our own and other "mass societies," by contrast, the adolescent finds himself confronted with a bewildering array of alternatives. The sheer volume of educational, occupational, economic, moral, and other choices is staggering. The present-day *Occupational Dictionary,* for example, lists over 20,000 job titles. Realistically, these do not represent true choices for every youth, but certainly the task of choosing and preparing for one's life's work is more complicated than it was under a hundred years ago when it was estimated that there were but several hundred different occupations. And so it is for choices in other areas. Caught up in the swollen stream of cultural alternatives, with its frequent crosscurrents, it is not surprising to find numerous adolescents consciously or otherwise "giving up" in their struggle to make decisions.

LACK OF RATIONALE FOR DECISION MAKING. It is somewhat paradoxical that a culture replete with alternatives is found wanting in the preparation for choosing among them. We force the child to make moral choices for which he is unprepared. We stress the importance of "right" and "wrong" and yet can provide no really satisfactory rationale for what acts are clearly to be regarded as right and wrong. What is even worse, we teach the child, more perhaps by example than by formal instruction, that certain things are wrong, yet we, the adults, do those same things, either characteristically or under certain extenuating circumstances. Smoking, drinking, and sexual behavior illustrate this moral category well. Adults who smoke and drink tell adolescents that they should not smoke and drink "because it is not good for you." "Is it good for you?" asks the adolescent. The adult has no satisfactory answer because there is none. Moreover, in the sexual realm the adolescent is overstimulated by a culture which places great emphasis on sexual matters, manifesting this sexual preoccupation in advertising soft drinks with pictures of near nudes in highly suggestive poses, meanwhile pouring forth from radios, television and "juke boxes" a plethora of productions with almost exclusively romantic, if not downright sexual, themes. In this panorama of taboo and indulgence, of inconsistent preachment and example, the adolescent is supposed to make moral choices with greater discretion than his parents!

NEGATIVE CONDITIONING. Not only do we require the adolescent to make decisions for which he is not prepared—and for which many adults are not either—we actually *unfit* him for wise choices during the adolescent period. Again, we do not do this consciously, and certainly not with the desire to make life difficult for him. But regardless of our intentions, the consequences are the same. In no area of life is this more true than in the area of sex. Here the characteristic adult mode of handling the "problem" is a combination of withholding pertinent information from the child for as long as possible, and then, when procrastination is no longer expedient, of presenting him with a pattern of fears and phobias which are designed to keep him "pure," but which are more likely to make him neurotic. In this atmosphere of too little information coming too late and distorted by instilled fears, the adolescent is expected by righteous adults to make wise decisions in sexual matters and is condemned brutally when he fails.

EMPHASIS ON "PEER COMPETITION." From the time the child enters school, great stress is placed upon competition, and high standing is attached to being successful in competition with those of older age levels. From the time that "mama" takes great pride in the fact that "Junior, only two, wears suits sized 3½!" until the same mother boasts that Junior has "graduated from college, the *youngest* member of his class," he is almost constantly subjected to competition that drives him to be like someone older than he. Then, when Junior wishes to reap the rewards of his successful emulation of older persons, he is promptly told that he is too young for them. Seen in this way, the so-called adolescent rebellion is not difficult to understand and almost impossible to solve.

IMPERSONAL SOCIAL RELATIONSHIPS. As we have shifted from a predominantly rural to a predominantly urban society, there has been a decline in the personal, face-to-face type of social relationship. The social control previously exerted by almost daily association with members of a tightly knit primary group is not felt to the same degree in the more fleeting contacts with secondary-group members. Modern urban living readily allows the average adolescent to escape from the watchful eye of parent and sibling, church and neighbor. Where he goes and what he does no one knows—and shortly no one really cares.

THE ROLE OF MATERIAL CULTURE. Our material culture, that is the objects or "things" that we have created, has contributed its share of hazard and confusion to adolescence. As accident statistics indicate, an automobile in the hands of an adolescent is a 200 percent more lethal device than when it is in the hands of an adult over thirty-five. This is not opinion, it is sheer statistical fact. In other less dramatic ways the automobile multiplies adolescent problems. The automobile parked a few blocks or a few miles from home may be used almost as effectively for a boudoir as for a vehicle of transportation. While certainly sex was invented before the automobile, and equally obviously morality did not end with it, it is no less true that the anonymity and intimacy fostered by the modern automobile are contributing factors in the difficulties that many adolescents have in working out a code of sexual conduct which will give them a maximum of long-term life fulfillment.

Adolescent Trauma Begin Early

It cannot be stressed too forcibly that much of the adolescent's difficulty, hostility toward parents, maladjustment in school, mental-health problems, and the like, does not *originate* with adolescence. These symptoms are merely more *conspicuously* manifest at that time. There is much comment, for example, concerning "adolescent rebellion," which term usually refers to the fact that very often during adolescence children rebel against their parents and other authority and give other evidence of their refusal to act as they are expected to. What is frequently overlooked is that such behavior is the *end product* of all of the child-rearing practices to which the child has been subjected. If parental disciplining is inconsistent, if parents are not honest in answering children's questions about sex, if the parents' own moral conduct is not consistent with their moral preachment, an intelligent adolescent can hardly be expected either to rely on his parents' advice or to feel too kindly toward them when they attempt to force it on him. This is not to be taken as a categorical assertion that adolescents are always blameless or that all adolescent irresponsibility is to be tossed like a dead cat on the doorstep of parents. Obviously, in individual cases other circumstances besides child-rearing practices operate. But taking the society *as a whole,* the evidence is clear that much of the tempest in the adolescent experience is the consequence of the accumulation of little whirlwinds of parental ineptitude.

Nor can it be stressed too forcibly that we are not here speaking of the *individual* parent and his *individual* offspring. This is a *societal* problem, rather than an individual one. Some particular parents, for example, may rear their children with wisdom and empathy, only to find their best efforts defeated because their child has come under the influence of other children who were not so fortunate in their parental influence, but who serve thereafter as a sort of emotional contamination. In other words, this is a *social* problem and cannot be solved solely, even somewhat effectively, by the individual parent working alone, as if he lived in a vacuum. *How other people rear their children can be a decisive factor in the eventual fate of one's own.* Long ago we learned this lesson with respect to contagious-disease control—the same principle holds for the mental hygiene of adolescence.

INDICES OF ADOLESCENT DIFFICULTY

The purpose of this section is to bring together some of the lines of evidence now available which demonstrate either the nature of typical adolescent difficulty in our society or the extent to which these difficulties exist. It must be admitted at the outset that for many of the most serious adolescent difficulties, notably those in the realm of mental hygiene, there are no clear or convincing statistics of the true extent of difficulties. If a child does not commit a delinquency that results in his getting caught (and very, very few ever get caught), if he avoids failure or major disciplinary action in school or court martial in the army, or if he is not cornered somewhere by an ambitious researcher who pries into his private life,[2] the torments of his adolescence go unrecorded and unknown. Certainly one is no alarmist if he points out that for every school failure that is recorded there must be many near-failures and many who find the going very, very painful. For every child who commits a delinquent act and gets caught there must be many more who suffer considerable indecision, conscience trouble, and other emotional discomfort, caught as they are in the same crosscurrents of cultural inconsistency as is the technical delinquent. Realizing, then, that only the more extreme and more dramatic instances become matters of record, it may be useful to look at the record for more tangible evidence of the difficulty of the adolescent period in American society.

School Failures

By "school failures" are meant not merely those persons who fail to maintain minimal standards of academic achievement, but rather the much larger group of adolescents who remain in school, but for whom the school experience is a continuously frustrating one, or one that does not provide for them the degree of satisfaction and growth in experience that it could and should. It is customary for many superficial adults to jump hastily to the conclusion that it is the adolescent's fault if he fails to "get enough out of" his school experience. Just what is meant by that is not always clear, but the implication apparently is that the school is a sort of reservoir of goodness from which a good child drinks long and heartily and the wayward or willful or "problem" child refuses to drink at all. What is overlooked in such a conception of the matter is that not all of the responsibility rests with the adolescent. To return to our figure of speech, if the water supply is contaminated, it may be a sign of good judgment rather than poor judgment if one refuses to drink. Many of our more penetrating students of education have come to the conclusion that the phrase "failure *of* the *school*" to interest the adolescent is a more accurate way of putting it than is the more familiar "failure *of* the *adolescent*" to be interested in school. In many schools the curriculum content, the teaching skills of the staff, and the whole concept of child development is so foreign to what we know scientifically about the needs of adolescents that "failure of the school" rather than "failure of the adolescent" seems a more accurate way of stating the case.

[2] See Chapter 14 on Mental Health.

Morals

The tendency of adults to decry the morals of youth is older than Methuselah. Each generation seems to torture itself with the "certain" knowledge that its youth is going to the dogs! Careful research on moral conduct is not as abundant as one might expect in a scientifically minded nation. Moreover, "morals" is a slippery concept to manipulate. It means different things to different people, and different things to the same person in various contexts. To many persons "morals" is synonymous with sexual conduct. Just why a breach of conduct in the sexual area should be more serious or important than a breach of conduct in business dealings is not wholly clear. Many students of adolescent behavior feel there has been a far greater revolution in moral precepts in the realm of business ethics than in sexual ones.

Moreover, phrases like "moral degeneracy" are frequently misleading, because they imply a static concept of moral conduct. Many people in our society and in others adhere to a static concept of moral conduct, accepting the idea that a given behavior is right or wrong per se, and that it makes no difference *when* the behaving is done. To such persons it is futile to argue that it once was wrong for a woman to smoke or wear shorts in public, but that it is not so today. To them, morals are morals, and they go on forever unchanged and unchangeable. History, however, has it otherwise. It records a continuously changing concept of right and wrong in every society that has a written history, and a great variation in moral conduct among societies at any one time. Thus many of the "immoral" acts of adolescents as seen by older adults may be the "moral" acts of the next generation. This is evidenced most vividly in the recent history of women's conduct, although it could be illustrated in many other ways as well.

Insofar as there have been careful studies of the sexual morality of persons of different ages, notably those by Alfred Kinsey and his staff, the differences alleged between present-day adolescents and their elders do not show up. Kinsey's research fails to show that there is any marked difference in the sexual conduct of American adolescent males, their fathers, and their grandfathers. Much of our so-called moral revolution may lie in the realm of conscience and tolerance rather than in overt action. Adolescents today may talk more freely about sexual matters and judge violators of the expected codes less severely than they used to. Moreover, there appears to be a greater freedom to experiment with erotic satisfactions short of coitus than there was in the past, and a greater casualness with respect to the identity of the partner. Whether such acts and such judgments are immoral or not would seem to depend largely upon the point of view of the evaluator. That is why it is difficult to say whether the freer conduct of adolescents in this area of life constitutes immorality or not.

A sociological sage once wrote, "The imaginations which people have of one another are the solid facts" of human life. In this frame of reference the frequent adult charge that adolescents are immoral is both real and important. It is real in that adults base their judgments of adolescents and their efforts to control adolescents on the supposition of juvenile immorality. Whether that assumption is right or wrong, they act and talk as if it were correct, and for practical purposes, therefore, it might almost as well be. In a second sense, the adolescent-immorality charge may be socially significant, namely, in its effect upon the adolescent. There is an adage that "one may as well have the game, since one has the name." Just how far such a realization may influence present-day adolescents is of course not known, but it would not be surprising if it had some influence, nor if that influence were in the direction of encouraging some adolescents at least to take greater liberties with the traditional code than they otherwise would.

Economic Frustration

Theoretically, an adolescent in America may choose, after he has fulfilled the minimum compulsory school attendance, whether he shall go on to college or go to work. Whichever role he chooses, there are many more impediments in his path than are ordinarily recognized. If he chooses "to go on to college and make something of himself," he may encounter any one or more, or possibly even all, of the following serious hurdles: (1) He and his parents may not have the money necessary to enable him to go to college. (2) If he belongs to certain minority groups, he may find himself excluded categorically or by a "quota system" from some or all of the colleges he wishes to attend. (3) He may find, after admission to college, that his skills, abilities, temperament, intelligence, or what not, may not be suited to the requirements of the school or the profession he has chosen. (4) He may find that his desire to get married, or the fact that he is already married, interferes with his attending school. (5) Even after the successful completion of four or more years of study he may find that he is still expected to "start at the bottom" in his chosen career at a salary that suggests still further postponement of marriage. A moment's reflection will indicate that these hazards are by no means to be minimized. The adolescent who wishes to attend noncollegiate training schools faces the same type of problems, but not, perhaps, to so sharp a degree.

If, however, the adolescent chooses not to go to school, he encounters serious difficulties too: (1) Even in times of relatively full employment, he may discover that what he considers a "good job" is hard to find. A common complaint is that most of the better jobs require "experience," and this the youth fresh from high school does not have. (2) The job he finally accepts and its pay may not be too much to his liking. There is almost certain to be disappointment when he realizes that being financially "on his own" means that, for some time at least, he may have a lower standard of living than he had while living with his parents. (3) He will shortly, probably, wish to get married. Wage rates for unskilled workers of comparative inexperience do not conduce to marriage. Even with husband and wife both working, frustrations are numerous. With or without children the couple's standard of living cannot be very high. Advertisements for "dream homes," new automobiles, and northland vacations leave an understandably bad taste. (4) Not infrequently there is some "unfinished business" with parents, relatives, and friends who may have expected the young man to further his education, there being a widespread American ideal that a young man ought to start out at a somewhat better job than his father had. Parents and friends frequently let it be known, in rather less than subtle ways, that he is something of a disappointment!

Thus, whether he chooses the narrow and somewhat demanding path of higher education or the somewhat less exciting path of early and romantic "independence," the adolescent finds the adult world difficult to "crack." Perhaps that is why he finds it necessary to "zoom" in and out of the lines of traffic with his "hot-rod jalopy," just to show his middle-aged elders in their shiny cars that he can do *something* conspicuously!

THE JUVENILE COURT

A second background area of our problem concerns the juvenile court, which includes detention services and probation services for delinquents. The juvenile court is a product of the twentieth century, whereas most of our legal concepts go back several centuries.

The juvenile court would not strike most adults as a court at all. There is no jury, no contentious lawyers, no complicated evidence and legalism. In fact, in the larger cities there is often not even a judge. The hearings of the court are often presided over by a *referee,* usually appointed by the judge to act for him in a judicial capacity. The procedure is informal to such an extent that sometimes it resembles a domestic crisis more than it does a court of law. The court is only incidentally concerned with whether or not the offense was committed in the manner claimed by the complainant; it is charged by law to be more concerned with how the child is to be treated than with whether the child is to be punished and if so, how. Judges and referees are, of course, human, and despite statutory requirements to the contrary, may assume a very punitive stance because they have become personally outraged by what they have learned, by the incalcitrant attitudes of the juvenile or his parents, or because of embarrassing pressures from newspapers and other outside sources. Nevertheless, by and large there appears to be a reasonably consistent tendency in juvenile courts, especially in the larger cities, to carry out the purposes of a nonpunitive, treatment-oriented public institution to handle the juvenile offender.

Most imperfections in the juvenile court system appear to stem from two sources. First, there is the human equation. If an elected judge has an authoritarian attitude toward children, much of the treatment philosophy inherent in the juvenile code will understandably fail to get through to him. He has wide discretionary powers, most of his actions are nonpublic (even the names of juvenile offenders in some states may not be given to the newspapers), and few of his decisions are subject to ordinary judicial review. If he wishes, he may practice the role of petty tyrant over the lives and fortunes of the delinquents brought before him. The same problem applies to probation officers and detention home personnel and others on whose testimony the judge must almost completely rely in reaching his decision. Other deviations from the theory of the juvenile court grow out of imperfections in the communication process among complainants, the delinquents themselves, their parents and the probation officer. The latter is often not well trained, typically overworked and in general is forced to function under conditions not conducive to efficiency.

In the second place, most juvenile courts are forced to operate with grossly inadequate budgets. They are often unable to hire competent personnel because they cannot pay enough to attract them. They are chronically understaffed in all departments, which means that the probation officer and other court personnel are often forced to make recommendations on the basis of insufficient evidence because they have had insufficient time to make a thorough investigation. In addition, despite the legal safeguards to insure informality and privacy in the proceedings, there is a considerable amount of harassment and interference, quite illegally, from the outside. Influential people in the community, sometimes parents of the delinquents themselves, "get to" the court or its officers in various ways, which has the effect of influencing decisions for reasons that ought to be extraneous.

In recent years the traditional juvenile court philosophy and procedures have come under *increasing criticism,* not so much because the underlying idea is basically incorrect but rather because certain of the practices that have been introduced to implement the philosophy have tended, it is alleged, to pervert it instead.

1. The juvenile courts in many cities have permitted themselves to be "used" by hostile and unreasonable adults with trivial complaints against juveniles. In almost any court on any given day the telephone calls and letters and visits concerning relatively trivial matters are considerable—a broken window from a well-hit foul ball, "obscene language" (which often

turns out to be normal adolescent language, even in better homes), smoking on the school grounds, staying out all night (no evidence of any specific wrongdoing), and so on. Many such acts strike a realist as simply normal behavior for adolescents, which admittedly the adult solid citizen would wish to be otherwise. An inordinate amount of court work goes into these trivial cases and, particularly when the complainant is a person of substance in the community, the court finds it difficult to ignore him. It would seem that the critics are right when they insist that the juvenile court should be concerned with more serious offenses than those of Halloween pranksters and "delinquencies" of the sort mentioned above.

2. Juvenile court judges and referees, when dealing with more serious cases requiring treatment, frequently find themselves blocked because the community (or state) has failed to supply them with the kind of institutions and agencies that can actually help the delinquent overcome his difficulties. Sometimes the problem is one of overcrowding, so that the personnel in the existing facilities is too busy and harassed to do the kind of rehabilitation job it could do under more sensible workloads. In other instances the pay scales are so low that the personnel actually employed does not measure up to professional standards required. Much too often so-called diagnostic and treatment centers for juvenile delinquents are not much better than jails and come to have the same deleterious effects that jails do. They become "schools of crime."

3. A charge more difficult to document conclusively has to do with the tendency of some courts to assume jurisdiction too soon, without sufficient evidence of the adolescent's guilt and without sufficient time being devoted to alternative sources of treatment for the offender. Just as law enforcement officers have been known sometimes to be "trigger happy" so have juvenile courts sometimes become "disposition happy"—the urge to dispose of the case too promptly and get on with the next one. The delinquent's common charge that he was "railroaded" is no doubt often an exaggeration, but there are cases in the informal operation of the juvenile court in which this does happen. It is a serious matter for a preadult to lose confidence in the police and the judicial system as sources of his protection. If they are his enemies from this time on, it is small wonder that incorrigibles are so common. To solve this problem, however, is no easy task. Some have suggested that juveniles should have the same benefit of counsel as do adult criminals. This opens up the whole procedure, however, to the kind of theatrics and overattention to the technical aspects of guilt or innocence, the evils of which brought about the juvenile court in the first place. Perhaps the best solution is simply one of higher professional standards for court personnel and sufficient budgets so that judges, referees, and probation officers can work more deliberately and give their attention to the important cases.

The realistic interpreter of the situation with practical experience such as a juvenile court referee (the writer of this chapter has held such a position), can certainly attest to the legitimacy of the above criticisms and others as well, but there is danger when attacking the problem wholesale of throwing the baby out with the bath water. Despite its evils, the juvenile court system, particularly where it has had adequate financing and freedom from harassment by newspapers and other sometimes irresponsible critics, has performed an acceptable public service. Obviously, during the period in which the juvenile court has existed, delinquency has not disappeared and very probably has increased. To blame this on the juvenile court is analogous to blaming the medical profession for the increased incidence of heart disease and cancer. The roots of delinquency run deep into American society, and all that can be realistically expected of a court is that it carry out with a minimum of error its function of treating individual instances which come before it as well as is humanly possible. The large amount of juvenile recidivism, as in adult crime, can be construed as one kind of evidence that the court is not doing a perfect job. But no one knows what adequate success is. The influence of the court is not the only influence that determines the outcome in a given case. The juvenile offender in addition to having the influence of the court, good or bad, also is affected by his parents, his peer groups, school and job experience, the section of the city he lives in, recreational patterns—indeed, a host of social influences, good and bad. It is always easy to blame some one or another fragment in the kaleidoscope, but a sterner objectivity would seem to suggest that human behavior should be seen in the light of *total* impact from the *total* society.

NEW MODES IN JUVENILE DELINQUENCY

Like all other aspects of society, delinquency varies with time. Fifty years ago, for example, automobile stealing and traffic crimes were virtually nil as forms of delinquency. Now they loom large. Sex offenses are difficult to evaluate not so much because we have evidence that the incidence of sexual irregularity has increased, as that consciousness of the problem and changing conceptions about appropriate sexual behavior have varied. In the period since World War II, however, at least three relatively new aspects of juvenile behavior have reached such proportions that attention needs to be given them.

Middle-class Delinquency

Traditionally, juvenile delinquency has been primarily a lower-class phenomenon. Children of the slums and poorer working-class sections, housed in substandard dwellings, aimlessly roaming the streets, born and reared by parents of dubious morality and casual family life were responsible for a large amount of *reported* and *adjudicated* delinquency. Insofar as there was wrongdoing in the middle and upper-middle classes, such misbehavior largely missed police detection, and if detected was "handled" unofficially, chiefly by the parents. Since World War II, however, a larger amount of delinquency has occurred among the so-called better homes in the better sections of the city, often among the *over*privileged rather than the *under*privileged children. The offenses of the middle-class children run the whole gamut from auto stealing and gang warfare to the more "normal" kinds of mischief such as minor sex offenses and truancy. The difference appears to be not merely in reporting and differential treatment, but rather in a true increase of delinquent behavior among middle-class children. No one knows precisely, or even approximately, why this change has taken place. The old explanations in terms of poverty, unstable family life, absence of religious instruction, and substandard schooling obviously do not supply realistic answers. Perhaps psychiatric interpretations are in order, but here again careful scientific evidence is lacking which would permit one to reach definitive conclusions. We simply do not know why there has been this rise in middle-class delinquency.

Vandalism

One of America's leading criminologists says that "the symbol of delinquency in the present era is the growing pattern of vandalism." [3] A U.S. Senate committee in 1957 reported that vandalism "is either a form of protest, an explosion of suppressed resentment or the release of feelings of aggression by children who, given a large measure of freedom . . . are unable to control their impulses because they lack the quality of self discipline. . . . The amount of maliciousness and hostility expressed in vandalism is an index to the degree (young people) feel they have been imposed upon." [4] Reckless points out that much of this behavior is to be regarded as simple bedevilment of adults, not so much specific adults as adults in general. Thus, public property—schools, parks, road signs, and shrubbery— parked automobiles, and theatres in the better neighborhoods are more or less standard objects of malicious attack. Vandalism, Reckless reports, is primarily a middle- and upper-middle class delinquent pattern.

The promiscuous or impersonal aspect of delinquency and the absence of any personal material benefit to the delinquent continues to baffle the person who seeks for causes. All that the individual delinquent can gain from vandalism is some sort of subjective feeling of gratification, but it is

[3] Walter C. Reckless, *The Crime Problem* (New York: Appleton-Century-Crofts, 1961), p. 368.

[4] "Juvenile Delinquency," *Report of the Committee on the Judiciary*, U.S. Senate, 85th Cong., 1st Sess. (Washington, D.C.: Government Printing Office, 1957), p. 129.

mostly an impersonal feeling, since the persons whose property has been damaged are largely unknown. It appears to be sufficient gratification that *somebody's* property has been damaged. It would appear, then, that psychiatric reasons rather than rational self-gain or simple revenge are at the root of vandalism. But what psychiatric problems? And why is gratification achieved in this way?

Gang Violence

The inimitable portrait of gang violence presented in *West Side Story* may be somewhat overplayed and some of the characters stereotyped, nonetheless the picture of juvenile irrationality and compulsive loyalty which this American classic reveals is *not* basically overdrawn. Nor is the pattern restricted to New York city, or for that matter exclusively to urban gangs. Rather generally across the country, groups of preadults organize into bands based upon territorial, racial, ethnic, class, and even religious bonds. Sometimes these gangs do violence to other gangs, sometimes engage in collective vandalism, but their most generic attributes are their spontaneous organization, their indulgence in delinquent acts, and their stubborn resistance to established methods of delinquent detection and control. Again, no one really knows the reasons for the growing violence, nor is there any consensus, even among the experts, as to how this form of delinquency can effectively be dealt with.

Summary

In this section we have presented some background understandings pertaining to juvenile delinquency under three general rubrics: (1) the nature of the adolescent and the world in which he lives; (2) the juvenile court tradition for dealing with the juvenile deviant, and (3) some of the newer modes of delinquent behavior which have recently complicated the problem. We turn our attention next to varying conceptions in our society concerning what should be done about the problem of delinquency.

PROPOSED SOLUTIONS

Everyone, it seems, has a solution for the adolescent problem. These solutions vary markedly in their approach, their basic assumptions, their feasibility, and certainly in their comprehension of the problem. Loosely classified, they seem to fall into two main categories: (1) repressive measures, and (2) constructive measures. A brief consideration of each type will enable almost anyone to supply further illustrations based upon his own observations of persons and communities with which he is familiar.

Repressive Measures

"Now, when I was a boy, parents got tough with kids. When I was seventeen, my father and I made a trip to the woodshed. . . ." Anyone can finish the sentence. So usually begins the "get-tough" orator. The supposition here is that there are adolescent problems because adolescents willfully refuse to follow what adults know to be appropriate courses of action, which, if followed, would solve all of the adolescents' problems. The trouble, as these persons see it, is that adolescents are willfully disobedient or heedless. Consequently, the correct course of action is to get tough with them. A student on a campus of 20,000 is involved in a traffic accident, and immediately the "get-tough" advocates wish to deny all students the right to drive cars! Juvenile delinquency authorities who try to solve personality difficulties by removing the causes are constantly subjected to ridicule for being "too easy" and "soft." The local newspaper plays up some juvenile delinquency, and the town fathers are barraged with petitions to invoke curfews requiring all persons under eighteen to be "off the streets" by 10 P.M.! Parents are admonished to make their children work harder, but no one knows how to *find* work enough in a five-room apartment for the mothers, much less for the children. And so on and on. What all of these measures have in common is a rather transparent disregard for (1) the need to examine the *causes* of the difficulty, and (2) the fact that times have changed and that, therefore, measures presumably appropriate to another era may no longer be appropriate to this one. The chief sociological significance of the "get-tough" policy is its nuisance value to the advocates of careful analysis of the problem and of intelligent effort to solve the problem in accordance with reality.

Constructive Measures

Under this caption are subsumed a number of widely variant proposals that have one basic and important attribute in common, namely, they seek to reduce some problem for the adolescent either by removing the cause or in some way counterbalancing it. Some of these proposals are undoubtedly more effective or more feasible than others, but this attribute of rational attack is the common ingredient.

IMPROVED PARENT EDUCATION. As we have seen earlier in this chapter, adolescent problems are largely mental hygiene problems and, as such, go back to the child-rearing practices of the adolescent's parents. It is important, therefore, that parents learn how and why the consequences of their child-rearing techniques do not show up today or tomorrow, but ten or twenty years from now. For example, it might solve today's disciplinary problem with Billy to compare Billy unfavorably with his older brother Jack, but if such disciplinary techniques create sibling rivalry in Billy, we may develop an adolescent who hates both his brother and his parents and is not too much at peace with anybody. This is undoubtedly an oversimplified illustration, but it is accurate as far as it goes, and typifies the point we are discussing. A very important part of this parental education should consist in teaching parents the necessity of not pushing children beyond their own real abilities and desires, because to do so is to aggravate adolescent turmoil.

EDUCATIONAL REFORM. There is great need for a more realistic approach in American education. Generally speaking the school system is unrealistically predicated on concepts of adolescence, how learning takes place, and ways to teach morality that are hopelessly out of line with our scientific knowledge about these things. Generally speaking, professional educators are aware of this but cannot institute reforms as rapidly as they would like for fear of incurring community disapproval. Regardless of the reason, however, the fact remains that we can do much better in implementing sound and realistic educational philosophies than we now do. The result would be a lessening of school failures, fewer "dropouts" in high school and college, less unhappiness about school work, and surely an improved mental hygiene in general.

FREE EDUCATION. It has been revealed by almost every relevant study made that numerous persons of talent are prevented from furthering their education because of inadequate funds. Not very many unskilled workers' families could afford to send a promising son to college, even if assured of his exceptional competency. It was recommended to the President by the Commission on Higher Education that there should be made available, on a competitive basis, a considerable number of scholarships at federal expense to insure the education of capable young men and women in the lower-income groups. The so-called G.I. educational program demonstrated that there are many persons of talent who wish to and can successfully attend college. The argument runs that they should be encouraged to do so, not only in their own interests but for the good of the nation as a whole.

IMPROVED COMMUNITY RECREATION. Adolescents, like adults, frequently have time on their hands. They have no desire, as a rule, to use it in antisocial or harmful ways, but they may do so because there is often no real alternative. Commercialized recreation does not fully meet the need, partly because of cost, but more importantly because it does not create, as a rule, sufficiently consuming and enduring interests. Accordingly, it is often argued that communities should provide extensive year-round public recreation for adolescents. While the total cost of such a program seems impressive, the per capita cost to the taxpayer is very low. Parks, playgrounds, athletic leagues, swimming pools, hobby clubs—the list is almost endless.

Not only do such activities use up available recreational time and super-abundant physical energies, but participation in them creates and cultivates recreational skills which may be useful and pleasurable over the years.

Other kinds of constructive proposals have been made. We have singled out these four as being fundamental, widespread, and typical of the approach.

ADOLESCENT PROBLEMS ARE
GENERIC TO THE SOCIETY

In separating the problem of the adolescent from the rest of the social problems of our time, we have of course committed a certain violation of reality. Most, if not all, of the adolescent's problems are present in the larger society and are only *reflected in* the adolescent. Problems of job frustration, bad mental health, and delinquent conduct are certainly not unique with the adolescent. They may even be less prevalent among adolescents than among adults, and may only be brought to a focus in adolescence because of our sharper scrutiny and stricter control of the young. Other problems, like the failure of the school to inspire a larger proportion of adolescents, are really not adolescent problems at all. They represent the failure of the society to do an effective job in rearing its own young. To be sure, the adolescent bears the brunt of adult ineptitude here as elsewhere, but this should not obscure the fact that the root cause is societal, not individual. It has been suggested that what we call "adolescent problems" are merely the outward sign of an unhealthy and inefficient society so far as rearing its young is concerned, that the troubled adolescent is the symptom, not the disease.

In the problem of the adolescent we find a cardinal expression of the sociological principle that a refusal to be realistic aggravates a social problem. Another way of saying this is that when values are predicated upon inaccurate and unrealistic assumptions, programs based on those values either fail to solve the problem or make it worse.

The foregoing paragraph may seem to oversimplify the adolescent problem. If we left the matter at that, it would, but we hasten to add that there is a second aspect which may be even more important. Numerous observers have pointed out that ours is a society trying to "face both ways," that is, we face choices that we will not make or cannot make. The alternatives may be dilemmas such as the following. We know the hazards of child labor, so we have abolished it. We now have the hazard of enforced adolescent idleness, especially among the lower-class adolescents. Who can prove which is worse? The dilemma is even more pronounced in the case of sex. We are aware of the hazards of early marriage, but what of the hazards of delayed marriage? Who can say in which course of action, fostering early marriage or delaying marriage, the greater social good lies? And, even if we can decide objectively, can we translate our decision into effective action, and are we prepared for the consequences of our decision? Both appear doubtful.

Dilemmas also appear with respect to philosophies of solution. We have pointed out that the "get-tough" philosophy breeds resentment, hostility, or further alienation from adults and from the values that adults are fostering. But a "get-soft" policy could conceivably be worse. What we have called constructive solutions sound good in theory, but may have consequences in fact that may render them impractical. Values are in great chaos: adolescents' needs versus archaic adult conceptions, adults of varying philosophy and familiarity with the problem working at cross-purposes. Meanwhile the problem persists.

CONCLUSION

Despite the unfortunate amount of "sloppy sentimentality" and equally sloppy malice written about the real and imagined problems of the adolescent, there is a certain grain of truth in some of the clichés. To the adolescent, whether delinquent or nondelinquent, the adult world is a new and complex one. Some things about this new and complex world the child is adequately taught, but in many respects he is not adequately prepared and sometimes is deliberately misprepared. There is a large amount of deliberate concealment of reality by adults, usually for the misguided but well-intentioned reason that this protects him. But concealment seldom works for long. When accurate perceptions dawn, the young adult is left not only to his own devices and to the newfound sophistication of his peers but feels cut off from adult sources of guidance by the fact that adults have not come clean with him in the first place. This applies not only to the "birds and bees" conception of sex but to the whole gamut of personal relations, routes to success, recreational modes, and the like. As every sophisticated adult knows, or ought to, the modern world is schizoid. Inconsistencies between practice and preachment occur on every hand and the discrepancies are frequently great. Schoolboy conceptions of democracy, justice, and success are early dashed on the rocks of reality, and this may have a good deal to do with the disillusionments that often are at the root of obvious wrongdoing.

Delinquency rates as measured by statistics should be understood to be as much a function of the amount and kind of repressive measures taken by the communities as they are accurate measures of actual delinquency. Certainly no realistic person should need to be told that, as with crime, there are a great many more delinquent acts than there are cases of apprehended and punished delinquents. The cynical adolescent who offers as part of his defense that he is only doing what countless others also are, but had the misfortune of getting caught, has the facts securely on his side.

This obviously cannot be taken to mean that his acts are any less delinquent or that the community can be casual about his delinquency, but it does nevertheless point up a solid fact of life.

Juvenile delinquency presents a familiar paradox of human behavior: It is normal but it cannot be tolerated. Just as it may be normal for a toddler to smash dishes and windows or choke the cat to death, so, much of the delinquency of preadults poses a threat both to life and property in the adult community and even to the delinquent himself. Because delinquency is in a measure a natural and normal condition in our society, it is here to stay, but eternal vigilance to minimize its effects, to reduce its incidence, and to save delinquents as much as is possible from their own immaturity is normal and natural too. The latter calls for truly creative effort in finding new modes for attacking the problem, but at the same time preserving the tremendous potentials in the lives of many of the young adults whose delinquency is often only a passing phase of a few years of their lives. In a certain idealistic sense, each delinquency is a tragedy and ought to be prevented. This is equally true for each illness. Yet a knowledgeable person must realize that in spite of all known efforts there will occur in fact, substantial incidences of both delinquency and illness. The challenge is to understand the problem better and to devise methods for reducing the incidence to the lowest possible level.

SUGGESTED READINGS

BLOCH, HERBERT A., and FRANK T. FLYNN, *Delinquency: The Juvenile Offender in America Today.* New York, Random House, 1956.

BUELL, BRADLEY, *Is Prevention Possible?* New York, Community Research Associates, Inc., 1959.

CLINARD, MARSHALL B., and ANDREW L. WADE, "Toward the Delineation of Vandalism as Sub-Type in Juvenile Delinquency," *Journal of Criminal Law, Criminology and Police Science,* 48:5 (1958), pp. 493–499.

DUNHAM, WARREN H., "The Juvenile Court: Contradictory Orientations in Processing Offenders," *Law and Contemporary Problems* (Summer 1958).

GLUECK, SHELDON, ed., *The Problem of Delinquency.* Boston, Houghton Mifflin Company, 1959.

JENKINS, RICHARD L., "Motivation and Frustration in Delinquency," *American Journal of Orthopsychiatry,* 27:3 (1957), pp. 528–537.

RECKLESS, WALTER C., *The Crime Problem.* 3d ed. New York, Appleton-Century-Crofts, 1961. Chapters 19, 20, 21.

RECKLESS, WALTER C., SIMON DINITZ, and ELLEN MURRAY, "Self Concept as an Insulator against Delinquency," *American Sociological Review,* 21:6 (1956), pp. 744–746.

ROBISON, SOPHIA M., *Juvenile Delinquency: Its Nature and Control.* New York: Holt, Rinehart and Winston, Inc., 1960.

SOME CONVENTIONAL DEVIATIONS 18

The title of this chapter suggests a logical, and to some extent also a socio-logical contradiction. The term *deviation* is generally conceded to refer to some minority practice that is in conflict with or in violation of established majority norms. The word *conventional* on the other hand, while less pre-cise, refers primarily to some widespread practice that, by implication at least, is a widespread mode. Yet the phrasing is apt. There do exist in American society a number of practices, often paralleled and sustained by established institutions, that are deviant in the sense that they run counter to law or to the established and sometimes also time-honored norms of this and other societies. Some of these folkways are so widespread as to suggest strongly, in the absence of definitive data, majority or near majority ob-servance; yet when interrogated the majority of people seem to say that the practices are ill advised, wrong, sinful, or otherwise taboo. In some instances there are long established laws as well as strong ecclesiastical rules against them, nonetheless the practices flourish, sometimes quite openly. Cases in point are prostitution, gambling, heavy alcoholic consumption, homosexu-ality and other sexual deviations—the list could be expanded considerably.

Needless to point out, these have all become problems to the society precisely because of discrepancies between practice and preachment, or more concretely, between the participants in these behaviors and those members of society who would deny them the right to so behave. Oddly enough, there is also a psychological dimension to the matter, since it is not uncommon for persons who behave in these conventionally deviant ways to assert, when asked, that such acts are undesirable and ought to be stopped, yet at the same time seem unable or unwilling to act in accordance with their own assertions. It all adds up to a curious confusion. It will be the purpose of this chapter to select four of these problem areas and to attempt to unravel such parts of the skein as research provides one with authority so to do. Specifically, we shall select from the larger group: alcoholism, sexual deviation, gambling, and prostitution.

The concept *norm of evasion* is useful in understanding many aspects of these problem areas. The gist of the matter seems to be that there co-exist in the society two contradictory cultural patterns—values, practices, social groupings, recruitment patterns, and all the rationalizations and protections to keep both a legitimate and a *sub rosa* system going. The realist must conclude that the basic value structure of our society is sufficiently pluralistic so that majority values, even when codified into law, cannot effectively control the behavior of minorities of substantial size who hold to contradictory values. In a literal sense there is an underworld, sometimes not very far submerged, of homosexuals, drug addicts, and their suppliers, prostitutes and their patrons, gambling interests and their various associated personnel, all of whom normally function in this and other societies. In order to operate as effectively as they do in the face of a hostile majority opinion, repressive laws, and even half-hearted policing, it is evident that their activities must fulfill the "needs" or desires of a clientele. Not as much is known about the nature of these needs, their genesis, or their elimination, but a few cause and effect inferences are reasonably well accepted among investigators and these will be pointed out from time to time in this chapter.

ALCOHOLIC CONSUMPTION AND ALCOHOLICS

There is no single problem of "alcohol" or "alcoholism"; rather the term refers to a vague collection of more or less separate and distinct "problems." Following are five more or less distinct focuses of attention, each of which involves one or more clashes of values with respect to (1) the existence or nonexistence of the alleged problem, (2) whether the problem ought to or can be "treated," and (3) what measures for treatment seem appropriate, feasible, and effective.

(1) To many in our society (no one knows how many) any and all consumption of alcoholic beverages in any form or any degree is categorically undesirable. Sometimes these persons and groups reason from religious and moral premises, and at other times from essentially practical, almost scientific premises. Regardless of the source of their value judgments, there is a "total abstinence" point of view in our society. Obviously, these persons and organizations are in direct opposition to others who see nothing wrong, morally *or* practically, with alcoholic consumption in varying degree.

(2) To other persons the main problem is to set up peripheral controls so that alcohol consumption is restricted to adults and to nonproblem drinkers. There is considerable difference of opinion as to the appropriate age to be considered as adult, and, of course, as to what the term "problem drinker" really means.

(3) "Regulation" of alcoholic consumption is the focus for others. The laws of almost every community stipulate hours and days of sale, kinds of businesses that may be licensed to sell alcoholic beverages, the location of dispensaries only at stipulated distances from schools and churches, and forbid the sale of alcohol to persons who show evidences of having already drunk excessively. Driving an automobile while intoxicated is almost everywhere a serious offense.

(4) To still others "the problem" is one of so educating and indoctrinating the population as to keep alcoholic consumption "under control" —at the "social drinking" level.

(5) There are those for whom the problem of alcohol is synonymous with the problem of the alcoholic—the compulsive consumer of alcohol, one who is an addict in the technical sense and who usually needs some kind of psychiatric and/or medical treatment, if he is to regain control of his own conduct.

In order to complete the picture of value confusion, it is also necessary to point out that despite a prodigious amount of research effort which has gone into the problem, we know very little reliably about what "causes" alcoholism—or for that matter the social drinker either—and how the problem drinker and the alcoholic should be treated in order to expedite "recovery." All kinds of theories, more or less scientific, abound, and no small amount of forensic endeavor and political machination has gone into one group's or another's efforts to impose programs of action, which are presumed to solve the "problem" as the proponents see it. It should be obvious to the objective student of the matter that many of these confidently endorsed programs have been conspicuously unsuccessful in practice (for example, prohibition), and, on a somewhat more sophisticated level, that courses of action in the absence of reliable knowledge about true causes are not likely to meet with much success. Some may easily worsen the situation.

The caution implied in the foregoing paragraph should certainly not be taken to mean that the various problems associated with the consumption of alcohol may not be serious either directly in the lives of many people or potentially so for everybody. The driver under the influence of alcohol, to take but one aspect of the problem, is a threat to the life and safety of everyone else who drives or rides in a car, or who walks along the sidewalk. Nevertheless to jump uncritically from the gravity of a problem to some a priori "solution" is neither intelligent nor practical.

The various problems of alcoholism are not likely to be materially eased and certainly not eliminated in our time. While our knowledge of cause and effect is, as we have said, exceedingly limited, enough is known to establish the inference that the roots of the problem lie deep in the society, and are therefore not amenable to any quick solution. Among these roots are at least the following:

(1) Established traditions and conventions like the cocktail party, the corner tavern, the night club, and the "night cap." For millions of Americans recreation is intimately associated with drinking. While, of course, problem drinking and alcoholism are not intended consequences, any more than automobile accidents are intended consequences of driving, they are accepted as inherent hazards in much the same way.

(2) The liquor industry itself is an important part of the American economy. Liquor, wine, and beer production, distribution, and advertising enterprises are enormous. Ironically enough, several American states support their educational systems in substantial measure either by taxing the liquor traffic heavily or by actually owning and operating liquor dispensaries.

(3) Harder to describe objectively is another underpinning for the consumption of alcohol that stems from the deeper psychological needs which it apparently fulfills. Perhaps in the amateur psychiatry of informal conversation, drinking for the purpose of "getting away from it all" is an oversimplification of a more complicated process. Nonetheless, it does point up an almost universally acknowledged fact that psychological discomfort of various kinds can be eased by drinking—at least temporarily—that many people generally know this, and that many act from this knowledge. Further buttressing this condition is the fact that the kind of work, play, and political orders within which most Americans live are fraught with deeply frustrating and tension-producing circumstances, many astute observers insisting that these frustrating circumstances are becoming more and more acute as time goes on. Men are typically alienated from their work, bored by too much leisure, discouraged by too little, unhappy for many reasons in their man-woman worlds, collectively fearful of the possibility of a nuclear holocaust, and in surprising numbers are in manifest degree mentally ill. The temporary escape through alcohol is to many people a more or less "rational" way of "learning to live with it all." Thus the "social drinker" is born.

It should be obvious by now that there is no sure, quick, or easy solution to whatever problems alcohol and alcoholism present. If solutions were easy, we would have no problem. Even the drastic solution, with the colossal power of the federal government behind it, of the prohibition (Eighteenth) amendment appears not to have been sufficient to solve the problem, but quite likely even worsened it. "Cures" like Alcoholics Anonymous and other more professionally directed programs and treatments solve the problem only for some, no one knows exactly what proportion, of those alcoholics who present themselves for treatment. The great majority of problem drinkers, and many alcoholics too, do not regard themselves in need of treatment, submit to none, and pursue their inefficient and troubled ways alone. Meanwhile, no one is satisfied with the state of affairs. The prohibitionists would like to see the whole business again declared illegal, either on a local option or on a national basis. The liquor industry, meanwhile, functions as a secure and powerful commercial and manufacturing enterprise. Governments collect colossal revenue and support important public enterprises out of liquor taxes or liquor distributing enterprises. Educational campaigns are waged against the evils of alcohol and on the importance of extreme moderation, yet the per capita consumption of alcoholic beverages continues to rise. The total situation is not only utterly confusing but shows no likelihood of important change in the foreseeable future.

GAMBLING

The term *gambling* derives from a popular rather than a technical nomenclature. It suggests a wide variety of activities—the penny ante poker game among friends, the church bingo party to buy playground equipment for the kids, legal gambling in Las Vegas, millionaire gambling at Monte Carlo, the "numbers racket," especially among the poorer and uneducated Negro communities, football pools, parimutuel betting at the races. What do all of these things have in common? The obvious answer is that they all represent, to the participant, risk taking in the form of relatively small investment with the prospect of relatively large return. It has been contended by many that this kind of playing with the odds is rooted deeply in human nature, by others that it is a perversion of rational intelligence. In any event, gambling in this and in other cultures as well, is widely practiced and in this culture especially, value judgments concerning its desirability and its consequences vary widely.

A number of distinctions are in order to achieve a more than pedestrian understanding. One relatively innocuous form of gambling operates among equals, where the odds are also equal and well understood, as in the case of the friendly poker game. Usually in this configuration the amounts of money wagered are relatively small and over a long period tend to be canceled out, with allowance, of course, for differential skill. At the opposite extreme is commercialized gambling, an enterprise engaged in by one party as a business, with the odds, therefore, necessarily less than equal for the two "players." Since there are laws and other traditions in our society that condemn this type of gambling, the industry tends to operate *sub rosa,* with some exceptions to be sure, and is frequently tied in with prostitution, drug traffic, and the vice racket congeries. This tends to be true even where gambling is legal and ostensibly supervised by the government. A further distinction, especially important to some, has to do with the ultimate purpose. Here three types are clearly manifest in the culture: (1) gambling chiefly for amusement with the odds equal and the stakes either purely nominal or financially innocuous; (2) gambling for charitable purposes, the proceeds acknowledgedly going to charitable or religious enterprises, the participants knowing this and also, therefore, that the probabilities of winning are reduced thereby; and (3) gambling as economic enterprise, with large stakes and a recognition that the maintenance of the structure is someone's commercial business. The latter is further subdivided into those activities like parimutuel betting at the racetracks, which are quite legal, and other forms of gambling like "numbers," which are in most places illegal. The participant in these latter can hardly help knowing that he is functioning in illegal activity.

Value conflicts concerning gambling are so numerous as almost to defy listing in a general work of this sort. We shall, however, make an attempt at a partial listing of some of the grosser juxtapositions in American society at this time.

1. The most extreme value position is that of the person who categorically disapproves of gambling—all kinds, all forms, for everyone.

2. A second position, close to this but seemingly more realistic, recognizes that the conventional forms of gambling do not exhaust the practice of gambling. For example, various forms of business enterprise, particularly "playing the stock market," have many aspects of gambling: outcomes are uncertain even for the expert; if purchase is on margin, the ratio of potential profit to original investment is great; there is considerable evidence also that the temptation to manipulate, cheat, or otherwise interfere with the process is sufficiently strong so that constant vigilance on the part of the government is required to regulate even this quite legitimate economic institution. Other forms of "business"—where the venture capital is, indeed, venturesome—may assume the structure of a gambling rather than a more normally legitimate enterprise. How is one to draw the line? Can a line be drawn?

3. There is a substantial opinion in American society that all forms of *commercial* gambling should be outlawed and by diligently enforced laws. Persons with this view typically feel frustrated for two reasons. First, because in the present haphazard legal system some kinds of gambling are illegal, while other kinds are legal, the variations occurring from state to state. It is very difficult, consequently, to make a strong case for the wrongness of acts on which there is so small a degree of consensus. What is even

worse to these people is that everywhere there are seemingly equivocal laws, enforcement is atrocious in some communities, and a "wide open" *sub rosa* gambling enterprise flourishes. In the second place, there is objection to the apparently enormous profit of the successful gambling enterprise, which together with the already mentioned tie-in with prostitution, illicit liquor and drug traffic, sets up a racketeering empire which is almost untouchable by established legal machinery. It is argued by some that the most vulnerable aspect of the unholy alliance is gambling and that if this financial underpinning were completely extirpated, it would be easier to handle the others.

4. There is also a body of opinion, no one knows how large numerically, that obviously must condone gambling since its patrons are numerous and some of them prestigious. Here again one must use the evidence of action rather than words, for everywhere the analyst of social behavior encounters the familiar dualism—one set of negative opinions and a contrary set of actual behavior. This is not to deny, however, that there is a body of articulate opinion that purports to see nothing wrong with wide open gambling. A minority of this group have openly stated that since the urge to gamble seems to be so deeply entrenched in "human nature," the society might as well face this fact and have all gambling enterprises run by the government, thus permitting the tremendous profits to accrue to the public treasury. The "tax income" would obviously be enormous. At least three American states (New Hampshire, Nevada, and until 1965 under current legislation, Maryland) have legalized gambling in one form or another.

5. Finally, there are the compromise value positions. There are those who disapprove of gambling but reluctantly grant that others approve and insist on practicing it. The compromise position then is one of "regulation" —classified forms and places of gambling, supervision of the gambling machinery and financial records of gambling enterprise, the location of gambling institutions, and a host of other devices, some of which are actually in effect in particular places.

Quite obviously, then, the situation is confused. Individuals are not necessarily confused but the coexistence of so many radically different value positions and assumptions of fact underlying them make it almost impossible to reach collective agreement even on fundamentals.

The parallel to alcohol and alcoholism is striking. There are in both cases the total abstainers. Paralleling the social drinkers are the petty gamblers who play for fun, seldom risking much or gaining much. There are the problem gamblers like the problem drinkers, who occasionally get out of hand doing themselves and others serious damage. And at the extreme there are the gambling addicts who, like the alcoholics, operate outside the realm of rationality and present a miserable picture of human entrapment. The life histories of such persons are strewn in the same ignoble remnants of ruined potential, broken careers, compromised health, poor interpersonal relations, just about the whole spectrum of human misery. Finally, there is the organized, institutional enterprise that supplies the consumer for gain. The liquor and gambling industry apologists say simply, and technically correctly, that both these industries produce only what the customers want and actually have little to gain and much to lose from the behavior of persons who consume their services to excess. Yet the companion fact remains that the enterprises do exist and in their existence provide a kind of *de facto* legitimation for participation by the members of society. They present their commodities attractively and to a certain extent create or at least encourage wants on the part of the consumers. This is a part of normal American business technique; yet to be altogether frank about the matter, the gambling and liquor industries actually have fewer avenues of advertising and public relations open to them than do their competitors for the American public's time and money.

No one but the most naïve expects the gambling problem, any more than the liquor problem, to be solved in our time, however one chooses to define their problem aspects. This does not mean that there may not be gains in mutual understanding and some kinds of compromises among persons and groups of differing positions, which may at least have the effect of narrowing the areas of confusion. The problem is solved for many people by avoidance—by association with persons of like-mindedness and by largely ignoring, to the extent possible, what persons of other persuasions do. Finally, as we have pointed out again and again in this book, a great many people solve the problem of their own confusion and inconsistency by living in two logic-tight compartments—idealization, taking the form of pious preachment particularly when talking to the young, and pragmatic practices that often depart markedly therefrom.

SEXUAL "DEVIATIONS"

For a variety of reasons the professionally known extent of sexual "deviation" tends to be played down by others. Perhaps the best evidence that this is the case was brought out when the famous Kinsey reports were made public. Most professionals were not surprised by the proportions of the population who had or had not performed various unapproved acts. Lay people, on the other hand, as well as professionals operating in protected environments, were astounded and said so. (It is a curious reinforcement of this point that when faced with a discrepancy between personal impressions and carefully collected data, the discrepancy is solved for many not by acknowledging their innocence but by questioning the accuracy, if not even the integrity, of the scientists who made the study.) It is not our purpose here to catalogue the extent and kinds of sexual deviation that the Kinsey and other reliable studies have revealed. We simply make the summary point that such verbally disapproved practices as the following are exceedingly common in American society; coitus between persons unmarried, coitus between pairs, one or both of whom are married to someone else, homosexuality, forms of sexual gratification often called perversions actually widely practiced as supplementary or substitutive of what is regarded as normal sexual behavior, and, of course, prostitution in its many forms.

Reactions to these facts bring out a wide variety of differing value positions. At the one extreme it is held that these data are highly encouraging, since they indicate that many persons have found it possible to free themselves from what are regarded in their view, as oppressive, Victorian, unduly inhibitive and archaic expectations for human conduct. At the other extreme the fact that so many people defy the God-given eternal verities for male and female conduct is considered abhorrent. In between, of course, are many other positions. Some people simply believe that what a couple do in their intimate relationship ought to be "their own business," but often qualify the statement in terms of the age of the participants and the nature of relationship within which the behavior takes place. Almost any group can be brought into serious controversy when someone brings up some aspect of sexual behavior and focuses on whether it is to be approved or disapproved, and why.

This raises again the whole question concerning the legitimacy of the use of the term *deviant*. The confusions are no mere quibble over decimal points or adjectives. If, for example, "deviation" represents minority practice, then one must be prepared for the conclusion that certain *approved* behaviors are by definition the "deviant" ones. Thus, abstinence from the use of contraceptive devices and probably also premarital chastity would need to be called "deviant" in American society, at least certainly so with respect to large and influential subgroups. Sometimes, however, the term *deviant* is used in a moralistic sense, that is, the deviant is the person who does the disapproved thing, whether such actions are majority or minority practice. Then there is the whole question of deviation *from which set* of moral dictates—Catholic or Protestant, liberal or traditional, existential or more austere?

One must conclude that there is a curious ambivalence, so widespread in American society as to be regarded as almost typical, concerning sex conduct. Actual behavior and statements of what ought to be are in sharp contrast, not only for various groups in the society but for many specific individuals within it. Kinsey pointed out, for example, almost as an aside, that he had observed the most condemnatory attitudes concerning certain deviations on the part of the people who had practiced them with greatest impunity. Moreover, there is a general anxiety about sex which innumerable professionals have pointed out. No one seems satisfied with the situation as he sees it, notwithstanding the fact that the situation is seen differentially in the first place. Some hold that our problem is sexual inhibition, others that it is sexual license. Parents are said to be too vague and dishonest and withholding in the sex education of their children; others say that they are too frank, indelicate, and forthright. Thus, the realistic observer of the scene shares the same kind of ambivalence, only perhaps for different reasons. It has been pointed out many times that American society does not seem to know where it is going or where it wants to go, and there is certainly license for such a view. In this maelstrom of disputed fact, disputed morality, and inconsistent judgment and practice, it is exceedingly difficult, if one is realistic, to avoid such contradictory phrasings as the "conventional deviation." Some observers have gone so far as to call it a schizoid configuration.

PROSTITUTION

Prostitution in the United States has followed an interesting pattern of oscillation between the opposed values of health and morality, on the one hand, and business interests and sexual desires, on the other. Until about the second decade of the twentieth century business and sex dominated societal treatment of prostitution, and it was permitted to exist relatively undisturbed in the segregated districts of most American cities. The antivice campaign that preceded World War I, however, forced public officials to cease open toleration of prostitution. This brought about the concealing, not the permanent closing, of houses of prostitution.

During World War II the federal government was empowered to proceed against prostitution in military and defense factory centers. This forced local authorities to curb much more efficiently and consistently than they had previously the business of prostitution. Hence, as an open practice, prostitution almost disappeared during World War II. Although the wartime federal powers of enforcement on local authorities have been continued, the effectiveness is apparently gradually falling below the wartime level.[1]

Changing Types of Prostitution

Today it may be difficult (but by no means impossible) to go down to the "red-light" district of a major American city and point out the houses of prostitution. We rarely read of unsuspecting and naïve girls being lured from home and forced into a great prostitution ring by "white slavers." Even the somewhat overweight and overrouged "street walker" is less seldom seen. There is some evidence that the form of prostitution may have changed; this does not necessarily mean that the extent has been reduced.

[1] Walter C. Reckless, *The Crime Problem* (New York: Appleton-Century-Crofts, 1950), pp. 222–223.

Where once the prostitute more or less openly plied her trade individually or was connected with a "house," now she may be quietly and anonymously living in her own apartment where she is informed where and when to meet a customer. A number of "call girls" may be loosely organized by some central figure who makes "appointments" for them, or the individual prostitute may make her own arrangements for securing contacts with potential customers. It is always difficult to obtain accurate information on the extent of prostitution and the activities of prostitutes. And this is particularly true of the clandestine activities of the "call girl." It is well to remember that lack of obvious signs of prostitution does not necessarily mean that the activity does not exist.

Sources of Prostitution

One of the chief sources of prostitution would seem to be the desire on the part of a considerable number of males for an easily achieved, nonbinding sexual outlet and their willingness to pay for such an outlet. Without this demand, the supply of prostitutes would quickly disappear.

This desire of some males for such sexual experiences as prostitutes may provide is aided by various business interests not directly involved in prostitution itself. Hotel employees, taxicab operators, restaurant proprietors and waiters, bartenders, and various other types of commercial persons know that there is "money in it for them," directly or indirectly, if they can provide their customers with or refer them to prostitutes.

A third factor is the belief on the part of girls themselves that prostitution is an easier way to make a living than other pursuits open to them. However correct or mistaken the particular girl may be in this judgment, the belief undoubtedly lures many into the occupation.

With demand set up in the form of males ready to pay, with channels of communication improved by greedy merchants, and with the lure of "easy money," the girl herself still has to be vulnerable to such attractions. The girls from whom prostitutes are recruited seem to be, to a large extent, those who come from poor social backgrounds, who have mental or emotional inadequacies (low intelligence, high degree of emotional immaturity, psychopathic tendencies, and the like), who have had previous sexual experience (mostly unfortunate), and who have had contact with persons in or on the fringe of prostitution.[2]

Effects of Prostitution

Whatever the beginning of the road to prostitution for the woman, the chances of demoralization, ultimately to be a derelict, are great. A few prostitutes probably permanently improve their economic and social status.

[2] *Ibid.*, pp. 228–230.

Others get out in time to escape the occupational hazards. But it would appear that most meet with one or more of the following undesirable consequences: "arrests and institutional sentences, venereal infection, sickness, gynecological complications, marginal living, alcoholism, drug addiction, and so forth." [3]

The effects of prostitution on the rest of society are less easily discerned. According to the official morality of the ages, prostitution is an unmitigated vice. And yet, side by side with this morality, sometimes openly and sometimes partially hidden, prostitution has continued to exist. What the effect on the strength and health of society is of this perpetual clash of values, and the hypocrisy behind which many members of society hide in an attempt to deny the clash, is difficult to ascertain. That the effect is undesirable to some degree can scarcely be disputed.

Suppression and Prevention

As with any social problem, the reduction or elimination of prostitution postulates a strong public opinion in favor of the laborious study and effective action necessary. Such public opinion has never been consistently present in American society (or, for that matter, in any other large urban society). Any program of complete suppression or prevention would seem to be out of the question.

Some methods for reducing the number of active prostitutes are (1) insistence on federal surveillance of local officials with the same diligence as was accomplished during World War II (this is legally possible through the permanent extension in 1946 of the May Act); (2) reestablishment of social-protection assistance to the states of the type used during the war; (3) more adequate readjustment programs for sex-delinquent girls in juvenile courts and training schools; (4) better assistance to the unattached or stranded woman in finding employment, lodging, and approved recreations; (5) surveillance and protection of female workers and patrons in taverns, restaurants, bars, and other places of moral hazard; (6) creation and application of a more effective sex-education program in the public schools; and (7) provision of far-reaching marriage, vocational, and educational counseling programs.

Such activities as the foregoing would take more time, money, and effort than the American people are now ready to expend. So long as anything less than these things are done, however, any long-term reduction of prostitution seems unlikely.

---

[3] *Ibid.,* p. 234.

SUGGESTED READINGS

BACON, SELDEN D., ed., special issue on "Understanding Alcoholism," *Annals of the American Academy of Political and Social Science* (January 1958).

BERGLER, EDMUND, M.D., *Homosexuality: Disease or Way of Life?* New York, Hill and Wang, Inc., 1956.

ERIKSON, KAI T., "Notes on the Sociology of Deviance," *Social Problems,* 9:4 (Spring 1962), pp. 307–314.

GINSBERG, M., "The Enforcement of Morals," *British Journal of Sociology,* 1961, 12:1 (March 1961), pp. 65–68.

JELLINEK, E. M., "Social, Cultural and Economic Factors in Alcoholism," *Quarterly Journal for the Study of Alcoholism,* 21:4 (December 1960), pp. 565–583.

KITSUSE, JOHN I., "Societal Reaction to Deviant Behavior: Problems of Theory and Method," *Social Problems,* 9:3 (Winter 1962), pp. 247–256.

PLOSCOWE, MORRIS, and EDWIN J. LUKAS, eds., special issue on "Gambling," *Annals of the American Academy of Political and Social Science* (May 1950).

REISS, IRA L., *Premarital Sexual Standards in America.* New York, The Free Press of Glencoe, 1960.

SCHUR, EDWIN M., "Drug Addiction in America and England," *Commentary,* 30:3 (September 1960), pp. 241–248.

SEELEY, JOHN R., "Alcoholism Prevalence: An Alternative Estimation Method," *Quarterly Journal for the Study of Alcoholism,* 1960, 21:3 (September 1960), pp. 500–505.

STATE OF CALIFORNIA DEPARTMENT OF MENTAL HYGIENE, *California Sexual Deviation Research.* Sacramento, California State Printing Office, 1953.

"SYMPOSIUM ON ALCOHOLISM," *Social Problems,* 5 (Spring 1958), pp. 292–338.

ZOLA, IRVING K., "Observations on Gambling in a Lower-Class Setting," *Social Problems,* 10:4 (Spring 1963), pp. 353–361.

PRESSURE GROUPS 19

To some, the expression "pressure group" conveys the image of a sinister group of men who lurk about the halls of government trying, more by foul means than fair, to coerce legislators to vote "their way." In reality, however, a pressure group is simply a special interest group that attempts to impose its policies on the larger society. Its policies can be good or evil, its techniques subtle or direct, and its membership can be large or small. As long as one of the purposes of the organization is to compete for power and influence in the give and take between the government and the governed, it can rightly be called a pressure group.

If everyone had the same interests and held them with equal intensity there would scarcely be a need for special groups to exert "pressures" in behalf of these interests. Thus, the existence of pressure groups represents the crystallization of value conflict; to ignore such groups and their activities would be to ignore some of the noisiest, if not the most severe, value clashes in American society. In addition to the value conflict manifested by the divergent interests of pressure groups, there is some evidence of a clash of values concerning the *fact* of pressure groups. That is, regardless of why or what they are "pressuring," some hold that such groups are not only unnecessary but downright "dangerous." Others see pressure groups as completely compatible with democracy and indeed part of the "American way" of getting things done. But it seems that not everyone on either "side" of the issue fully understands the nature and workings of pressure groups. In this chapter, then, we will take a look at the activities and operations of pressure groups and investigate some of the major groups in existence today. We will then be in a position to evaluate the extent to which such activities constitute a "problem."

THE NATURE OF PRESSURE GROUPS

We have said that a pressure group can be defined as an organization engaged in the struggle for the control of power. Pressure groups work to protect or to further the interests and privileges of *certain* people. Frequently the "certain people" are a specific segment of the population with similar economic or occupational interests. But pressure groups also have been formed to protect or further a host of values other than strictly economic ones. Some examples of such groups that immediately come to mind are the Anti-Saloon League, the Anti-Vivisection Society, and the Council on Christian Social Progress.

Scope of Pressure Group Activities

Pressure groups vary, too, with regard to their scope and power. The "big" groups like the National Association of Manufacturers and the American Medical Association are fairly well known, but the majority of pressure groups are far more limited in scope. The activities of the Clothespin Manufacturers of America or the Committee Against Discrimination on Small Catalog Postage Rates are relatively specific and restricted. Occasionally pressure groups are at least purportedly organized in the interests of the whole citizenry. The American Civil Liberties Union is an example of this type of pressure group, for it "pressures" for the defense and advancement of the civil rights of all citizens.

Growth of Pressure Groups

The federal Regulation of Lobbying Act of 1946 requires the registration of all organizations collecting money to be used to influence legislation by Congress.[1] Any individual paid to influence legislation must also register and must state his employer and his purpose. The resulting list of paid lobbyists becomes a matter of public record. Despite this convenient catalogue of lobbyists, we still do not know how many pressure groups exist in our society. There are several reasons for this. In the first place, a pressure group could operate without a Washington lobby; it could attempt to promote its interests solely through other channels, such as by attempting to mold opinion through mass-media advertising. In the second place, the existing law has sufficient "loopholes" to allow an estimated 75 percent of paid lobbyists to remain unregistered without fear of reprisals. Presumably many such lobbyists represent real pressure groups.

[1] For the text of the Lobbying Act see Franklin L. Burdette, *Lobbyists in Action* (Manassas, Va.: National Capitol Publishers, 1950), appendix.

Judging from their increasing numbers, there is some justification for the belief that pressure groups are fast becoming the third house of Congress. Today over 500 organizations have registered under the Lobbying Act. This represents an increase of one third over 1941 and is more than double the number of pressure groups thought to be in existence twenty-five years ago.[2]

More important than sheer numbers, however, is the amount and extent of influence exerted by pressure groups. It is interesting that some of the most notorious victories of pressure groups involved an influential and vociferous minority influencing legislation that affected the country as a whole. The famous Yazoo land frauds of the early 1800s cost the taxpayers $8 million, the sum voted by Congress as compensation to a handful of land speculators. No less a personage than the Postmaster General acted as lobbyist for the claimants. Americans will long remember, too, the powerful influence of the Anti-Saloon League. Judging from the initial response to prohibition and its eventual repeal, the wishes of the majority of Americans were ignored or misconstrued on this issue.

Many more famous or infamous examples of influential pressure groups can be gleaned from history. There is some evidence, however, that pressure groups are becoming increasingly more influential. Literally millions of dollars are spent annually by pressure groups in their twofold task of shaping public opinion and directly influencing legislation. If we turn to an examination of the "workings" of pressure groups, we shall gain a better idea of just how influential and important such groups have become.

THE WORKINGS OF PRESSURE GROUPS

In order to impose their policies on the larger society, pressure groups operate in two general ways: (1) by attempting to influence and mold public opinion, and (2) by striving to influence government agencies, particularly the legislative branches. These channels are by no means completely separable. A public conditoned by the activities of a pressure group may itself elect legislators who hold the values it has been taught are "right." Again, a pressure group working to defeat a bill before Congress may attempt both to influence legislators directly and to "educate" the public who, in turn, may let their views be known to their representatives.

[2] Data on lobbies taken from House of Representatives, House Select Committee on Lobbying Activities, *Lobby Index* (Washington, D.C.: Government Printing Office, 1950). Data on lobbying activities in earlier years cited in Donald C. Blaisdell, "Government Under Pressure," Publc Affairs Pamphlet No. 67, New York, Public Affairs Committee, 1946.

Influencing Public Opinion

Pressure groups cannot ignore public opinion. New laws can be "pressured through" or attempts at legislation can be blocked by frontal attacks upon legislators, but a sufficiently aroused public can undo both. In the long run, a pressure group is better off if it manages to mold public opinion to its liking. If it can sell an idea to the public, or arouse public opinion on an issue, or sometimes just create good will for its interests, the pressure group has a chance of making a stronger and more lasting impression on the American scene.

The specific techniques used to influence public opinion are many. Even a superficial survey of advertisements in magazines and newspapers shows that many are selling ideas rather than, or in addition to, products. An industrial organization may utilize a full newspaper page to explain its version of the "American way." A union may buy newspaper space to present "labor's side" of a current management-labor dispute. The public utilities annually spend hundreds of thousands of dollars for disseminating the message that it is somehow better, and even more American, for power to be produced by "investor-owned" companies rather than by the government. Not many people, probably, have failed to notice the seemingly perpetual attempts by both the railroads and interstate trucking associations to convince the public that *the other group* pays too few taxes or otherwise has an unfair advantage due to existing laws. The aim of both groups is the same —to create a sympathetic attitude toward the group and, ultimately, popular support for legislation favorable to its special interests.

Pressure groups are well aware of the potential value of the written word for molding public opinion. Such special interest groups prepare pamphlets, books, and periodicals which they distribute themselves or through other groups sympathetic with their purpose. The true extent of the quantity distribution of such materials is amazing. The Committee for Constitutional Government set its sights on distributing 2½ million copies of a single book, *The Road Ahead*.[3] The National Association of Real Estate Boards was so pleased with the contents of the pamphlet, "Roofs or Ceilings," published by the Foundation for Economic Education, that it purchased 500,000 copies for distribution through local member boards.[4] During one nine-month period, the National Association of Manufacturers produced over 800,000 copies of forty-five pamphlets, booklets, leaflets, and the like. Obviously, such efforts at mass persuasion are costly, and can only be engaged in by the larger and wealthier groups.

[3] Daniel Katz *et al.*, eds., *Public Opinion and Propaganda* (New York: Holt, Rinehart, and Winston, 1954), p. 217.
[4] *Ibid.*

It is not always easy to recognize the source or sponsor of attempts at opinion molding. A pressure group may be organized as an educational foundation, thereby being exempt from federal taxes, and, in addition, it may publish with a certain anonymity or at least obscurity. Even if the name of the organization appears on the literature, the average citizen may not realize the intent of the organization, or the source of its support. For example, the major function of the Foundation for Economic Education was described by a Congressional committee investigating its activities as "the preparation of pamphlets, booklets, and articles presenting one side of public issues." [5] This foundation, which considers its functions as purely educational, receives the bulk of its support from "big business." It has published such titles as *So You Believe in Rent Control?, The TVA Idea,* and *Illusions of Point Four.* An estimated total of 4 million booklets and pamphlets were distributed by the foundation during its first four years of operation. During this time it received about two thirds of its support from twenty large business organizations and the remainder chiefly from a number of other similar organizations. Although the foundation prints its name on its publications, it is unlikely that many of the message recipients recognize its sponsorship or are aware of the Buchanan Committee's conclusion that it consistently presents but one side of public issues. And this is but one example. It is doubtful that an impartial committee would judge many of the publications of the former CIO Political Action Committee as anything but one-sided. Sometimes the public fares even less well, for the message it reads or hears is apparently unsponsored. Some group is behind it, but which one? Somebody has paid for it, but who? The simple fact is that educators, clergy, labor leaders, and millions of private citizens are almost constantly being exposed to the opinion-molding activities of pressure groups. Frequently, the sponsorship of the activities is obscure or unknown.

Many private citizens probably are not aware that some of the editorials and columns they read in their local newspaper have been prepared, wholly or in part, by a special interest group, and that the identical information was sent to newspapers across the land. An example of just such a tactic is recorded in the report of the House Select Committee on Lobbying Activities: [6]

> An even bolder example of stereotyped materials is provided by the "Sylvester Says" series of the National Retail Lumber Dealers Association. These quarter column releases, many of which take stands on legislative issues, are distributed in mats to 1,400 newspapers by Western Newspaper Union, a nationwide syndicated news service. The source is indicated on the mat, but not in the individual releases. In this way, the lumber dealers

[5] Reported in Karl Schriftgiesser, *The Lobbyists* (Boston: Little, Brown and Company, 1951), p. 180.
[6] Katz, *op. cit.,* p. 219.

have presented their views to at least 4,000,000 readers who had no inkling of the material's source.

Political, Legislative, and
Administrative Pressures

Many pressure groups do not restrict themselves to the shaping of public opinion but carry on activities more directly related to the influencing of actual legislation. If its policies are reflected in laws, the pressure group has come a long way in the struggle for power and influence. In their attempts at influencing legislation, pressure groups operate at various levels and employ a host of techniques.

PRESSURE GROUPS AND POLITICAL PARTIES. Pressure groups do not usually form political parties with their own total platforms and their own slates of candidates. Rather, working through existing parties, they attempt to influence the party policies and to elect the "right" candidates. No political party can completely ignore the views of large organized pressure groups. Such groups are powerful and may be able to influence a sizable bloc of voters. Such groups also may make sizable financial contributions to the party. Party platform drafters sometimes find diametrically opposed pressure groups clamoring for their attentions. They can either "choose up sides," or, more likely, they can write their party policies with sufficient lack of lucidity to accomplish the well-known feat of fence straddling. But while party platform drafters may keep one ear tuned to the large but somewhat vague "public," it is politically expedient that the other give its attention to the vociferous minority represented by pressure groups.

If the pressure group fails to exert its influence at the platform-drafting stage, there is always the matter of election. The pressure group does not usually endorse a particular party consistently or even all members of a party in a given election. The best pressure group is nonpartisan, or better, omnipartisan. Its work must continue regardless of the party in power. During a give election, however, a pressure group may well openly support one candidate and oppose another. Its force and skill in propaganda may be aimed at the outcome of an election. The pressure group's financial contribution to individual or party "war chests" can be important at this stage. Thus, by influencing party platforms and by helping to elect legislators and administrators who are friendly toward its interests, legislation unfavorable to pressure group interests can be prevented from ever making its appearance.

MAINTENANCE OF A LOBBY. The expression "lobby" obviously grew out of the name for a public waiting room where persons could meet and attempt to influence public officials. A lobby thus consists of those who attempt to bring pressure on public officials, particularly legislators. Lobbying is as old as legislation, it is legal, and it is big. We have already commented upon some of the influential lobbies of the past. These and their modern counterparts operate within the law, protected by the first amendment to the Constitution which provides that Congress shall make no law abridging the people's right to petition the government for a redress of grievances.

Lobbyists use various techniques in their attempts to assure the passage of legislation. It is well known that many of the bills introduced by members of Congress have been painstakingly prepared by the legal force of a lobby. When a bill reaches the committee stage, the lobbyist can often exert sufficient pressure to bring about a public hearing on the bill. If the hearing is granted, the lobbyists may arrive like a well-tutored and effective sales team. Hours of preparation allow the lobbyist to have on hand minute facts about the bill in question, the testimony of influential citizens, and perhaps the results of public opinion polls conducted at the expense of the lobby. The material is usually artfully presented and witnesses are strategically introduced. Lobbying is a big business; it is also something of an art and a science.

Pressure groups also maintain lobbies in Washington and state capitals to attempt to *prevent* passage of legislation contrary to their aims and purposes. The lobbying techniques may be similar to those employed when acting *for* passage of a bill. The lobby becomes thoroughly acquainted with the proposed measure and its legality and is prepared to exert pressures at various points to assure that the bill never becomes a law. The "tricks of the trade" are legion and many are apparently quite effective. Lobbies have instigated the timely arrival of thousands of messages from the legislator's own constituents demanding the defeat of a bill. What legislator can remain impervious to the opinions of his supporters even though it may have taken a strong pressure group to create or intensify the opinions?

PRESSURE AT OTHER POINTS. If the battle to prevent the passage of inimical legislation, or to render it relatively ineffective by "crippling amendments," is lost, pressure groups by no means withdraw from the fight. Veto of the legislation by the administration can be sought, and, failing that, adequate appropriations for administering the new law can be prevented, and, failing that, pressure may be brought to bear for the appointment of administrators of the law who are friendly to the pressure group. Furthermore, the act may be repealed or rendered ineffective by later legislation. And, as a last resort, interpretations of the law may be made by the courts that reduce or remove its disagreeable characteristics.

MAJOR PRESSURE GROUPS
IN THE UNITED STATES

As indicated previously there are literally hundreds of pressure groups actively at work in the United States. The pressure groups we have selected for further analysis are important because taken together they frequently represent major value clashes, they collectively include a large number of people, and they are apparently quite powerful. These groups fall into three major divisions: (1) business, led by the National Association of Manufacturers and the Chamber of Commerce of the United States, (2) organized labor, major representatives of which are the combined American Federation of Labor–Congress of Industrial Organizations, the United Mine Workers, the International Brotherhood of Teamsters, and the railway brotherhoods, and (3) farmers, represented principally by the National Grange, the American Farm Bureau Federation, the National Farmers' Union, and the National Farmers Organization.

Business, the "American Ruling Class"

Some four hundred national organizations have permanent representatives in Washington, and a preponderant number of these groups are directly or indirectly attached to general or specific business interests. Business pressure groups are of two types, principal and satellite. The former range from groups lobbying for interests that business enterprises hold in common (Chamber of Commerce and National Association of Manufacturers) down to specific business or industrial interests (Edison Electric Institute's lobby, National Coal Association, American Short Line Railroad Association, and the like). The satellite groups are many of the professional associations, revolving about business and partly dependent upon it for their support (American Bankers Association, American Pharmaceutical Association, American Bar Association, American Newspaper Publishers Association, and the like).

Although there have been and continue to be challenges, the business control of power has been such, at least since the Civil War, that many students believe business may be properly referred to as the "ruling class." Social critics hold that, since power has come to reside largely in the hands of business, most of its activities as a class, especially in its manifestations as a pressure group on government, have been to maintain that power.

PUBLIC "GOOD WILL." Power rests ultimately upon public acceptance of it, and business has come more and more to realize the importance of a public opinion favorably disposed toward it. In a social environment traditionally hostile to monopolies, business has been able to achieve and maintain a tremendous accumulation of power and apparently to concentrate the control of this power into ever fewer hands. It is contended that through various propagandistic channels, both revealed and concealed, the public has been led to believe that general social welfare and business-class welfare are synonymous, that, in other words, the interests of society in general are identical with the interests of the business class.

LEGISLATIVE BATTLES. Any bills proposed for significantly extending the power of any other group, be it farmer, labor, government, consumer, or the general public, arouse open or covert business opposition. When a group has obtained a position of overwhelming power in a society, its chief function inevitably becomes the protection of that power from either direct reduction or indirect reduction (through extension of more power relatively to other groups in the society).

As seen above, the main pressure of business has apparently been brought to bear against proposed legislation directly or indirectly limiting its power, but it has also sought to extend its power through positive legislation. The chief type of positive legislation successfully advocated has been the protective tariffs, which amount to an indirect subsidy. Some businesses, notably the shipping industry, have obtained direct governmental subsidy.

ADVANTAGES OF BUSINESS IN THE STRUGGLE FOR POWER. As principally obstructors of legislation, however, business pressure groups have had a tremendous advantage over other class interests in their propagandistic and lobbying activities. Because of the human tendency to cling to the comforts of the customary, it is almost always easier to convince people of the undesirability, rather than the desirability, of experimenting with new social patterns. The greater burden of proof tends to fall upon the proponent, not the opponent, of change. It is only when a people is close to desperation (as in the early days of the New Deal) that it is very receptive to tampering with the status quo.

Linked to this fundamental advantage of business is the equally important one of great financial resources. Not only is the bulk of the nation's wealth represented by business, but a very considerable percentage of the wealth is concentrated in a relatively few large corporations. Since in our society wealth and power are to a considerable extent inseparable, the amount of pressure that can be brought to bear upon the American people and their government by business in general and large corporations in particular is terrific. By no accident, business lobbies are the most consistently successful lobbies. We are reminded of the adage concerning the relationship between the ability to pay a piper and the privilege of calling tunes.

These two outstanding advantages of the business class can be successfully combated on specific issues only by an intensely and consistently aroused public opinion contrary to the position of business on these issues. It is rarely that such arousal of opinion occurs with sufficient intensity and staying power to combat the powers of business. So consistently, in fact, are the American people given propaganda friendly to business that nothing short of crises of the magnitude of a major economic depression or a war seems to bring about the passing of legislation fundamentally curtailing the control of power by the business class.

It is not here contended that business always uses its control of power in efforts that are contrary to the public welfare or that all legislation inimical to the interests of business is for the public good. Much proposed regulatory legislation is probably unworkable, and much more is undoubtedly suggested and undertaken without sufficient information in regard to the complicated problems and possible consequences involved. We have merely attempted to demonstrate that the *balance of power in pressure politics is heavily weighted in favor of the business class* and that this class pressures for its own interests, whether or not these interests are in harmony with the general welfare.

BUSINESS SATELLITES. The pressure groups representing the professions have traditionally had two important roles, the first of which has been to gain control of the making and administering of laws vitally affecting their members and the second of which has been, to a large extent, the support of the interests of the business class in matters of public policy. The two most powerful professional pressure groups are the American Bar Association and the American Medical Association, and the policies of these two organizations have been almost without exception probusiness policies. A growing minority of physicians are indicating their disagreement with the AMA on some issues (such as compulsory health insurance), and a cleavage among lawyers gained official status with the organization of the more liberal National Lawyers Guild in opposition to the very conservative ABA. On the whole, however, physicians and lawyers, and the majority of the membership of the other main professions as well, have been, and apparently continue to be, largely identified with the business class.

Rise of Organized Labor

The greatest potential challenge to the business ruling class comes from organized labor. It is only very recently in our cultural history that any organization of labor as a class has been sufficiently effective to constitute a real threat to the concentration of control of power in the hands of business. There have been two main reasons for the historical ineffectiveness of labor organization. First, the control of government by business had been so complete and absolute prior to the 1930s that most attempts upon the part of labor to gain more control of power were efficiently smashed. Secondly, and still more important, the nongovernmental controls of business, especially in the use of propaganda, were so effectively wielded that until very recently a vast majority of labor has believed that its interests were synonymous with and well represented by the interests of the ruling class. Many working people did, and not a few still do, so identify their interests with those of the business class that they felt that the very organization of labor to bargain with management was "wrong," "un-American," and contrary to their welfare.

During the first century of our national history practically no legislation for the benefit of labor was even attempted by our government. After about a decade of agitation by labor groups, Congress finally, in 1884, created a Bureau of Labor in the Department of Interior. The function of this bureau was solely to gather information. Not until 1913 was a Department of Labor established with a head of Cabinet rank. At this time, to the information-gathering functions were added the directions to attempt to mediate labor disputes. No real power over either business or labor was given to this Conciliation Service.

As interpreted by the Supreme Court, the Sherman Antitrust Act of 1890 had had, in many respects, a more restrictive effect on labor than on business, for the Court held that the Act applied to such concerted acts of workers as strikes and boycotts when designed to interfere with interstate commerce. An attempt by labor organizations through pressure on Congress to include in the Clayton Act of 1914 several provisions removing labor activities from the Sherman Antitrust Law was nullified by the Supreme Court. It was not until the Norris–La Guardia Anti-injunction Act of 1932 that the federal courts were prohibited from issuing injunctions in labor disputes; contained in this Act was the first general statement by Congress that labor organization and collective bargaining are desirable.

LABOR BECOMES "RECOGNIZED." Not, then, until 1932 was labor officially recognized as having the right to organize and meet the business class as a theoretical equal in the struggle for control of power. The major economic depression that had begun in 1929 had reached a sufficient state of crisis by 1932 to create a public opinion in support of legislation that organized labor had long desired. In that year a majority of Congress and a President were elected on a platform that promised the enactment of legislation establishing old-age pensions and unemployment insurance and regulating wages and hours. The assumption of duties by this Congress and President Roosevelt in 1933 marked a major turning point in the attitude of government from a weak toleration to a program of positive assistance to organized labor.

The first legislative act of positive assistance to labor in guaranteeing its right to organize and to bargain collectively was Section 7A of the National Industrial Recovery Act of 1933. When NIRA was invalidated by the Supreme Court, the National Labor Relations Act was passed in 1935. This Act guarantees to employees "the right to self-organization, to form, join, or assist labor organizations, to bargain collectively through representatives of their own choosing, and to engage in concerted activities, for the purpose of collective bargaining or other mutual aid or protection." It also prohibits certain specified "unfair practices" on the part of employers which are calculated to prevent or discourage collective bargaining. The National Labor Relations Board was given semijudicial powers to decide when "unfair practices" interfering with collective bargaining were being used by employers and to determine the legitimate bargaining unit in an establishment.

The greater power equality which labor had achieved in its struggle with business under the National Labor Relations Act was somewhat reduced by the Labor-Management Act of 1947 (passed June 23, 1947, this Act is more popularly known as the Taft-Hartley Law). Although there is considerable difference of opinion regarding the amount of curtailment of labor's rights by the Taft-Hartley Law, all of the major unions have bitterly attacked the Act as a severe restriction on the rights of organized labor.

LABOR'S STRENGTHS AND WEAKNESSES. Although organized labor is in a position relatively weaker than that of business, it has won a number of victories through collective bargaining with industry. Labor's big continuing pressure battle is to maintain these gains. But it has a more positive program for which it has already begun to fight. Two of the principal aims of this program are guaranteed full employment and a guaranteed annual wage. For labor fully to achieve these aims and for it even to maintain its present position, it will be necessary for it to build further upon its strengths and to control its weaknesses.

While labor has an advantage in the sheer number of people who qualify for membership in its ranks, its potential strength has not been realized because of the number of workers who remain outside labor organizations. The AFL-CIO has a membership in excess of 15 million. Over 3 million workers belong to other unions. But these figures do not seem so impressive when placed against the fact that the total labor force, not including farmers, is about 55 million. It is estimated that about three fourths of all blue-collar workers belong to a union. However, of all workers, blue-collar and white-collar alike, only about a third are union members. Clerks, typists, teachers, and other white-collar workers have been difficult to "organize."

In the decade 1935–1945 the proportion of workers who belonged to a union, farmers again excluded, grew from about 13 percent to almost 36 percent. Since then union memberships have fluctuated around this latter proportion. The increasing proportion of white-collar workers in America, and the aforementioned difficulty of getting them to join a union, probably accounts for most of the lack of a gain in union memberships. There is some indication of apathy toward unions, however, even on the part of the blue-collar worker.

LABOR RACKETEERING. One internal weakness of the labor movement is the existence of a number of local unions whose leadership consists of racketeers. These gangster elements have been shown to have intricate connections with the underworld, with its connotations of widespread illegal activity not stopping short of the murder of organizational opponents. Racketeers have also introduced the "kickback" in their employment practices, which requires a worker to pay the racketeering union official for the right to work. Outright thievery of goods, "shakedowns" of employers, and other practices not tolerated by the overwhelming majority of trade unions, have been well documented in several investigations conducted by federal and local governments. Finally, since the racketeer-led union is a purely rapacious enterprise, it bears no resemblance to the concept of a union as a democratically functioning organization that serves the interests of its members.

"FEATHERBEDDING." Still another internal weakness of organized labor is the occasional (and, when it happens, highly publicized) practice of "featherbedding." Featherbedding is the union practice of creating superfluous jobs, preventing the introduction of modern machinery, and forcing unnecessary work to be done. It is a procedure comparable to that of some employers in buying up patents to prevent the introduction of superior methods of production and of restricting output of needed goods to obtain higher profit. Just as employer featherbedding arises from desire for profit, labor featherbedding arises from desire for employment. Partly, again, because of the effectiveness of business control of propaganda, labor featherbedding has been considered more reprehensible in the eyes of the public than has its employer counterpart.

Farmers

Various pressure groups representing the interests of farmers have at times come in conflict with the interests of business, although at other times they have conceived of their interests as nearly identical with those of business. While the farmer, like the worker, has sometimes sought control of power at the expense of the business class, he has seldom felt his interests to be merged with those of organized labor, has, in fact, often bitterly opposed the rise of organized labor. Politically, and often directly contrary to his rather obvious interests, the farmer has most frequently had his vote counted on the side of the business class. And yet pressure groups representing some of these same farmers have frequently achieved tremendous strength in getting legislation designed to benefit various groups of farmers.

The greatest periods of prosperity for the farming interests in the United States in the past several decades have been during the course of two world wars. Shortly after World War I, foreign demand for American agricultural products declined, and the farmer entered a period of economic depression which, despite various relief measures provided during the 1930s, lasted until the beginning of World War II. Most of the current activities of pressure groups representing farmers may be understood in the light of the farmers' attempts to maintain the favorable economic position they had achieved during World War II and to prevent a recurrence of the economic disasters following upon World War I. Farmers are not in a position to maintain their economic welfare by a laissez-faire governmental policy; positive governmental protection is needed. Farmers lack economic security both because of the decline in relative importance of agriculture in our national economy and because of the increasing susceptibility of agriculture to financial maladjustments in our growingly complex and interdependent society.

The various pressure groups representing farmers do not have identical interests. The three main groups are the National Grange, the American Farm Bureau Federation, and the National Farmers' Union. The more recently formed National Farmers Organization is coming to have considerable influence. While each group attempts to "speak for the American farmer," each represents sectional and other specialized interests that influence its policies. Of course, the potential strength of farmers is reduced because of the disunity within their ranks.

THE NATIONAL GRANGE. The oldest and most conservative group is the National Grange, which draws its membership heavily from the traditionally Republican northeastern states. Its policies reflect the fact that many of its farmer members produce for strictly domestic consumption, reside in traditionally conservative areas, and are advantageously situated in relation to rich domestic markets. The Grange is opposed, for example, to the continuance of the Reciprocal Trade agreements and stands with manufacturing interests in supporting a strong tariff and in demanding curbs on labor groups along the lines followed in the Taft-Hartley Act. The Grange has likewise showed little enthusiasm for various programs for the control of agricultural production, in part, presumably, because eastern farmers have less to gain by such programs than do farmers in other sections of the country. Although it favors government subsidy for domestically consumed agricultural products, it is against federal subsidies for agricultural exports.

Through its publication, the *National Grange Monthly,* the Grange informs its members on how the organization evaluates existing farm programs and of the organization's policy on numerous issues. Some of these issues seem only vaguely related to problems of agriculture. For example, among the thirty-five items listed under the heading, *The Grange Favors,* were, "The principle of the Peace Corps," "Driver education in high schools," and "Intensified efforts to halt distribution of obscene literature through the U.S. mails." [7] It was further stated that the group opposed a national lottery and the use of public funds for private schools. [8]

As a pressure group The Grange thus engages in "grass-roots lobbying," attempting to influence the opinions of its three quarters of a million members on a variety of issues. It does, of course, have a Washington office and at one time it labeled its annual policy meeting as a "little Congress." While not as powerful an organization as it once was, the National Grange can still exert considerable influence.

[7] *National Grange Monthly,* 59 (January 1962), p. 11.
[8] *Ibid.*

THE FARM BUREAU. The American Farm Bureau Federation comes closer to covering the country than does the National Grange, but its principal strength is concentrated in the midwestern area from Ohio to Kansas to Minnesota. Although it agrees with the Grange on many issues, the Federation's policies have been less conservative, less friendly toward big business, more friendly toward labor. Since more of the farmers represented by the Farm Bureau are dependent on the world market, it has supported reciprocal trade agreements and compulsory production control.

The Farm Bureau, with almost a million and three-quarters members, is the largest and probably the most influential farmers' organization. It frequently testifies before legislative committees in Washington and in the state capitals. In almost every issue of its magazine, *The Nation's Agriculture,* its members are told of the Farm Bureau position on current or pending laws, not all of them dealing with agriculture. Following a roll-call vote on the 1962 Farm Bill, there appeared in *The Nation's Agriculture* a complete listing of how the members of the House and Senate voted on the various aspects of the bill, and, for each aspect, whether the "Yea" or "Nay" vote was in support of the Farm Bureau position.[9] The Farm Bureau is a highly organized and thorough group. In its dual role of influencing legislation and molding the opinions of its members, it is also an effective group.

THE NATIONAL FARMERS' UNION. The mildly "radical" element among the American farmers is represented by the National Farmers' Union. Many of the members of the union are farmers on the western margin of tillable lands (Colorado, Oklahoma, Iowa, Kansas, Nebraska, and the Dakotas). Its policies often differ sharply not only from those of the Grange, but also of the Farm Bureau Federation (reputedly composed chiefly of the more prosperous farmers).

From the Farmers' Union comes the strongest support for legislative proposals to bring to the farmer a return guaranteed to be equal to his cost of production. The Union further demands gradual movement of our economy away from private enterprise to cooperative business that is "owned by producers and consumers."

THE NATIONAL FARMERS ORGANIZATION. The newest major farmers' group is the highly aggressive, rapidly growing National Farmers Organization. Incorporated in 1955, the NFO is concentrating on a twelve-state area in the midwest and probably is strongest in Iowa, Illinois, and Missouri.

The unique feature of the NFO is that it is primarily a collective bargaining organization. Members authorize the NFO to be their bargaining agent with food processors and to write contracts with them governing the price of farm products. In order to show its strength and ultimately to get more food processors to sit down at the bargaining table with them, the NFO has been conducting "holding actions." That is, upon direction of the

[9] *Nation's Agriculture,* 37 (October 1962), pp. 12–13.

organization, members withhold specified farm products from the market for a stated period of time.

While so far the NFO has concentrated its efforts on becoming a true collective bargaining agent for farmers, the organization openly takes a stand on legislation that affects the pricing, handling, and processing of farm products.[10] It has pledged itself to fight for the passage of some laws and to fight against others. In so doing, the NFO is operating as a pressure group. Indeed, if it continues to grow in influence and numbers it could become a most significant farmers' pressure group.

VALUE CONFLICTS REGARDING PRESSURE GROUPS

Democracy, Representative Government, and Pressure Groups

Earlier it was pointed out that there is a certain amount of conflict over the very existence of pressure groups. Some look upon them as an abortion of democracy and claim that our "founding fathers" never intended that all of us should be governed according to the dictates of powerful and influential cliques of some of us.

Ours is said to be a government "by the people," meaning that the laws and regulations that are enacted are in keeping with the will of the people, or at least the majority of them. To be sure, it is often difficult to determine what the majority of people want. But in a democracy, each person should be able to express his wishes; each voter should have a real and equal share of power, and thus an equal opportunity to influence the decisions on the laws under which he and his fellow men must live.

Contrary to the ideal state of affairs, it is quite apparent that in our society "some are more equal than others." Speaking bluntly, small but powerful minority groups have better opportunities to influence legislative decisions than has the unorganized majority. Some years ago, for example, it was reported that the National Electric Light Association was spending $20 million a year in an all-out crusade against public ownership and regulation of public utilities.[11] More recently, the American Medical Association spent at least $1 million in its campaign against compulsory health insurance.[12] Whether these were selfish, economic interests of the groups in question or honest efforts in behalf of the common good is not here the

---

[10] See, for example, its statement with regard to the support of legislation in its publication, *NFO Reporter* (Corning, Iowa: January 1961), p. 2.

[11] Cited in James MacGregor Burns and Jack Walter Peltason, *Government By the People* (2d. ed.; New York: Prentice-Hall, 1954), p. 257.

[12] *Ibid.*

question. The point is that strong pressure groups such as these have more power and have altogether a better chance of influencing the laws of the land than do millions of unorganized private citizens.

All people are consumers of farm products and most are consumers of medical services, but "the masses" are not organized into special interest groups that represent the consumers' point of view with regard to farm or medical legislation. Obviously if they were so organized they could speak with a louder voice than the American Farm Bureau Federation or the American Medical Association. Because of the lack of organization of the private citizens who will be affected by the laws, and in view of the process by which laws are passed or repealed, it is quite possible that a small minority, speaking in unison as a pressure group, can drown out the voices of the majority.

In addition to the fact that pressure groups represent only a small part of society, such groups are said to be unrepresentative even of those people they purportedly represent. A farm group, as we have seen, may act only for a certain segment of farmers, and the millions of nonunion workers are not really represented by labor organizations. In a related manner, the leaders of a special interest group may not, in fact, speak for all members of the group. One wonders, for example, whether the majority of the members of the American Farm Bureau Federation were actually in accord with the stand that group took against federal aid to education, or even whether the bulk of the members approve of the group seemingly going beyond its purpose.[13]

Regardless of specific issues and specific groups, there would seem to be a great deal of truth in the general assertion that pressure groups are sometimes unrepresentative of their own membership, often unrepresentative of those with related interests who do not belong to the organization, and almost always unrepresentative of the masses. Under such conditions, and in view of the influence of pressure groups, representative government becomes distorted and something happens to the idea of government by the people.

The Ethics of Pressure Tactics

The second major conflict with regard to pressure groups concerns the techniques that they sometimes use, rather than their existence. That is, among those who feel that pressure groups can never be abolished and even among those who feel they have a certain utility, there is real concern over the methods they use to influence legislation and sway public opinion.

The technique, still in use, of flooding a legislator's office with letters,

[13] See "Farm Bureau Opposes Federal Aid to Education," *Iowa Farm Bureau Spokesman,* June 17, 1961.

telegrams, or telephone calls whose contents were dictated by a pressure group but appear to come from his constituents "back home," has been severely criticized. Most of the time, probably, this general technique is legal, although there have been instances of out-and-out fakery as when pressure groups sent the messages themselves using fictitious names or the names of actual people picked from a directory. But whether or not there is actual fraud involved, and whether or not the legislators are "taken in" by the verbal barrage, many people feel that the technique is basically dishonest.

Such practices as entertaining legislators, giving parties for them, and performing personal services such as finding a house to rent, are sometimes referred to as "social lobbying." Very likely, the operation of a social lobby by a pressure group is not an effective way to insure that legislators will work toward the passage of favored legislation. Still, as one authority puts it, "it is harder to refuse someone who has been kind to you than to turn away a more or less complete stranger." [14] Many people find the existence of this technique offensive and feel that there is something unethical about even trying to influence legislation in this way. Of course, if it is at all effective, it places at a disadvantage those who cannot, or will not, "wine and dine" their congressmen.

Perhaps the most serious complaint against pressure group techniques concerns the anonymity with which they are sometimes shrouded. Some feel that anyone who attempts to influence legislation should be made to tell who he is, what he wants, and who is paying his way. Some feel, too, that there is no place in a democracy for anonymous propaganda or out-and-out attempts to sway public opinion under the guise of publicity or education.

It is no easy matter to secure legislation that will force the activities of pressure groups out into the open. This has been demonstrated by the only partial effectiveness of the federal Regulation of Lobbying Act which has been in existence for almost twenty years. The act provides for the registration of anyone paid to influence the passage or defeat of a bill. Such a person must state his employer, and must file statements of money collected and used for lobbying purposes. The law is so written, however, that many true pressure groups can continue their attempts to influence legislation without registering under the act. In addition, the constitutionality of some aspects of the act has been questioned.

Any attempts to regulate or control the propagandizing efforts of pressure groups are likely to be met with cries about invasion of basic rights and liberties. It is generally agreed that freedom of speech does not give one the right falsely to cry "Fire!" in a crowded theater, but it is not always so easy to set forth just what is covered by this "first freedom." Does one, or should

[14] David B. Truman, "The Dynamics of Access in the Legislative Process," in Katz, *op. cit.,* p. 170.

one, have the right anonymously to propagandize his neighbors for whatever cause or interest? Who is to decide what is and what is not propaganda? And what restrictions, such as disclosure of sponsor, should be placed on that which is found to be propaganda? These are all serious questions and the fact that simple answers are not immediately forthcoming should not discourage serious thought. For as long as strong minorities, largely making their own rules as they go along, can directly and indirectly influence the legislation affecting the majority, there is likely to be some discontent within the pressured public.

Pressure Groups as Functional Representatives

Pressure groups, particularly in their attempts to influence legislation, operate as the spokesmen for people who have been drawn together by some common, special interest. In a sense, the pressure group represents these people in Washington, complementing our system of geographical representation. Considered in this way, it is not difficult to account for the rise of pressure groups or to understand the need they fill in our legislative process.

When our society was smaller and more homogeneous, an elected representative could speak with greater certainty for the people in his district. The differences among his constituents were not great, and he had at least a good chance of being able to determine what their interests really were. The increasing specialization in our society has meant that more and more segments of the population have interests, problems, or needs unique to themselves. And so it becomes more difficult for a legislator to represent and speak for all the specialized segments in his increasingly more diversified district.

In view of the highly specialized and diversified nature of our mass society, and in view of our particular form of representative government, there are those that hold that pressure groups are not only permissible but necessary. Such individuals contend that some type of functional representation is needed to complement the geographical representation on which our system of government rests. A manufacturer in Iowa, for example, probably shares far more interests with fellow manufacturers throughout the country than he does with many fellow Iowans. In a very real sense our manufacturer may find that he is unrepresented in Congress, particularly if the bulk of people in his district are farmers. Thus, there is said to be need for representation at the legislative level along economic and other lines and that pressure groups fill this need.

The need for functional representation is not difficult to accept. Of course, the more fully one accepts the proposition, the more he is concerned with the nature and working of pressure groups. This takes us back to the matters of how well and how fully pressure groups represent their membership. And if functional representation is actually so necessary and important, then the question of who so represents the unorganized also is important.

Pressure Groups as Sources of Information

Stemming from the same diversity and complexity of our society that suggest the desirability of functional representation, is the need that legislators feel for technical knowledge of proposed laws and for information as to their consequences.

No legislator can be an expert on the myriad issues on which he has to decide, to render an opinion, and to vote. Because of their obvious involvement in an issue and because it is their business to be expert in a particular field, pressure groups are in a position of supplying valuable technical information to legislators. To take a fairly simple example, meatpackers are in a position to explain why they have been in the practice of adding fairly large amounts of water to processed hams, how they do this, and what effects the process has on the flavor of the ham, its price, and so on. It would be necessary for a legislator to have all of this information before he could act intelligently on a law designed to forbid, to regulate, or to supervise the procedure.

No legislator is completely without the need for information on the political and social consequences of legislation. Indeed, the desire for such information may at least be equal to his quest for technical knowledge. How do people feel about the bill? What possible repercussions can he expect if he votes against the bill? Will he satisfy opposing factions or make two groups of enemies, if he suggests certain amendments to a law? As anyone with a rudimentary knowledge of politics knows, these are the sorts of questions that legislators must continually consider. Special interest groups, of course, can make it their business to conduct polls and investigations and provide the desired information.

The need of legislators for both technical and political information on laws is too obvious to be denied. Equally as obvious is the fact that pressure groups are not above exaggerating their claims for support, withholding or distorting technical facts, or otherwise supplying misinformation. As long as the informational function of pressure groups needs to be performed, there will be those people, many congressmen among them, who are genuinely concerned lest the activities of pressure groups be unduly curtailed. But as long as the information-giving function of pressure groups can be mishandled, and as long as the ability to provide information gives some citizens more influence than others on the legislative decision making process, we can expect an equally genuine desire for more stringent regulation of pressure groups.

SUGGESTED READINGS

BLAISDELL, DONALD C., *American Democracy Under Pressure*. New York, The Ronald Press, 1957.

BURNS, JAMES MACGREGOR, and JACK WALTER PELTASON, *Government by the People*. 2d ed. Englewood Cliffs, N.J., Prentice-Hall, 1954.

CHRISTENSON, REO M., and ROBERT O. MCWILLIAMS, eds., *Voice of the People*. New York, McGraw-Hill Book Company, Inc., 1962.

KATZ, DANIEL, *et al.*, eds., *Public Opinion and Propaganda*. New York, Holt, Rinehart, and Winston, 1954.

KEY, V. O., JR., *Politics, Parties, and Pressure Groups*. 4th ed. New York, Thomas Y. Crowell Company, 1958.

———— *Public Opinion and American Democracy*. New York, Alfred A. Knopf, 1961.

LOWI, THEODORE J., ed., *Legislative Politics U.S.A.* Boston, Little, Brown and Company, 1962.

BROADER IMPLICATIONS: THE WORLD BACKGROUND

20

Up to this point we have discussed value conflicts that form the backdrop and much of the dialogue of American social problems as if the United States were a self-contained society. Every school child knows, or ought to, that no society is, or for our time ever can again be, a self-contained society. What goes on in the most remote part of the world can affect us no less than our own value conflicts and compromises affect these same remote parts of the planet. A quick review of the international events of 1962 and 1963, in the context of which this is being written, should convince even the skeptic of this interaction.

RICH NEIGHBORS: POOR NEIGHBORS

Most informed people are aware that changes in public policy, such as abandoning a weapons system, resumption or deferment of nuclear testing, "quarantines" against hostile powers, and the like, have world-wide importance. Back of them lie far more tremendous potentials for explosive world events. Our own ethnocentrism often blinds us to the fact that some of the societal conditions of which the American is most proud are in themselves extremely unsettling to much of the rest of the world. If there is anything, for example, upon which Americans can reach something close to unanimous agreement, it would be the high level of living this country enjoys. Some of the facts are well known. The American people constitute but 6 percent of the world population, yet own the vast majority of the world's automobiles and television sets, and so on and on. Less familiar is the observation that the garbage from the average middle-class American family's kitchen would feed two or three Asiatic families on a level of luxury, by their standards. The average American's expenditures for tobacco and liquor would be more than enough to feed, clothe, and house several families on a level of living that would be regarded as high by a majority of the people of the world. (See Figure 6.) Some informed people are uncomfortable with such observations.

FIGURE 6   POPULATION AND INCOME

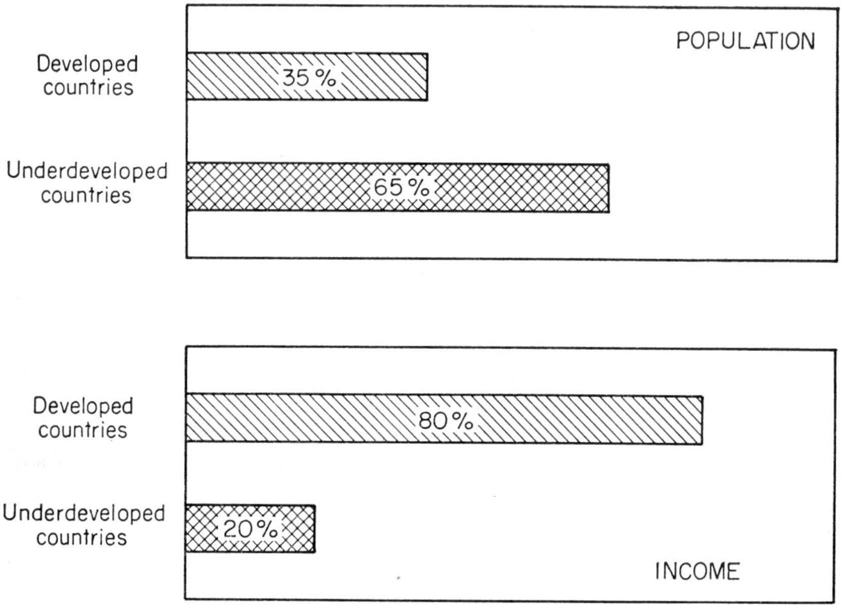

SOURCE: John F. Cuber, Sociology: A Synopsis of Principles (5th ed., New York: Meredith Publishing Company, 1963), p. 394. Copyright © 1963 by the publisher.

One of the consequences of America's fabulous affluence derives from the fact that with modern communications this opulence is widely known and deeply resented by many of the other 94 percent of the world's population. It is easy enough to point out that this well-being is enjoyed because of the superior know-how which has been built up by enterprising Americans and other technological masters of the Western world. But it does not look this way to many on the other side of the economic watershed. The apparent facts strongly support the inference, which the "Ugly American" does little to dispel, that some uncommon insensitivity, if not some intent to exploit, is also part of the American way of life. Programs like foreign aid and the Peace Corps, coupled with the older missionary movement, appear to some to be only feeble sharings with the underdeveloped countries.

The impressive military power of which we are so proud and which stands between us and any forced relinquishment of our political system and economic affluence, appears to people in many parts of the world as a kind of brutish device to maintain a lion's share of the world's goods, if not an actual "dog in the manger" enactment. Numerous careful observers have pointed out that often our aid programs are resented for various reasons by the people for whom they are intended, but chiefly because they represent no significant sacrifice to the Americans who send them and because they are coupled almost always with alleged ulterior motives, a sort of bribe to win friends to the Western side of the Cold War. In the past seemingly philanthropic help has often been used to open the way for economic penetration that has not been motivated by any clear desire to help the people in the underprivileged country.

BACKGROUND

The United States, and most of the colonial powers of Europe as well, have since World War II inherited some exceedingly knotty international problems as a result of earlier short-sighted economic and political policies formulated to maintain a domestic economy of abundance. Large-scale investment of capital abroad in factories, mines, and plantations has enabled the economy of the United States to draw raw and partially fabricated materials in quantity from all over the world. To be sure, this has brought employment to native populations and has undoubtedly raised their level of living somewhat, but the wage rates and employment conditions of these corporations have been pitifully poor as compared to those of the same corporations in their continental American operations. In pointing this out we are not implying that corporations doing a foreign business have any necessary obligation, moral or legal, to do anything other than what they did, nor that corporations of other nations may not also have acted unwisely for long-run amity, nor that the native populations may not have in many instances clearly been better off as a result of corporate policies. The point is rather that under present kinds of contact and methods of communication the contrasts between the way in which Americans live and the way in which the native populations must live are dramatic and deeply frustrating to the people of the less developed countries. It is a question of exposure and interpretation—but these are socially real.

The problem is complicated and compounded by the fact that there is a world-wide struggle between the two radically different ideologies of communism and that of the Western world. In this Cold War the leaders both of the Communist countries and of the indigenous Communist groups found almost everywhere take advantage of these discrepancies between American affluence (and the arrogance that sometimes goes with it) and the pitiful plight of many of the peoples who are contributing to it but seemingly not sharing the benefits. Accusations of exploitation and imperialism and the like have a prima facie appeal. That they are oversimplifications and not wholly true is easy enough for us to explain to each other, but these explanations have little appeal, in fact often seem insulting, to those who regard themselves as the victims of oppression.

TO MAINTAIN THE STATUS QUO

In international policy the federal government, whether Republican or Democratic, is forced by the prevailing American values to use economic pressure, diplomatic skills, and, if necessary, military force to maintain American privilege in foreign nations. There are two aspects to this bind. First, the American society needs sugar, nitrates, special kinds of crude oil, certain metals, and several other materials not available in continental United States in order to maintain the civilian economy and the military structure as well. And it needs to secure these at favorable cost, again in order to maintain the level of consumption to which we are accustomed. If, for example, an automobile had to cost two or three times as much as it now does in order to enable us to pay native populations wage rates comparable to the American, the American level of living would be seriously reduced and this would obviously not be well taken by the American people. Second, to maintain our position the government must countervail the efforts of the Communists to make capital of what Americans are and have been doing. Regardless of our intentions, even of our honest humanitarian efforts, and regardless of the long-run benefit to the countries involved, present policies can easily be made to *appear* to be exploitative and imperialistic. Thus, the peoples of so many of the underdeveloped countries, and some of the more developed ones as well, are in the hard realities of our century being manipulated like pawns in the Cold War.

Certainly no easy solution, that is to the more fully informed individual, is at hand. Before speaking of solutions, however, we should perhaps outline more precisely what concrete problems have grown out of this climate of native resentment fanned by larger world struggles.

NATIONALISM

First of all are the so-called nationalistic, independence ambitions of almost all small "nations." By breaking their ties with the so-called imperialistic nation, they hope to be free to capitalize on their own resources and not be forced to divide their national produce with a foreign power. On the surface this is convincing. Many of them have found, however, often too late, the fallacy in their hopes. Many do not have the necessary capital and often lack the technical know-how involved not only in the physical production but in the sale and distribution of their products. But the urge to be independent is still there and has a prima facie appeal. Almost every year since World War II has seen substantial amounts of American capital nationalized by one country or another. Similarly in the case of Great Britain, the Netherlands, and other European nations with comparable economies. Sometimes this nationalization involves a fair payment to American corporations, while in other instances it amounts to something closer to confiscation. What may be even more important to the American economy is that crucial sources of supply are threatened—at least at prices we have been accustomed to pay. Strategic materials may then go to the Communist bloc and thus indirectly aid it in its struggle for world dominance. Further, the economy of the small countries may become integrated with the Russian and Chinese economies and dislocate the world balance of power.

Allies

But not all international involvements are tied up with underdeveloped countries and Cold War considerations. Others involve relationships with countries in a family of nations essentially like ourselves. In 1963 the disruption of the political and quite possibly also economic relations with Canada was threatened as a result of a largely technical decision of our defense and state departments concerning the arming of allied planes with nuclear war heads. The Canadian government fell largely as a result of the announcement, and no one knows what the final consequences of the ensuing political discussion may be. A comparable situation arose with respect to another military decision, namely, to discontinue the Skybolt missile system on which NATO was to rely and to substitute the Polaris missile based on submarines instead of airplanes. In neither case was there any attempt or any intention to embarrass either of our staunch allies—the decision was essentially a technical one, but it had large implications which have caused embarrassment to ourselves as much as to Canada and Great Britain. Friendly governments have been embarrassed, traditional allies placed at odds with one another. The hard lesson seems to be that it is very difficult in the modern world to mind one's own business, for very little anymore seems clearly to be only one nation's business. No one knows precisely or even approximately how serious these disruptions may be but no one can deny that potentially, and possibly indirectly, they create additional difficulties for international cooperation even among friends.

Trade

Less dramatic and more constant are problems of trade relations, again among friendly nations. The long history of tariff policy is an excellent and continued illustration. Historically we have had two schools of thought in this country and elsewhere concerning protective tariffs. The ethnocentric view is essentially that it is better to restrict the national market to producers within the nation to facilitate employment and reward investment and thus build up the national economy. There are many other justifications for protective tariffs which practically everyone has studied in courses in economics and history. The chief value involved, however, is this insistence on a direct self-interest by keeping out foreign competitors. The other, or free trade view, is more broadly based. It holds in effect that every nation, ourselves included, should produce what it can produce most efficiently in competition with everyone else. If other nations follow this practice, the net effect for everyone will be to maximize efficiency, promote a large amount of mutually advantageous trade, with everyone gaining thereby.

In practice neither the free trade nor the high protectionist position has been completely or consistently followed. Each time Congress writes a new trade act the battle lines are drawn and the familiar arguments repeated. Most interpreters seem agreed that the high protectionism of the 1920s has largely disappeared and that various kinds of reciprocal tariffs, "most friendly nations" agreements, are likely to continue. This by no means solves the problem, however. Other nations have their own policies and their attempts to protect their own infant industries, national security, and high wages may prompt them to follow a high protectionist policy. The net effect is one of a continued need for negotiation and the ever-present danger that tariff policies of one nation may seriously disturb the economy of another one and strain relations between countries previously cooperative. In the crudest sense this takes the form of continued concern lest tariff policies force allies to trade with the other "side" in the Cold War, thus increasing the political power of the Communist bloc. The Communists have the same concern for the same reasons.

Immigration

Immigration policies present a similar, continuing problem. Varying values underlie the desires of one group or another to ease or tighten the established immigration quotas. Some considerations are humanitarian, others economic. Organized labor has tended to take the view that immigration should be restricted in order not to flood the labor market. Similarly, certain professional groups have taken a dim view of admitting too many foreign trained specialists who might disrupt current employment. The point is, whether our immigration policy is liberal or strict, it has effects good or bad upon other economies as well as upon our own, and these in turn affect relations among nations, economically and usually also politically. No one can appraise, for example, the possible impetus toward Japan's alliance with Germany and Italy in World War II that may have resulted in part from our

Japanese Exclusion Acts of the preceding decades. Certainly the kind of clearly implied rejection could hardly be expected to make for a friendly atmosphere. Similarly on the current scene (1962–1963), what is the effect upon future United States–Cuban relations of our encouragement of Cuban immigration? In the present context to be sure, relations are so strained that this one policy is not likely to make much difference, but it does illustrate with a current case that no nation, not even a large one, can go about its own problems without seriously affecting broader international relationships.

Communication

It is a current platitude that the world has shrunk. It is conventional to make this observation in terms of the decreased time required in the jet age to travel from, say, New York to London to Peiping. Further evidence is supplied by intercontinental missiles and bombing planes capable of reaching almost any place on earth from almost any other. But this is only the technological dimension. The real shrinkage is with respect to communication— the virtual impossibility of maintaining a national secret about anything. Newspapers on every continent give as much attention to racial problems in the United States as do our own. Sometimes occurrences in the United States are distorted by the foreign press; this should not be surprising. Occurrences here are distorted by our own press too. But they are reported, and America is more and more judged by its record of performance and not by some mystique of national character which some would have us present.

THE NEW REALISM

Nor are we permitted to solve our own problems—unless we do so totally without conscience—without becoming aware of world-wide consequences. Our agricultural problem is a case in point. Superficially it would seem that the solution to the problem of agricultural surplus would be simply to sell our agricultural products at discounted prices to those peoples of the world who need food. Yet to do so would in many instances be seriously disturbing to the economies of other countries who must depend upon the sale of their agricultural surpluses for their very existence. For us to undersell them, Canada for example, would be to plunge their economies into disastrous depression. Even giving away agricultural surpluses could create international problems for some friendly nations. So a totally intelligent course of action, as distinct from impulsive self-interest, requires that solutions be worked out that are mindful of broader implications.

The foregoing might appear to be far removed from the legitimate concerns of rank and file Americans. After all, our social problems are *our* problems, and it is up to us to work out our own solutions in terms of our own needs and objectives and values, regardless of the deleterious effects on someone else. In the seventeenth or eighteenth centuries this philosophy could in substantial measure be an effective one. We were a self-contained nation to a considerable extent, although not completely. In the twentieth century, however, many of the old rules need to be reversed. The longest way around *may* be the shortest way home.

Perhaps a hypothetical illustration or two—at least we hope they remain hypothetical—will illustrate the point. Suppose we solve the problem of American agriculture by dumping agricultural commodities on the world market. This will disturb the economies, as we have said, of several of our allies who will then be obliged to do something to protect their markets. Since several of the Communist countries have food shortages, they might be quite willing to accept these agricultural commodities at prices satisfactory to, say, the Canadians in return for other considerations such as missile bases in Windsor or airfields in Saskatchewan.

Or again, suppose we solve the competition from foreign automobiles produced in West Germany by raising the tariff and largely restricting the American market to American producers. In order to sell their cars, the West Germans might be willing to convert their factories, say, to the manufacture of tractors for Russia in return, of course, for a pro-Communist government in West Germany.

While the above illustrations are hypothetical, strikingly parallel ones have occurred in fact. The sequence of events in Cuba comes strongly to mind. When an unfriendly regime took over by revolution in Cuba and had some forthright and embarrassing things to say about the way in which American corporations had handled their affairs there, strong feelings arose in this country demanding that we refuse to buy sugar and in other ways to do business with Cuba. This greatly improved the opportunity for the Russians to move in with various and sundry economic aids to the embarrassed Cubans, including, of course, missile bases and other military paraphernalia. In the autumn of 1962, everyone agrees, the world was perilously close to war, the consequences of which could have been beyond description—and all over a small island which relied for its economic existence largely upon the production of sugar! No nation, it appears, lives unto itself. "No man is an island"—and the truth of this looms large in the twentieth century.

Generally speaking the American character appears to be much more continent-bound than that of other Western peoples. For a long time in history this stood us in good stead—foreign involvements were minimal. But that was in a horse-drawn world. Today we can no longer take our national security by isolationist policy for granted. The shift from an isolationist mentality to world community responsibility is a hard one for many to make. It is a much bigger shift than attention to specific issues such as the extent to which we should cooperate with the United Nations, how much and what kind of foreign aid should be appropriated, and how to present a case before a disarmament conference. These are relatively specific and concrete problems which might conceivably be worked out fairly well within an isolationist mentality. It is on the preventive side that our chronic localisms give us trouble—the tacit assumption that we can go our own way with what appear to be national problems, not realizing that it is exceedingly difficult to draw the line between what is a domestic problem and what is an international problem *for us*. The matter is further compounded by the fact that whatever our influence upon other countries, that influence is filtered for most of the peoples of the world through a resentment of our opulence and almost always fanned to maximum heat by the political intentions of those of Communistic philosophy. Uneasy rests the head that wears this kind of crown. And it is not impossible that for the decades to come the most important skills that Americans ought to cultivate are those of realistic international diplomacy. And this out of no necessarily altruistic motive, but rather out of an urgent desire for national survival. A 6 percent minority whose affluence is deeply resented by a majority of the other 94 percent can ill afford to be primarily concerned with matters of national and local scope, because almost no matters are of clearly national or local scope any more.

SUGGESTED READINGS

BAKAL, CARL, "The Mathematics of Hunger," *Saturday Review* (April 27, 1963), pp. 16–19.

BUCHANAN, WILLIAM, "How Others See Us," *Annals of the American Academy of Political and Social Science,* 195 (September 1954), pp. 1–11.

DRUMMOND, ROSCOE, "Beyond the Cuban Crisis," *Saturday Review* (November 10, 1962), pp. 16–18.

FEINSTEIN, OTTO, "American Scholars Analyze U.S. Foreign Policy," *The Bulletin of Atomic Science,* 16:10 (December 1960), pp. 395–399.

FULBRIGHT, J. WILLIAM, "The First Fifteen Years of the Fulbright Program," *Annals of the American Academy of Political and Social Science,* 335 (May 1961), pp. 21–27.

STOCKWELL, EDWARD G., "The Relationship Between Population Growth and Economic Development," *American Sociological Review,* 27 (April 1962), pp. 250–252.

Part III

OVERVIEW

RATIONALISM AND VALUE ANALYSIS

The core thesis of this book has been that social problems are characterized by "clashes of values" concerning their nature, their importance, or their treatment. It is easy to demonstrate that wide differences of opinion exist concerning every social problem from the quest for national security to the inconsistencies of marriage laws. It remains now to delve somewhat further into the factors that underlie this value diversity and to consider the probabilities that there may be emerging some sort of value agreement that may yet make it possible for the various value adherents to "get together" on some positions at least. Repeatedly it has been asked, by poet and scientist alike, why cannot reasonable, thinking men come to some measure of agreement upon the fundamental value ends of human activity at least within our own society and for our own time? Must we ever resign ourselves to accept divergent opinion, and the ill will that generates, as an inherent part of the American way of life?

FACTORS UNDERLYING VALUE DIVERSITY

In so far as it is possible to isolate the factors that appear to be responsible for the present heterogeneity of values in America, we shall list and explain those influences that seem to us to contribute to the current disunity.

Differential Vested Interest

Throughout this book we have recurrently shown that social problems affect persons of differential social position in greatly varied ways. So great is this variation in effect that conditions that may be problems to people in one social class may not be problems at all to people in other social classes. And even where it can be shown that a given condition is a problem to all strata of the society, it can almost always be also shown that there are vast differences in the severity of the effect. Finally, and in the extreme, conditions that are deplorable to certain persons and groups may actually be beneficial to the interests of other persons and groups. This latter is illustrated by the disprivilege afforded Negroes, by permitting the payment of less than subsistence wages to certain persons, or by permitting persons to manufacture and sell commodities that are harmful to the physical or mental welfare of the consumers. Under such conditions it is hardly to be expected that agreement could be reached relative to the desirability or undesirability of the condition in question.

Under the existing American value of individuation—the right and the desirability of each person to amass the largest income possible to himself so long as he violates no law thereby—the payer of less than a living wage or the possessor of superior privilege because he is fortunate enough to be white or Gentile or educated or "well bred," can hardly be blamed for failing to see that someone else is being injured or that the system is not a just one. To be sure, idealistically one is expected to be mindful of the needs of other people and sympathetic to their disprivileges, but the point is that it may be asking more magnanimity of him than he is capable of manifesting, after he has been conditioned to the rightness of the individualistic success system. This is not to deny that *some* people are not capable of the degree of identification necessary to understand opposing sides of a value position with comparable vividness, for obviously there are such people. As early as 2000 years ago, it is written, at least one socially prominent man had the temerity to give his goods to the poor in an attempt to realize new values which he had come to believe were worthy. And in our time there are more than a few who, while perhaps not going so far as to resign themselves to poverty, more or less consistently take positions on social issues that are antithetical to their own vested interests. But the proportion of such persons seems not to be large enough now to alter the basic condition of personal alignment in terms of vested interest.

Cultural Pluralism

American society has been referred to as a "melting pot" of diverse heritages from most of the rest of the advanced cultures of the world. To some extent this heterogeneous collection of cultures has been assimilated into a unique American culture, but there are evidences of the continued existence of schisms which should not be overlooked. Some nations, whatever their economic differences, have the unifying influence of a single or a predominant religion, such as Italy and Catholicism or England and Anglicanism. But the United States is torn by the ideological conflicts between Catholicism and Protestantism which are, of course, not exclusively matters of religion but vitally affect such matters as birth control, divorce, education, censorship, and many others.

Cultural pluralism, however, seems to affect social problems in other ways than simply providing a source for diversity in viewpoint. It has given us traditions that are incongruous and, therefore, a source of conflict. During the period of high immigration from Europe and Asia, for example, the low social status of the immigrant established patterns of disprivilege which the immigrant groups were forced to accept or tolerate because they were powerless to do otherwise. A more specific example of this is the intolerable slum housing conditions characteristic of the industrial cities in which many immigrants settled. As the immigrant group has lost its identity through assimilation into American culture, first- and second-generation descendants, even though often doing the same kind of work as their immigrant ancestors, have become increasingly unwilling to accept some of the disprivileges that their parents and grandparents had adjusted to. These people are now demanding their "American rights of freedom of opportunity." Meanwhile the more fortunate Americans are attempting to retain the superior privileges they originally had and deeply resent "the ingratitude" of working-class people of foreign extraction who are pressing for more tangible expression of the equality of opportunity which they have been taught is the essence of America. Sooner or later, apparently, American society will have to make up its mind whether our traditional patterns of differential social privilege will be modified in greater conformity to the democratic ideal of equality of opportunity, or whether we will candidly say that the democratic ideal was a mistake and set about to rationalize a nondemocratic or castelike social system. Whatever may be said for either choice, it would appear that some of our confusion over values would be reduced if our practice became more nearly consistent with our preachment.

Extrarational Nature of Values

We have referred a number of times to the nonrational or extrarational nature of some specific social form or value. At this point we should perhaps examine the value structure as a whole in order to determine, if possible, whether the traditional and basic values of American society are not inherently extrarational phenomena.

It would probably not be difficult to reach agreement, even among persons of diverse value orientation, that the following values are conspicuous parts of American culture. There would probably be disagreement concerning the relative importance or the acceptance of certain values in the list, but seemingly not upon the existence of the following value ends toward which Americans are oriented.

(1) *Monogamous marriage:* that is, one mate at a time, preference for stability and for children to be born within wedlock.

(2) *Freedom:* by which is usually meant holding only minimum arbitrary limitations on the will of people to do as they please.

(3) *Acquisitiveness:* the desirability of securing as great a proportion as possible of income, wealth, and material objects, even far beyond the volume necessary to sustain an abundant physical existence.

(4) *Democracy:* There is a somewhat circumscribed application of the equality of opportunity principle—that is, of the belief that almost everyone should have a right to vote and have access to at least some of the "good things" which the society provides, such as the free use of the schools, the highway system, equality before the law, and the like.

(5) *Education:* There is faith that despite its limitations and its needed modifications, the education of as many people as possible, as much as possible, is a worthy objective, limited to some extent, to be sure, by varying judgments of how much we can afford to spend for this purpose.

(6) *Monotheistic religion:* Although regular, weekly participation in organized religion is probably not a majority practice in America, adherence to at least some of the traditional tenets of the Christian and Jewish faiths is still taken for granted and taught to children.

(7) *Technology and Science:* There is great respect for the specific findings of science and the "miracles" that it has explained. To a vastly lesser degree there is respect for scientific method per se. But the chief orientation is toward what science and the man of science can do to help one to achieve desired objectives. Thus it may be more accurate to say that "technology" rather than "science" is held to be the great good, although in the minds of many people the two are inseparably mixed.

What, now, is "extrarational" or nonrational about these seven dominant American value patterns? Is it not self-evident that they are sound, worthy of one's allegiance, important enough, in fact, to die for? The point we are making, however, is not that these values are *ir*rational—that is, contrary to rational judgment—but that they are in themselves judgments rather than being either inherent in human life or objectively demonstrable as representing the greatest possible good. To put our point more simply, such values as democracy, monotheism, science, and so on can be rationalized by intelligent people—that is, can be defended by logical reasoning. The defense is easier, however, to the extent that one is defending the given value to a similarly prejudiced person. If a person, for example, is already a Christian and accepts the admonition that he is his brother's keeper and that all human beings are equal in the sight of God, then it will be easier, probably, to convince him that the freedom-of-opportunity value is an objective worth espousing. In other words, to the extent that the democratic value is similar to or consistent with the Christian value it will appear rational to the Christian.

It is necessary to point out in this connection that antithetical values can both be logically and rationally justified. This can be demonstrated either historically or contemporaneously. At one time slavery was morally right and acceptable in the eyes of God, so far as intelligent people and very Christian people were concerned. Now it seems not to be so. To some contemporaries the practice of birth control is akin to murder and should immediately cease, while to others it is a moral imperative that no more children be conceived than can, so far as one can anticipate, be able to participate liberally in the benefits of modern society. Obviously there is a logic and a rationale to both sides, and people of both high and low intelligence can be found who adhere to either of the two opposite positions.

The foregoing, then, is what is meant by the "extrarational" character of values; one cannot prove the validity of a value like democracy or of capitalism or of Christianity in the way that he can prove that the hypotenuse of a right-angle triangle is equal to the square root of the sum of the squares of the other two sides. There is a great element of faith and previous indoctrination that underlies a person's acceptance of any of these value positions. Even science is basically a matter of faith: we believe or hope that, as a result of examining selected phases of the universe by the inductive method, we will uncover laws that will be useful in our lives. Actually we do not know, except by faith, whether we are on the right track. Certainly, up to the present point in the "atomic age," the results of science have been far from an unmixed blessing. But the faith persists that some day, somehow, if "the bomb" does not kill us all, we will be better off for using the scientific method of inquiry as we have.

But people regard their values not only as if they were strictly rational but often even as if they constituted "eternal verities with which man has not the right to tamper." Thus we find in all societies and all times men who have been willing to die for what they have called "principles"; simultaneously on the other side of the ideological or physical battle other men have also been willing to die for the antithesis of the same principles. Possibly, someone has been misinformed, although it is not always easy to determine which one should so be regarded. History is a long record of the coming and going of "eternal" values, of wars and struggles over values, the believers in which apparently ignored the rest of history which shows how relative and temporary most values really are. But the illusion persists that my values are eternal verities and yours, if they differ from mine, simply show that you have been "misguided." So long as individuals and groups persist in these thought ways, agreement as to what to do about specific social problems seems very remote.

Coexistence of Inconsistent Values

Within a given society, and also within the mind of a given person, two or more opposing values may coexist, even though from a strictly logical point of view they are inconsistent with one another.[1] Thus a man may loudly and sincerely proclaim that he believes in freedom of opportunity for all men, yet oppose permitting Negro children to attend the same school with his children or, if segregation is operative, refuse to permit his community to spend as much per child on Negro education as upon white education. Or again, while proclaiming his adherence to Christianity and specifically to the Golden Rule, he also proclaims that it "doesn't pay" to be generous to other people "because they take advantage of you," or "in this world it's dog eat dog, and I'm glad I'm a bigger dog."

On the surface it might seem relatively easy for a society, and especially for some one person, to discover such inconsistencies as these, evaluate the two positions, choose one, and discard the other. All this, of course, in the interest of being consistent. But in practice it seems not to be so easy an undertaking. In the first place, *logical inconsistency may constitute social consistency*—that is, a person whose values seem inconsistent when analyzed by a third party may regard himself to be quite consistent. Both values seem to him to be quite tenable because he can point out other persons in the society as authority for the rightness of each position. There are further complications when an entire society attempts to make up its mind, so to speak, concerning some concrete course of action that always involves some underlying value positions. Requiring people to put governors on their automobiles so that they will run only forty miles per hour, for example, would undoubtedly help to achieve the value of saving some lives, but few people would vote for such a law because other values like saving time and personal freedom would be jeopardized. So the problem persists because we attain one value at the expense of another.

The persistent and very serious problems of income inequality, racial inequality, and inequality between men and women stem in considerable measure from value inconsistency. While we try to apply the equality-of-opportunity value, our other values stand in the way of its complete and direct application to the situation. Along with the democratic ideology we have the traditional white assumptions of the inherent inferiority of the Negro, the social necessity of keeping him "in his place," and an unwill-

[1] Read Bain, "Our Schizoid Culture," *Sociology and Social Research,* 19 (January–February 1935), pp. 266–276.

ingness to give up the benefits that white exploitation has brought. So solutions to specific problems of race relations are made from time to time within the framework of value conflict, but no clear-cut solution is reached because there is no clear-cut consensus on underlying values.

Thus we have seen that American society, like others, is based upon a number of values which have come down through the past and are *regarded as* eternal principles. The fact that we have pointed this out, of course, or that a relatively small fragment of the population realizes this, does not alter the basic fact that most persons and groups in the society make their decisions *as if* their value positions were self-evidently the right ones. Meanwhile, inconsistencies among values are patent, and much energy is devoted by various groups to indoctrinating as many people as possible with the values that these groups believe are the right ones. There is, however, another factor in the American intellectual climate that is relevant to the relation of values and social problems, namely, the philosophy of rational examination of values. In the following section we shall examine this philosophy and discuss its relation to the social problem situation in contemporary American society.

RATIONALISM IN THE ANALYSIS OF VALUES

Relatively recently in Western civilization a point of view has emerged that stresses the necessity and propriety of approaching values rationally, or at least more rationally than has been traditional. There is, to be sure, considerable sociological naïveté in this rational position, in that it tends to overlook the fact that while some people may be capable of manipulating values rationally, many others, probably a majority, are unwilling or unable so to do. Nevertheless, there is considerable evidence of the impact of this so-called rational approach upon social-problems thinking and action.

As this rational philosophy is examined historically and logically, it is apparent that it consists of at least three separable phases.

Identification of Values as Phenomena

It will probably already be clear that students of society may regard values as distinguishable "things." Of course they are not tangible things, but they may have very tangible results. They are what social theorists term "constructs." The idea of "value" is thus identified as a more or less distinct phase of any society, which for purposes of discussion and analysis we may abstract from the rest of the totality. Having learned, then, to recognize such values as the democratic ideology or Christian ideology or the ideology of science, the student of society, whether theorist or practical man of affairs, has taken a significant step in the direction of greater rationality. Being able automatically to identify values *as data* places a person one step along the way toward "doing something about" his or his society's specific values.

Conception of Values as Secular Elements

Being able to abstract values as distinct phenomena in the total context of a culture will not in itself make for rationality in thinking about values until a second intellectual skill is achieved, namely, the ability to think about values in a secular manner. So long as one identifies values but attributes them to transhuman forces, such as God, the devil, Nature, or some other presumably uncontrollable source, no attempt at value modification would be probable. But to the extent that it becomes apparent, both to the theoretical analyst and to the practical man, that values are man-made, it becomes relatively obvious that man has the power, perhaps the responsibility, to remake, modify, or discard what he has created when it has outgrown its usefulness.

This point of view has been termed "secularism" in contrast to the more "sacred" conception of values which preceded it. Students of social history have indicated that they have reason to believe that one of the most significant over-all trends in human development has been the emergence of a more secularlike ideology in some modern societies.[2] While they do not contend that any existing society is entirely secular, they make a good case for the increasing secularization of the thinking of modern man.

It may be too obvious to mention that secularism is itself a value—the belief that it is good for persons and groups to view their society as a man-made thing subject to more or less modification at his will. We point this out merely to show that there probably is no position which people now take concerning the evaluation of their society that is not, in some measure at least, derived from extrarational value considerations.

Objective Evaluation of the Values as Means

Once we have recognized that values are abstractable phenomena, and have granted the moral rightness of values being subject to the human will, the way becomes open for a scientific testing of at least some of our value positions. We can illustrate this point in numerous ways. On a commonsense level it is implied in Abraham Lincoln's famous clause that "no nation can exist half slave and half free." Factually, of course, Lincoln's statement was incorrect because the United States then was half slave and half free and yet was very much in existence. What Lincoln obviously referred to

[2] Robert Redfield, "The Folk Society," *American Journal of Sociology,* 52 (January 1947), pp. 293–309.

was the fact that the slavery system and the values that supported it were inconsistent with other values that the American society at that time held. Consequently, he reasoned, either the slavery system would have to go or some other values would have to go. In short, he was applying rationality to the analysis of the social problem of Negro slavery in the society of his time.

But rational value analysis can be, and is now to some extent being, approached in a much more formal manner. Numerous studies have attempted to attain this objective, and some of them at least have yielded results of theoretical and practical importance. The general *modus operandi* of value analysis consists of testing factually any subordinate value that is claimed to have a cause-and-effect relationship. If, for example, it is held that "poverty is good because it makes for better character," then we can study a group of people reared in poverty, compare them with another group reared in comfort, and discover whether the alleged value position holds up under factual analysis or not. At several points in this book attention has been called to research of precisely this sort, but a few additional examples may help to explain the procedure and philosophy.

One of the arguments often advanced against the teaching by schools of "liberal" points of view concerning politics and economics is the assumption that once a person has modified his conservative values in these areas he will also "lose his devotion to religion," "conservative family life," "respect for law and order," and so on. Research has failed to establish the validity of such a point of view. Conservatism in one area of life does not necessarily bring about conservatism in other areas.

One of the most significant over-all studies which attempts by scientific-logical procedures to examine a large sector of American values was discussed at length in the chapter on Race, namely, Myrdal's *An American Dilemma*. Myrdal's analysis, when very simply generalized, is much the same as a number of other analyses that we made throughout this book: it stresses the fact that once a society becomes committed to the democratic ideal of equality of opportunity, it must be expected that such existing inequalities as are found—for example, in race relations, education, income distribution, and health benefits—will become increasingly difficult to rationalize. They would not be difficult to rationalize in a nondemocratic society where differential privilege is either taken for granted or rationalized as a social good. In other words, by a rational examination of the value make-up of a society, it is possible to explain why certain social problems come to the fore rather than others, and even in considerable measure to predict what further issues will arise as long as the value structure remains as it is. Thus it is relatively safe to say, for example, that so long as the democratic ideology continues, so long as American technology is capable of producing the abundance of physical goods that it now does, and so long as America remains a sovereign power, we may expect continuing conflict around such conspicuous inequalities as race relations, income distribution, class-biased education, and underrepresentation of certain groups in government. Should, of course, a fascist ideology, for example, supersede the democratic ideology, then presumably such conflicts as these will be reduced because a disfranchised proletariat is hardly in a position to be assertive about its rights—if it can be said to have rights as we know them in contemporary America.

SUMMARY AND CONCLUSION

In the preceding section we have shown, then, that in relatively recent times, in Europe and in the United States at least, a new philosophy pertaining to values has been superimposed upon the older sacred system of extrarational valuation. This new point of view begins with the identification of values as phenomena that can be abstracted from a total social context. Having separated values from the rest of the system, the observer is then in a position to view them secularly—that is, as man-made and man-modifiable conditions. As a basis for possible modification, however, values may be tested to determine whether their cause-and-effect assumptions are valid and what values may coexist with what other values without creating conflict.

Much of the value conflict in American society stems from the crucial inconsistencies between the older nonrational acceptance of value positions and the somewhat rational procedures which we have just discussed. At numerous places in this book we have in one way or another called attention to this important conflict. For instance, some people simply see wage inequalities as the inevitable outgrowth of differences in native ability. It is not uncommon, even, to hear people say that God so ordained the world. At the same time we have the rationalists who point out, by comparing social systems past and present, that there is nothing inevitable about any particular system of income distribution, that any system can appear inherent in the scheme of things, provided one is sufficiently ignorant of other systems or of the nature of the processes involved. The ideological difference between these two positions is no mere quibble over the details of wage rates or the provisions of social security; it is a fundamental and irreconcilable conflict of basic values. We do not mean to imply that there is any simple device for the empiric discovery of the correct answers to such questions as these, because some value positions are still so held, facts to the contrary notwithstanding; people do not alter their value position in response to factual revelations. We do mean to imply that at least some men can at least some of the time apply their minds to the task of rational analysis of values and that such effort is both proper and practicable.

Our treatment of values and social problems has repeatedly raised, and at no point answered, a fundamental question with respect to man's thinking processes: Undoubtedly man thinks, and apparently values are a conspicuous part of his thinking about social problems, but *how* does he use his thinking processes in relation to values? Does he use his intellect merely to rationalize the values with which he has been indoctrinated before he was able to think critically? Or does his thinking faculty provide him with a somewhat detached point of view that enables him truly to "choose" which values he shall espouse? Putting the issue in still another way: is it possible for men in our time to formulate a rational system of values or is value formulation inherently a matter of rationalization of extralogical positions? To be sure it does depend upon the individual, and it is apparent that individuals manipulate values differently. But the central problem persists: how rational *can* our society be—how rational does it *want* to be?

SUGGESTED READINGS

BAIN, READ, "Our Schizoid Culture," *Sociology and Social Research,* 19 (January–February 1935), pp. 266–276.

BENSMAN, JOSEPH, and BERNARD ROSENBERG, *Mass, Class, and Bureaucracy.* Englewood Cliffs, N.J., Prentice-Hall, Inc., 1963. Chapter 16, "Changing Institutions and Ideologies."

GUSFIELD, JOSEPH R., "Mass Society and Extremist Politics," *American Sociological Review,* 27:1 (February 1962), pp. 19–30.

LIPSET, SEYMOUR MARTIN, "The Value Patterns of Democracy: A Case Study in Comparative Analysis," *American Sociological Review,* 28:4 (August 1963), pp. 515–531.

————— "A Changing American Character?" Institute of Industrial Relations, Reprint No. 180, Berkeley, University of California, 1962.

LUNDBERG, GEORGE, *Can Science Save Us?* New York, Longmans, Green & Co., 1947.

LYND, ROBERT, *Knowledge for What?* Princeton, Princeton University Press, 1939.

MYRDAL, GUNNAR, *An American Dilemma.* New York, Harper & Row, Publishers, 1944.

REDFIELD, ROBERT, "The Folk Society," *American Journal of Sociology,* 52 (January 1947), pp. 293–309.

AMERICAN IDEOLOGY AND THE HOPE FOR RATIONAL ACTION | 22

FAITH AND REALITY

Practically everyone in America has been taught by an entourage of history and civics teachers, politicians, pundits of various vintage, and even by the philosophical bits slipped into the commercials by Madison Avenue, that the great genius of America rests on two or three basic assumptions. These are, first, that we have a wide, not quite universal, suffrage, and that "the will of the people" through election is "the law of the land." A companion idea found in the Bill of Rights, the first ten amendments to the Constitution, is that minorities, groups with religious, political, and other value structures different from those of the majority, will be allowed a decent respect for their ideas and practices, so long as they do not seriously interfere with similar rights of the larger group. Another idea, more an inference than a clearly stated principle, is that we can somehow trust the collective judgment as shown through elections and the legislative process as worked out by the elected officials, to reach decisions that are not only popular but somehow inherently right. The will of the majority is a near-sacred thing in the American intellectual climate. And the individual (or party) who wins the coveted "mandate of the people" has reason to claim a kind of vindication for the authenticity of his stated views and, if reelected, for his record. Many Americans who think about such matters as these (and by no means all do) tend to a kind of quiet confidence that so long as these ideals are held inviolate, the present and future security of the American nation and "the things for which it stands" are in no serious jeopardy.

404

Nevertheless there are many facts and reasonable inferences documented in this book and many more documentable from other sources that cast a long gray shadow of doubt across these easy assumptions. Historically our ideals have stood us in good stead. But a new world has evolved, a world as different from the old one as a jet plane is different from a horse and buggy, and as an astronaut is from a woodsman. We have said repeatedly throughout this book that the modern world is amazingly intricate and complex, that problems are therefore also intricate and complex, and solutions even more so. We have pointed out over and over again that the professionals, the experts who devote their lives to trying to understand problems, are often forced to admit that there are no ready solutions or that the solutions that they believe will work involve courses of action and deviations from tradition which the rank and file will often not grant. Mental health problems or juvenile delinquency, for example, could be materially reduced if collectively we would spend the necessary money (less than we now spend for liquor and tobacco), but the will of the people, as expressed through legislatures which must appropriate the necessary funds, refuses so profligate an expenditure of public money.

Tradition continues to ride high. The "man on the street," who outvotes the expert "umpteen times to one," takes little heed of the expert typically, except to second-guess him and often to refute him by recourse to the wisdom derived from another era. The opinions of the rank and file, moreover, are constantly manipulated by a barrage of propaganda, by "the hidden persuaders" who make complicated problems seem easy. Personality tends to triumph over real issues in reaching serious and vital political decisions. People of different classes, sections, religions, colors, tend to live in their own logic-tight worlds where problems tend to be seen chiefly in special perspectives. The Negro sees the problem of discrimination in terms of his being denied access to the collective fruits, not realizing, as a rule, that others suffer similarly in American life. The ability of the Roman Catholic to solve the problem of the population explosion and its terrifying consequences is, of necessity, circumscribed by his basic commitment to a non-contraceptive solution. The farmer, the coal miner, and other victims of sick or obsolescent industry see the stark realities of life not in terms of economic concepts like supply and demand or technological change, but in terms of poverty, rejection, and fear of the future.

SPECIALIZATION AND INTEGRATION

One critic of the scene held that human existence is "a mad race between education and catastrophe," the obvious point being that in any of several respects man could easily annihilate himself unless somehow he learned how to *control* the effects of the society he has created. (This point was made before the nuclear age.) Another formulation has it that the larger human problem lies in man's emotional immaturity. Erich Fromm has said that we are trying to live intellectually in the twentieth century, with the scientific power of the nuclear age, but that psychologically we are still in the cave man age. The obvious point is that primitive emotions like fear and ambition and intolerance were less dangerous in an age when rivals fought hand to hand, when the vanquished could retreat to some unoccupied place, and in various other ways could handle problems of human aggression and fear by common sense adaptations. In the nuclear age survival itself is tenuous for almost the entire population of the globe. No one can win an all-out war, and yet it is not uncommon to hear rational people speak of "teaching" this or that nation a "lesson," through warfare if necessary, as if this objective were achievable.

The point to giving serious consideration to such ideas as these is not that they are necessarily completely right, but rather that at least they raise the more significant, cosmic questions. We live in a scientific world and unwittingly our thinking tends to focus on only one aspect at a time. Science and engineering have achieved their rather remarkable accomplishments in large part because they have isolated smaller units from large complexities for analysis and eventual control. Not only has there been specialization of subject matter, but a more basic separation has occurred—that of moral and humane considerations from the merely technical. By ignoring, for example, the larger moral question it has been possible to proceed ethically unencumbered to the production of the awesome nuclear weapon. This seems natural to us. Yet to thinking men in other times, the Athenians for example, the moral callousness and ethical irresponsibility necessary to achieve this scientific miracle might have precluded a rational man's even attempting it.

Less dramatically the same point can be made for the kind of social-scientific one-thing-at-a-time approach that social scientists utilize and which to some extent has been used in this book. Human life is chopped up for analytical purposes into separate areas like juvenile delinquency, sick industries, pressure groups, urban living, and mental health, as if each of these were something different and as if its causes and effects and the value judgments concerning them are something apart from the others. A moment's reflection readily reveals, if we start for example with urban living, that this relatively new mode of life relates significantly to delinquency and mental health, makes possible our affluence on the one hand and contributes to the sick industry on the other, while the pressure groups, regardless of their objectives tend so to muddy the waters that most human dialogue on social problems is myopic, distorted, and yields only the most modest rationality.

KNOWLEDGE AND WISDOM

It has been said that for all his increased education modern man has achieved only knowledge, not wisdom. Knowledge tells him how best to get what he wants, how things work, and how to make them serve his purposes. But knowledge is morally neutral. It cannot answer the question of *what* he should want or whether the things he wants are good or bad, destructive or ennobling. The latter he derives from his wisdom, if any. The prevailing tendency in American society, of course, is to beg the whole question of wisdom as it relates to the larger purposes and human objectives. The clear tendency is to disparage the egghead's concerns with the good, the true, and the beautiful and to get on quickly with the faster plane, the food with the longer shelf life, and the better advertising gimmick.

In the intellectual climate of contemporary America, then, objectives tend to be both short-sighted and inconsistent. The clear tendency is to want each problem solved as if it were separate from the rest of the human skein. Thus, typically, the solutions demanded by a person for different problems are such that if his stated wishes were all granted, he would be frustrated at as many points as he would be satisfied. He wants the problem of juvenile delinquency solved by a more rigorous policing and a return to parental authority and more supervision over children. Yet he wants a low tax rate and believes in freedom and wants to indulge his various and sundry conventional vices which he wishes concealed from his own children. He probably follows an occupation and a social life that takes him away from home a great deal, so the return to more adult responsibility and supervision turns out to be something that he wants someone else to do for their children but cannot possibly do for his own. He wants his children to get a good up-to-date education in the sciences but charges "subversion" or worse when the moral neutrality of the scientific method is learned and acted upon by his "integrated scion." This discussion could go on indefinitely but enough has been said to suggest the general point which can be embellished very quickly by any thoughtful person.

The purpose of the foregoing is obviously not to contribute to a genteel cynicism about solutions for social problems, any more than it is intended that we throw in the sponge. Rather our intention has been to set forth bluntly some of the larger aspects of social problems consciousness in the context of which the smaller, conscious value judgments operate. A sophistication about broad principles alone is in itself as inadequate as is a solid erudition about isolated details. The obvious need is for both—to know as much as is humanly possible about the more minute aspects of juvenile delinquency, mental illness, sick industries, the population explosion, the family, leisure. But there is an equally urgent need for an awareness of the over-all concern, to understand not only the interrelatedness of all of the separate problems but the even more elusive idea that unless and until there is better understanding than there now is of some inclusive conception of the good life (central values), all of the detailed knowledgeability will not help us much.

Unfortunately we do not have as neat a recipe to achieve wisdom as we do to achieve knowledge. The philosopher is not much heeded in the twentieth century in the Western world. We prefer to act as if the larger questions have already been solved, as if we know the dimensions of the good life, the nature of man, and other philosophical master enigmas, and all we need to discover therefore are solutions to more circumscribed questions.

Future historians would have to say that twentieth-century America, along with much of the rest of the Western world, was an exceedingly capable and scientifically oriented collectivity, but that it was much more scientific and capable about material things than about deeper aspects of the human plight. It seems likely also that the record would have also to say that in the neglect of the quest for wisdom, many of the potentials of the scientific power were lost in a rather primitive scramble for naked power among nations, classes and races, and even neighbors.

A NOTE ON CULTURAL LAG

It has been said so often that it now amounts almost to a cliché, that the problems of human living together remain as serious as they now are because the social sciences are behind the physical sciences. By "behind" is usually meant that the social sciences cannot match the definiteness of the physical and biological sciences in many matters, nor can action based upon current research completely control outcomes as in the case of the older sciences. This is true enough as stated, but an important omission tends to be made. Throughout this book we have pointed out that there exists rather reliable expert knowledge on many problems, even extending into the area of control, but that for some reason or another—tradition, religion, competing vested interests, simple ignorance—the program is not put into operation, or, if so, is surrounded by conditions almost certain to limit its success. This would be analogous, say, to denying the physical scientist the necessary funds with which to build a space ship, admonishing the astronauts that there is nothing in the Bible or the Constitution advising space travel, harassing one way or another the technicians at Cape Canaveral, and then complaining because so many attempts fail. Quite obviously an important difference in the two cases is that we are thoroughly committed to the importance of space travel and investigation, practically ignoring the colossal costs involved, and are quite tolerant with our experts' failures in these efforts.

It has been forecast that it may cost $30 billion to "put a man on the moon." But how much is $30 billion?

It is sobering to think of an alternative set of projects that might be financed with this sum. We could: give a 10 per cent raise in salary, over a ten-year period, to every teacher in the United States, from kindergarten through universities, in both public and private institutions (about $9.8 billion); give $10 million each to 200 of the best smaller colleges ($2 billion); finance seven-year fellowships (freshman through Ph.D.) at $4,000 per person per year for 50,000 new scientists and engineers ($1.4 billion); contribute $200 million each toward the creation of ten new medical schools ($2 billion); build and largely endow complete universities, with medical, engineering, and agricultural faculties for all fifty-three of the nations which have been added to the United Nations since its original founding ($13.2 billion); create three more permanent Rockefeller Foundations ($1.5 billion); and still have $100 million left over to popularize science.

Whether you are primarily concerned with national welfare, international prestige, or science, weigh these alternatives against a man on the moon.[1]

CONCLUSION

It is difficult to end a treatment such as this. There is always more that could be said on the almost infinite subject of values and human action. It is in the nature of every inquiry, however, that it must and should be incomplete. As this is being written new values are in process of formulation, old ones are being modified, and new human action is being attempted. It is quite possible that many of the documented assertions about human values and actions contained in this book will some day be no longer true. No values and no action based upon values have ever been eternal, except perhaps those which spring directly from the biopsychic nature of man, but even they, through socialization, take ever-changing forms.

We end with a restatement of the objectives with which we opened, namely to present a study of social problems organized around the idea that values and the conflicts among them constitute a fertile approach to understanding these trouble spots in the human plight—in this age or in any other one. If we have succeeded in sharpening this kind of awareness for the serious student, this limited but not modest objective will have been approximated.

[1] Warren Weaver, "What a Moon Ticket Will Buy," *Saturday Review* (August 4, 1962), p. 38. Copyright by the *Saturday Review*.

AUTHOR INDEX

Allen, Francis R., 101
Anderson, Nels, 211
Apple, Dorrian, 251
Ashmore, Harry S., 233

Back, Kurt W., 133
Baber, Ray E., 147, 148
Bain, Read, 398, 403
Bakal, Carl, 389
Barnes, Harry Elmer, 307
Barron, Milton L., 300
Beattie, Ronald H., 324
Bensman, Joseph, 403
Bereday, George Z. F., 174
Bergler, Edmund, 359
Bernard, Jessie, 153
Berry, Brewton, 215
Bestor, Arthur E., 174
Bettelheim, Bruno, 276
Blaisdell, Donald C., 362, 380
Bloch, Herbert A., 346
Boskoff, Alvin, 104, 113, 116
Brickman, William W., 174
Bronowski, J., 25
Brown, Lawrence Guy, 39
Buchanan, William, 389
Buell, Bradley, 346
Burdette, Franklin L., 361
Burgess, Ernest W., 280, 285, 300
Burns, James MacGregor, 375, 380
Bush, Vannevar, 101

Calverton, V. F., 329
Campbell, Arthur A., 133
Cavan, Ruth, 280
Cayton, Horace R., 233
Christenson, Reo M., 380

Churchill, Henry S., 116
Clinard, Marshall B., 346
Comas, Juan, 218
Cottrell, Fred W., 91, 101
Cressey, Donald R., 324
Cuber, John F., 13, 39, 153, 382
Cumming, Elaine, 300
Curtiss, John Shelton, 191

Dedman, Jean, 191
Denny, Reuel, 19
Dinitz, Simon, 324, 346
Donahue, Wilma T., 282, 300
Drake, St. Clair, 233
Draper, William H., 127
Drucker, Peter, 101
Drummond, Roscoe, 389
Dunham, H. Warren, 346
Dunlop, John T., 25, 85
Durand, John D., 119

Erikson, Kai T., 359

Fein, Rashi, 270
Feinstein, Otto, 389
Feld, Sheila, 253, 254, 276
Form, William H., 85
Freedman, Ronald, 130, 133
Freeman, Howard E., 276
Friedmann, Georges, 212
Fulbright, J. William, 389
Fuller, Richard C., 36, 38, 39
Furfey, Paul H., 39

Galbraith, John K., 17, 82, 84, 85, 101
Gallup, George H., 189

Gardner, Martin, 59
Garfinkel, Herbert, 233
Gillin, John P., 32, 39
Ginsberg, M., 359
Glazer, Nathan, 19
Glueck, Eleanor, 324
Glueck, Sheldon, 324, 346
Goldhamer, Herbert, 280
Gordis, Robert, 191
Gottman, Jean, 116
Grabill, Wilson H., 133
Greer, Scott A., 115, 116
Griffin, John Howard, 233
Gulick, Luther H., 115
Gurin, Gerald, 253, 254, 276
Gusfield, Joseph R., 403

Haar, Franklin B., 251
Hager, Don J., 59
Handy, William F., 324
Harrington, Michael, 85
Harroff, Peggy B., 39, 153
Hauser, Philip M., 119, 133
Havighurst, Robert, 280, 285
Haworth, Laurence, 116
Henry, William, 300
Hollingshead, August B., 268, 276
Huff, Darrell, 41, 59
Hughes, Charles C., 85
Hulburd, David, 175
Hunt, Elgin F., 25
Huxley, Aldous, 31

Irwin, John, 324

Jaco, E. Gartly, 276
Jellinek, E. M., 359
Jenkins, Richard L., 346
Jewett, Robert E., 175
Johnson, Thomas, 117
Josephson, Eric, 276
Josephson, Mary, 276

Kane, John J., 192
Kaplan, Mary, 212
Karlin, Jules, 25
Katz, Daniel, 363, 364, 377, 380
Kenkel, William F., 42, 45
Key, V. O., Jr., 380
King, Martin Luther, Jr., 233
Kinsey, Alfred C., 153, 334
Kiser, Clyde V., 133

Kitsuse, John I., 359
Kleemeier, Robert W., 212, 300
Klein, David B., 264
Kolb, William L., 39
Kolko, Gabriel, 66, 85
Kramer, Alfred, 192

Larrabee, Eric, 212
Lewisohn, Sam A., 314
Lindeman, Eduard C., 211
Lipset, Seymour Martin, 403
Lowi, Theodore J., 380
Lundberg, George, 403
Lukas, Edwin J., 359
Lyle, Jack, 212
Lynd, Robert S., 95, 403

McGinnis, R. J., 44
MacIver, Joyce, 276
Mack, Raymond W., 219, 227
McKee, James B., 59
McWilliams, Robert O., 380
Malthus, Thomas R., 121
Marx, Karl, 86
Mead, Margaret, 329
Meir, Richard L., 133
Melby, Ernest O., 175
Mendelson, Wallace, 233
Merton, Robert K., 217
Meyersohn, Rolf, 212
Miller, Norman P., 212
Mills, C. Wright, 20
Milner, Esther, 85
Montague, Ashley, 219, 233
Morgan, James N., 70, 85
Muelder, Alfred, 192
Myers, Jerome K., 269, 276
Myrdal, Gunnar, 230, 233, 403

Newman, Donald J., 324
Nisbet, Robert A., 217
Nordskog, John Eric, 25
Nosow, Sigmund, 85

O'Brien, John A., 127
Ogburn, William F., 86
Organski, A. F. K., 133
Organski, Katherine, 133
Orshansky, Mollie, 287

Packard, Vance, 15
Parker, Edwin B., 212

Peltason, James Walter, 375, 380
Petersen, William, 133
Pfeffer, Leo, 192
Pike, James A., 127
Pittman, David J., 324
Ploscowe, Morris, 359
Puner, Morton, 175

Raymond, Allen, 21
Read, Gerald, 174
Reckless, Walter C., 21, 313, 318, 324, 340, 346, 356, 357
Redfield, Robert, 400, 403
Redlich, Fredrick C., 268, 276
Reichard, Suzanne, 300
Reiss, Ira L., 153, 359
Riesman, David, 19, 20, 82, 101, 174
Roberts, Bertram H., 269, 276
Robinson, Duane M., 212
Robison, Sophia M., 346
Rogers, Everett, 101
Rose, Arnold M., 217, 229, 324
Rosenberg, Bernard, 25, 403
Rossi, Peter H., 117
Rowan, Carl T., 233
Rowe, Clarence J., 256
Ruchames, Louis, 224, 232
Ryans, David G., 175

Salisbury, Harrison E., 25
Sauvy, Alfred, 133
Scarpitti, Frank R., 324
Scheinfeld, Amram, 261
Schlesinger, Ina, 174
Schmalhausen, S. D., 329
Schnore, Leo F., 59
Schorr, Alvin L., 117
Schramm, Wilbur, 15, 212
Schriftgiesser, Karl, 364
Schur, Edwin M., 359
Schwartz, Richard D., 324
Seeley, John R., 359
Sheldon, Henry D., 278
Simmons, Ozzie G., 276
Simpson, George E., 233

Sirjamaki, John, 117
Skolnick, Jerome H., 324
Smith, Ralph Lee, 251
Smith, T. Lynn, 282
Smolensky, Jack, 251
Sofen, Edward, 117
Somers, Anne R., 247, 251
Somers, Herman M., 247, 251
Soule, George, 212
Spergel, Irving, 324
Spiro, Audrey G., 153
Spiro, Melford E., 153
Srole, Leo, 276
Stewart, George R., 175
Stewart, Robert L., 189, 192
Stockwell, Edward G., 389
Strauss, Anselm L., 117

Taylor, R. S., 324
Teeters, Negley K., 307
Terman, Lewis M., 44
Thompson, Craig, 21
Tibbitts, Clark, 288, 291, 293, 295, 300
Trasler, Gordon, 324
Truman, David B., 377
Turmin, Melvin M., 233

Vedder, Clyde B., 300
Vernon, Glenn M., 189, 192
Veroff, Joseph, 253, 254, 276

Wade, Andrew L., 346
Weaver, Warren, 409
Whelpton, Pascal K., 133
White, David M., 25
Whyte, William, Jr., 18
Woytinsky, E. S., 131
Woytinsky, W. S., 131

Yinger, J. Milton, 233
Young, Kimball, 181

Zanden, James W., 233
Zola, Irving K., 359

SUBJECT INDEX

Adolescence, indices of difficulties, 332–336
  intercultural view of, 328–329
  morals, 334–335
  school failures, 333
  as stage of life, 326–332
  trauma, 329, 332
  See also Juvenile delinquency
Affluent society, and belief in waste, 80–81
  and consumption morality, 79–81
  decline of "traditional virtues" in, 79–80
  effect on the comfortable and wealthy, 79–80
  and extended public services, 82–85
  extent of affluence in, 70–71
  and extent of unemployment, 75–76
  fact or myth, 65–72
  and the "good life," 81–82
  and poverty, 70–71, 72–74
  value conflicts in reducing problems of, 82–85
  See also Income, Wealth
Aged, *see* Old age
Agriculture, *see* Farming
Air pollution, 239–240
Alcoholism, diversity of problems, 348–349
  societal causes of, 350
Amelioration vs. curative treatment of social problems, 53–54, 93–98
American Bankers Association, 367
American Bar Association, 367, 369
American Civil Liberties Union, 361
American Farm Bureau Federation, 94, 367, 373, 374, 376

American Federation of Labor–Congress of Industrial Organizations, 367, 371
American ideology, faith vs. reality, 404–405
  knowledge and wisdom, 407–408
  specialization, 405–406
  See also Rationalism
American Medical Association, 361, 369, 375
American Newspaper Publishers Association, 367
American Pharmaceutical Association, 367
American Short Line Railroad Association, 367
American society, changes in recent past of, 6–13, 89–92
  perspective for viewing changes of, 4
Anti-intellectualism, *see* Education, Rationalism
Anti-Saloon League, 361
Anti-Vivisection Society, 361
Anxiety states, 261–262
Asia, population growth in, 122–123
Automation, 87
Averages, and facts of social problems, 47–49

"Big Lie," and facts of social problems, 41–42
Birth control, and U.S. population, 130
  and world population problems, 127–128
Birth rate, and industrialization, 121
  and population growth, 120–122

Business, as American ruling class, 367–368
  power advantages of, 368–369
  as pressure group, 367–369
  satellites of, 369

Censorship, *see* Religion
Chamber of Commerce of the U.S., 367
The Church of Jesus Christ of the Latter Day Saints, 180, 181
City, financial problems, 111–112
  government problems, 114–116
  growth in number of, 103
  human needs in, 105–107
  income taxes, 111
  individualism in, 105–107
  management problems, 110–114
  and metropolitan area, 104
  and metropolitan area government, 115–116
  planning, 112–114
  population growth, 8, 102–103
  sales taxes, 111–112
  service problems of, 107–110
  slums in, 109–110
  and suburb annexation, 112
  traffic problems in, 107–109
  value clashes in, 104–116
  zoning, 112–113
City manager system, 114–115
Civilization, cyclical theory of changes in, 4–5
  "mutation" theory of changes in, 1, 5–6
  panoramic view of history of, 4–6
  and theory of gradual social progress, 4
Clothespin Manufacturers of America, 361
Coercion vs. persuasion, in treatment of social problems, 54–56
Committee Against Discrimination on Small Catalog Postage Rates, 361
Committee for Constitutional Government, 363
Consumption morality, 79–81
Conventional deviations, concept defined, 347–348
Conversion hysteria, 262–263

Correlations, and facts of social problems, 45–46
Council on Christian Social Progress, 361
Culture change, *see* Social change, Economic change
Crime, career crime, 306–307
  causation, 310–311
  changing conceptions of, 305–310
  differential contagion, 317–318
  distinguished from sin, 302
  and law, 301–305, 321
  penalties and, 312–314
  popular proposals for reducing, 311–316
  professional conclusions on sources, 317–320
  professional recommendations for amelioration, 320–323
  risk factors in, 317–318
  social norms and, 307–309
  See also Juvenile delinquency
Culture lag, 86, 408–409

Death rate, and population growth, 120–121
Democratic values, and pressure groups, 375–376
Deviancy, concept of, 31–32
  conventional deviations, 347–348
  sexual deviations, 354–356
Divorce, as evidence of poor mental health, 255
  See also Marriage
Drug addiction, as escapist activity, 257

Economic change, adapting to,
  kinds of distress, 87–92
  meliorative efforts, 93–98
  value conflicts, 92–98
Economic distress, kinds of, 87–92
Economic interpretation of history, 86
Edison Electric Institute, 367
Education, for adults, 167
  anti-intellectualism, 163–164
  class bias in, 164–165
  contemporary issues in, 159–164
  federal aid to, 171–174
  growth of, 10–11
  projected school enrollments, 11

Education (*continued*)
  purpose of, 157–159
  and treatment of social problems,
    54–56
  See also Schools
Employment of older persons, 288–
    289
Everson v. Board of Education, 179

Facts, difficulties in interpretation of,
    49–50
  difficulties in obtaining and present-
    ing, 40–49
  and frame of reference, 50–51
Fair Employment Practices Act, 224
Family, incomes of, 70–71, 287–288
Farm Bureau, 367, 373, 374, 376
Farmers, declining number of, 9, 89
  increased output of, 9
Farming, employment, 89
  farm mortgage debt, 90
  farm price index, 89
  farm subsidies, 96–97
  Farmers Union, 94
  as sick industry, 88–91
Foundation for Economic Education,
    363, 364
Fuel production, 88

Gambling, value conflicts concerning,
    352–354
  varieties of, 351–352
Government, of cities, 114–116
  metropolitan area, 115–116
  See also, Pressure groups

House Select Committee on Lobbying
    Activities, 364
Humanitarianism, as criterion for so-
    cial problems, 28–31

Illness, *see* Mental illness, Physical ill-
    ness
Income, city tax of, 111
  definition of, 65
  distribution of family, 70–71
  distribution of national, 66–67
  and medical costs, 241–242
  of older persons, 287–288
  and physical illness, 237
  real vs. money, 68–69

Income (*continued*)
  total national, 67–68
  and use of physicians' services, 242–
    243
  See also Affluent society, Wealth
Industrialization, and birth rate, 121
  and population growth, 120–123
  and U.S. population, 130
Industrial revolution, broad effects of,
    5–6
International Brotherhood of Team-
    sters, 367
Inventions and innovations, effects of
    material and social, 12–13

Juvenile delinquency, as evidence of
    poor mental health, 255
  generic to the society, 344–345
  juvenile court, 336–339
  middle class, 339–340
  new modes in, 339–341
  proposed solutions, 341–344
  vandalism, 340–341
  See also Crime

Labor, AFL–CIO unions, 367, 371
  "featherbedding," 372
  growth of, 369–370
  legal recognition of, 370–371
  as pressure group, 369–372
  racketeering, 371–372
  strengths and weaknesses of, 371–
    372
Laissez faire, 93–95
  and treatment of social problems,
    52–53
Leisure, amount of available, 193–195
  "bulk," 194
  community planning for, 209–210
  and do-it-yourself movement, 198–
    199
  meaning of, to people, 195–196
  and "moonlighting," 199–200
  national planning for, 210–211
  potential and achieved values, 195–
    198
  research on, 209
  state planning for, 210
  value conflicts on remedies, 207–
    211
  See also Recreation

Libraries, 206
Lobby, *see* Pressure groups
Lobbying Act, 361

McCollum v. Board of Education, 179
Manic-depressive psychosis, 260–261
Marriage, American tradition, 135–136
  counseling, 151
  de facto and *de jure*, 136–138
  defunctionalization of, 139
  divorce, 141–142
  education for, 150–151
  legal aspects, 145–149
  modern setting, 136–145
  proposals for treating problems of, 145–152
  sense of maladaptation, 139–141
  sexual morality, 143–144
Mass society, characteristics, 13–17
  consequences, 17–22
  as world-wide concept, 22–25
Medical services, and compulsory health insurance, 247–249
  costs of, and income, 241–242
  distribution of, 244–245
  increasing costs of, 241
  meeting need for, 249–250
  private payment for, 246
  use of, and income, 242–243
  use of, and race, 242
  value conflicts over payment methods, 245–249
  and voluntary health insurance, 246–247
Mental health problems, and costs of mental illness, 269–270
  delinquency as evidence of, 255
  and differential proneness to mental illness, 268–269
  divorce as evidence of, 255
  escapist activities as evidence of, 257–258
  explanations of, 265–269
  extent of, 253–259
  mental illness rates, 258–259
  occupational maladjustment as evidence of, 256–257
  people's view of, 253–255
  and preventive measures, 273–274
  psychoneurosis, 261–264

Mental health problems (*continued*)
  psychopathic personalities, 264–265
  psychosis, 259–261
  psychosomatic disorders as evidence of, 256
  schizoid culture theory as explanation of, 267–268
  societal complexity theory as explanation of, 266–267
  treatment of, 271–272
  and value conflicts, 274–275
  value issues in amelioration of, 269–275
Mental hospitals, admissions to, 258–259
  improvement of, 271–272
  patient-personnel ratio in, 272
Mental hygiene clinics, 273
Mental illness, classification of, 259–265
  costs of, 269–270
  differential proneness to, 268–269
  prevention of, 273–274
  psychoneurosis, 261–264
  psychopathic personalities, 264–265
  psychosis, 259–261
  rates of, 258–259
  treatment of, 271–272
Metropolitan area government, 115–116
Mormon Church, 180, 181

National Association of Manufacturers, 361, 363, 367
National Association of Real Estate Boards, 363
National Coal Association, 367
National Electric Light Association, 375
National Farmers Organization, 367, 374–375
National Farmers' Union, 367, 373, 374
National Grange, 367, 373
National Health Survey, 235
National Industrial Recovery Act, 370
National Labor Relations Act, 370–371
National Lawyers Guild, 369
Neurasthenia, 263
Norris-La Guardia Act, 370

Objectivity and problem analysis, 98–100

Obsessive-compulsive reactions, 263–264

Occupations, changing patterns of, 9–10

Old Age, ameliorative programs for, 298–299

attitudinal changes required in, 299

autonomous vs. dependent role, 285–286, 293–294, 295

economic problems, 287–293

employment, 288–289

health problems, 294–295

income, 287–288

income sources and role, 293–294

industrial pensions, 292–293

institutional care, 297, 299

insurance for, 289–291, 294

lack of meaningful roles in, 295–297

and life expectancy, 277–279

nature of, 280–285

need for subcategories of, 284–285

number and growth of, 11–12, 279–280

physical, 281

problems of, and value conflicts, 285–297

proportion in society, 11–12, 280

psychological, 281–282

public assistance, 291–292, 294

research needs, 298

sociological, 282–284

Old-age Assistance, 291–292, 294

Old-age, Survivors', and Disability Insurance, 289–291, 294

Percentages, and facts of social problems, 46–47

Personality disorders, see Mental illness

Physical health, and costs of medical care, 241–243

Physical health problems, and distribution of doctors, 244–245, 249–250

needs in U.S., 234–238

of older people, 294–295

psychosomatic disorders, 256

and public health problems, 238–240

Physical health problems (*continued*)

and rates of illness, 234–238

social explanations of problems, 240–245

U.S. values, 234

value conflicts and amelioration of, 245–251

See also Physical illness, Public health

Physical illness, acute, 236

chronic, 235–236

disabilities, 236–238

impairments, 236

and income, 237

rates of, 234–238

See also Physical health problems, Public health

Population, Asian growth, 122–123

capacity of U.S., 130–131

in cities, 8, 102–103

effects of birth rate on, 120–122

effects of death rate on, 120–121

effects of level of living on, 124

effects of natural resources on, 123

effects of technical knowledge on, 123–124

and family planning in U.S., 130

future U.S., 130

growth by continents, 122

growth in U.S., 6–8, 128–130

and industrialization in Asia, 122–123

and industrialization in Europe, 120–122

and industrialization in U.S., 130

reducing world problems, 126–128

rural-urban makeup of, 8

U.S. problems, 128–132

value conflicts over U.S. growth, 131–132

value conflicts over U.S. responsibility, 125

world growth, 119–123

world problems and birth control, 127–128

world problems and economic assistance, 126

world problems and the U.S., 124–125

world's capacity, 123–124

Poverty, extent of, 70–71

and fiscal policy, 77

Poverty (*continued*)
  meaning of, in affluent society, 72–74
  and monetary policy, 77
  reduction of, through higher wages, 74–75
  and reduction of unemployment, 75–77
  reduction of, and value conflicts, 74–78
Pressure groups, anonymity of, 377–378
  in business, 367–369
  definition of, 360
  ethics of tactics, 376–378
  and farmers, 372–375
  as functional representatives, 378–379
  growth of, 361–362
  influence on public opinion, 363–365
  as information sources, 379
  in labor, 369–372
  and legislation, 365–366
  and lobbies, 365–366
  and mass media of communication, 363–365
  nature of, 361–362
  and political parties, 365
  regulation of, 377–378
  and representative government, 375–376
  scope of activities, 361
  value conflicts regarding, 375–379
  workings of, 362–366
Psychoneurosis, classification of, 261–264
Psychopathic personalities, 264–265
Psychosis, classification of, 259–261
  treatment of, 271–272
  See also Mental illness
Public health, advances in, 238
  and air pollution, 239–240
  opposition to, 238
  scope of, 238–239
  value conflicts over reducing problems, 250–251
Public services, extension of, 82–85

Race, amelioration of problems of, 230–232

Race (*continued*)
  biological basis of prejudice, 221–222
  biological superiority of given race, 218–219
  concept of, 213–216
  criteria for classification, 214–215
  cultural evidence of superiority of given race, 220–221
  definition of, 213
  discrimination, 217, 223–230
  discrimination and democracy, 230–231
  discrimination reduction, 232
  economic basis of prejudice, 222–223
  economic costs of discrimination, 229
  economic discrimination, 223–224
  educational discrimination, 225–226
  and fair employment practices, 224
  and future of race relations, 232–233
  housing discrimination, 224–225
  and intelligence, 219–220
  myth of, 215–216
  perpetuation of prejudice, 223
  political discrimination, 227
  prejudice, 217–223
  prejudice reduction, 231–232
  prejudice sources, 221–223
  psychological basis of prejudice, 222–223
  psychological superiority of given race, 219–220
  and racism, 217–218
  social costs of, 229–230
  social discrimination, 227–228
  and use of medical services, 242
Rationalism, 399–402
  extrarationality, 396–399
Recreation, commercial, 200–202
  community planning for, 209–210
  complexity of private, 202–203
  and contact with nature, 197
  and do-it-yourself movement, 198–199
  and esthetic creation, 197
  and fuller use of mind and body, 196
  and group participation, 197

Recreation (*continued*)
  growth of public, 204–205
  inadequacies of private, 203–204
  and libraries, 206
  national planning for, 210–211
  and occupation of time, 197–198
  and perception of freedom, 196
  popularity of commercial, 201–202
  potential and achieved values, 195–198
  preparation for, 207–209
  private nonprofit programs, 202–204
  public programs for, 204–207
  and the schools, 205–206
  state and national, 206–207
  state planning for, 210
  time available for, 193–195
  value fulfillment by commercial, 200–201
  youth groups for, 202–203
  See also Leisure
Religion, censorship, 181–185
  church and state, 176–181
  parochial school issues, 177–180
  religiosity, 189–191
  and social action, 185–189
  Supreme Court decisions, 179
Roman Catholic Church, 177–178, 179, 183, 184
Rural, declining number of farmers, 9
  population decline, 8

Sampling, and facts of social problems, 42–43
Schizophrenia, 260
Schools, need for counseling in, 273
  projected enrollments in, 11
  and recreation activities, 205–206
  See also Education
Sexual deviations, 354–356
  prostitution, effects of, 357–358
    sources of, 357
    treatment, 358
    types of, 356–357
Sherman Antitrust Law, 370
Sick industry, 88
Slums, 109–110
Social change, and changing educational patterns, 10–11
  and changing occupational patterns, 9–10

Social change (*continued*)
  cyclical theory of, 4–5
  and Industrial Revolution, 5–6
  and inventions, 12–13
  and mass society, 13–25
  "mutation" theory of, 5–6
  panoramic view of, 4–6
  rate of, 6
  in recent American society, 6–13
  and social disorganization, 33–34
  and theory of gradual social progress, 4
Social disorganization, concept of, 33–34
  and social change, 33–34
  and social problems, 33–35
Social problems, amelioration vs. curative treatment of, 53–54
  coercion vs. persuasion in treatment of, 54–56
  difficulties in obtaining and presenting facts of, 40–49
  disapproved deviancy as criterion of, 31–33
  evolutionary vs. revolutionary treatment, 56–57
  humanitarianism as criterion of, 28–31
  laissez faire vs. purposive control of, 52–53
  nature of, 26–39
  and need for societal perspective, 3–4
  piecemeal vs. total attack on, 56–57
  role of experts in defining, 27–28
  and social disorganization, 33–35
  treatment of, 40–59
  undesirability of condition as criterion of, 26–28
  value conflicts as source of, 35–39
  value conflicts in treatment of, 37–38, 51–58
  world background, 381–389
Social Security Act, 289–291
Social scientists, as social problems experts, 28
Socialized medicine, 247–249
Society, panoramic view of changes in, 4–6
Standard Statistical Metropolitan Area, 104
Supreme Court decisions, *see* Religion

Taft-Hartley Act, 371
Traffic, problems in city, 107–109
Trend data, and facts of social problems, 44–45

Underdeveloped countries, population and income, 381–383
problems resulting from, 383–387
Unemployment, extent of in U.S., 75–76
Unions, labor, *see* Labor
United Mine Workers, 367
Urban, *see* City

Value conflicts, and recognition of social problems, 36–37
as source of social problems, 35–39

Value conflicts (*continued*)
and treatment of social problems, 37–38, 51–58
two main phases of, 36–38
Value diversity, sources, 393–395
Values, basic American orientation, 396
as basis of social problems, 35–39
as data, 35–36

Wealth, definition of, 65
extent of, 70–71
See also Affluent society, Income
Women, employment of, 10

Yazoo land frauds, 362